Pocket Atlas of the World

Editors:
Dr. Manfred Reckziegel
Willi Stegner
Werner Thiele
Gerhard Treger

Cartography:
Klett-Perthes

Flags:
Jiří Tenora, Das Flaggenkabinett, Berlin

Cover:
Grafikdesign Brüning, Gotha

Printed and bound in Germany by:
Salzland Druck & Verlag, Staßfurt

First published 1999

http://www.klett-verlag.de/klett-perthes

First published for United States and Canada by:
Barron's Educational Series, Inc.
250 Wireless Boulevard
Hauppauge, NY 11788
http://www.barronseduc.com

International Standard Book Number 0-7641-1130-2
Library of Congress Catalog Card Number 99-73144

Preface

Haack Pocket Atlas of the World constitutes a handy state-of-the-art presentation of the world in maps. Like the more than 100 preceding editions this one also stands out by its solid craftsmanship and graphic diversity. The completely new and up-to-date look of the Pocket Atlas has been achieved by computer-assisted cartography and technically innovative design. The core of the atlas is the map section with a wealth of geographical information. The discreet coloring chosen to distinguish political units ensures that names and signatures are easily readable. The exceptionally high density of information, with more than 14,000 entries in the index, in no way interferes with the well-balanced cartographic design. The map scales chosen are unusually large for a Pocket Atlas. Another asset is its selection of thematic maps of the world and individual continents. But there is even more to it: the map section is followed by a set of basic statistics comprising all countries of the world, thereby expanding the atlas to a geographical reference book.

This atlas was produced with the utmost care, but of course we welcome any suggestions for further improvements of content and design.

The publisher

Contents

Key to Regional maps

	International boundary
	Disputed / Undefined boundary
	Demarcation line
	Internal boundary
	Indication of country extent
MEXICO	Independent country
Réunion (Fr.)	Dependent territory
Karnataka	Federal state / Province
<u>Washington</u>	National capital
<u>Nashville</u>	Administrative center

	Highway / Road
	Railway
	Railway tunnel
	Rail ferry
	Canal
✈	International airport
⚓	Major port
⸫	Historical site
	River
	Seasonal river / Wadi
	Marsh, swamp
	Salt flat
· 4807	Mountain height (in m)
· -116	Depression depth (in m)

Settlements

■ BERLIN	more than 1,000,000 inhabitants
● Dublin	500,000 – 1,000,000 inhabitants
● Verona	100,000 – 500,000 inhabitants
⊙ Marbella	50,000 – 100,000 inhabitants
○ Kórinthos	10,000 – 50,000 inhabitants
○ Hammerfest	fewer than 10,000 inhabitants
	Urban agglomeration

Measures

1 m = 3.2808 feet

1 km = 0.6214 mile

1 km² = 0.3861 square mile

1000 m	
900 m	3,000 feet
800 m	2,500 feet
700 m	
600 m	2,000 feet
500 m	1,500 feet
400 m	
300 m	1,000 feet
200 m	500 feet
100 m	
0 m	0 foot

Comment on Ethnic maps

For reasons of scale the maps on "Peoples" can only present a selection of the major peoples and ethnic groups. There are different definitions of "people", depending on the context. In the field of ethnology the term comprises a linguistically and to a large extent culturally homogenous group that often lives in a territory of its own. The term as employed in these maps does not refer to the total population of a country, i.e. not to *Belgians* or *Moroccans*, but to the ethnic groups living there, namely *Flemings* and *Walloons* or *Arabs* and *Berbers*. Foreigners in the European Union and refugees are not shown.

In most cases the classification or grouping of the peoples follows general linguistic lines; there are some exceptions where cultural and geographic aspects have also been taken into account. Smaller ethnic groups are summed up under such familiar terms as *Papuans*, *Polynesians* or *Pygmies*.

The World at a Glimpse

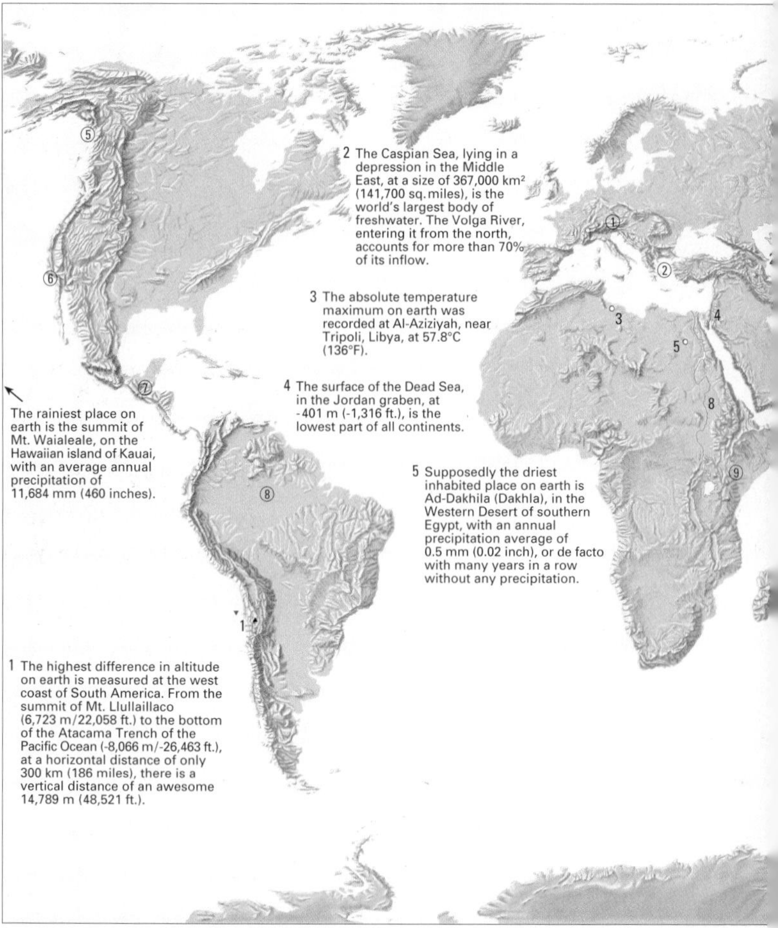

1 The highest difference in altitude on earth is measured at the west coast of South America. From the summit of Mt. Llullaillaco (6,723 m/22,058 ft.) to the bottom of the Atacama Trench of the Pacific Ocean (-8,066 m/-26,463 ft.), at a horizontal distance of only 300 km (186 miles), there is a vertical distance of an awesome 14,789 m (48,521 ft.).

2 The Caspian Sea, lying in a depression in the Middle East, at a size of 367,000 km² (141,700 sq. miles), is the world's largest body of freshwater. The Volga River, entering it from the north, accounts for more than 70% of its inflow.

3 The absolute temperature maximum on earth was recorded at Al-Aziziyah, near Tripoli, Libya, at 57.8°C (136°F).

4 The surface of the Dead Sea, in the Jordan graben, at -401 m (-1,316 ft.), is the lowest part of all continents.

5 Supposedly the driest inhabited place on earth is Ad-Dakhila (Dakhla), in the Western Desert of southern Egypt, with an annual precipitation average of 0.5 mm (0.02 inch), or de facto with many years in a row without any precipitation.

↖ The rainiest place on earth is the summit of Mt. Waialeale, on the Hawaiian island of Kauai, with an average annual precipitation of 11,684 mm (460 inches).

⑤ Glacier Bay, Alaska
(Rother, Schwäbisch Gmünd)

⑥ Los Angeles, United States
(Krauter, Esslingen)

⑦ Lake Atitlán, Guatemala
(Rother, Schwäbisch Gmünd)

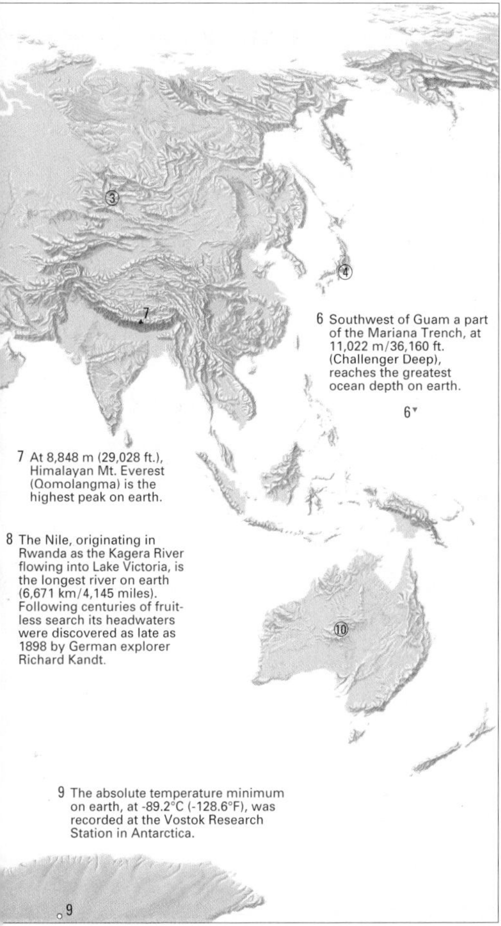

6 Southwest of Guam a part of the Mariana Trench, at 11,022 m/36,160 ft. (Challenger Deep), reaches the greatest ocean depth on earth.

7 At 8,848 m (29,028 ft.), Himalayan Mt. Everest (Qomolangma) is the highest peak on earth.

8 The Nile, originating in Rwanda as the Kagera River flowing into Lake Victoria, is the longest river on earth (6,671 km/4,145 miles). Following centuries of fruitless search its headwaters were discovered as late as 1898 by German explorer Richard Kandt.

9 The absolute temperature minimum on earth, at -89.2°C (-128.6°F), was recorded at the Vostok Research Station in Antarctica.

① The Alps, Europe
(Tauernkraft, Salzburg)

② Mýkonos, Greece
(Mauritius, Russell Kord)

③ Altai, Asia
(Sofinsky, Schwäbisch Gmünd)

④ Mount Fuji, Japan
(Mitsubishi, Rüsselsheim)

⑧ Rio Negro, Amazon Basin
(Rother, Schwäbisch Gmünd)

⑨ Dry Savanna, Kenya
(Rother, Schwäbisch Gmünd)

⑩ Kata Tjuta (Mt. Olga), Australia
(Rother, Schwäbisch Gmünd)

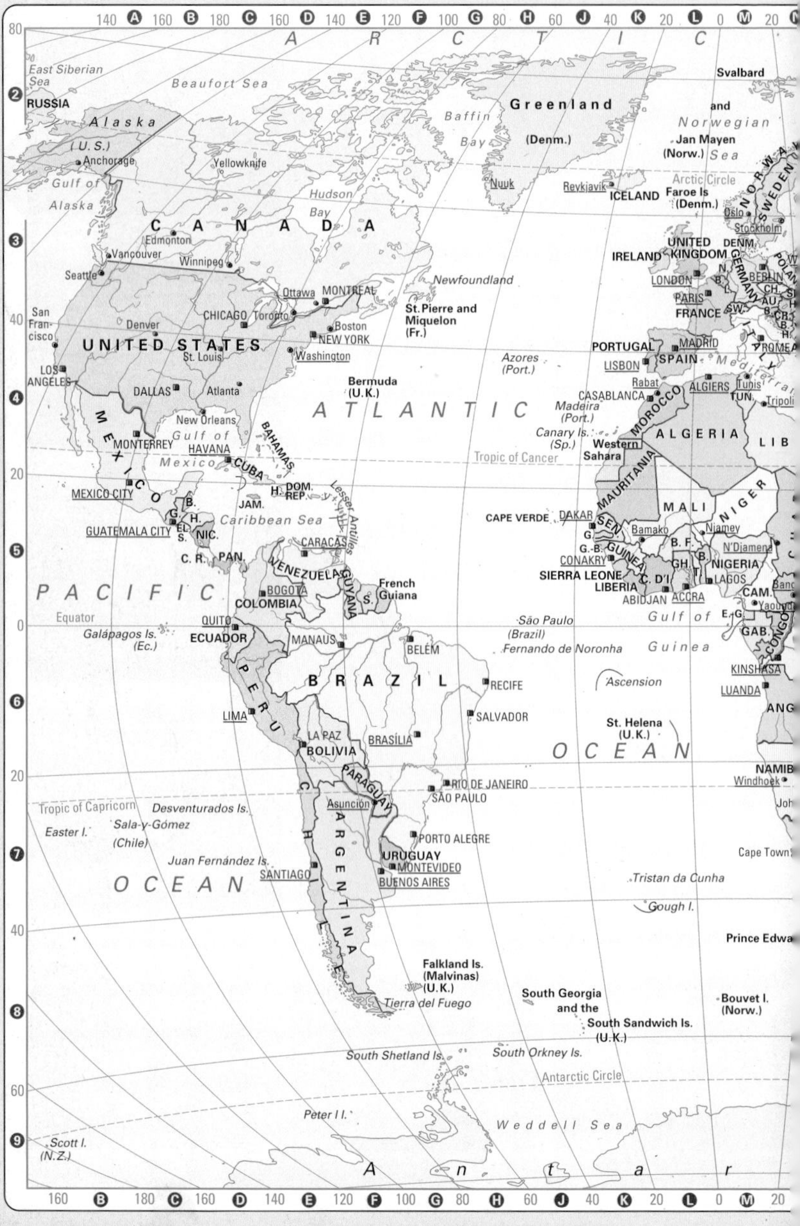
A R C T I C
East Siberian Sea
RUSSIA
Alaska
(U. S.)
Anchorage
Gulf of Alaska
Beaufort Sea
Yellowknife
Baffin Bay
Greenland
(Denm.)
Nuuk
Reykjavik
ICELAND
Svalbard
and
Norwegian Sea
Jan Mayen
(Norw.)
Arctic Circle
Faroe Is
(Denm.)
NORWAY
SWEDEN
Oslo
Stockholm
Hudson Bay
C A N A D A
Edmonton
Vancouver
Winnipeg
Seattle
Newfoundland
St. Pierre and Miquelon
(Fr.)
Ottawa
MONTREAL
Toronto
CHICAGO
Boston
NEW YORK
Washington
San Francisco
Denver
UNITED STATES
St. Louis
LOS ANGELES
DALLAS
Atlanta
New Orleans
Bermuda
(U.K.)
IRELAND
UNITED KINGDOM
LONDON
DENM.
N.
B.
L.
GERMANY
BERLIN
POLAND
CH.
PARIS
FRANCE
SW.
AU.
CR.
ITALY
ROME
PORTUGAL
LISBON
MADRID
SPAIN
Mediterranean
Azores
(Port.)
Rabat
CASABLANCA
MOROCCO
ALGIERS
Tunis
TUN.
Tripoli
Madeira
(Port.)
Canary Is.
(Sp.)
Western Sahara
ALGERIA
LIB
A T L A N T I C
MEXICO
MONTERREY
Gulf of Mexico
HAVANA
CUBA
BAHAMAS
Tropic of Cancer
MAURITANIA
MEXICO CITY
B.
G.
H.
EL S.
NIC.
GUATEMALA CITY
JAM.
H.
DOM. REP.
Lesser Antilles
Caribbean Sea
CAPE VERDE
DAKAR
SEN.
G.
G.-B.
MALI
NIGER
Bamako
Niamey
B. F.
N'Djamena
C. R.
PAN.
CARACAS
VENEZUELA
GUYANA
S.
French Guiana
CONAKRY
GUINEA
GH.
T.
B.
NIGERIA
SIERRA LEONE
LIBERIA
C. D'I.
LAGOS
ABIDJAN
ACCRA
CAM.
Yaoundé
P A C I F I C
BOGOTÁ
COLOMBIA
Equator
QUITO
ECUADOR
Galápagos Is.
(Ec.)
MANAUS
BELÉM
São Paulo
(Brazil)
Fernando de Noronha
Gulf of Guinea
E. G.
GAB.
CONGO
KINSHASA
LUANDA
ANG
PERU
BRAZIL
RECIFE
Ascension
LIMA
SALVADOR
St. Helena
(U.K.)
LA PAZ
BOLIVIA
BRASÍLIA
O C E A N
PARAGUAY
RIO DE JANEIRO
SÃO PAULO
NAMIB
Windhoek
Asunción
Tropic of Capricorn
Desventurados Is.
Easter I.
Sala-y-Gómez
(Chile)
CHILE
ARGENTINA
PORTO ALEGRE
URUGUAY
MONTEVIDEO
BUENOS AIRES
Cape Town
Juan Fernández Is.
SANTIAGO
O C E A N
Tristan da Cunha
Gough I.
Prince Edwa
Falkland Is.
(Malvinas)
(U.K.)
Tierra del Fuego
South Georgia and the South Sandwich Is.
(U.K.)
Bouvet I.
(Norw.)
South Shetland Is.
South Orkney Is.
Antarctic Circle
Peter I I.
Weddell Sea
Scott I.
(N.Z.)
A n t a r

O C E A N
Franz Josef Land
Severnaya Zemlya
Novaya Zemlya
Barents Sea
Kara Sea
Laptev Sea
New Siberian Is.
East Siberian Sea
Wrangel I.
CANADA
Alaska (U.S.)
Anchorage
Norilsk
Yakutia
Yakutsk
Bering Sea
Sea of Okhotsk
Aleutian Is.
R U S S I A
ST. PETERSBURG
YEKATERINBURG
OMSK
NOVOSIBIRSK
MOSCOW
NIZHNIY NOVGOROD
SAMARA
Irkutsk
Petropavlovsk-Kamchatskiy
Kurile Is.
Khabarovsk
Astana
KIEV
UKRAINE
KAZAKHSTAN
MONGOLIA
Ulan Bator
Manchuria
CHANGCHUN
Vladivostok
ALMATY
TASHKENT
KYRG.
ÜRÜMQI
UZBEK.
TAJ.
TURKM.
BULG.
G.
AZ.
ANKARA
TURKEY
PEKING
N. KOREA
S.
SEOUL
TOKYO
JAPAN
OSAKA
TEHRĀN
IRAN
AFGH.
Kabul
SYRIA
C.
L.
I.
IRAQ
BAGHDAD
JORD.
K.
PAKISTAN
LAHORE
DELHI
New Delhi
Tibet
CHINA
XI'AN
CHENGDU
WUHAN
SHANGHAI
Ryukyu Is.
Bonin Is.
PACIFIC
Volcano Is.
CAIRO
EGYPT
SAUDI ARABIA
RIYADH
B.
Q.
U.A.E.
KARACHI
NEPAL
BH.
B.
CALCUTTA
INDIA
GUANGZHOU
HONG KONG
TAIWAN
JIDDAH
OMAN
MUMBAI
MYANMAR
HANOI
LAOS
VIETNAM
Hainan
Northern Mariana Is. (U.S.)
Arabian Sea
Bay of Bengal
RANGOON
THAILAND
BANGKOK
C.
MANILA
PHILIPPINES
Guam (U.S.)
Khartoum
ER.
Sana
YEMEN
Socotra
CHENNAI
(Ind.)
SUDAN
DJ.
ADDIS ABABA
ETHIOPIA
SOMALIA
SRI LANKA
Colombo
Ceylon
MICRONESIA
KUALA LUMPUR
BR.
MALAYSIA
PALAU
OCEAN
Mogadishu
UG.
KENYA
NAIROBI
MALDIVES
SINGAPORE
S.
Sumatra
Borneo (Kalimantan)
Celebes (Sulawesi)
Equator
R.
B.
TANZANIA
DAR ES SALAAM
Brit. Indian Ocean Terr. (U.K.)
SEYCHELLES
INDONESIA
JAKARTA
SURABAYA
Java
PAPUA NEW GUINEA
COMOROS
INDIAN
Christmas I. (Austr.)
Port Moresby
ZAMBIA
M.
MOZAMBIQUE
Cocos Is. (Austr.)
HARARE
ZIMB.
MADAGASCAR
ANTANANARIVO
Coral Sea
Réunion (Fr.)
MAURITIUS
Maputo
SW.
L.
AUSTRALIA
BRISBANE
OCEAN
PERTH
Amsterdam
Saint-Paul
ADELAIDE
SYDNEY
Canberra
French Southern and Antarctic Terr.
MELBOURNE
Tasman Sea
Marion Is. (S. Afr.)
Crozet Is.
Tasmania
NEW ZEALAND
Wellington
Kerguelen Is.
Chatham Is.
Heard and McDonald Is. (Austr.)
Macquarie (Austr.)
Balleny Is.
Scott I.
t i c a
Ross Sea

A R C T I C
Greenland (Denm.)
Svalbard and Jan Mayen (Norw.)
Franz Josef Land
Severnaya Zemlya
Barents Sea
Novaya Zemlya
Kara Sea
Laptev Sea
New Siberian Is.
East Siberian Sea
Wrangel I.
NORWAY
SWEDEN
FINLAND
Oslo
Stockholm
Norilsk
Arctic Circle
E.
ST. PETERSBURG
R U S S I A
Yakutsk
LIT.
B.
NIZHNIY NOVGOROD
MOSCOW
YEKATERINBURG
SAMARA
NOVOSIBIRSK
KIEV
UKR.
OMSK
Astana
Irkutsk
Sea of Okhotsk
Petropavlovsk-Kamchatskiy
Bering Sea
Aleutian Is.
KAZAKHSTAN
Ulan Bator
MONGOLIA
Khabarovsk
Kurile Is.
G.
A.
AZ.
UZBEK.
ALMATY
TASHKENT
KYRG.
ÜRÜMQI
Manchuria
CHANGCHUN
Vladivostok
TURKM.
TAJ.
PEKING
TEHRAN
Kabul
AFGH.
IRAN
C H I N A
N. KOREA
S.
SEOUL
TOKYO
Tibet
XI'AN
OSAKA
LAHORE
PAKISTAN
CHENGDU
WUHAN
SHANGHAI
J A P A N
P A C I
Midway (U.S.)
DELHI
NEPAL
BH.
New Delhi
Ryukyu Is.
Bonin Is.
U.A.E.
KARACHI
OMAN
I N D I A
B.
GUANGZHOU
CALCUTTA
MYAN-
HANOI
HONG KONG
TAIWAN
Wake (U.S.)
MUMBAI
MAR
LAOS
VIETNAM
Hainan
Northern Mariana Is. (U.S.)
Johnston Atoll (U.S.)
Arabian Sea
Bay of Bengal
RANGOON
THAI-LAND
MANILA
MARSHALL ISLANDS
CHENNAI
(Ind.)
BANGKOK
C.
Guam (U.S.)
PHILIPPINES
Caroline Is.
O
SRI LANKA
Ceylon
Colombo
MALAYSIA
BR.
KUALA LUMPUR
PALAU
MICRONESIA
Howland I.
Baker I.
MALDIVES
Equator
SINGAPORE
S.
Sumatra
Borneo (Kalimantan)
Celebes (Sulawesi)
Gilbert Is.
NAURU
Phoenix Is.
KIRI
Brit. Indian Ocean Terr. (U.K.)
I N D O N E S I A
PAPUA NEW GUINEA
SOLOMON ISLANDS
Tokelau (N.Z.)
JAKARTA
SURABAYA
Java
TUVALU
Port Moresby
Wallis and Futuna (Fr.)
SAMOA
Christmas I. (Austr.)
Cocos Is. (Austr.)
VANUATU
Coral Sea
New Caledonia (Fr.)
FIJI
TONGA
I N D I A N
MAURITIUS
Réunion (Fr.)
Tropic of Capricorn
A U S T R A L I A
BRISBANE
Norfolk (Austr.)
Kermadec (N.Z.)
PERTH
ADELAIDE
SYDNEY
Canberra
MELBOURNE
O C E A N
Tasman Sea
NEW ZEALAND
Wellington
Amsterdam
Saint-Paul
Tasmania
Chatham Is.
French Southern and Antarctic Terr.
Bounty Is.
Auckland Is.
(N.Z.)
Antipodes
Crozet Is.
Kerguelen Is.
Macquarie (Austr.)
Prince Edward and Marion Is. (S. Afr.)
Heard and McDonald Is. (Austr.)
Balleny Is.
Scott I.
Ross S
A n t a

| 0 | 1000 | 2000 | 3000 km |
| 0 | 1000 | 2000 | miles |

O 140 P 120 Q 100 R 80 S 60 T 40 U 20 V 0 W 20 X 40 Y 60 Z 80 100

O C E A N

Franz Josef Land

Barents
Sea Novaya Zemlya

Svalbard
and *Norwegian* RUSSIA
Jan Mayen FINLAND
(Norw.) *Sea* NORWAY SWEDEN

Greenland
(Denm.)

Baffin ICELAND Stockh. ②

Beaufort Sea Bay Reykjavik Oslo 60

Faroe Is.
(Denm.) DENM.

Alaska Nuuk UNITED N.
(U.S.) KINGDOM

Anchorage Yellowknife Hudson IRELAND LONDON ③

Gulf of C A N A D A *Bay* FRANCE
Alaska Edmonton

Newfoundland

Vancouver Winnipeg St. Pierre and 40
Seattle MONTREAL Miquelon
Ottawa Toronto (Fr.)

CHICAGO Boston Azores
San Francisco Denver St. Louis NEW YORK (Port.)

U N I T E D S T A T E S Washington ④

LOS Atlanta Bermuda A T L A N T I C
ANGELES DALLAS (U.K.)

Tropic of Cancer

Hawaiian Is. New Orleans BAHAMAS
(U.S.) Gulf of HAVANA O C E A N 20

Revillagigedo Is. M E X I C O *Mexico* CUBA Lesser Antilles ⑤
(Mex.) MEXICO CITY B. DOM.
GUATEMALA CITY H. JAMAICA REP.
E EL
A N EL S. Caribbean Sea
Clipperton NIC.
(Fr.) C.R. PAN. VENEZUELA CARACAS

BOGOTÁ G. French
COLOMBIA S. Guiana

ngman Reef QUITO Equator 0
Palmyra Atoll Galápagos Is. ECUADOR
rvis I. Kiritimati (Ec.) MANAUS BELÉM

TI RECIFE

ok Is. French P E R U B R A Z I L ⑥
an LIMA SALVADOR
N.Z. Polynesia LA PAZ BRASÍLIA

BOLIVIA
20
Pitcairn Desventurados Is. RIO DE JANEIRO
(U.K.) Easter I. Sala-y-Gómez SÃO PAULO
(Chile) Asunción PARAGUAY

Juan Fernández Is. PORTO ALEGRE ⑦
SANTIAGO URUGUAY
BUENOS MONTEVIDEO
AIRES

A R G E N T I N A 40

Falkland Is.
(Malvinas)
(U.K.) ⑧
Tierra del Fuego South Georgia
and the
South Sandwich Is. Bouvet I.
Antarctic Circle (U.K.) (Norw.)

South Shetland Is. 60
Peter I I. South Orkney Is.

Weddell Sea ⑨

c t i c a

O 140 P 120 Q 100 R 80 S 60 T 40 U 20 V 0 W 20 X 40 Y 60

A R C T I C
Queen Elizabeth Is.
East Siberian Sea
Wrangel I.
Beaufort Sea
Point Barrow
Sverdrup Is.
Parry Is.
Ellesmere I.
Devon I.
Bering Str.
Alaska
Victoria I.
Baffin Bay
Baffin I.
Greenland
Spitsbergen
Norwegian Sea
Mt. McKinley 6194
Alaska Range
Anchorage
Gulf of Alaska
Kodiak I.
Yukon
Mackenzie
Yellowknife
Davis Str.
Gunnbjørn Fjeld 3700
Denmark Str.
Nuuk
Reykjavik
Iceland
2119
Arctic Circle
Hudson Bay
Coast Mts.
Canadian Shield
Labrador
Labrador Sea
Cape Farewell
British Isles
North Sea
Oslo
Stockholm
Edmonton
Vancouver
Seattle
Winnipeg
NORTH AMERICA
Newfoundland
LONDON
BERLIN
Land's End
PARIS
Alps
Mont Blanc 4807
MONTREAL
Cape Race
Rocky Mountains
Great Plains
Missouri
Mississippi
Toronto
Boston
Appalachian Mts.
San Francisco
Sa. Nevada
4418
Mt. Whitney
4399
Denver
St. Louis
CHICAGO
NEW YORK
Washington
Mt. Mitchell
2037
C. Finisterre
MADRID
ROME
LISBON
ALGIERS
Mediterranean
Tunis
Tripoli
LOS ANGELES
DALLAS
Atlanta
Cape Hatteras
CASABLANCA
Madeira
Toubkal 4165
Atlas
Canary Is.
New Orleans
Florida
ATLANTIC
Sa. Madre Occ.
MONTERREY
Gulf of Mexico
Bahama Is.
HAVANA
Cuba
Tropic of Cancer
C. San Lucas
Ahaggar
2918
Sahara
Pico de Orizaba 5675
MEXICO CITY
Hispaniola
Greater Antilles
Lesser Antilles
C. Nouadhibou
Cape Verde Is.
DAKAR
C. Verde
Niger
Caribbean Sea
Punta Gallinas
GUATEMALA CITY
Bamako
Niamey
L. Chad
N'Djamena
5775
CARACAS
Llanos
CONAKRY
LAGOS
PACIFIC
2810
Guiana Highlands
BOGOTÁ
3014
Cameroon Mtn. 4095
ABIDJAN
ACCRA
Equator
Galápagos Is.
QUITO
São Paulo
Gulf of Guinea
C. Lopez
Chimborazo 6272
MANAUS
Amazon
BELÉM
Fernando de Noronha
C. de São Roque
Selvas
Punta Negra
Huascarán 6768
RECIFE
Ascension
LUANDA
Campos
SOUTH AMERICA
LIMA
SALVADOR
Andes
LA PAZ
BRASÍLIA
Brazilian Highlands
St. Helena
6542
Pico da Bandeira 2890
OCEAN
RIO DE JANEIRO
SÃO PAULO
Windhoek
Tropic of Capricorn
Desventurados Is.
Asunción
Sala-y-Gómez
Easter I.
Gran Chaco
PORTO ALEGRE
Pampas
Aconcagua 6959
Cape Town
Cape of Good Hope
Juan Fernández Is.
SANTIAGO
MONTEVIDEO
Tristan da Cunha
OCEAN
BUENOS AIRES
Río de la Plata
Gough I.
Patagonia
4058
Falkland Is.
South Georgia
Tierra del Fuego
Bouvet I.
Str. of Magellan
Cape Horn
Scotia Sea
South Sandwich Is.
Drake Passage
South Shetland Is.
South Orkney Is.
Antarctic Pen.
Antarctic Circle
Bellingshausen Sea
Peter I I.
Alexander I.
Mt. Jackson 4191
Weddell Sea
Queen Maud
Amundsen Sea
Scott I.
Ellsworth Land
Berkner I.
A N T A R C
140 160 180 160 140 120 100 80 60 40 20 0 20
A B C D E F G H J K L M

O C E A N
Franz Josef Land
Severnaya Zemlya
C. Chelyuskin
New Siberian Is.
East Siberian Sea
Point Barrow
Beaufort Sea
Victoria I.
Novaya Zemlya
Kara Sea
Taimyr Pen.
Laptev Sea
Bering Str.
Alaska
Yukon
Barents Sea
North Cape
1701
Norilsk
Central Siberian Plateau
Cherskiy Ra.
6194
Mt. McKinley
Alaska Ra.
Anchorage
Narodnaya 1895
Ural Mts
West Siberian Plain
Yenisey
Lena
Yakutia
Yakutsk
Bering Sea
ST. PETERSBURG
NIZHNIY NOVGOROD
MOSCOW
YEKATERINBURG
OMSK
NOVOSIBIRSK
Ob
Stanovoy Ra.
Sea of Okhotsk
Kamchatka
Klyuchevskaya Sopka 4750
Aleutian Is.
7822
Petropavlovsk-Kamchatskiy
SAMARA
Volga
E
P
KIEV
4506
Altai
Sayan
Irkutsk
L. Baykal
Amur
Khabarovsk
Sakhalin
Kurile Is.
10900
Ulan Bator
Manchuria
Vladivostok
Hokkaido
Caucasus
Elbrus 5642
Black Sea
-28
Caspian Sea
Aral Sea
ALMATY
ÜRÜMQI
TASHKENT
Tien Shan
Gobi
CHANGCHUN
Sea of Japan
Honshu
A S I A
ANKARA
Anatolia
ATHENS
Elburz Mts.
5671
TEHRAN
7495
Altun Shan
7723
Hindu Kush
Kabul
Kunlun Shan
PEKING
SEOUL
Korea
Japan
Mt. Fuji 3776
TOKYO
OSAKA
10062
Iranian Plateau
Tibet
XI'AN
Yellow R.
SHANGHAI
Kyushu
BAGHDAD
CAIRO
-133
-401
LAHORE
Himalayas
CHENGDU
WUHAN
7556
Yangtze
Ryukyu Is.
Bonin Is.
Nile
Red Sea
Arabian Pen.
DELHI
Mt. Everest 8848
PACIFIC
Volcano Is.
9156
RIYADH
KARACHI
CALCUTTA
GUANGZHOU
3952
Taiwan
HONG KONG
Mariana Is.
JIDDAH
2980
Ras al-Hadd
India
HANOI
Hainan
Luzon
MUMBAI
Arabian Sea
Bay of Bengal
RANGOON
Further India
BANGKOK
South China Sea
Philippines
MANILA
Khartoum
3071
4620
Sana
3620
Socotra
C. Guardafui
CHENNAI
Challenger Deep 11022
Ethiopian Highlands
ADDIS ABABA
2695
10497
Caroline Is.
Somali Pen.
Cape Comorin
Colombo
2524
Ceylon
Kinabalu 4101
Mindanao
5824
Mogadishu
Maldives
KUALA LUMPUR
SINGAPORE
OCEAN
L. Victoria
Borneo (Kalimantan)
Equator
NAIROBI
Kilimanjaro 5895
Sumatra
3805
Celebes (Sulawesi)
3455
Bismarck Arch.
New Guinea
DAR ES SALAAM
Seychelles
Chagos Is.
Greater Sunda Is.
Puncak Jaya 5030
JAKARTA
SURABAYA
Java
3676
Lesser Sunda Is.
4073
Cabo Delgado
Comoro Is.
INDIAN
7450
C. York
Port Moresby
Lusaka
2876
3002
Cocos Is.
Mozambique Ch.
Madagascar
ANTANANARIVO
HARARE
Mascarene Is.
Coral Sea
North West Cape
Maputo
Johannesburg
3482
Drakensberg
1510
Great Dividing Range
6400
AUSTRALIA
Great Victoria Desert
-12
BRISBANE
OCEAN
1011
PERTH
Cape Leeuwin
ADELAIDE
Amsterdam
Saint-Paul
Austr. Alps
2228
Mt. Kosciusko
SYDNEY
5671
MELBOURNE
North Island
Tasman Sea
Crozet Is.
Tasmania
5267
New Zealand
2797
Wellington
Prince Edward I.
South East C.
Mt. Cook 3764
South Island
Kerguelen Is.
Heard
South West C.
Macquarie
6250
Height of Land
4000 m (13124 ft.)
2000 m (6562 ft.)
1000 m (3281 ft.)
500 m (1640 ft.)
200 m (656 ft.)
0 m (0 ft.)
Depression
Depth of Sea
200 m (656 ft.)
2000 m (6562 ft.)
4000 m (13124 ft.)
6000 m (19686 ft.)
8000 m (26248 ft.)
Inland ice, glaciers
Balleny Is.
Wilkes Land
4163
Mt. Erebus 3794
Ross I.
Ross Sea
T I C A
40 O 60 P 80 Q 100 R 120 S 140 T 160 U 180 V 160 W 140 X 120 Y 100 Z 80
2 3 4 5 6 7 8 9
60 40 20 0 20 40 60

A B C D E F G H J
150 180 150 120 90 60 40 0
ARCTIC
New Siberian Is.
East Siberian Sea
Bering Str.
Point Barrow
Beaufort Sea
Queen Elizabeth Is.
Magnetic Pole
Ellesmere I.
Greenland
Spitsbergen
Victoria I.
Baffin Bay
Baffin I.
Norwegian Sea
Alaska Ra.
6194 Mt. McKinley
Yukon
Mackenzie
Barrengrounds
3700
Davis Str.
Denmark Str.
Iceland
2119
Reykjavik
Nuuk
Faroe Is.
Gulf of Alaska
Hudson Bay
Labrador Sea
Cape Farewell
Gulf Stream
Stockholm
Labrador
Labrador Current
British Isles
North Sea
Baltic
NORTH AMERICA
Rocky Mountains
Prairies
Great Lakes
New-foundland
Cape Race
MONTREAL
LONDON
BERLIN
PARIS
EU
Missouri
Great Basin
Sa. Nevada
4418
Mont Blanc 4807
Alps
CHICAGO
NEW YORK
Gulf Stream
C. Finisterre
MADRID
ROME
Azores
3478
Mediterranea
Mississippi
LOS ANGELES
ATLANTIC
CASABLANCA
ALGIERS
Bermuda Is.
Madeira
4165
Atlas
Canary Is.
Gulf of Mexico
Bahama Is.
HAVANA
Cuba
Canary Current
MEXICO CITY
P. de Orizaba 5675
Greater Antilles
North Equatorial Current
Sahara
3415
Lesser Antilles
Caribbean Sea
Cape Verde Is.
DAKAR
C. Verde
Sahel
L. Ch
GUATEMALA CITY
Pta. Gallinas
Niger
AFR
CARACAS
Trinidad
South Equatorial Current
LAGOS
Cameroon M 4095
Equatorial Counter Current
Llanos
BOGOTA
Guiana Highlands
Guinea Current
ABIDJAN
São Paulo
São Tomé
MANAUS
Selvas
Galápagos Is.
Amazon
Fernando de Noronha
C. de São Roque
Benguela Current
Punta Negra
SOUTH AMERICA
Ascension
LUANDA
PACIFIC
Campos
Brazil Current
LIMA
6613
Brazilian Highlands
OCEAN
Humboldt Current
Andes
St. Helena
Namib
OCEAN
Atacama
Gran Chaco
RIO DE JANEIRO
SÃO PAULO
Easter I.
Sala-y-Gómez
Aconcagua
SANTIAGO
6959
BUENOS AIRES
Cape Town
Cape of Good Hope
30
Juan Fernández Is.
Río de la Plata
Pampas
Tristan da Cunha
Gough I.
Patagonia
Falkland Is.
South Georgia
Bouvet I.
Punta Arenas
Tierra del Fuego
Str. of Magellan
West Wind Drift
Cape Horn
Drake Passage
South Sandwich Is.
South Orkney Is.
South Shetland Is.
Antarctic Circ
60
Antarctic Pen.
Peter I Island
Alexander Island
4191
Weddell Sea
AN
1 2 3 4 5 6
Inland ice, glaciers
Tundra, high mountains
Forest tundra
Northern (coniferous) boreal forest, taiga
Tropical rain forest, humid monsoon forest
Other tall-treed forests
Heathlands, grasslands of the northern boreal forest zone
Agricultural lands, intensively used meadows and pastures
Steppe, dry grassland
Humid savanna (grasslands and savanna fore
Dry savanna (grassland and seasonally dry fo
Semi-desert, desert

K L M N O P Q R
60 90 120 150 180 150 120 90
O C E A N
Franz Josef Land
Severnaya Zemlya
C. Chelyuskin
New Siberian Is.
Laptev Sea
East Siberian Sea
Point Barrow
Beaufort Sea
Victoria I.
Novaya Zemlya
Barents Sea
Kara Sea
North Cape
Norilsk
Arctic Circle
Bering Str.
Yukon
Alaska Ra.
6194
Mt. McKinley
Yakutsk
Siberia
Ural Mts.
Yenisey
Ob
Lena
Bering Sea
Sea of Okhotsk
Klyuchevskaya Sopka
4750
Kamchatka
Aleutian Is.
ST. PETERSBURG
CHELYABINSK
NOVOSIBIRSK
Irkutsk
Baykal
Sakhalin
Kurile Is.
Oya Shio
MOSCOW
Volga
EUROPE
ASIA
4506
Altai
Ulan Bator
Amur
Khabarovsk
KIEV
PEST
Kazakh Steppe
Aral Sea
Caucasus
5642
Black Sea
Casp. Sea
Kyzyl Kum
TASHKENT
Tien Shan
Gobi
SHENYANG
PEKING
Yellow R.
Japan. Meer
Hokkaido
Honshu
3776
TOKYO
Kuro Shio
ISTANBUL
BAKU
Kara Kum
Takla Makan
7723
SEOUL
ATHENS
TEHRAN
Hindu Kush
Kabul
8611
XI'AN
East China Sea
SHANGHAI
Sea
DAMASCUS
Himalayas
Tibet
-401
CAIRO
DELHI
Mt. Everest
8848
Yangtze
Ryukyu Is.
Bonin Is.
Tropic of Cancer
Libyan Desert
RIYADH
KARACHI
Taiwan
PACIFIC
Arabian Pen.
Ras al Hadd
CALCUTTA
HANOI
HONG KONG
Hainan
Mariana Is.
Nil
Red Sea
Rub al-Khālī
MUMBAI
Deccan
Bay of Bengal
RANGOON
South China Sea
Philippines
North Equatorial Current
Arabian Sea
BANGKOK
MANILA
3620
4620
G. of Aden
Socotra
CHENNAI
Caroline Is.
Cape Guardafui
Ceylon
C. Comorin
Sudd
AFRICA
ADDIS ABABA
North Equatorial Current
4101
Equatorial Counter Current
OCEAN
Maldives
SINGAPORE
Borneo
Equator
Sumatra
Celebes
South Equatorial Current
NAIROBI
Kilimanjaro
5895
Lake Victoria
Indian Counter Current
Greater Sunda Is.
5030
New Guinea
Seychelles
DAR ES SALAAM
Chagos Is.
JAKARTA
Java
Lesser Sunda Is.
C. Delgado
Comoro Is.
South Equatorial Current
C. York
Solomon Is.
Cocos Is.
INDIAN
Gt. Barrier Reef
Coral Sea
Mozambique Ch.
Madagascar
Mauritius
Réunion
Tropic of Capricorn
North West C.
New Caledonia
OCEAN
AUSTRALIA
Great Victoria Desert
3482
Agulhas Current
PERTH
Norfolk I.
East Australian Current
C. Leeuwin
SYDNEY
Amsterdam
St-Paul
Mt. Kosciusko
2228
Auckland
MELBOURNE
Tasman Sea
West Wind Drift
Crozet Is.
2797
Prince Edward I.
Tasmania
New Zealand
Kerguelen Is.
South East C.
3764
West Wind Drift
South West C.
Chatham Is.
Heard
Macquarie Is.
Magnetic Pole
Balleny Is.
Scott I.
ANTARCTICA
0 30 60
1 2 3 4 5 6
Intermittently flooded land
Swamp or marsh
Salt lake, salt pan (sebkha)
Mangrove swamp
Antarctic shelf ice
Permanently frozen Polar Sea
Ocean frozen in winter
Ocean frozen episodically
Frequent icebergs
Cold upwelling water
Ocean current, colder than its surroundings
Ocean current, warmer than its surroundings
Coral reef

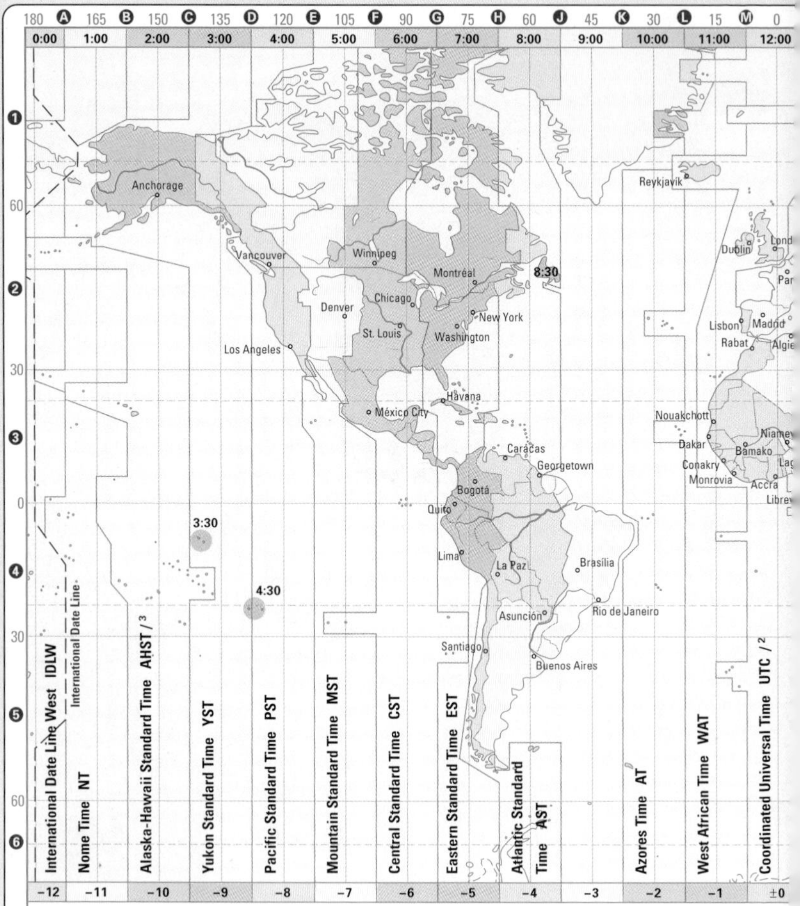

Zonal time (disregarding daylight (saving) time/ summer time)

National time

1 Middle European Time MET
Middle European Winter Time MEWT

2 Western European Time WET
Greenwich Mean Time GMT

3 Central Alaska Time CAT
Hawaii Standard Time HST

4 New Zealand Standard Time NZST

Countries with their own time (at 12 a. m. UTC/GMT):

Afghanistan 16:30

Australia:
Northern Territory 21:30
South Australia 21:30

India 17:30

Iran 15:30

Canada:
Newfoundland 8:30

Cocos Islands 18:30

Marquesas Islands 3:3

Myanmar (Burma) 18:3

Nepal 17:45

New Zealand:
Chatham Islands 0:45

Norfolk Island 23:30

Pitcairn Island 4:30

The earth turns around its axis once in 24 hours. Therefore along the upper margin of the map the nominal 24 time zones are marked, with a time difference of one hour from zone to zone (e. g. Central European Time, CET). The real delimitation of the time zones, especially on the land surface of the earth, deviates from the meridians in many ways, frequently following political boundaries. Along the lower margin of the map the differences in time are given that exist between the various zonal times and Coordinated Universal Time. Countries and islands where a special time is used that deviates from the world time zones system are designated by a different color and the zonal time in relation to 12 a. m. Coordinated Universal Time.

The International Date Line, which largely follows the 180th meridian, marks the line along which a calendar day has to be repeated while crossing it from west to east, and has to be skipped while crossing it from east to west.

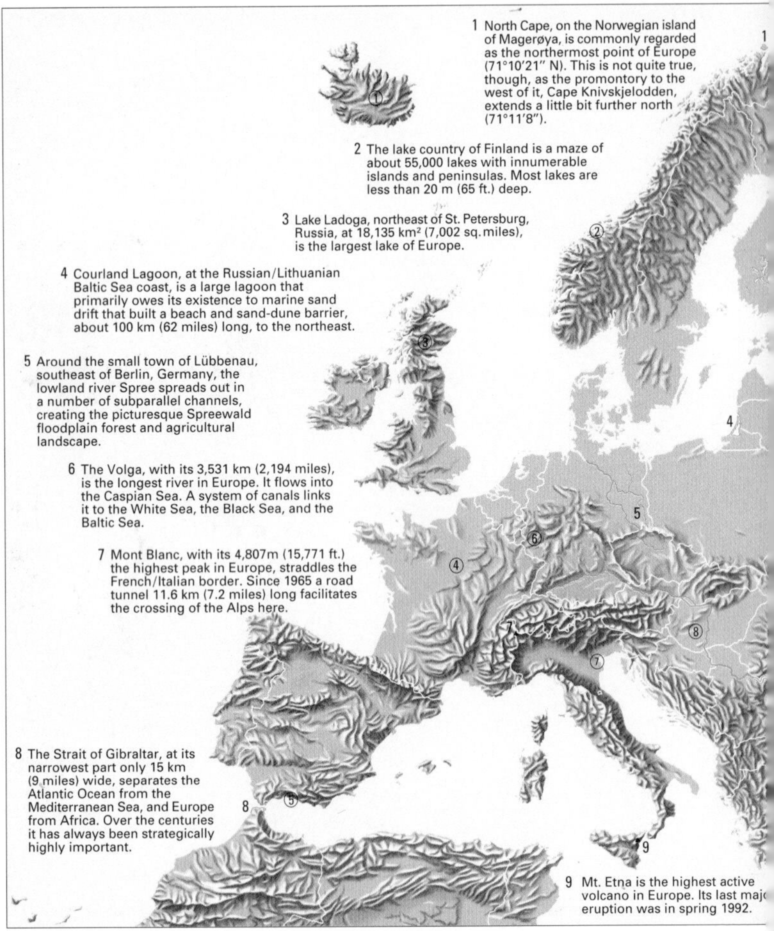

1 North Cape, on the Norwegian island of Magerøya, is commonly regarded as the northermost point of Europe (71°10′21″ N). This is not quite true, though, as the promontory to the west of it, Cape Knivskjelodden, extends a little bit further north (71°11′8″).

2 The lake country of Finland is a maze of about 55,000 lakes with innumerable islands and peninsulas. Most lakes are less than 20 m (65 ft.) deep.

3 Lake Ladoga, northeast of St. Petersburg, Russia, at 18,135 km² (7,002 sq. miles), is the largest lake of Europe.

4 Courland Lagoon, at the Russian/Lithuanian Baltic Sea coast, is a large lagoon that primarily owes its existence to marine sand drift that built a beach and sand-dune barrier, about 100 km (62 miles) long, to the northeast.

5 Around the small town of Lübbenau, southeast of Berlin, Germany, the lowland river Spree spreads out in a number of subparallel channels, creating the picturesque Spreewald floodplain forest and agricultural landscape.

6 The Volga, with its 3,531 km (2,194 miles), is the longest river in Europe. It flows into the Caspian Sea. A system of canals links it to the White Sea, the Black Sea, and the Baltic Sea.

7 Mont Blanc, with its 4,807m (15,771 ft.) the highest peak in Europe, straddles the French/Italian border. Since 1965 a road tunnel 11.6 km (7.2 miles) long facilitates the crossing of the Alps here.

8 The Strait of Gibraltar, at its narrowest part only 15 km (9 miles) wide, separates the Atlantic Ocean from the Mediterranean Sea, and Europe from Africa. Over the centuries it has always been strategically highly important.

9 Mt. Etna is the highest active volcano in Europe. Its last maj eruption was in spring 1992.

⑤ Andalusia, Spain
(Rother, Schwäbisch Gmünd)

⑥ Cochem/Mosel, Germany
(Mauritius, Power Stock)

⑦ Grand Canal, Venice
(Mauritius, Visa Image)

3
⑩
6
⑨
10 The Danube, 2,858 km (1,776 miles) long and navigable below Regensburg, Bavaria, links 10 European states.

① Iceland
(Schulz, Schwäbisch Gmünd)

② Geirangerfjorden, Norway
(Mauritius, HPM)

③ Scotland
(PhotoDisc)

④ Paris
(Rother, Schwäbisch Gmünd)

Balaton, Hungary
(MTI Foto Archiv)

⑨ Moldova
(Itar Tass, Moscow)

⑩ Southern Ural Mountains
(Itar Tass, Moscow)

Denmark Strait
Jan Mayen (Norw.)
ARCTIC
Reykjavik
ICELAND
Norwegian Sea
Arctic Circle
ATLANTIC OCEAN
Faroe Is. (Denm.)
Ålesund
Trondheim
Sognefj.
Shetland Is.
Orkney Is.
Bergen
British Isles
Stavanger
Oslo
Scotland
Aberdeen
UNITED KINGDOM
Glasgow
Edinburgh
Kristiansand
Skagerrak
Kattegat
North Sea
Belfast
Newcastle
IRELAND
Dublin
Irish Sea
England
COPENHAGEN
DENMARK
Cork
Manchester
Wales
BIRMINGHAM
HAMBURG
Land's End
Bristol
LONDON
Amsterdam
NETHERLANDS
Bremen
Szczecin
Greenw.
ROTTERD.
Hannover
BERLIN
English Channel
Lille
Brussels
Düsseldorf
Channel Is.
Le Havre
BELGIUM
Cologne
Leipzig
Elbe
LUX.
GERMANY
Rennes
PARIS
Meuse
Frankfurt
Luxembourg
CZE
Seine
Rhine
Stuttgart
Nantes
Loire
Strasbourg
Danube
Bay of Biscay
Dijon
MUNICH
VIE
FRANCE
Berne
SWITZERLAND
AUSTR
Drau
C. Finisterre
Gijón
Bordeaux
Lyon
Vigo
Turin
MILAN
Ljubljana
Bilbao
Venice
Porto
Po
Toulouse
Montpellier
Genoa
Bologna
Valladolid
Ebro
Nice
Florence
AND.
MON.
PORTUGAL
Marseille
S.M.
Zaragoza
Aragon
Ligurian Sea
Adriatic
MADRID
Catalonia
LISBON
Tagus
BARCELONA
Corsica
SPAIN
VAT.
ROME
ITALY
Cape Saint Vincent
Valencia
Seville
Córdoba
Balearic Is.
Menorca
NAPLES
Palma
Mallorca
Andalusia
Ibiza
Sardinia
Tyrrhenian Sea
Madeira (Port.)
Murcia
Strait of Gibraltar
Málaga
Cagliari
Tanger
Gibraltar (U.K.)
Mediterranean
Str. of Sicily
Palermo
Melilla (Sp.)
Oran
ALGIERS
Sicily
CASABLANCA
Rabat
Fez
Annaba
Oujda
Constantine
Tunis
La Palma
Canary Is. (Sp.)
Pantelleria
Moulouya
Marrakech
Sousse
Tenerife
MALTA
Valletta
Las Palmas
Agadir
MOROCCO
TUNISIA
Gran Canaria
Fuerteventura
Laghouat
Sfax
G. of Gabès
Djerba
Béchar
Touggourt
El Aaiún
Tripoli
Western Sahara
ALGERIA
West from Greenwich 0 East from Greenwich

OCEAN
North Cape
Kolguyev
Barents Sea
Vadsø
Tromsø
Salekhard
Ob
Nizhnevartovsk
Surgut
Naryan-Mar
Murmansk
Pechora
Khanty-Mansiysk
Lapland
Inari
Kirovsk
Mezen
Ukhta
Irtysh
Rovaniemi
White Sea
Tobolsk
Karelia
Arkhangelsk
Severodvinsk
Luleå
Oulu
FINLAND
SWEDEN
NORWAY
Serov
Tobol
Ishim
Onega
North. Dvina
Vychegda
Syktyvkar
Tyumen
Umeå
Gulf of Bothnia
Berezniki
Nizhniy Tagil
Petropavl
Kurgan
Kotlas
Kama
Vaasa
L. Onega
Sukhona
PERM
YEKATERINBURG
Sundsvall
Petrozavodsk
Vyatka
CHELYABINSK
Tampere
RUSSIA
Izhevsk
Gävle
Turku
Helsinki
Vologda
Kostanay
L. Ladoga
Rybinsk Res.
Yoshkar-Ola
UFA
Åland Is.
G. of Finland
ST. PETERSBURG
KAZAN
Naberezhnyye Chelny
Magnitogorsk
Stockholm
Tallinn
Novgorod
Yaroslavl
Sterlitamak
Ural
ESTONIA
Ivanovo
Norrköping
L. Peipus
Tver
Volga
NIZHNIY NOVGOROD
Orsk
Baltic Sea
Simbirsk
SAMARA
Orenburg
Gotland
Riga
LATVIA
Western Dvina
MOSCOW
Öland
Aktöbe
LITHUANIA
Vitsyebsk
Ryazan
Penza
Kaunas
Oral
Bornholm
Kaliningrad
Vilnius
Smolensk
Oka
Tula
KAZAKHSTAN
Gdańsk
MINSK
Dnieper
Orël
Tambov
Saratov
Bryansk
Voronezh
Emba
BELARUS
Kursk
Aral Sea
POLAND
Homyel
Poznań
Brest
Don
Atyrau
WARSAW
VOLGOGRAD
UZBEKISTAN
Łódź
Zhytomyr
KIEV
KHARKIV
Wrocław
Lublin
UKRAINE
Vistula
Kraków
Lviv
Bug
Vinnytsya
Luhansk
Astrakhan
Brno
DNIPROPETROVSK
DONETSK
Dniester
Kryvyy Rih
ROSTOV
SLOVAKIA
Bratislava
MOLDOVA
Mariupol
Aktau
Caspian Sea
Tisza
Mykolayiv
Chişinău
Sea of Azov
Kuban
Stavropol
BUDAPEST
Debrecen
Iaşi
HUNGARY
Transylvania
Prut
ODESA
Krasnodar
Makhachkala
Crimea
Novorossiysk
Grozny
Timişoara
Galaţi
Vladikavkaz
TURKMENISTAN
ROMANIA
Sevastopol
Turkmenbashi
Sava
BELGRADE
Wallachia
Sochi
Sukhumi
GEORGIA
BAKU
BOSNIA AND HERZEGOVINA
YUGOSLAVIA
BUCHAREST
Constanţa
TBILISI
Sarajevo
Black Sea
Gänca
Danube
Kura
AZERBAIJAN
Montenegro
Niš
Varna
ARMENIA
BULGARIA
Trabzon
YEREVAN
Araks
SOFIA
Samsun
Skopje
Plovdiv
Bosporus
Erzurum
Naxçivan
MACED.
TABRĪZ
Tirana
ALBANIA
İSTANBUL
Van
TEHRĀN
BURSA
Kizilirmak
Sivas
L. Van
L. Urmia
ANKARA
TURKEY
Thessaloniki
Diyarbakir
Orūmiyeh
Eskişehir
Malatya
Kurdistan
GREECE
Anatolia
Kayseri
Tigris
Hamadān
Qom
Ionian Sea
Aegean Sea
Gaziantep
Urfa
IRAN
Euboea
Konya
Mosul
Ionian Is.
İZMİR
Kirkūk
ADANA
Bākhtarān
ISFAHAN
Patras
ATHENS
Mersin
Euphrates
ALEPPO
Antalya
SYRIA
Rhodes
Nicosia
BAGHDAD
Dezfūl
Homs
IRAQ
Ahvāz
CYPRUS
Crete
BEIRUT
LEBANON
DAMASCUS
Mediterranean Sea
Basra
The Gulf
ISRAEL
Kuwait
Tel Aviv-Yafo
Amman
KUWAIT
Jerusalem
Gaza
Dead Sea
JORDAN
Benghazi
Sirte
ALEXANDRIA
Port Said
Ad-Dammām
LIBYA
EGYPT
SAUDI ARABIA
15 20 25 30 35 40 45 50 55 60 65 70 75 80
60 55 50 45 40 35 30
M N O P Q R S T U V W X Y Z
3 4 5 6 7 8 9 10

Denmark Strait
Jan Mayen
2544
ARCTI
Iceland
Reykjavik
Hekla 1491
Vatnajökull 2119
Norwegian Sea
Arctic Circle
3041
3921
3008
ATLANTIC OCEAN
Faroe Is.
Ålesund
Trondheim
Jostedalsbreen 2286
Galdhøpiggen 2469
Sognefj.
Bergen
Oslo
Stavanger
Kristiansand
Skagerrak
Kattegat
Jylland
COPENHAGEN
Rockall
British Isles
Hebrides
Orkney Is.
Shetland Is.
Ben Nevis 1343
Scotland
Aberdeen
Glasgow
Edinburgh
North Sea
Belfast
Newcastle
Ireland
Dublin
Irish Sea
Great Britain
1041
Cork
1085
Manchester
England
Wales
BIRMINGHAM
Land's End
Bristol
LONDON
Greenw.
Amsterdam
ROTTERDAM
HAMBURG
Bremen
Hannover
Szczecin
BERLIN
5080
English Channel
Channel Is.
Lille
Brussels
Düsseldorf
Cologne
Leipzig
Le Havre
Normandy
Brittany
Rennes
PARIS
Seine
Meuse
Frankfurt
Ore Mts.
Bohemian Forest
PRAGUE
Elbe
6325
Nantes
Loire
Burgundy
Strasbourg
Rhine
Stuttgart
Danube
Dijon
MUNICH
Bay of Biscay
Jura Mts.
Berne
Grossglockner 3798
C. Finisterre
Gijón
Vigo
Galicia
Cantabrian Mts.
Bordeaux
Bilbao
Mt. Dore 1886
Massif Central
Lyon
4807
Mt. Blanc
Turin
MILAN
Ljubljana
Venice
Porto
Valladolid
Old Castile
Ebro
Toulouse
Pyrenees
Montpellier
Provence
Po
Genoa
Bologna
Alps
3404 Aneto
Aragon
Marseille
Nice
Tuscany
Florence
Adriatic
Tagus
Iberian Peninsula
2592
Zaragoza
Catalonia
Ligurian Sea
LISBON
MADRID
BARCELONA
Corsica
2706
Gran Sasso 2912
5145
New Castile
ROME
Apennines
Cape Saint Vincent
Seville
Córdoba
Valencia
Balearic Is.
Menorca
NAPLES
Vesuvius
Andalusia
Murcia
Palma
Mallorca
Sardinia
1834
Tyrrhenian Sea
Madeira
Strait of Gibraltar
Ibiza
Sa. Nevada
Mulhacén 3481
Málaga
Cagliari
Tanger
Mediterranean
2887
Str. of Sicily
Palermo
Sicily
Rabat
Er Rif
2465
Oran
ALGIERS
CASABLANCA
Fez
Little Atlas
Annaba
Oujda
Moulouya
Constantine
Tunis
Pantelleria
La Palma
Canary Is.
Middle Atlas
Marrakech
3737
Saharan Atlas
2328
Sousse
P. de Teide 3718
Tenerife
High Atlas
Lampedusa
Las Palmas
Agadir
4165 Toubkal
Laghouat
-30
Sfax
Gran Canaria
Fuerteventura
Antiatlas
Béchar
G. of Gabès
Djerba
Touggourt
El Aaiún
Great Western Erg
Tripoli
Misrata
Great Eastern Erg
West from Greenwich 0 East from Greenwich

1 : 30 000 000

0 250 500 750 1000 km

0 250 500 750 miles

Peoples with Indo-European languages

Celtic group
1 Irish
2 Gaels
3 Welsh
4 Bretons

Romance group
5 Portuguese
6 Galicians
7 Spaniards
8 Catalans
9 French
10 Walloons
11 French Swiss
12 Italians
13 Italian Swiss
14 Corsicans
15 Sards
16 Rhaetian peoples
17 Romanians
18 Moldavians
19 Aromani (Vlachs)

Germanic group
20 Icelanders
21 Norwegians
22 Faroe Islanders
23 Danes
24 Swedes
25 Germans
26 German Swiss
27 Austrians
28 Luxemburgers
29 Dutch
30 Flemings
31 Frisians
32 English
33 Scotch
34 Northern Irish

Slavic group
35 Poles
36 Sorbs
37 Czechs
38 Slovaks
39 Slovenes
40 Croats
41 Bosnian Muslims
42 Serbs
43 Montenegrins
44 Macedonians
45 Bulgarians
46 Russians
47 Belorussians
48 Ukrainians

Balts
49 Letts (Latvians) 50 Lithuanians

51 Albanians

52 Greeks

53 Armenians

Iranian peoples
54 Ossetes

Gypsies

55 **Basques**

Caucasian peoples
56 Georgians
57 Abkhaz
58 Circassians and Adyghians
59 Kabardinians
60 Chechens and Ingushes
61 Dagestanian peoples

Peoples with Semitic languages
62 Maltese

Uralic peoples

Finno-Ugric group
63 Finns
64 Karelians
65 Estonians
66 Lapps
67 Mari
68 Mordvinians
69 Komi and Komi-Permyaks
70 Udmurts
71 Hungarians (Magyars)

Samoyeds
72 Nentsy

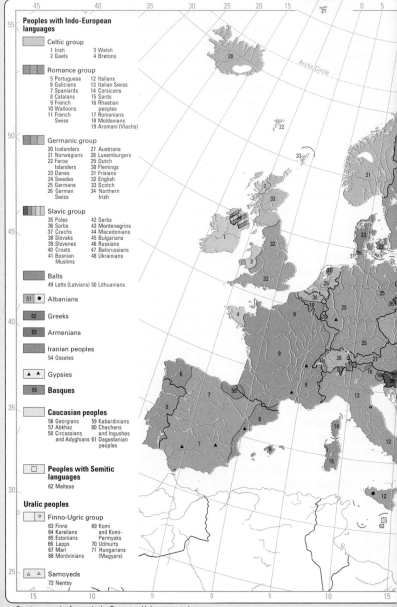

Foreigners and refugees in the European Union are not shown.

1 : 30 000 000

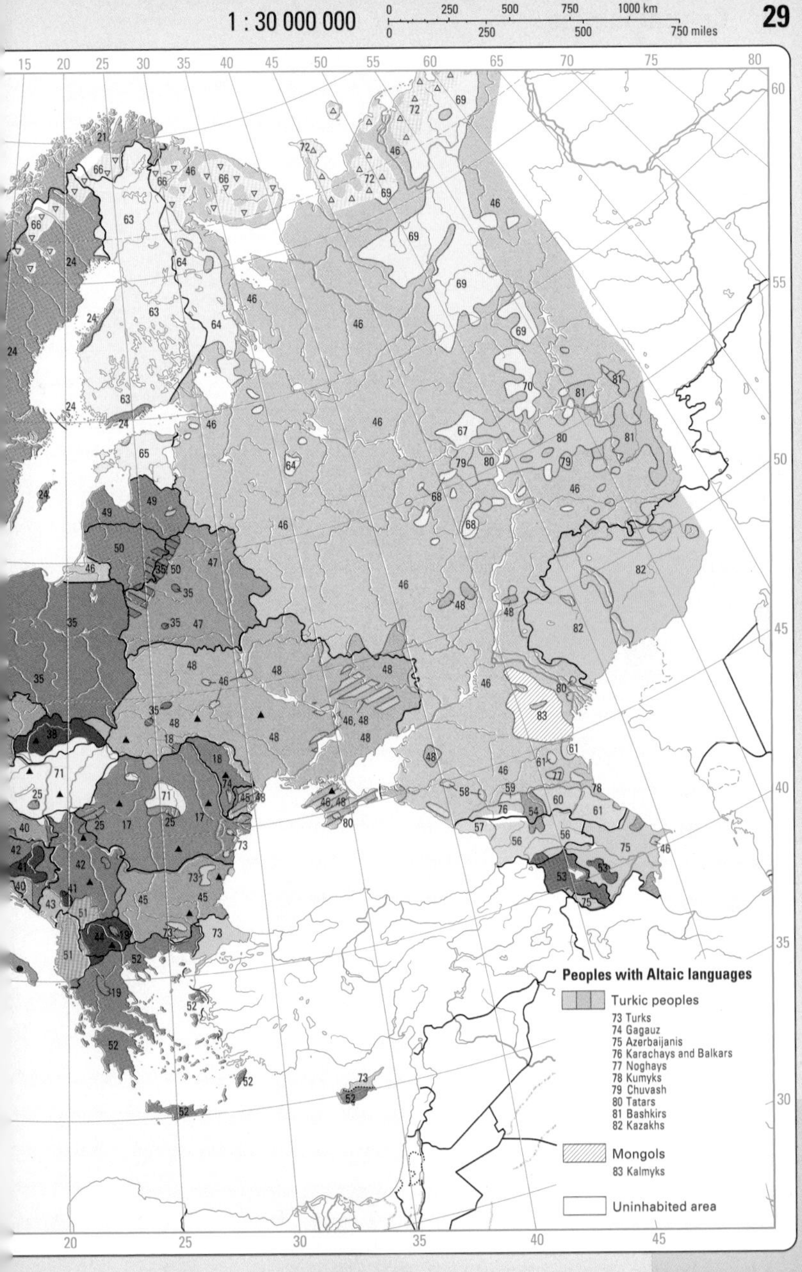
0 250 500 750 1000 km
0 250 500 750 miles
Peoples with Altaic languages
Turkic peoples
73 Turks
74 Gagauz
75 Azerbaijanis
76 Karachays and Balkars
77 Noghays
78 Kumyks
79 Chuvash
80 Tatars
81 Bashkirs
82 Kazakhs
Mongols
83 Kalmyks
Uninhabited area

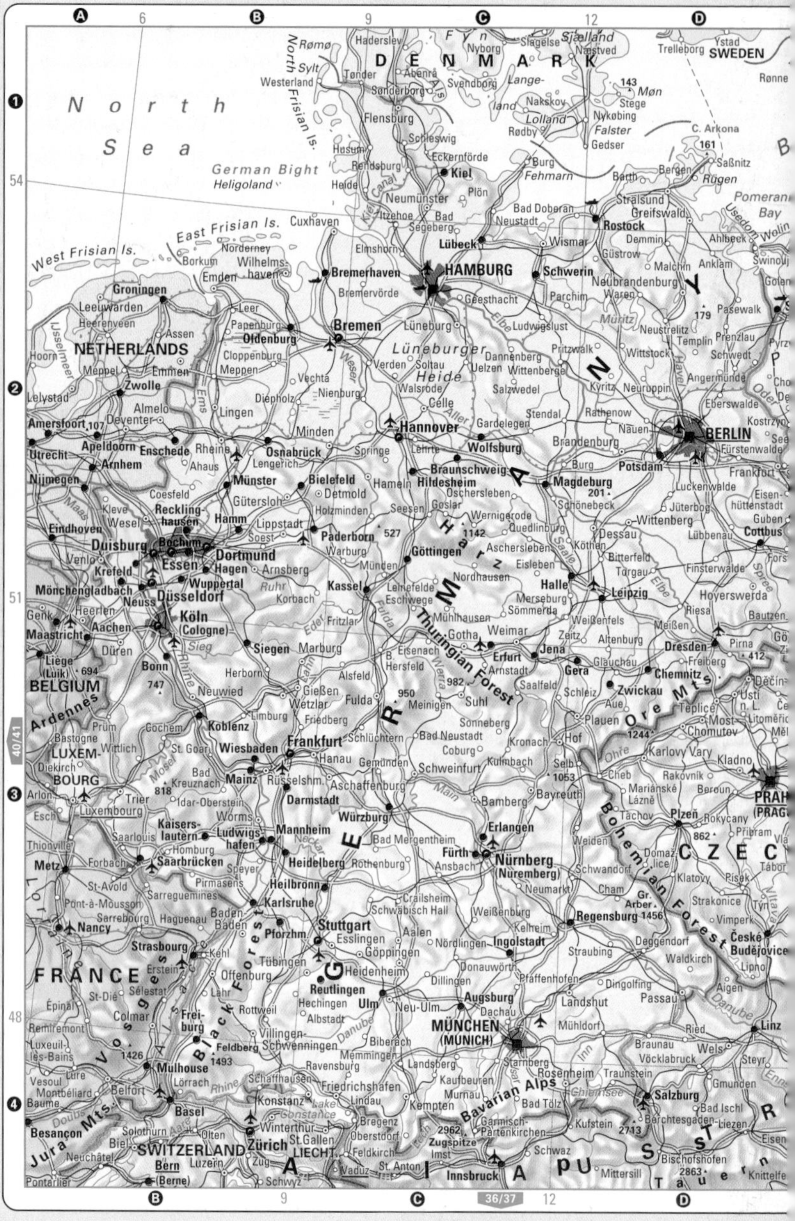

A
B
C
D
6
9
12
1
2
3
4
54
51
48
North Sea
German Bight
Heligoland
East Frisian Is.
West Frisian Is.
North Frisian Is.
Rømø
Sylt
Westerland
DENMARK
Haderslev
Tønder
Aabenraa
Sønderborg
Als
Fyn
Nyborg
Svendborg
Slagelse
Sjælland
Næstved
Lange-land
Nakskov
Lolland
Rødby
Nykøbing
Falster
Gedser
Møn
Stege
143
Trelleborg
Ystad
SWEDEN
Rønne
C. Arkona
161
Flensburg
Schleswig
Husum
Eckernförde
Kiel
Rendsburg
Heide
Kiel Canal
Neumünster
Plön
Burg
Fehmarn
Itzehoe
Bad Segeberg
Bad Doberan
Neustadt
Cuxhaven
Lübeck
Wismar
Rostock
Stralsund
Greifswald
Bergen
Rügen
Saßnitz
Barth
Pomeranian Bay
Usedom
Wolin
Ahlbeck
Swinoujście
Demmin
Güstrow
Malchin
Anklam
Norderney
Borkum
Emden
Wilhelmshaven
Bremerhaven
Elmshorn
HAMBURG
Schwerin
Neubrandenburg
Waren
Parchim
Groningen
Leeuwarden
Heerenveen
Assen
Leer
Papenburg
Oldenburg
Bremen
Bremervörde
Geesthacht
Lüneburg
Ludwigslust
Müritz
Neustrelitz
Templin
Prenzlau
Pasewalk
179
Schwedt
IJsselmeer
Hoorn
NETHERLANDS
Emmen
Meppel
Zwolle
Lelystad
Cloppenburg
Meppen
Vechta
Nienburg
Weser
Verden
Soltau
Lüneburger Heide
Dannenberg
Uelzen
Wittenberge
Pritzwalk
Wittstock
Angermünde
Oder
Havel
Elbe
Ems
Diepholz
Walsrode
Celle
Salzwedel
Kyritz
Neuruppin
Eberswalde
Almelo
Lingen
Aller
Stendal
Rathenow
Amersfoort
107
Deventer
Minden
Hannover
Gardelegen
Nauen
BERLIN
Kostrzyn
Apeldoorn
Enschede
Rheine
Osnabrück
Springe
Lehrte
Wolfsburg
Brandenburg
Utrecht
Arnhem
Ahaus
Lengerich
Braunschweig
Burg
Potsdam
Fürstenwalde
Nijmegen
Münster
Bielefeld
Detmold
Hameln
Hildesheim
Magdeburg
201
Frankfurt
Coesfeld
Gütersloh
Oschersleben
Schönebeck
Luckenwalde
Eisenhüttenstadt
Kleve
Wesel
Recklinghausen
Hamm
Holzminden
Seesen
Goslar
Wernigerode
Jüterbog
Guben
Maas
Eindhoven
Lippstadt
Soest
Paderborn
527
1142
Quedlinburg
Wittenberg
Lübbenau
Cottbus
Duisburg
Bochum
Dortmund
Warburg
Harz
Aschersleben
Dessau
Köthen
Venlo
Essen
Hagen
Arnsberg
Göttingen
Eisleben
Bitterfeld
Krefeld
Wuppertal
Ruhr
Münden
Nordhausen
Torgau
Finsterwalde
Spree
Mönchengladbach
Düsseldorf
Neuss
Korbach
Kassel
Leinefelde
Eschwege
Halle
Merseburg
Leipzig
Hoyerswerda
Genk
Heerlen
Aachen
Köln
(Cologne)
Eder
Fritzlar
Fulda
Mühlhausen
Sömmerda
Saale
Weißenfels
Riesa
Bautzen
Maastricht
Düren
Sieg
Siegen
Marburg
Gotha
Weimar
Zeitz
Altenburg
Meißen
Dresden
Pirna
Liège
(Luik)
694
Bonn
Rhine
Herborn
Lahn
Eisenach
Bad Hersfeld
Erfurt
Jena
Arnstadt
Gera
Glauchau
Chemnitz
Freiberg
412
BELGIUM
747
Neuwied
Gießen
Alsfeld
Werra
982
Thuringian Forest
Saalfeld
Schleiz
Zwickau
Ore Mts.
Děčín
Ústí n. L.
Ardennes
Wetzlar
Fulda
950
Meiningen
Suhl
Aue
Teplice
Most
Litoměřice
Limburg
Friedberg
Sonneberg
Plauen
Chomutov
Mělník
1244
Prüm
Cochem
Koblenz
Schlüchtern
Bad Neustadt
Coburg
Kronach
Hof
Bastogne
LUXEMBOURG
Wittlich
St. Goar
Wiesbaden
Frankfurt
Hanau
Gemünden
Schweinfurt
Kulmbach
Selb
Ohře
Karlovy Vary
Kladno
Diekirch
Mosel
Bad Kreuznach
Mainz
Rüsselsheim
Aschaffenburg
1053
Cheb
Rakovník
PRAHA
(PRAGUE)
818
Arlon
Trier
Idar-Oberstein
Darmstadt
Main
Bayreuth
Mariánské Lázně
Beroun
Luxembourg
Esch
Worms
Würzburg
Bamberg
Bohemian Forest
Tachov
Plzeň
Rokycany
Kaiserslautern
Ludwigshafen
Mannheim
Neckar
Erlangen
Příbram
Thionville
Saarlouis
Homburg
Bad Mergentheim
Weiden
862
Metz
Forbach
Saarbrücken
Speyer
Heidelberg
Rothenburg
Fürth
Ansbach
Nürnberg
(Nuremberg)
Schwandorf
Domažlice
CZECH
Tábor
St-Avold
Pirmasens
Heilbronn
Neumarkt
Klatovy
Písek
Pont-à-Mousson
Sarreguemines
Karlsruhe
Crailsheim
Schwäbisch Hall
Cham
Arber
Gr. Arber 1456
Strakonice
Vltava
Sarrebourg
Haguenau
Baden-Baden
Weißenburg
Regensburg
Vimperk
Nancy
Pforzheim
Stuttgart
Aalen
Kelheim
České Budějovice
Strasbourg
Kehl
Esslingen
Nördlingen
Ingolstadt
Straubing
Deggendorf
Tübingen
Göppingen
Waldkirch
FRANCE
Erstein
Offenburg
Heidenheim
Donauwörth
Pfaffenhofen
Dingolfing
Lipno
Sélestat
Lahr
Reutlingen
Dillingen
Passau
Aigen
St-Dié
Black Forest
Hechingen
Ulm
Neu-Ulm
Augsburg
Landshut
Danube
Épinal
Colmar
Freiburg
Rottweil
Albstadt
Dachau
Remiremont
Villingen-Schwenningen
Biberach
MÜNCHEN
(MUNICH)
Mühldorf
Ried
Linz
Vosges
Feldberg
1493
Memmingen
Inn
Braunau
Wels
Luxeuil-les-Bains
1426
Ravensburg
Landsberg
Vöcklabruck
Steyr
Mulhouse
Kaufbeuren
Starnberg
Rosenheim
Traunstein
Enns
Lure
Lörrach
Schaffhausen
Friedrichshafen
Isar
Gmunden
Vesoul
Belfort
Rhine
Lindau
Murnau
Bavarian Alps
Chiemsee
Montbéliard
Lake Constance
Konstanz
Bad Tölz
Salzburg
Baume
Basel
Kempten
Bad Ischl
Doubs
Jura Mts.
Aare
Winterthur
Bregenz
2962
Garmisch-Partenkirchen
Kufstein
2713
Berchtesgaden
Liezen
Besançon
Solothurn
Olten
Zürich
St. Gallen
Oberstdorf
Zugspitze
Eisenerz
Biel
SWITZERLAND
LIECHT.
Feldkirch
Imst
Schwaz
Bischofshofen
Neuchâtel
Bern
(Berne)
Luzern
Zug
Vaduz
St. Anton
Innsbruck
Mittersill
2863
Knittelfeld
Pontarlier
Schwyz
AUSTRIA
Tauern
GERMANY
40/41
36/37

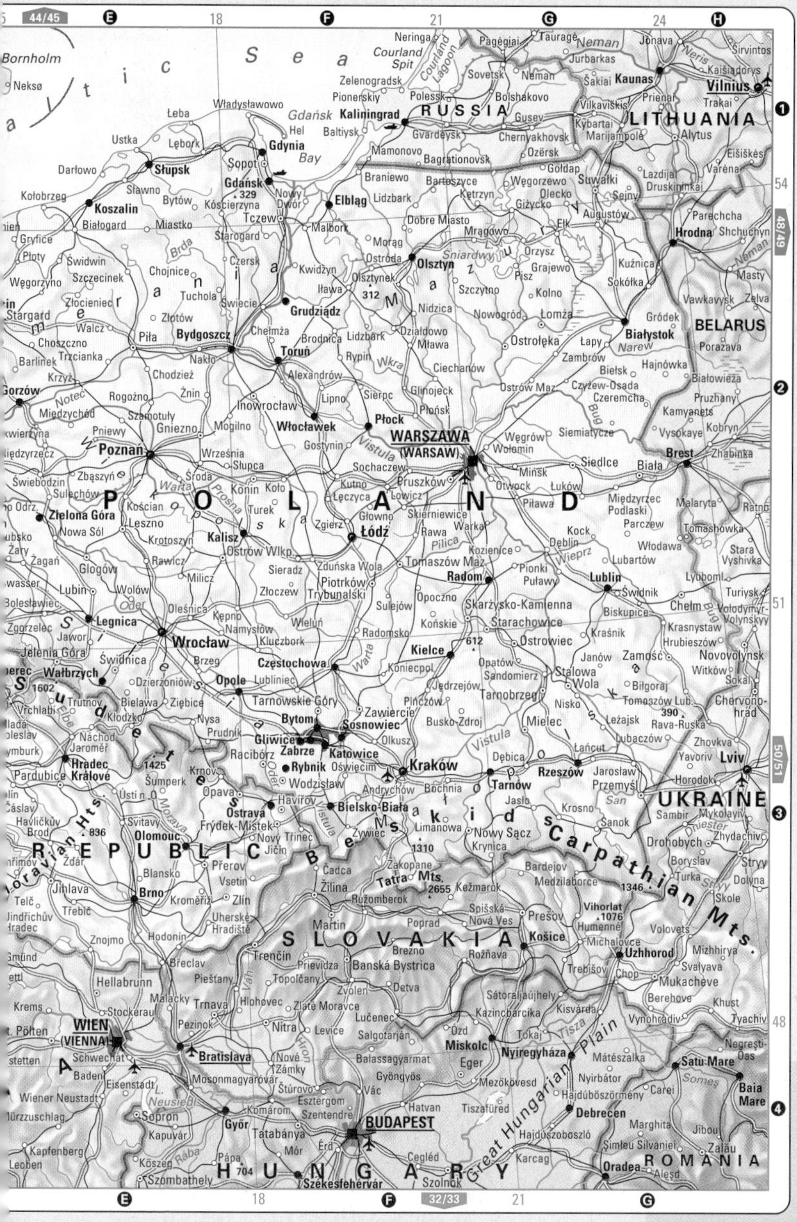
44/45
48/49
50/51
32/33
E
F
G
H
18
21
24
54
51
48
Baltic Sea
Bornholm
Neksø
Courland Spit
Courland Lagoon
Neringa
Pagėgiai
Tauragė
Neman
Jonava
Neris
Širvintos
Jurbarkas
Kaišiadorys
Sovetsk
Zelenogradsk
Šakiai
Kaunas
Vilnius
Pionerskiy
Polessk
Bolshakovo
Trakai
Władysławowo
Gdańsk
Kaliningrad
RUSSIA
Vilkaviškis
Prienai
Łeba
Hel
Baltiysk
Gusev
Kybartai
LITHUANIA
Ustka
Gdynia
Gvardeysk
Chernyakhovsk
Marijampolė
Alytus
Lębork
Bay
Mamonovo
Ozërsk
Darłowo
Słupsk
Sopot
Bagrationovsk
Gołdap
Lazdijai
Varėna
Eišiškės
Sławno
Gdańsk
329
Braniewo
Bartoszyce
Węgorzewo
Suwałki
Druskininkai
Kołobrzeg
Bytów
Kościerzyna
Nowy Dwór
Elbląg
Lidzbark
Kętrzyn
Olecko
Sejny
Koszalin
Giżycko
Augustów
Białogard
Miastko
Tczew
Dobre Miasto
Parechcha
Gryfice
Malbork
Mrągowo
Ełk
Hrodna
Shchuchyn
Starogard
Morąg
Płoty
Brda
Ostróda
Olsztyn
Śniardwy
Orzysz
Świdwin
Czersk
Kwidzyn
Grajewo
Kuźnica
Neman
Chojnice
Olsztynek
Pisz
Węgorzyno
Szczecinek
Iława
Szczytno
Sokółka
Masty
312
Kolno
Złocieniec
Tuchola
Świecie
Vawkavysk
Zelva
Stargard
Złotów
Grudziądz
Nidzica
Nowogród
Łomża
Walcz
Gródek
Chełmża
Działdowo
BELARUS
Piła
Bydgoszcz
Brodnica
Lidzbark
Mława
Ostrołęka
Łapy
Białystok
Choszczno
Nakło
Toruń
Rypin
Narew
Porazava
Trzcianka
Wkra
Zambrów
Barlinek
Chodzież
Alexandrów
Ciechanów
Bielsk
Hajnówka
Krzyż
Białowieża
Gorzów
Żnin
Glinojeck
Ostrów Maz.
Czyżew-Osada
Noteć
Rogoźno
Lipno
Sierpc
Pruzhany
Inowrocław
Ciechanów
Czeremcha
Międzychód
Szamotuły
Płońsk
Bug
Kamyanets
Gniezno
Mogilno
Włocławek
Płock
Węgrów
Siemiatycze
Pniewy
WARSZAWA
(WARSAW)
Vysokaye
Kobryn
Międzyrzecz
Poznań
Wrześnica
Gostynin
Wołomin
Brest
Zhabinka
Słupca
Vistula
Siedlce
Biała
Świebodzin
Zbąszyń
Środa
Sochaczew
Mińsk
Sulechów
Warta
Prosna
Konin
Koło
Kutno
Pruszków
Otwock
Łuków
Odrz.
POLAND
Łęczyca
Łowicz
Piława
Międzyrzec Podlaski
Malaryta
Ratno
Zielona Góra
Kościan
Turek
Głowno
Skierniewice
Warka
Parczew
Leszno
Zgierz
Łódź
Rawa
Kock
Tomashowka
Nowa Sól
Krotoszyn
Kalisz
Pilica
Dęblin
Włodawa
Stara Vyshivka
Żary
Ostrów Wlkp.
Kozienice
Wieprz
Żagań
Rawicz
Sieradz
Zduńska Wola
Tomaszów Maz.
Pionki
Lubartów
Głogów
Milicz
Radom
Puławy
Lublin
Lyuboml
Lubin
Wołów
Piotrków Trybunalski
Złoczew
Opoczno
Świdnik
Turiysk
Bolesławiec
Oder
Oleśnica
Sulejów
Skarżysko-Kamienna
Biskupice
Chełm
Volodymyr-Volynskyy
Legnica
Kępno
Wieluń
Końskie
Starachowice
Kraśnik
Krasnystaw
Zgorzelec
Jawor
Namysłów
Radomsko
612
Ostrowiec
Hrubieszów
Jelenia Góra
Wrocław
Kluczbork
Kielce
Zamość
Novovolynsk
Świdnica
Brzeg
Częstochowa
Janów
Witków
Wałbrzych
Koniecpol
Opatów
Sandomierz
Stalowa Wola
Sokal
1602
Dzierżoniów
Opole
Lubliniec
Jędrzejów
Tarnobrzeg
Biłgoraj
Trutnov
Bielawa
Ziębice
Tarnowskie Góry
Pińczów
Nisko
Tomaszów Lub.
Chervonohrad
Vrchlabí
Kłodzko
Nysa
Bytom
Zawiercie
Busko-Zdroj
Mielec
390
Rava-Ruska
Elbe
Náchod
Prudnik
Gliwice
Sosnowiec
Leżajsk
Jaroměř
Zabrze
Katowice
Olkusz
Lubaczów
Zhovkva
Hradec Králové
1425
Racibórz
Rybnik
Oświęcim
Kraków
Dębica
Łańcut
Yavoriv
Lviv
Pardubice
Šumperk
Krnov
Wodzisław
Bochnia
Tarnów
Rzeszów
Jarosław
Przemyśl
Horodok
Ústí n.O.
Opava
Andrychów
Jasło
San
UKRAINE
Čáslav
Havířov
Bielsko-Biała
Krosno
Sambir
Mykolayiv
Havlíčkův Brod
Svitavy
Ostrava
Frýdek-Místek
Limanowa
Nowy Sącz
Sanok
Dniester
836
Olomouc
Nový Jičín
Třinec
Żywiec
Krynica
Drohobych
Zhydachiv
REPUBLIC
Beskids
Carpathian Mts.
Boryslav
Žďár
Přerov
Čadca
Zakopane
1310
Bardejov
Turka
Stryy
Moravian Hts.
Vsetín
Tatra Mts.
2655
Medzilaborce
1346
Dolyna
Jihlava
Blansko
Žilina
Kežmarok
Skole
Telč
Brno
Kroměříž
Zlín
Ružomberok
Spišská Nová Ves
Viborlat
1076
Jindřichův Hradec
Třebíč
Uherské Hradiště
Martin
Poprad
Prešov
Humenné
Volovets
Znojmo
Hodonín
SLOVAKIA
Košice
Michalovce
Mizhhirya
Gmünd
Trenčín
Brezno
Rožňava
Uzhhorod
Svalyava
Břeclav
Prievidza
Banská Bystrica
Trebišov
Chop
Mukacheve
Piešťany
Topoľčany
Váh
Zvolen
Detva
Hellabrunn
Malacky
Hlohovec
Zlaté Moravce
Sátoraljaújhely
Berehove
Krems
Stockerau
Trnava
Lučenec
Kazincbarcika
Kisvárda
Khust
Pezinok
Nitra
Levice
Hron
Ózd
Tisza
Vynohradiv
Tyachiv
WIEN (VIENNA)
Salgótarján
Miskolc
Tokaj
St. Pölten
Bratislava
Nové Zámky
Balassagyarmat
Eger
Nyíregyháza
Mátészalka
Negrești-Oaș
Schwechat
Great Hungarian Plain
Satu Mare
Baden
Mosonmagyaróvár
Štúrovo
Gyöngyös
Mezőkövesd
Nyírbátor
Someș
Eisenstadt
Vác
Baia Mare
Wiener Neustadt
Neusiedl
Esztergom
Hatvan
Hajdúböszörmény
Carei
Mürzzuschlag
Sopron
Komárom
Szentendre
Tiszafüred
Debrecen
Kapuvár
Győr
Tatabánya
BUDAPEST
Hajdúszoboszló
Marghita
Jibou
Kapfenberg
Rába
Mór
Érd
Şimleu Silvaniei
Zalău
Leoben
Kőszeg
Pápa
Cegléd
Karcag
Oradea
ROMANIA
Szombathely
704
HUNGARY
Székesfehérvár
Szolnok
Aleşd
1
2
3
4

A
B
C
15
18
21
30/31
36/37
1
2
3
4
48
45
42
GERM.
IT.
AUSTRIA
SLOVAKIA
HUNGARY
SLOVENIA
CROATIA
BOSNIA AND HERZEGOVINA
YUGOSLAVIA
Serbia
Montenegro
Vojvodina
Kosovo
ALBANIA
MACEDONIA
Alps
Tauern
Karawanken
Julian Alps
Karst
Dinaric Alps
Dalmatia
Istria
Great Hungarian Plain
Abruzzi
Apennines
Campania
Apulia
Adriatic Sea
Danube
Enns
Mur
Drava
Sava
Tisza
Váh
Hron
Rába
Sió
Una
Vrbas
Bosna
Drina
Neretva
Ofanto
Mureş
L. Neusiedl
Balaton
Lake Scutari
L. Ohrid
L. Prespa
Passau
Aigen
Lipno
Braunau
Ried
Wels
Linz
Vöcklabruck
Zwettl
Krems
Hellabrunn
Stockerau
St. Pölten
Steyr
Amstetten
Gmunden
Bad Ischl
WIEN (VIENNA)
Schwechat
Baden
Eisenstadt
Wiener Neustadt
Eisenerz
Liezen
Kapfenberg
Mürzzuschlag
Bischofshofen
2863
Leoben
Knittelfeld
Graz
Fürstenfeld
Spittal
St. Veit
Wolfsberg
Villach
Leibnitz
Klagenfurt
Maribor
1543
Triglav 2864
Jesenice
Velenje
Kranj
Tolmin
Celje
Trbovlje
Ptuj
Lenart
Gorizia
Ljubljana
Vrhnika
Trebnje
Postojna
Pivka
Monf.
Trieste
Koper
Snežnik 1796
Novo Mesto
Samobor
Rijeka
Poreč
Opatija
Labin
Rovinj
Pula
Rt Kamenjak
Krk
Cres
Crikvenica
Senj
Rab
Lošinj
Mali Lošinj
Pag
Karlobag
Gospić
Velebit
1758
Zadar
Ugljan
Dugi Otok
Pašman
Sali
Kornat
Šibenik
Primošten
Trogir
Split
Šolta
Brač
Makarska
Hvar
Vis
Korčula
Lastovo
Pelješac
Mljet
Palagruža
Pianosa.
Tremiti-Is.
Dubrovnik
Trebinje
Nikšić
Kotor
Podgorica
Bar
Břeclav
Trenčín
Prievidza
Brezno
Spišská-Nová-Ves
Humenné
Košice
Michalovce
Trebišov
Banská Bystrica
Piešťany
Topoľčany
Malacky
Trnava
Hlohovec
Zvolen
Detva
Rožňava
Pezinok
Zlaté Moravce
Bratislava
Nitra
Levice
Lučenec
Nové Zámky
Mosonmagyaróvár
Štúrovo
Sátoraljaújhely
Kazincbarcika
Ózd
Salgótarján
Miskolc
Balassagyarmat
Gyöngyös
Eger
Nyíregyháza
Vác
Esztergom
Mezőkövesd
Sopron
Győr
Komárom
Szentendre
Hatvan
Kapuvár
Tatabánya
BUDAPEST
Tiszafüred
Hajdúböszörmény
Kőszeg
Pápa
704
Mór
Érd
Debrecen
Hajdúszoboszló
Szombathely
Veszprém
Székesfehérvár
Szolnok
Karcag
Cegléd
Zalaegerszeg
Ajka
Kecskemét
Mezőtúr
Oradea
Siófok
Dunaújváros
Murska Sobota
Keszthely
Fonyód
Paks
Kiskőrös
Csongrád
Békéscsaba
Sarkad
Gyula
Čakovec
Nagykanizsa
Tamási
Kaposvár
Dombóvár
Kiskunhalas
Hódmezővásárhely
Varaždin
Szekszárd
682
Krapina
Koprivnica
Pécs
Komló
Baja
Szeged
Makó
Curtici
Arad
Đurđevac
Barcs
Mohács
Zagreb
Bjelovar
Siklós
Subotica
Sânnicolau Mare
Ivanić-Grad
Virovitica
Senta
Timişoara
Sombor
Karlovac
Daruvar
Valpovo
Kikinda
Kutina
Novi Bečej
Apatin
Buziaş
Velika
Osijek
Vrbas
Sisak
Našice
Srbobran
Ogulin
Vrginmost
Slavonska Požega
Vukovar
Bačka Palanka
Temerin
Zrenjanin
Slavonski Brod
Đakovo
Vinkovci
Novi Sad
Reşiţa
Bos. Novi
Bos. Gradiška
Šid
Sremska Mitrovica
Vršac
Prijedor
Derventa
Bela Crkva
Bihać
Banja Luka
Doboj
Brčko
BEOGRAD (BELGRADE)
Pančevo
Šabac
Kovin
Klekovača 1961
Srnetica
Teslić
Tuzla
687
Obrenovac
Smederevo
Požarevac
Loznica
Mladenovac
Jajce
Zavidovići
Zvornik
Valjevo
Lazarevac
Neresnica
Velika Plana
Travnik
Zenica
Kladanj
Knin
1132
Bugojno
Vareš
1537
Srebrenica
Kragujevac
Visoko
Užice
1509
Livno
Gornji Vakuf
Sarajevo
Svetozarevo
Paraćin
Sinj
Konjic
Pale
Višegrad
Čačak
Kraljevo
Jablanica
Goražde
2226
Imotski
Foča
Golija 1833
Ušće
Kruševac
Mostar
Pljevlja
Nevesinje
Raška
Niš
Bjelašnica 1867
Durmitor 2522
Sjenica
Prokuplje
Ploče
Metković
Bijelo Polje
Novi Pazar
Leskovac
Ivangrad
2382
Kosovska Mitrovica
Peć
Klina
Priština
Vranje
Gnjilane
2694
Tropojë
Đakovica
Uroševac
Prizren
Preševo
Kumanovo
Shkodër
Kukës
Skopje
Pukë
Tetovo
Rrëshen
Korab 2764
Lezhë
Peshkopi
Gostivar
Solunska Glava 2540
Veles
Bogomila
Laç
Krujë
Kičevo
Debar
Tiranë (Tirana)
Durrës
Librazhd
Struga
Sopotnica
Prilep
Ohrid
Kavajë
Elbasan
Bitola
Pogradec
2600
Lushnjë
Kuçovë
Gramsh
Fier
Berat
Patos
Flórina
San Benedetto
Penne
Pescara
Chieti
2793
Lanciano
Vasto
Termoli
Larino
Vieste
1056
Testa del Gargano
Campobasso
San Severo
Isernia
Lucera
Manfredonia
Gulf of Manfredonia
San Bartolomeo
Foggia
Benevento
Cerignola
Barletta
Caserta
Ariano Irpino
Molfetta
Andria
Bari
Vesuvius 1277
Avellino
Melfi
Mola di Bari
Pompei
Venosa
Altamura
Monopoli
NAPOLI
Avigliano
Gioia del C.
Ostuni
Salerno
Eboli
Potenza
Matera
Sorrento
Battipaglia
Martina Franca
Brindisi
Tricarico

1 : 6 000 000

0 50 100 150 200 km
0 50 100 150 miles

YUGOSLAVIA
Montenegro
Podgorica
Serbia
Priština
Surdulica
Vranje
Bosilegrad
Preševo
Gnjilane
Đakovica
Uroševac
Prizren
Peć
Klina
2694
Tropojë
L. Scutari
Bar
Shkodër
Drin
Pukë
Kukës
Tetovo
Skopje
Kumanovo
Kriva Palanka
Kyustendil
Pernik
SOFIYA
(SOFIA)
Balkan Mts.
Botev
2376
Gabrovo
Karlovo
Kazanlŭk
Sliven
Panagyurishte
BULGARIA
Samokov
Ikhtiman
Stara Zagora
Nova Zagora
Yambol
Rakovski
Pazardzhik
Rila
2925 Musala
Dupnitsa
Struma
Velingrad
Plovdiv
Chirpan
Maritsa
Dimitrovgrad
Tundzha
Elkhovo
Topolovgrad
Kharmanli
Svilengrad
Khaskovo
Asenovgrad
Blagoevgrad
Blansko
2914
Pirin
Rhodope Mts.
Devin
Kŭrdzhali
Arda
Edirne
Gotse Delchev
2191
Smolyan
Ivaylovgrad
Podkova
Orestiáda
Lezhë
Rrëshen
Korab
2764
ALBANIA
Laç
Peshkopi
Krujë
Tiranë
(Tirana)
Durrës
Kavajë
Elbasan
Librazhd
Debar
Kičevo
Gostivar
2540
Veles
Bogomila
Kočani
Štip
Dečevo
MACEDONIA
Radoviš
Sandanski
Petrich
Vardar
1746
Kavadarci
Strumica
Sopotnica
Struga
Ohrid
L. Ohrid
Prilep
Gevgelija
2030
Sidirókastro
Káto Nevrokópi
Chionótrypa
2232
Sérres
Dráma
Néstos
Xánthi
Komotiní
Soufli
Ergene
Uzunköprü
Lushnjë
Kuçovë
Gramsh
Pogradec
L. Prespa
Bitola
2600
Gouménissa
Kilkís
Fier
Berat
Patos
Korçë
Çorovodë
Vlorë
Vjosa
Memaliaj
Ersekë
Përmet
Gjirokastër
Flórina
Kastoria
Édessa
Giannitsá
Véroia
Nigríta
Lagkadás
Amfípoli
Kavála
Ávdira
Sápes
Malkara
Alexandroúpoli
Keşan
Enez
Thessaloníki
Chalkidikí
Polýgyros
Ólynthos
Ptolemaïda
Kozáni
Aliákmonas
Kateríni
Gulf of Thessaloníki
Thásos
1203
Thracian Sea
Samothráki
1600
Gulf of Saros
Gelibolu
Ierissós
Karyés
Áthos
2033
Gökçeada
Eceabat
Strait of Otranto
Sarandë
Kérkyra
Corfu
2637
Siátista
Kónitsa
Grevená
Sérvia
2917
Olympus
Litóchoro
Kalpáki
Métsovo
Pindus Mts.
Elassóna
Kalampáka
Tírnavos
Sykiá
Sithoniá
Kassándra
C. Palioúri
Límnos
Mýrina
Ímroz
Çanakkale
Dardanelles
Troy
Bayramiç
Ezine
Kazdağ
1774
Ioánnina
Ēpirus
Igoumenitsa
Párga
Paxoí
Fillippiáda
Árta
Tríkala
Thessaly
Lárisa
Palamás
Kardítsa
Achelóos
Vólos
Miléai
Fársala
Almyrós
Ágios Efstrátios
Aegean Sea
Míthymna
Ayvalık
Lésvos
Mytilíni
Polichnítos
968
Préveza
Lefkáda
Amfilochía
Domokós
Rentína
Lamía
Northern Sporades
Skópelos
Skýros
Istiaía
GREECE
Ionian Islands
Karpenísi
Agrínio
Gióna
2510
Amfissa
Atalánti
Euboea
1743
Kými
Psará
Karaburun
1267
Chíos
Çeşme
Ithákí
Mesolóngi
Náfpaktos
Delfoí
Livádia
Chalkída
Kefallinía
Argostóli
Antírrio
Aígio
Gulf of Corinth
Pátra
(Patras)
Thíva
Káto Achaïa
Kalávryta
2376
Kyllíni
Kiáto
Acharnés
C. Kafiréas
Kárystos
Kyllíni
Mégara
Peiraias
(Piraeus)
ATHÍNA
(ATHENS)
994
Ándros
Zákynthos
Amaliáda
Kórinthos
Pýrgos
Olympia
Árgos
Mycenæ
Aígina
Lávrio
Sámos
Ágios Kírykos
Ikaría
Foúrni
Zacháro
Levídi
Trípoli
Náfplio
Keá
Tínos
Mýkonos
Ermoúpoli
Kyparissía
Peloponnese
Filiatrá
Leonídi
Ýdra
Kýthnos
Sýros
Dílos
Pátmos
Ionian Sea
Kalamáta
Messíni
Spárti
Mirtoan Sea
Sérifos
Páros
Náxos
Léros
Pýlos
2407
Sífnos
Kálymnos
Gýtheio
Schíza
Gulf of Messíni
Mílos
770
Síkinos
Amorgós
Monemvasía
Íos
Folégandros
Gulf of Lakonia
C. Taínaron
C. Maléa
Thíra
Astypálaia
Anáfi
Cyclades
Southern Sporades
Kýthira
Sea of Crete
Antikýthira
C. Spánta
Chaniá
Kastélli
Crete
Réthymno
Irákleio
Ídi
2456
Knossos
Ágios Nikólaos
C. Síderos
Palaiochóra
Tympáki
Pýrgos
Siteía
Ierápetra
C. Líthino
Gávdos
Mediterranean
21
24
42
39
36
A
B
C
1
2
3
4
32/33
36/37

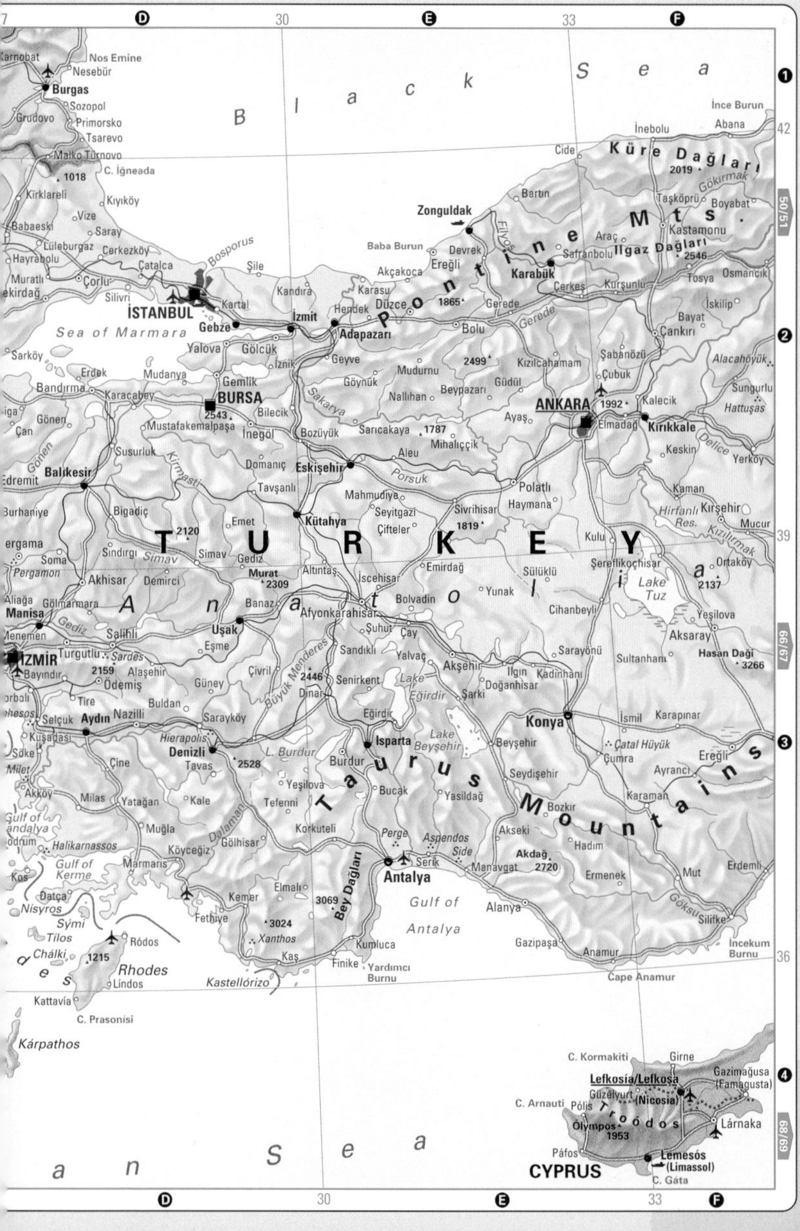
D
30
E
33
F
Black Sea
Nos Emine
Nesebür
Karnobat
Burgas
Sozopol
Grudovo
Primorsko
Tsarevo
Malko Türnovo
1018
C. İğneada
Kırklareli
Kıyıköy
Vize
Babaeski
Saray
Lüleburgaz
Çerkezköy
Hayrabolu
Çatalca
Muratlı
Çorlu
Tekirdağ
Silivri
Bosporus
Şile
İSTANBUL
Kartal
Gebze
Sea of Marmara
Şarköy
Erdek
Bandırma
Mudanya
Yalova
Gölcük
İznik
Gemlik
Karacabey
BURSA
2543
Gönen
Çan
Mustafakemalpaşa
İnegöl
Bilecik
Susurluk
Kirmasti
Balıkesir
Edremit
Burhaniye
Bigadiç
Emet
Tavşanlı
Domaniç
2120
Sındırgı
Simav
Gediz
Soma
Bergama
Pergamon
Akhisar
Demirci
Murat
2309
Aliağa
Gölmarmara
Manisa
Gediz
Menemen
Salihli
Uşak
Eşme
İZMİR
Turgutlu
Sardes
Bayındır
2159
Alaşehir
Ödemiş
Tire
Güney
Buldan
Çivril
Selçuk
Aydın
Nazilli
Sarayköy
Kuşadası
Hierapolis
Denizli
Söke
Milet
Çine
Tavas
2528
Akköy
Milas
Yatağan
Kale
Gulf of Mandalya
Bodrum
Halikarnassos
Muğla
Dalaman
Gölhisar
Köyceğiz
Gulf of Kerme
Marmaris
Kos
Datça
Nísyros
Sými
Tílos
Chálki
1215
Ródos
Rhodes
Líndos
Kattavía
C. Prasonísi
Kárpathos
Fethiye
Kemer
Elmalı
3069
Bey Dağları
3024
Xanthos
Kaş
Kastellórizo
Kumluca
Finike
Yardımcı Burnu
Zonguldak
Baba Burun
Devrek
Ereğli
Akçakoca
Karasu
Kandıra
Hendek
Düzce
İzmit
Adapazarı
1865
Geyve
Sakarya
Göynük
Mudurnu
Nallıhan
Bozüyük
Sarıcakaya
1787
Mihalıççik
Alcu
Eskişehir
Porsuk
Mahmudiye
Seyitgazi
Kütahya
Çifteler
Altıntaş
İscehisar
Banaz
Afyonkarahisar
Şuhut
Çay
Bolvadin
Emirdağ
Sandıklı
Senirkent
2446
Dinar
Yalvaç
Lake Eğirdir
Eğirdir
Akşehir
Isparta
L. Burdur
Burdur
Yeşilova
Tefenni
Bucak
Korkuteli
Perge
Aspendos
Side
Antalya
Serik
Manavgat
Gulf of Antalya
Alanya
Gazipaşa
Anamur
Cape Anamur
Taurus Mountains
Lake Beyşehir
Beyşehir
Yasildağ
Seydişehir
Akseki
Akdağ
2720
Hadım
Bozkır
Ermenek
Konya
Çatal Hüyük
Çumra
Karaman
Ayrancı
Ereğli
İsmil
Karapınar
Mut
Erdemli
Göksu
Silifke
İncekum Burnu
Kadınhanı
Ilgın
Doğanhisar
Şarki
Sarayönü
Sultanhanı
Hasan Dağı
3266
Aksaray
Yeşilova
Lake Tuz
Cihanbeyli
Yunak
Sülüklü
Şereflikoçhisar
Ortaköy
2137
Kulu
Mucur
Kızılırmak
Kırşehir
Hirfanlı Res.
Kaman
Polatlı
Haymana
Sivrihisar
1819
TURKEY
Anatolia
Pontine Mts.
Bolu
Gerede
2499
Kızılcahamam
Güdül
Beypazarı
Ayaş
ANKARA
1992
Elmadağ
Kalecik
Kırıkkale
Keskin
Delice
Yerköy
Çubuk
Şabanözü
Çankırı
Bayat
İskilip
Alacahöyük
Sungurlu
Hattuşaş
Karabük
Çerkeş
Kurşunlu
Tosya
Osmancık
Safranbolu
Araç
Ilgaz Dağları
2546
Kastamonu
Boyabat
Taşköprü
Gökırmak
Bartın
Filyos
Cide
Küre Dağları
2019
İnebolu
Abana
İnce Burun
C. Kormakiti
Girne
Lefkosía/Lefkoşa
Güzelyurt
(Nicosia)
Gazimağusa
(Famagusta)
C. Arnauti
Pólis
Troódos
Ólympos
1953
Lárnaka
Páfos
Lemesós
(Limassol)
CYPRUS
C. Gáta
50/51
66/67
68/69
1
2
3
4
42
39
36

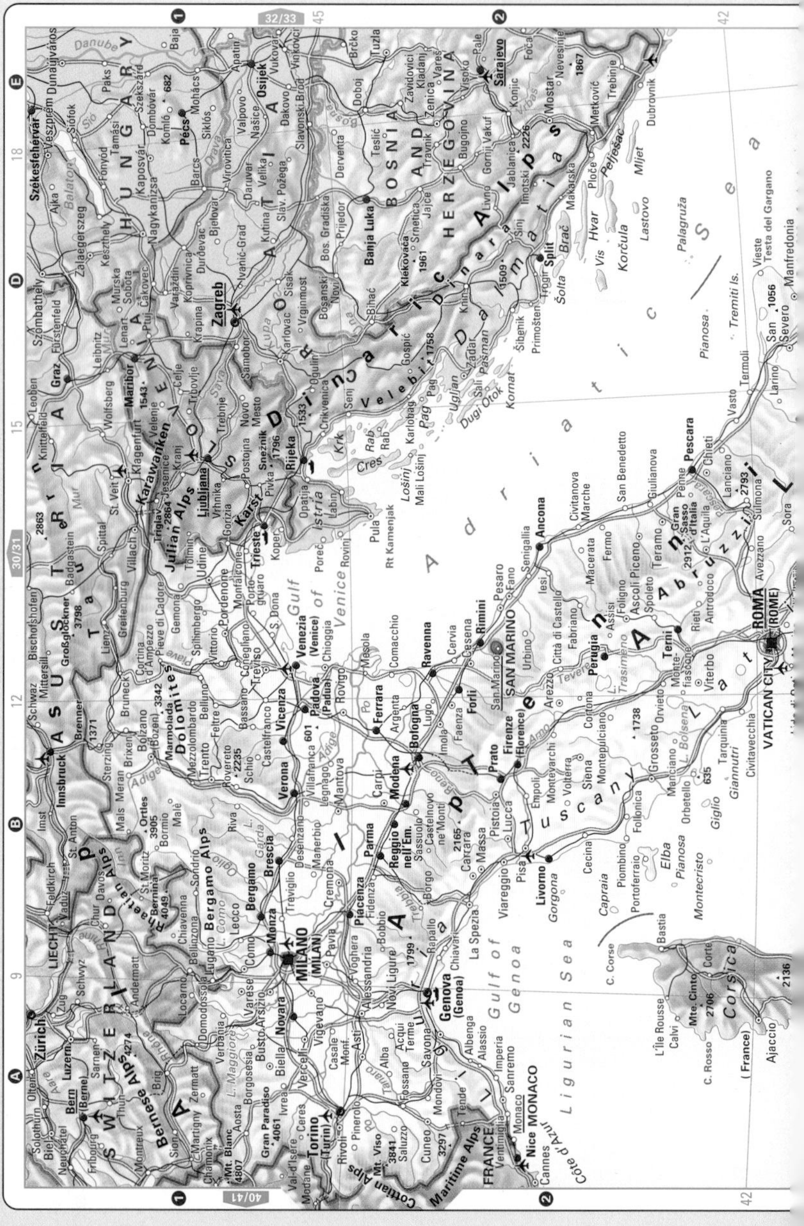

SWITZERLAND
AUSTRIA
HUNGARY
SLOVENIA
CROATIA
BOSNIA AND HERZEGOVINA
ITALY
SAN MARINO
MONACO
VATICAN CITY
FRANCE
LIECHT.
Adriatic Sea
Ligurian Sea
Gulf of Genoa
Gulf of Venice
Dinaric Alps
Alps
Apennines
Bernese Alps
Rhaetian Alps
Bergamo Alps
Julian Alps
Karawanken
Dolomites
Maritime Alps
Cottian Alps
Tuscany
Abruzzi
Latium
Istria
Corsica
(France)
Elba
Capraia
Gorgona
Pianosa
Montecristo
Giglio
Giannutri
Tremiti Is.
Palagruža
Vis
Hvar
Brač
Korčula
Lastovo
Mljet
Pelješac
Krk
Cres
Rab
Pag
Lošinj
Dugi Otok
Ugljan
Kornat
Šolta
Côte d'Azur
Danube
Drava
Sava
Mur
Po
Adige
Piave
Arno
Tevere
Rhône
Rhine
Inn
Balaton
L. Maggiore
L. Como
L. Garda
L. Trasimeno
L. Bolsena
Velebit
ROMA (ROME)
MILANO (MILAN)
Torino (Turin)
Genova (Genoa)
Venezia (Venice)
Firenze (Florence)
Padova (Padua)
Bologna
Verona
Vicenza
Trieste
Bolzano (Bozen)
Ljubljana
Zagreb
Sarajevo
Bern (Berne)
Zürich
Luzern
Innsbruck
Graz
Maribor
Rijeka
Split
Banja Luka
Pécs
Osijek
Székesfehérvár
Szombathely
Klagenfurt
Villach
Udine
Trento
Brescia
Bergamo
Monza
Novara
Parma
Piacenza
Modena
Reggio nell'Em.
Ferrara
Ravenna
Rimini
Forlì
Ancona
Pescara
Perugia
Terni
Prato
Livorno
Pisa
Lucca
Siena
Grosseto
La Spezia
Savona
Nice
Monaco
Sanremo
Cannes
Ajaccio
Bastia
Corte
Calvi
Mt. Blanc 4807
Gran Paradiso 4061
Mt. Viso 3841
Mte. Cinto 2706
Ortles 3905
Bernina 4049
Marmolada 3342
Großglockner 3798
Triglav 2864
Gran Sasso d'Italia 2912
Snežnik 1796

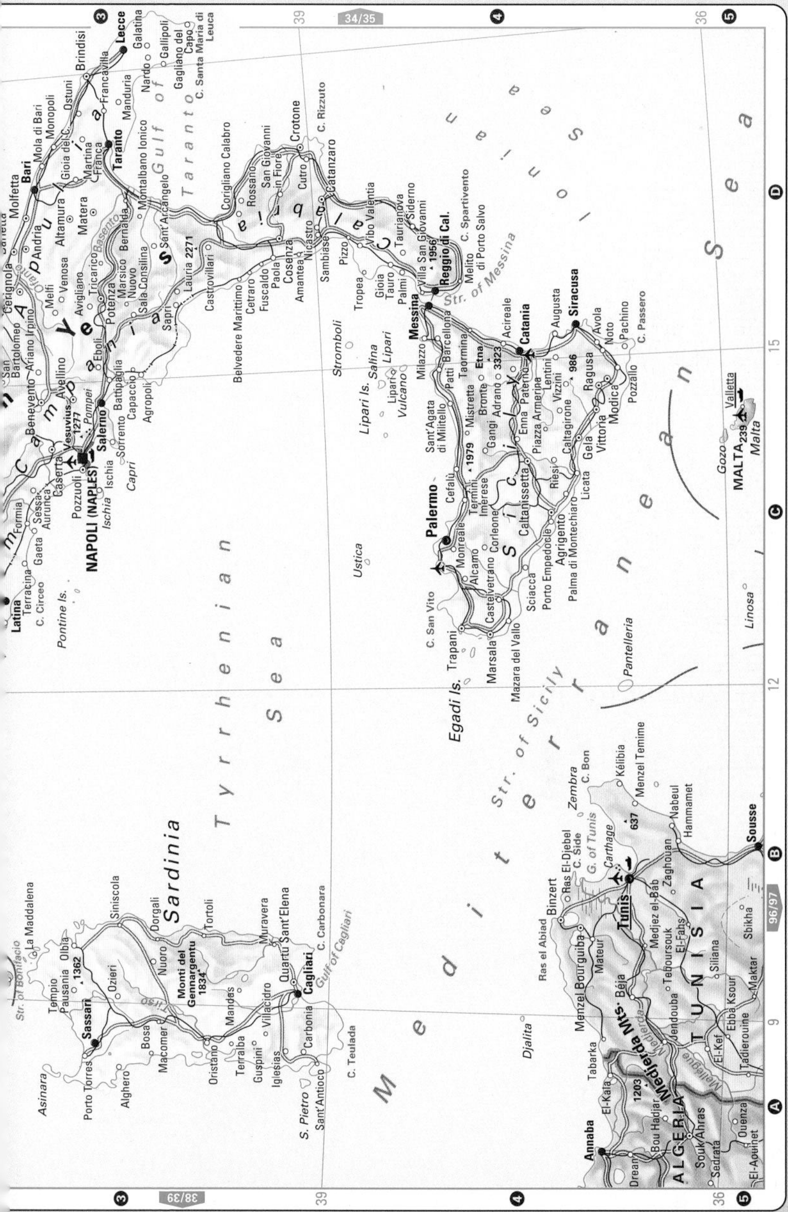
34/35
38/39
96/97
Tyrrhenian Sea
Mediterranean Sea
Ionian Sea
Sardinia
Sicilia
Calabria
Campania
Puglia
Basilicata
TUNISIA
ALGERIA
MALTA
Valletta
Gozo
Malta
NAPOLI (NAPLES)
Palermo
Messina
Catania
Siracusa
Reggio di Cal.
Cagliari
Sassari
Tunis
Bari
Taranto
Lecce
Brindisi
Salerno
Cosenza
Catanzaro
Crotone
Potenza
Matera
Foggia
Gulf of Taranto
Str. of Messina
Str. of Sicily
Str. of Bonifacio
Gulf of Cagliari
G. of Tunis
Lipari Is.
Egadi Is.
Stromboli
Salina
Lipari
Vulcano
Ustica
Pantelleria
Linosa
Etna
3323
Vesuvius
1277
Pompei
Capri
Ischia
Pontine Is.
Monti del Gennargentu
1834
Medjerda Mts.
C. Bon
Zembra
Sousse
Annaba
Bizerte
Trapani
Marsala
Mazara del Vallo
Agrigento
Gela
Ragusa
Caltanissetta
Enna
Cefalù
Milazzo
Tropea
Nuoro
Olbia
Oristano
Alghero
Iglesias
Carbonia
C. Teulada
C. Spartivento
C. Passero
C. Rizzuto
C. Santa Maria di Leuca
C. San Vito
Latina
Gaeta
Formia
Caserta
Avellino
Benevento
Eboli
Sorrento
Amantea
Paola
Vibo Valentia
Gallipoli
Manduria
Ostuni
Monopoli
Molfetta
Altamura
Melfi
Venosa
Noto
Modica
Vittoria
Licata
Sciacca
Alcamo
Corleone
Augusta
Acireale
Taormina
Bronte
Adrano
Paternò
Lentini
Avola
Pachino
Hammamet
Nabeul
Kélibia
Béja
Jendouba
El-Kef
Siliana
Maktar
Tabarka
El-Kala
Souk Ahras
Carthage

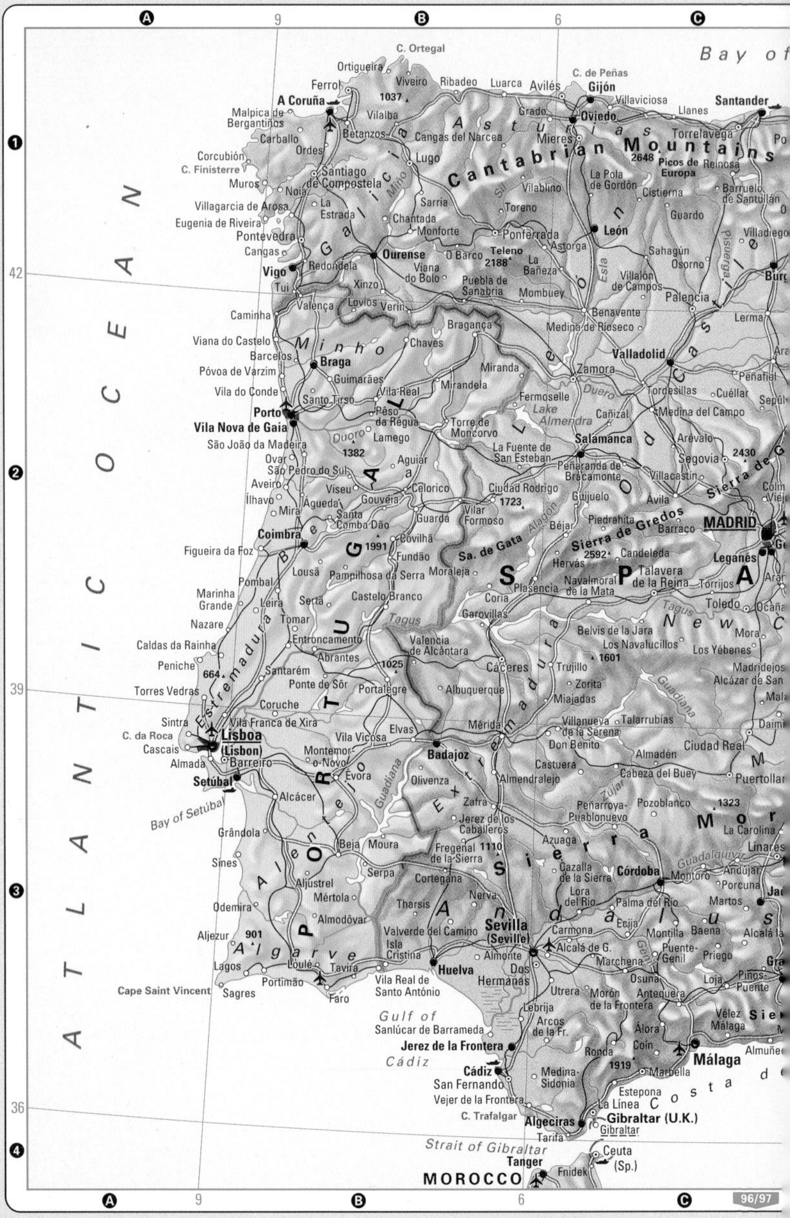
A
B
C
9
6
1
2
3
4
42
39
36
Bay of
C. Ortegal
Ortigueira
Ferrol
Viveiro
Ribadeo
Luarca
Avilés
C. de Peñas
Gijón
Villaviciosa
Santander
Llanes
A Coruña
1037
Vilalba
Grado
Oviedo
Malpica de Bergantiños
Betanzos
Asturias
Torrelavega
Carballo
Cangas del Narcea
Mieres
Ordes
Cantabrian Mountains
Corcubión
Lugo
2648
Picos de Europa
Reinosa
C. Fínisterre
Santiago de Compostela
La Pola de Gordón
Muros
Noia
Vilablino
Cistierna
Barruelo de Santullán
Villagarcia de Arosa
La Estrada
Sarria
Toreno
Guardo
Eugenia de Riveira
Chantada
León
Pontevedra
Monforte
Ponferrada
Villadiego
Cangas
Galicia
Miño
Sil
Esla
Pisuerga
Astorga
Sahagún
Ourense
O Barco
Teleno
2188
La Bañeza
Osorno
Vigo
Redondela
Viana do Bolo
Puebla de Sanabria
Villalón de Campos
Burgos
Tui
Xinzo
Mombuey
Palencia
Valença
Lovios
Verín
Benavente
Lerma
Caminha
Bragança
Medina de Rioseco
Viana do Castelo
Minho
Chaves
Barcelos
Braga
Miranda
Valladolid
Póvoa de Varzim
Guimarães
Zamora
Peñafiel
Vila do Conde
Mirandela
Vila Real
Tordesillas
Cuéllar
Santo Tirso
Fermoselle
Porto
Pêso da Régua
Lake Almendra
Cañizal
Medina del Campo
Sepúlveda
Vila Nova de Gaia
Torre de Moncorvo
Duero
Duoro
São João da Madeira
Lamego
Salamanca
Arévalo
Ovar
1382
La Fuente de San Esteban
São Pedro do Sul
Aguiar
Peñaranda de Bracamonte
Segovia
2430
Aveiro
Viseu
Villacastín
Ílhavo
Celorico
Ciudad Rodrigo
Guijuelo
Águeda
Gouveia
1723
Ávila
Old Castile
Sierra de Guadarrama
Colmenar Viejo
Mira
Santa Comba Dão
Guarda
Vilar Formoso
Alagón
Béjar
Piedrahita
Sierra de Gredos
MADRID
Coimbra
Beira
Barraco
Covilhã
1991
Sa. de Gata
Figueira da Foz
Fundão
2592
Candeleda
Getafe
Leganés
Hervás
Lousã
Pampilhosa da Serra
Moraleja
Talavera de la Reina
Pombal
Plasencia
Navalmoral de la Mata
Torrijos
Aranjuez
Marinha Grande
Sertã
Castelo Branco
Coria
Toledo
Leiria
Ocaña
Tomar
Garrovillas
Tagus
Nazare
Entroncamento
Belvis de la Jara
New Castile
Mora
Caldas da Rainha
Valencia de Alcántara
Los Navalucillos
Los Yébenes
Abrantes
Peniche
1025
Cáceres
Trujillo
1601
Madridejos
Alcázar de San Juan
664
Santarém
Zorita
Estremadura
Ponte de Sôr
Portalegre
Albuquerque
Miajadas
Guadiana
Torres Vedras
Coruche
Sintra
Vila Franca de Xira
Mérida
Villanueva de la Serena
Talarrubias
Daimiel
C. da Roca
Lisboa (Lisbon)
Elvas
Vila Viçosa
Don Benito
Cascais
Montemor-o-Novo
Badajoz
Almadén
Ciudad Real
Almada
Barreiro
Castuera
Extremadura
Évora
Cabeza del Buey
Setúbal
Olivenza
Almendralejo
Puertollano
Alcácer
Zújar
Zafra
Peñarroya-Pueblonuevo
Pozoblanco
1323
Bay of Setúbal
Jerez de los Caballeros
Sierra Morena
La Carolina
Grândola
Alentejo
Beja
Moura
Fregenal de la Sierra
1110
Azuaga
Linares
Sines
Serpa
Cazalla de la Sierra
Guadalquivir
Andújar
Aljustrel
Cortegana
Córdoba
Montoro
Porcuna
Mértola
Lora del Río
Jaén
Odemira
Tharsis
Nerva
Palma del Río
Martos
Almodôvar
Andalusia
Aljezur
901
Valverde del Camino
Sevilla (Seville)
Carmona
Écija
Montilla
Baena
Alcalá la Real
Algarve
Isla Cristina
Alcalá de G.
Genil
Puente-Genil
Priego
Lagos
Loulé
Tavira
Huelva
Almonte
Marchena
Granada
Portimão
Dos Hermanas
Osuna
Loja
Pinos-Puente
Cape Saint Vincent
Sagres
Faro
Vila Real de Santo António
Utrera
Morón de la Frontera
Antequera
Gulf of Cádiz
Lebrija
Vélez Málaga
Sanlúcar de Barrameda
Arcos de la Fr.
Álora
Jerez de la Frontera
Coín
Málaga
Almuñécar
Ronda
Cádiz
1919
Marbella
San Fernando
Medina-Sidonia
Estepona
Costa del Sol
Vejer de la Frontera
La Línea
C. Trafalgar
Algeciras
Gibraltar (U.K.)
Gibraltar
Tarifa
Strait of Gibraltar
Ceuta (Sp.)
Tanger
Fnideq
MOROCCO
SPAIN
PORTUGAL
ATLANTIC OCEAN
96/97

D
E
F
40/41
36/37
1
2
3
4
FRANCE
Gascony
Languedoc
Pyrenees
Navarra
Aragon
Catalonia
Valencia
Murcia
Castile
ANDORRA
ALGERIA
Tell Atlas
Biscay
Gulf of Lions
Gulf of Valencia
Balearic Islands
Mediterranean Sea
Costa Brava
Costa Dorada
Costa Blanca
Costa del Sol
Alborán
Condom
Grisolles
Lodève
Arles
Mont-de-Marsan
Aire
Graulhet
Montpellier
Capbreton
Dax
Adour
Auch
Toulouse
Castres
Mazamet
Pézenas
Bayonne
Biarritz
Peyrehorade
Gimont
Revel
Sète
Saintes Maries
Donostia
(San Sebastián)
Orthez
Pau
Castelnaudary
Canal du Midi
Béziers
Bilbao
Irún
Oloron-Ste.-Marie
Gave de Pau
Tarbes
St-Gaudens
Pamiers
Carcassonne
Narbonne
Tolosa
Durango
Lourdes
Garonne
St-Girons
Lavelanet
Quillan
Alsasua
Roncesvalles
2504
Bagnères-de-L.
Foix
1230
Vitoria
(Gasteiz)
Pamplona
Pierrefitte-Nestalas
Ax-les-Thermes
Millas
Perpignan
Argelès
Miranda
Estella
3404
Aneto
Vielha
Mont-Louis
Céret
Haro
Logroño
Tafalla
Jaca
Boltaña
Andorra la Vella
Puigmal
2918
Puigcerdà
Portbou
C. Creus
Figueres
2077
Calahorra
Sádaba
Huesca
Pobla de Segur
Olot
Alfaro
Sierra de la Demanda
Lorenzo
Cervera
Tudela
Ejea de los Caballeros
Berga
Girona
Barbastro
Segre
Solsona
Vic
Sant Feliu de Guíxols
Tarazona
Gallur
Agreda
Balaguer
Manresa
2313
Alagón
Tàrrega
Sabadell
Soria
Zaragoza
Lleida
(Lérida)
Terrassa
Mataró
El Burgo de Osma
Fraga
Les Borges Blanques
BARCELONA
Almazán
Duero
Mequinenza
Ebro
El Vendrell
Ariza
Calatayud
Quinto
Valls
Vilanova i La Geltrú
Medinaceli
Jalón
Reus
Sigüenza
Daroca
Híjar
Caspe
Flix
Tarragona
Alcolea del Pinar
Andorra
Alcañiz
Jadraque
Molina
Monreal del Campo
Tortosa
Trillo
Tagus
Montalbán
Amposta
C. Tortosa
Guadalajara
Alfambra
Morella
Serranía de Cuenca
Albarracín
Vinaròs
Benicarló
Peñarroya
2024
Menorca
Teruel
Cabriel
Ciutadella
Huete
Mahón
Cuenca
Sarrión
Onda
Castellón de la Plana
Alcúdia
Mentalbo
Carboneras de Guadazaón
Vilarreal de los Infantes
Sóller
1445
Vall de Uxó
Inca
Artà
Segorbe
Zancara
Motilla del Palancar
Turia
Almarcha
Utiel
Sagunto
Palma
Manacor
Quintanar de la Orden
Requena
Valencia
Llucmajor
Mallorca
Mota del Cuervo
Minglanilla
Torrente
Santanyí
Villarrobledo
Quintanar del Rey
Sueca
Cabrera
Tomelloso
La Roda
Júcar
San Juan Bautista
San Antonio Abad
Alzira
Chinchilla de Monte-Aragón
Gandia
Albacete
Eivissa
(Ibiza)
Ibiza
Játiva
Denia
La Solana
Almansa
Alcoy
C. Nao
Villena
Formentera
1558
Alcaraz
Tobarra
Yecla
Elche de la Sierra
Hellín
Jumilla
Elda
Villajoyosa
Cieza
Elche
Alicante
Nerpio
Segura
Molina de S.
Villacarrillo
Caravaca de la Cruz
Mula
Orihuela
Murcia
Torrevieja
2381
1579
Alcantarilla
Cazorla
Huéscar
La Unión
Lorca
Cartagena
Baza
Vélez Rubio
Huércal-Overa
Aguilas
Seron
2168
Níjar
Dalías
Almería
C. de Gata
Dellys
AL-JAZA'IR
(ALGIERS)
Bordj Menaïel
Lakhdaria
Tizi Ouzou
Cherchell
Hadjout
El-Arba
Ténès
El-Boulaida
(Blida)
Tablat
Bouïra
Miliana
Lemdiyya
Sour el-Ghozlane
Ech-Cheliff
Beni Slimane
Aïn Defla
Berrouaghia
1810
Sidi Ali
Chéliff
El-Attaf
Aïn Boucif
Bou Kadir
Ksar el-Boukhari
Sidi Aïssa
Mostaganem
1985
Arzew
Aïn Tédèles
Oued Rhiou
Ouahran
(Oran)
Relizane
Tissemsilt
Birine
42
39
36
3
0

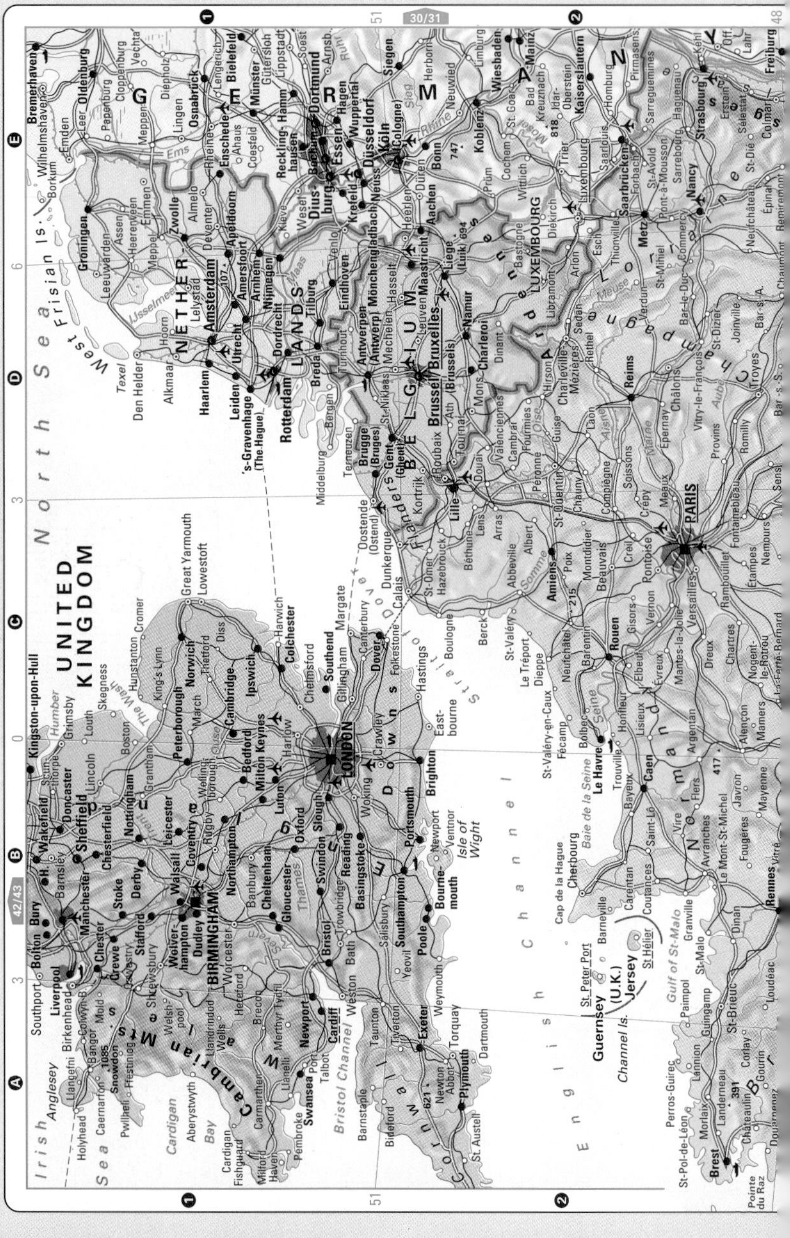
UNITED KINGDOM
NETHERLANDS
BELGIUM
LUXEMBOURG
North Sea
English Channel
Irish Sea
Bristol Channel
Cardigan Bay
Gulf of St-Malo
Strait of Dover
West Frisian Is.
Channel Is.
Isle of Wight
Cambrian Mts
Normandie
Bretagne
Flanders
Ardennes
Lorraine
Champagne
LONDON
PARIS
Brussel/Bruxelles (Brussels)
Amsterdam
Luxembourg
BIRMINGHAM
Manchester
Liverpool
Sheffield
Leeds
Bristol
Cardiff
Southampton
Rotterdam
's-Gravenhage (The Hague)
Antwerpen (Antwerp)
Gent (Ghent)
Brugge (Bruges)
Liège (Luik)
Lille
Rouen
Le Havre
Caen
Reims
Amiens
Calais
Dunkerque
Oostende (Ostend)
Köln (Cologne)
Düsseldorf
Essen
Dortmund
Aachen
Bonn
Koblenz
Saarbrücken
Metz
Nancy
Strasbourg
Rennes
Brest
Jersey
Guernsey
(U.K.)
St Helier
St Peter Port
Rhine
Maas
Meuse
Seine
Somme
Moselle
Thames
30/31
42/43
48

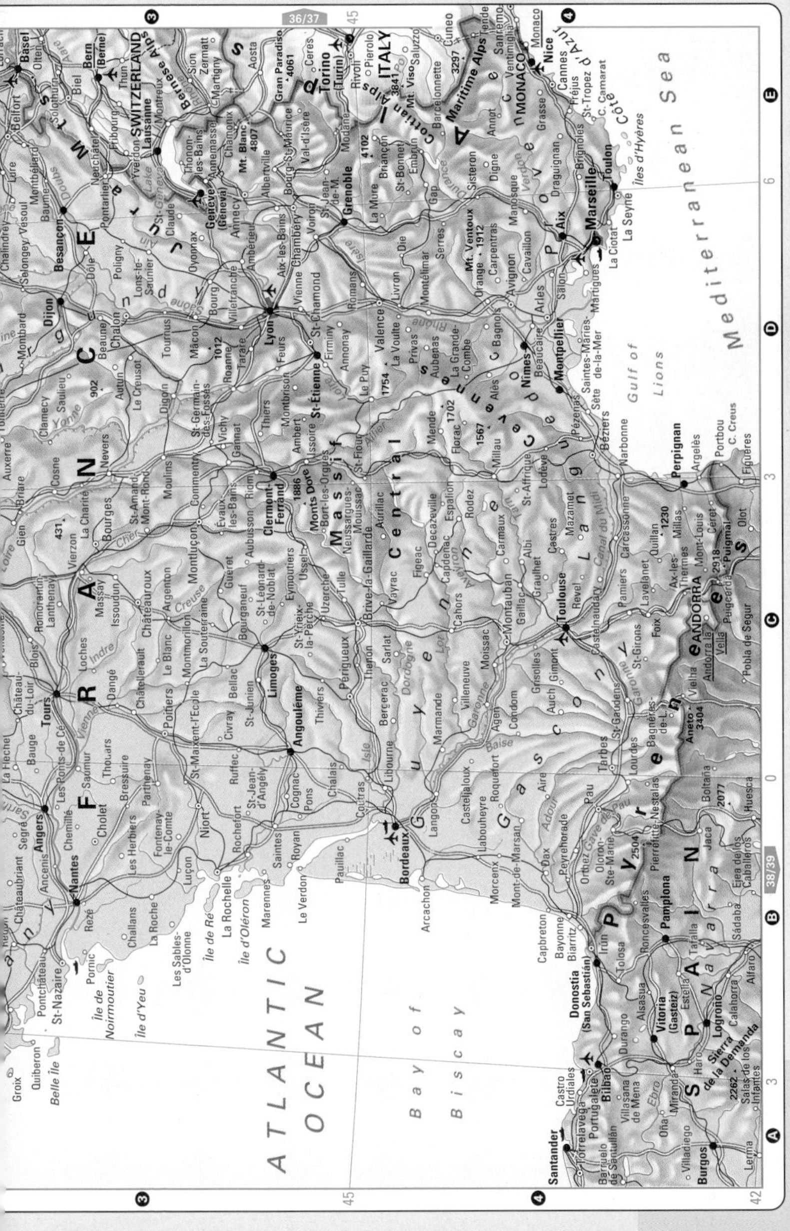
FRANCE
SWITZERLAND
ITALY
MONACO
ANDORRA
SPAIN
ATLANTIC OCEAN
Bay of Biscay
Gulf of Lions
Mediterranean Sea
Massif Central
Pyrenees
Maritime Alps
Cottian Alps
Bernese Alps
Côte d'Azur
Paris
Lyon
Marseille
Toulouse
Bordeaux
Nantes
Nice
Montpellier
Grenoble
Genève (Geneva)
Torino (Turin)
Bilbao
Donostia (San Sebastián)
Vitoria (Gasteiz)
Pamplona
Perpignan
Limoges
Clermont-Ferrand
Dijon
Besançon
Tours
Angers
Poitiers
Angoulême
Toulon
Aix
Nîmes
St-Étienne
Santander
Burgos
Logroño
Mt. Blanc 4807
Aneto 3404
Mt. Viso 3841
Mt. Ventoux 1912
36/37
38/39

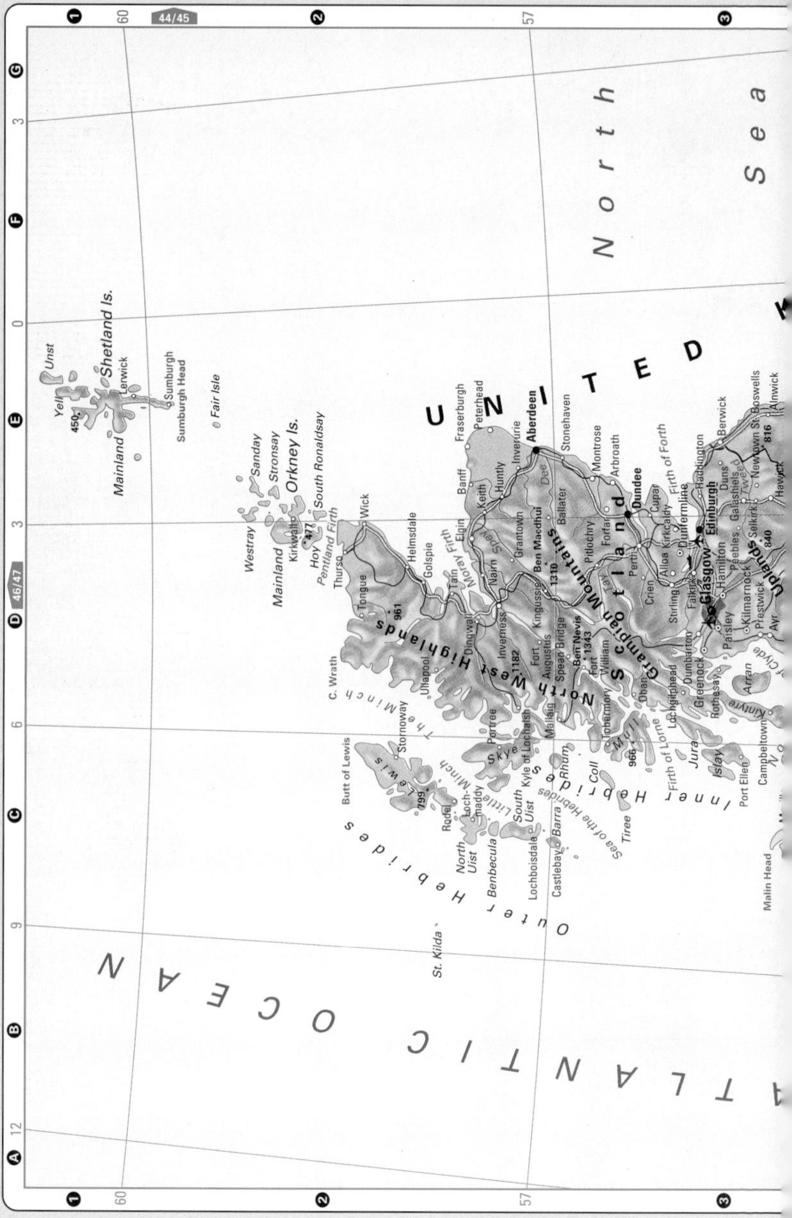
44/45
46/47
Shetland Is.
Unst
Yell
Lerwick
Mainland
450
Sumburgh
Sumburgh Head
Fair Isle
Orkney Is.
Sanday
Stronsay
Westray
Mainland
Kirkwall
Hoy
477
South Ronaldsay
Pentland Firth
Thurso
Wick
Helmsdale
Golspie
Tongue
961
C. Wrath
The Minch
Stornoway
Butt of Lewis
Lewis
799
Rodel
Little Minch
North Uist
Loch-maddy
Benbecula
South Uist
Lochboisdale
Castlebay
Barra
Outer Hebrides
St. Kilda
Sea of the Hebrides
Tiree
Coll
Rhum
Skye
Portree
Kyle of Lochalsh
Mallaig
Ullapool
North West Highlands
1182
Dingwall
Inverness
Tain
Moray Firth
Elgin
Nairn
Spey
Fort Augustus
Spean Bridge
Ben Nevis
1343
Fort William
Tobermory
Mull
966
Oban
Firth of Lorne
Jura
Islay
Port Ellen
Inner Hebrides
Kintyre
Campbeltown
Arran
Firth of Clyde
Rothesay
Greenock
Dumbarton
Lochgilphead
Paisley
Glasgow
Kilmarnock
Prestwick
Ayr
Hamilton
Peebles
Selkirk
840
Uplands
Edinburgh
Falkirk
Stirling
Crieff
Alloa
Kirkcaldy
Dunfermline
Firth of Forth
Perth
Pitlochry
Forfar
Dundee
Cupar
Arbroath
Montrose
Grampian Mountains
Scotland
Kingussie
1310
Ben Macdhui
Grantown
Ballater
Dee
Huntly
Keith
Banff
Fraserburgh
Peterhead
Inverurie
Aberdeen
Stonehaven
Haddington
Berwick
Duns
Galashiels
Tweed
Newtown St. Boswells
Hawick
816
Alnwick
Malin Head
UNITED
North Sea
ATLANTIC OCEAN

1 : 6 000 000

0 50 100 150 200 km
0 50 100 150 miles

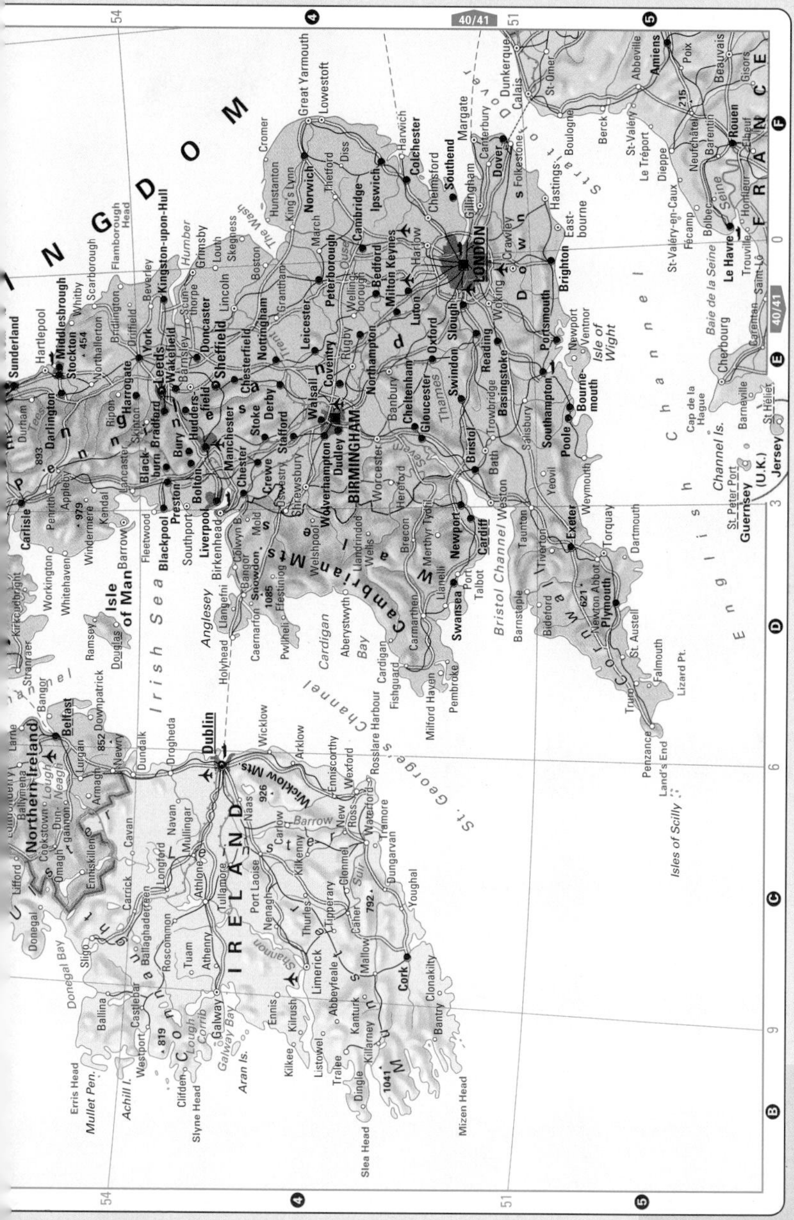

40/41
KINGDOM
IRELAND
FRANCE
Northern Ireland
Isle of Man
Isle of Wight
Channel Is.
Irish Sea
Bristol Channel
St. George's Channel
English Channel
Strait of Dover
Cardigan Bay
Galway Bay
Donegal Bay
Baie de la Seine
The Wash
Humber
Cambrian Mts.
Wicklow Mts.
Pennines
Downs
Midland
Cornwall
Wales
Connaught
Leinster
Munster
Ulster
Anglesey
Aran Is.
Achill I.
Mullet Pen.
Isles of Scilly
Lizard Pt.
Land's End
Erris Head
Slyne Head
Slea Head
Mizen Head
Flamborough Head
Lough Neagh
Lough Corrib
Shannon
Barrow
Suir
Thames
Severn
Trent
Ouse
Tees
Seine
LONDON
Dublin
BIRMINGHAM
Belfast
Cardiff
Douglas
St Peter Port
St Hélier
Guernsey
Jersey
(U.K.)
Carlisle
Sunderland
Middlesbrough
Stockton
Hartlepool
Darlington
Durham
Whitby
Scarborough
Bridlington
Driffield
Northallerton
York
Harrogate
Ripon
Skipton
Leeds
Bradford
Wakefield
Barnsley
Huddersfield
Sheffield
Doncaster
Scunthorpe
Beverley
Kingston-upon-Hull
Grimsby
Louth
Lincoln
Skegness
Boston
Grantham
Nottingham
Chesterfield
Derby
Leicester
Coventry
Rugby
Northampton
Peterborough
Wellingborough
Bedford
Milton Keynes
Luton
Cambridge
King's Lynn
Hunstanton
Cromer
Norwich
Great Yarmouth
Lowestoft
March
Thetford
Diss
Ipswich
Harwich
Colchester
Chelmsford
Southend
Harlow
Margate
Canterbury
Dover
Folkestone
Gillingham
Hastings
Eastbourne
Brighton
Crawley
Woking
Reading
Slough
Oxford
Swindon
Banbury
Cheltenham
Gloucester
Worcester
Hereford
Bristol
Bath
Trowbridge
Salisbury
Basingstoke
Southampton
Portsmouth
Newport
Ventnor
Bournemouth
Poole
Weymouth
Yeovil
Taunton
Weston
Exeter
Tiverton
Torquay
Dartmouth
Plymouth
Newton Abbot
Barnstaple
Bideford
St. Austell
Truro
Falmouth
Penzance
Swansea
Port Talbot
Llanelli
Carmarthen
Pembroke
Milford Haven
Fishguard
Cardigan
Aberystwyth
Merthyr Tydfil
Brecon
Llandrindod Wells
Welshpool
Shrewsbury
Oswestry
Wolverhampton
Dudley
Walsall
Stafford
Stoke
Crewe
Chester
Mold
Colwyn B.
Bangor
Caernarfon
Snowdon
Ffestiniog
Pwllheli
Holyhead
Llangefni
Liverpool
Birkenhead
Southport
Blackpool
Preston
Fleetwood
Barrow
Lancaster
Kendal
Windermere
Blackburn
Bury
Bolton
Manchester
Penrith
Appleby
Workington
Whitehaven
Kirkcudbright
Stranraer
Ramsey
Larne
Bangor
Lurgan
Downpatrick
Newry
Armagh
Dungannon
Omagh
Cookstown
Ballymena
Enniskillen
Lifford
Donegal
Sligo
Ballina
Castlebar
Westport
Clifden
Galway
Tuam
Athenry
Roscommon
Ballaghaderreen
Carrick
Longford
Cavan
Mullingar
Navan
Athlone
Tullamore
Dundalk
Drogheda
Naas
Wicklow
Arklow
Enniscorthy
Wexford
Rosslare Harbour
New Ross
Waterford
Tramore
Dungarvan
Carlow
Kilkenny
Port Laoise
Nenagh
Thurles
Tipperary
Clonmel
Cahir
Limerick
Ennis
Kilrush
Kilkee
Listowel
Tralee
Abbeyfeale
Kanturk
Mallow
Killarney
Dingle
Bantry
Clonakilty
Cork
Youghal
Dunkerque
Calais
St-Omer
Boulogne
Berck
Abbeville
Amiens
Poix
Beauvais
Gisors
St-Valéry
Le Tréport
Dieppe
Neufchâtel
Rouen
Elbeuf
Barentin
St-Valéry-en-Caux
Fécamp
Bolbec
Le Havre
Honfleur
Trouville
Saint-Lô
Carentan
Cherbourg
Barneville
Cap de la Hague
893
979
454
852
926
1085
792
819
1041
621
215

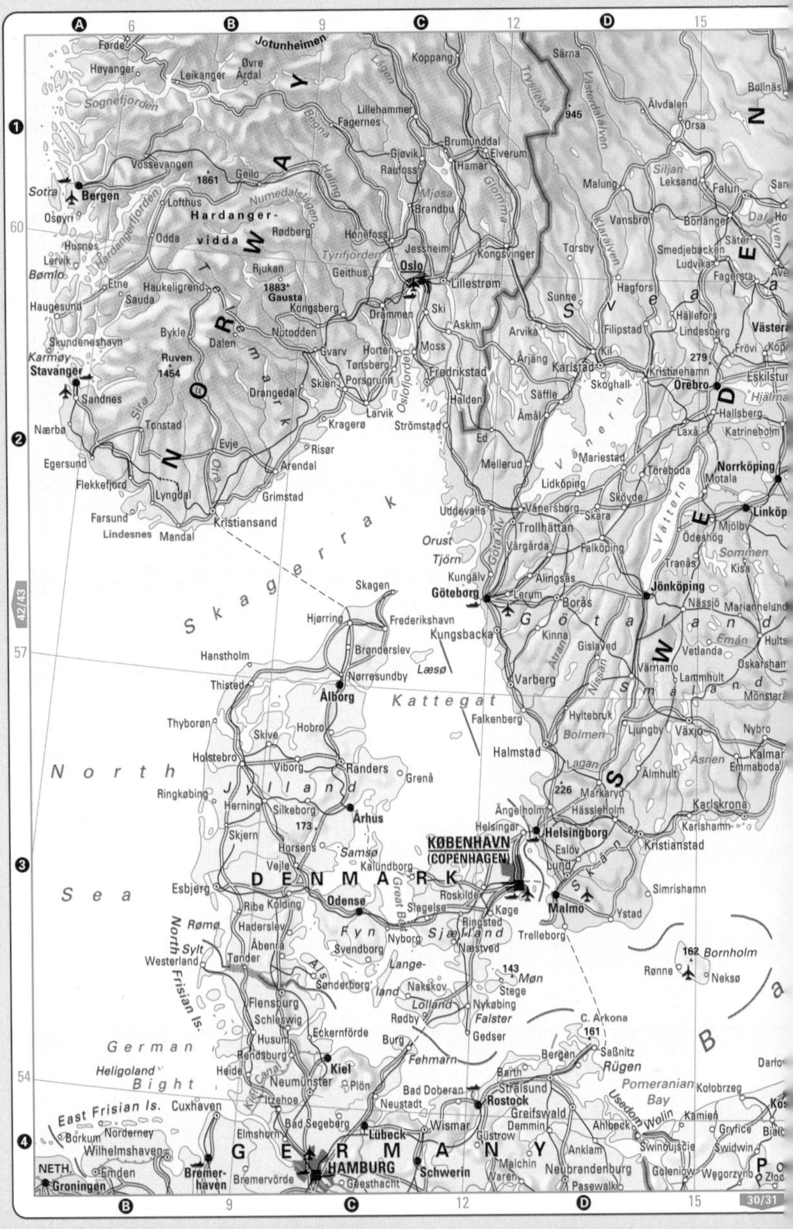
A
B
C
D
6
9
12
15
1
2
3
4
60
57
54
42/43
30/31
Førde
Jotunheimen
Høyanger
Leikanger
Øvre Årdal
Koppang
Särna
Bollnäs
Sognefjorden
Lillehammer
Fagernes
945
Älvdalen
Orsa
N
Y
A
W
R
O
Begna
Lågen
Trysilelva
Västerdalälven
Brumunddal
Elverum
Gjøvik
Raufoss
Hamar
Vossevangen
1861
Geilo
Sotra
Bergen
Malung
Siljan
Leksand
Falun
Lofthus
Numedalslågen
Mjøsa
Brandbu
Glomma
Osøyri
Hardanger-
vidda
Hardangerfjorden
Odda
Rødberg
Hønefoss
Jessheim
Kongsvinger
Vansbro
Borlänge
Husnes
Leirvik
Bømlo
Tyrifjorden
Rjukan
Geithus
Oslo
Lillestrøm
Torsby
Klarälven
Smedjebacken
Säter
Ludvika
Fagersta
Etne
Haukeligrend
Sauda
1883
Gausta
Kongsberg
Ski
Sunne
Hagfors
Haugesund
Drammen
Askim
Arvika
Filipstad
Hällefors
Lindesberg
Skudeneshavn
Bykle
Dalen
Notodden
Moss
Karmøy
Stavanger
Ruven
1454
Gvarv
Horten
Tønsberg
Årjäng
Karlstad
Kil
Kristinehamn
279
Örebro
Frövi
Sandnes
Skien
Porsgrunn
Fredrikstad
Skoghall
Eskilstuna
Drangedal
Halden
Säffle
Hjälmaren
Oslofjorden
Larvik
Åmål
Hallsberg
Nærbø
Sira
Tonstad
Kragerø
Strömstad
Ed
Laxå
Katrineholm
Egersund
Evje
Risør
Mellerud
Mariestad
Vänern
Arendal
Töreboda
Norrköping
Motala
Otra
Flekkefjord
Lyngdal
Grimstad
Lidköping
Skövde
Vänersborg
Uddevalla
Skara
Linköping
Farsund
Kristiansand
Trollhättan
Vättern
Mjölby
Lindesnes
Mandal
Skagerrak
Orust
Vårgårda
Falköping
Ödeshög
Tjörn
Sommen
Tranås
Kisa
Göta Älv
Kungälv
Alingsås
Skagen
Göteborg
Lerum
Borås
Jönköping
Nässjö
Mariannelund
Hjørring
Frederikshavn
Götaland
Kungsbacka
Kinna
Gislaved
Emån
Hultsfred
Brønderslev
Vetlanda
Hanstholm
Ätran
Nissan
Oskarshamn
Nørresundby
Læsø
Värnamo
Lammhult
Thisted
Ålborg
Varberg
Småland
Mönsterås
Kattegat
Thyborøn
Falkenberg
Hyltebruk
Ljungby
Växjö
Nybro
Skive
Hobro
Bolmen
Halmstad
Kalmar
Holstebro
Lagan
Åsnen
Emmaboda
North Sea
Viborg
Randers
Grenå
Almhult
Jylland
226
Markaryd
Ringkøbing
Herning
Silkeborg
Ängelholm
Hässleholm
Karlskrona
Århus
173
Helsingør
Helsingborg
Karlshamn
Skjern
KØBENHAVN
(COPENHAGEN)
Kristianstad
Horsens
Samsø
Eslöv
Skåne
Vejle
Kalundborg
Lund
DENMARK
Esbjerg
Roskilde
Simrishamn
Ribe
Kolding
Odense
Great Belt
Malmö
Slagelse
Køge
Ystad
Rømø
Haderslev
Ringsted
Fyn
Nyborg
Sjælland
Trelleborg
North Frisian Is.
Åbenrå
Næstved
Sylt
Svendborg
Bornholm
162
Westerland
Tønder
Als
Langeland
143
Møn
Rønne
Neksø
Sønderborg
Nakskov
Stege
Flensburg
Lolland
Nykøbing
Schleswig
Rødby
Falster
C. Arkona
Husum
Eckernförde
Burg
Gedser
161
German Bight
Rendsburg
Fehmarn
Bergen
Saßnitz
Kiel
Rügen
Baltic
Heligoland
Heide
Kiel Canal
Neumünster
Plön
Barth
Darłowo
Bad Doberan
Stralsund
Pomeranian Bay
Kołobrzeg
Itzehoe
Neustadt
Rostock
Usedom
East Frisian Is.
Cuxhaven
Greifswald
Wolin
Kamień
Norderney
Bad Segeberg
Wismar
Demmin
Ahlbeck
Gryfice
Borkum
Elmshorn
Lübeck
Güstrow
Wilhelmshaven
GERMANY
Anklam
Świnoujście
Świdwin
NETH.
Emden
Bremerhaven
HAMBURG
Schwerin
Malchin
Neubrandenburg
Goleniów
Węgorzyno
Groningen
Bremervörde
Geesthacht
Waren
Pasewalk

46/47
48/49
FINLAND
ESTONIA
LATVIA
LITHUANIA
RUSSIA
BELARUS
POLAND
Gulf of Bothnia
Gulf of Finland
Gulf of Riga
Baltic Sea
Åland Is.
Irbe Strait
Courland Lagoon
Gdańsk Bay
Lake Peipus
Tampere
Pori
Nokia
Valkeakoski
Vammala
Harjavalta
Kokemäki
Rauma
Toijala
Hämeenlinna
Lahti
Heinola
Sysmä
Päijänne
Mäntyharju
Saimaa
Imatra
Svetogorsk
Lappeenranta
Nastola
Kouvola
Vyborg
Vaalimaa
Hamina
Elimäki
Mäntsälä
Loimaa
Forssa
Riihimäki
Hyvinkää
Uusikaupunki
Mynämäki
Somero
Järvenpää
Porvoo
Kotka
Raisio
Turku/Åbo
Vihti
Kerava
Vantaa
Salo
Lohja
Helsinki/Helsingfors
Espoo
Pargas
Gogland
Moshchnyy
Ekenäs
Hanko
Purekkani Neem
Narva Bay
Ust-Luga
Kohtla-Järve
Ivangorod
Narva
Kunda
Loksa
Naisaar
Tallinn
Paldiski
Tapa
Rakvere
Kiviõli
Keila
Kose
Kauksi
Slantsy
Avinurme
Risti
Paide
Mustvee
Gdov
Rapla
Türi
Haapsalu
Jõgeva
Kallaste
Põltsamaa
Emajõgi
Virtsu
Suure-Jaani
Tartu
Pärnu
Sindi
Viljandi
Elva
Võrtsjärv
L. Pskov
Tõstamaa
Kilingi-Nõmme
Mõisaküla
Otepää
Põlva
Tõrva
Võru
Kihnu
Ruhnu
Ainaži
Rūjiena
Mazsalaca
Valka
Valga
Antsla
Pechory
318
Aloja
Strenči
Valmiera
Vireši
Ape
Limbaži
Smiltene
Alūksne
Gulbene
Vilaka
Gauja
Cēsis
Balvi
Pytalovo
Sigulda
Jaunpiebalga
Nītaure
Ērgli
Madona
Lubāna
Jūrmala
Rīga
311
Kārsava
Ogre
Varakļāni
Ludza
Pļaviņas
Aiviekste
Jēkabpils
Viļāni
Rēzekne
Aizkraukle
Jelgava
Western Dvina
Bauska
Līvāni
289
Preiļi
Viesīte
Biržai
Subate
Ilūkste
Krāslava
Pasvalys
Rokiškis
Daugavpils
Druya
Zarasai
Braslaw
Vidzy
Hiiumaa
Tahkuna nina
Vormsi
Kärdla
69
Emmaste
Muhu
Soela Väin
Drissaare
Mustjala
50
Kuressaare
Saaremaa
Sääre
Kolkasrags
Kolka
Mazirbe
Dundaga
Valdemārpils
Ventspils
Talsi
174
Piltene
Ugāle
Sabile
Tukums
Kuldīga
Venta
Aizpute
Saldus
Dobele
Auce
Liepāja
Durbe
Priekule
Mažeikiai
Naujoji Akmenė
Skuodas
Joniškis
Telšiai
Kuršėnai
Pakruojis
Palanga
Plungė
Šiauliai
Radviliškis
Kupiškis
Kretinga
Panevėžys
Klaipėda
234
Rietavas
Kelmė
Baisogala
Anykščiai
Gargždai
Šventoji
Utena
Ignalina
Raseiniai
Molėtai
Courland Spit
Šilalė
Kėdainiai
Ukmergė
Šilutė
Širvintos
Švenčionys
Pastavy
Neringa
Tauragė
Pagėgiai
Jurbarkas
Jonava
Pabradė
Narach
Neman
Neris
Svir
Sovetsk
Kaunas
Kaišiadorys
Šakiai
Vilnius
Astravets
Zelenogradsk
Pionerskiy
Polessk
Bolshakovo
Prienai
293
Vilyeyka
Smarhon
Kaliningrad
Vilkaviškis
Birštonas
Trakai
Baltiysk
Kybartai
Marijampolė
Ashmyany
Gvardeysk
Chernyakhovsk
Gusev
Alytus
Šalčininkai
Maladzyechna
Mamonovo
Ozërsk
Bagrationovsk
Varėna
Eišiškės
Goldap
Lazdijai
Valozhyn
Braniewo
Węgorzewo
Suwałki
Yuratsishki
Druskininkai
Lidzbark
Bartoszyce
Olecko
Sejny
Lida
Iwye
Ketrzyn
Giżycko
Augustów
Ełk
Parechcha
Hrodna
Shchuchyn
323
Navahrudak
Dzyatlava
Masty
Nyasvizh
Grajewo
Kuźnica
Sokółka
Orzysz
Pisz
Śniardwy
Szczytno
Mrągowo
Olsztyn
Olsztynek
Ostróda
Iława
312
Morąg
Dobre Miasto
Elbląg
Nowy Dwór
Malbork
Kwidzyń
Władysławowo
Hel
Łeba
Lębork
Gdynia
Sopot
Gdańsk
329
Słupsk
Bytów
Kościerzyna
Tczew
Starogard
Brda
Czersk
Chojnice
Tuchola
Hudiksvall
Söderhamn
Gävle
Gräsö
Tierp
Östhammar
Hallstavik
Väddö
Björkö
Åland
Godby
Mariehamn
Lemland
Uppsala
Norrtälje
Märsta
Sollentuna
Stockholm
Södertälje
Nynäshamn
Nyköping
Oxelösund
Gotska Sandön
Fårösund
Fårö
Visby
Slite
Gotland
Hemse
18
21
24
27
60
54

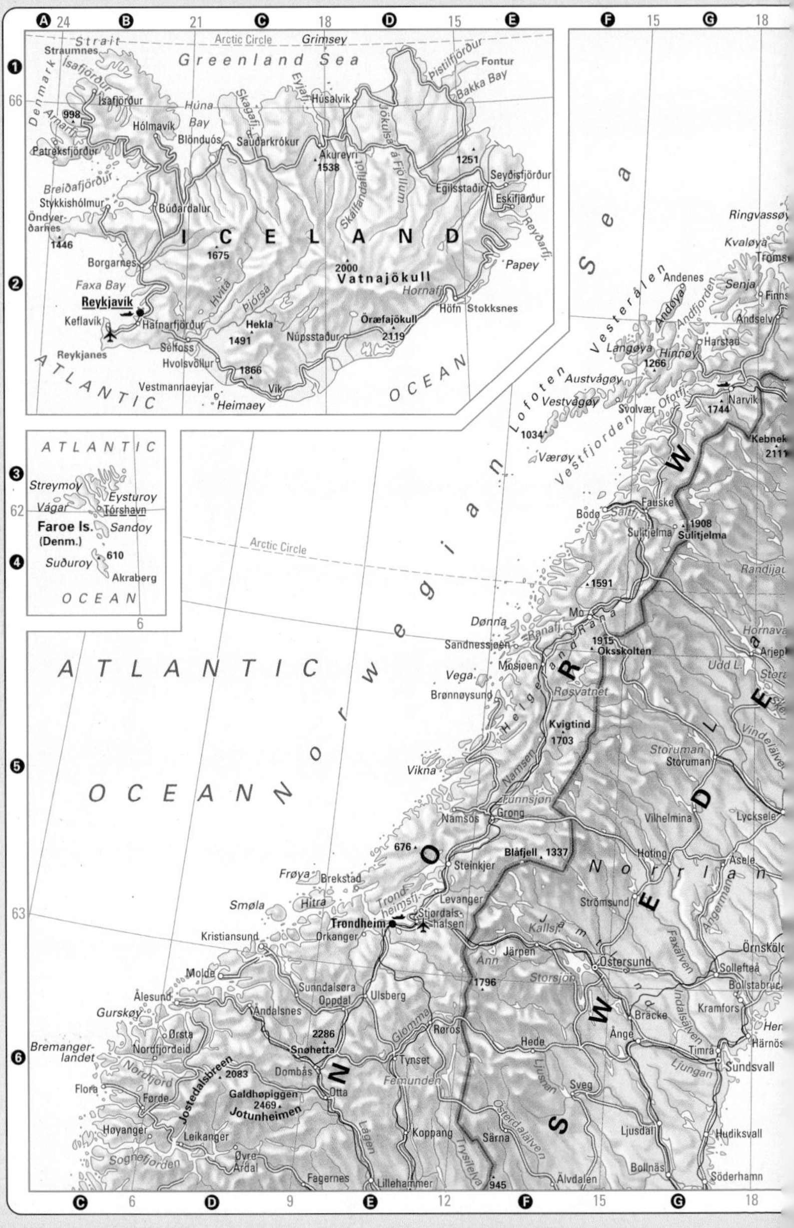

A
24
B
21
C
18
D
15
E
F
15
G
18
1
2
3
4
5
6
66
62
63
Strait
Arctic Circle
Grimsey
Straumnes
Ísafjörður
Greenland Sea
Pistilfjörður
Fontur
Bakka Bay
Denmark
Arnarfj.
Eyjafj.
Skagafj.
Húsavík
Ísafjörður
Húna Bay
998
Hólmavík
Blönduós
Sauðarkrókur
Jökulsá á Fjöllum
Patreksfjörður
Akureyri
1538
1251
Skjálfandafljót
Seyðisfjörður
Breiðafjörður
Egilsstaðir
Stykkishólmur
Búðardalur
Eskifjörður
Öndverðarnes
Reyðarfj.
1446
ICELAND
1675
Borgarnes
2000
Papey
Vatnajökull
Faxa Bay
Hvítá
Þjórsá
Hornafj.
Reykjavík
Höfn
Stokksnes
Keflavík
Hafnarfjörður
Hekla
Öræfajökull
1491
Núpsstaður
2119
Selfoss
Reykjanes
Hvolsvöllur
1866
Vestmannaeyjar
Vík
ATLANTIC
OCEAN
Heimaey
ATLANTIC
Streymoy
Eysturoy
Vágar
Tórshavn
Faroe Is.
(Denm.)
Sandoy
Suðuroy
610
Akraberg
OCEAN
6
Sea
Ringvassøy
Kvaløya
Tromsø
Andenes
Senja
Vesterålen
Andøya
Andfjorden
Finnsnes
Andselv
Langøya
Hinnøy
Harstad
1266
Austvågøy
Lofoten
Vestvågøy
Narvik
Svolvær
Ofotfj.
1744
1034
Kebnekaise
2111
Værøy
Vestfjorden
Norwegian Sea
Bodø
Saltfj.
Fauske
1908
Sulitjelma
Sulitjelma
Arctic Circle
Randijaure
1591
Mo
Rana
Dønna
Ranafj.
Hornavan
1915
Oksskolten
Sandnessjøen
Arjeplog
Mosjøen
Udd L.
Vega
Storavan
Brønnøysund
Røsvatnet
Helgeland
Kvigtind
1703
Vindelälven
Storuman
Storuman
Vikna
Namsen
Tunnsjøen
ATLANTIC
OCEAN
Grong
Namsos
Vilhelmina
Lycksele
676
Blåfjell
1337
Hoting
Åsele
Steinkjer
Norrland
Frøya
Brekstad
Trondheimsfj.
Levanger
Ångermanälven
Smøla
Hitra
Strömsund
Stjørdalshalsen
Trondheim
Kallsjön
Jämtland
Faxälven
Kristiansund
Orkanger
Örnsköldsvik
Åre
Järpen
Östersund
Sollefteå
Molde
Storsjön
1796
Bollstabruk
Sunndalsøra
Ålesund
Oppdal
Ulsberg
Indalsälven
Kramfors
Gurskøy
Åndalsnes
Bräcke
Härnösand
Glomma
Røros
2286
Ånge
Ørsta
Hede
Bremangerlandet
Nordfjordeid
Snøhetta
Timrå
Härnösand
Tynset
Ljusnan
Ljungan
Sundsvall
Nordfjord
Dombås
Jostedalsbreen
2083
Femunden
Florø
Otta
Sveg
Førde
Galdhøpiggen
2469
Jotunheimen
Lågen
Høyanger
Koppang
Särna
Ljusdal
Hudiksvall
Trysilelva
Österdalälven
Leikanger
Sognefjorden
Øvre Årdal
Bollnäs
Fagernes
Lillehammer
945
Älvdalen
Söderhamn
NORWAY
SWEDEN
SWEDEN
C
6
D
9
E
12
F
15
G
18

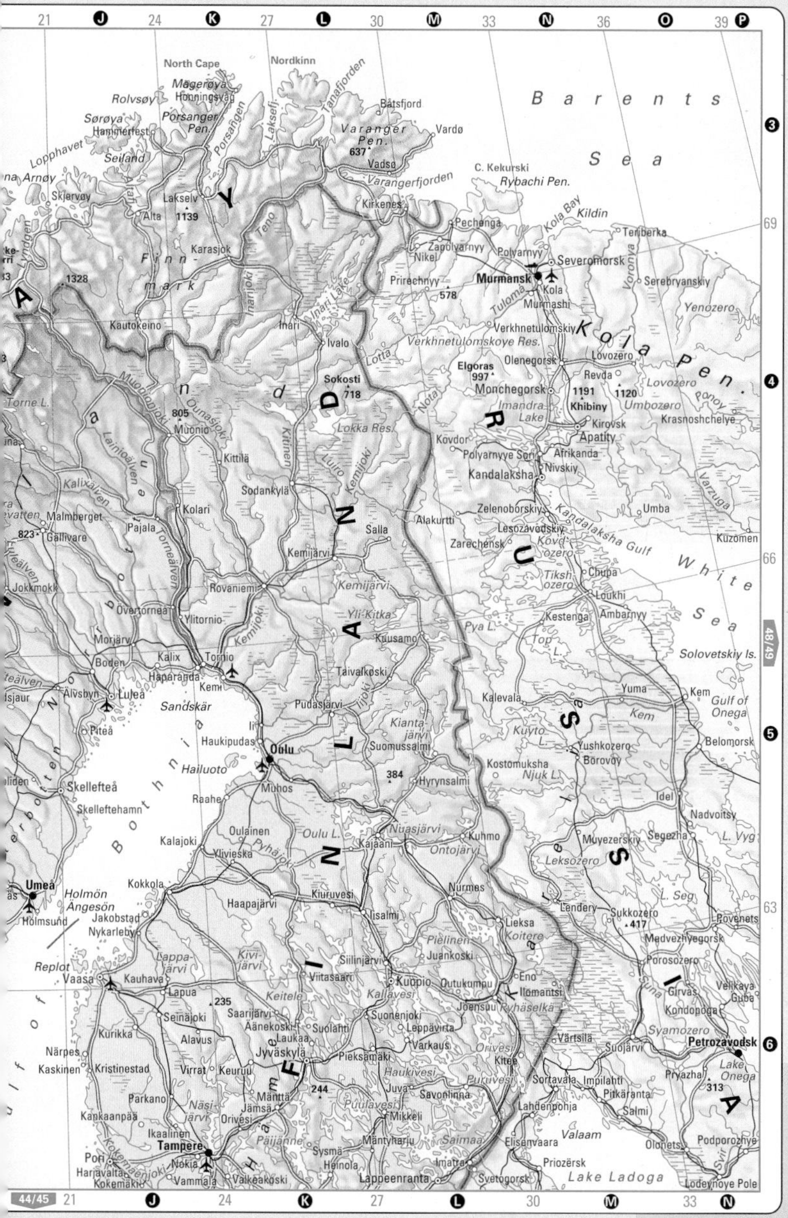
21
J
24
K
27
L
30
M
33
N
36
O
39
P
North Cape
Nordkinn
Magerøya
Honningsvåg
Rolvsøy
Sørøya
Hammerfest
Porsanger Pen.
Porsangen
Laksefj.
Tanafjorden
Båtsfjord
Varanger Pen.
637
Vardø
Vadsø
Varangerfjorden
Loppahavet
Seiland
Arnøy
Skjervøy
Lakselv
Alta
1139
Teno
Kirkenes
Pechenga
Zapolyarnyy
Nikel
B a r e n t s
S e a
C. Kekurski
Rybachi Pen.
Kola Bay
Kildin
Teriberka
Polyarnyy
Severomorsk
Murmansk
Kola
Murmashi
Tuloma
Prirechnyy
578
Voronya
Serebryanskiy
Yenozero
Lyngen
Karasjok
F i n n -
m a r k
1328
Inarijoki
Inari Lake
Inari
Ivalo
Kautokeino
Verkhnetulomskiy
Verkhnetulomskoye Res.
K o l a
P e n .
Lotta
Olenegorsk
Lovozero
Revda
Lovozero
Elgoras
997
Monchegorsk
1191
1120
Khibiny
Umbozero
Ponoy
Krasnoshchelye
Sokosti
718
Nota
Imandra Lake
Kirovsk
Apatity
Muonionjoki
Ounasjoki
805
Muonio
Torne L.
Kittilä
Kitinen
Lokka Res.
Luiro
Kemijoki
Kovdor
Polyarnyye Sori
Afrikanda
Nivskiy
Kandalaksha
Varzuga
Lainioälven
Kalixälven
Sodankylä
Kolari
Malmberget
823
Gällivare
Pajala
Torneälven
Salla
Alakurtti
Zelenoborskiy
Umba
Lesozavodskiy
Kandalaksha Gulf
Kovdozero
Zarechensk
Kuzomen
66
Luleälven
Jokkmokk
Kemijärvi
Kemijärvi
Tikshozero
Chupa
W h i t e
Loukhi
Rovaniemi
Övertorneå
Ylitornio
Yli-Kitka
Kestenga
Ambarnyy
S e a
Pya L.
Kemijoki
Kuusamo
Top L.
Morjärv
Boden
Kalix
Tornio
Solovetskiy Is.
48/49
Haparanda
Kemi
Taivalkoski
Älvsbyn
Luleå
Sandskär
Iijoki
Kalevala
Yuma
Kem
Gulf of Onega
Kem
Pudasjärvi
Kiantajärvi
Piteå
Ii
Kuyto L.
Haukipudas
Oulu
Suomussalmi
Yushkozero
Borovoy
Belomorsk
Hailuoto
Kostomuksha
Njuk L.
384
Hyrynsalmi
Skellefteå
Muhos
Raahe
Skellefthamn
Idel
Nadvoitsy
B o t h n i a
Oulainen
Oulu L.
Nuasjärvi
Kajaani
Kuhmo
Muyezerskiy
Segezha
L. Vyg
Kalajoki
Pyhäjoki
Ylivieska
Ontojärvi
Leksozero
Umeå
Holmön
Ängesön
Kokkola
Haapajärvi
Kiuruvesi
Nurmes
L. Seg
63
Jakobstad
Holmsund
Nykarleby
Iisalmi
Lieksa
Lendery
Sukkozero
417
Povenets
Koitere
Medvezhyegorsk
Pielinen
Juankoski
Porosozero
Lappajärvi
Kivijärvi
Siilinjärvi
Replot
Vaasa
Kauhava
Viitasaari
Kuopio
Outukumpu
Eno
Ilomantsi
Suna
Girvas
Velikaya Guba
Lapua
Keitele
Kallavesi
235
Saarijärvi
Joensuu
Pyhäselkä
Kondopoga
Seinäjoki
Äänekoski
Suolahti
Suonenjoki
Leppävirta
Syamozero
Kurikka
Alavus
Laukaa
Värtsilä
Suojärvi
Petrozavodsk
Närpes
Jyväskylä
Pieksämäki
Varkaus
Orivesi
Kitee
Kaskinen
Kristinestad
Virrat
Keuruu
Haukivesi
Puruvesi
Sortavala
Impilahti
Pryazha
Lake Onega
Parkano
244
Juva
Savonlinna
Pitkäranta
313
Mänttä
Näsijärvi
Jämsä
Puulavesi
Mikkeli
Lahdenpohja
Salmi
Kankaanpää
Orivesi
Ikaalinen
Päijänne
Mäntyharju
Saimaa
Elisenvaara
Valaam
Olonets
Podporozhye
Tampere
Pori
Sysmä
Harjavalta
Nokia
Heinola
Imatra
Priozërsk
Svir
Kokemäki
Vammala
Valkeakoski
Lappeenranta
Svetogorsk
Lake Ladoga
Lodeynoye Pole
Kokemäenjoki
H ä m e
F I N L A N D
L a p p l a n d
N o r r b o t t e n
G u l f o f
N O R W A Y
S W E D E N
R U S S I A
K a r e l i a
69
44/45
33

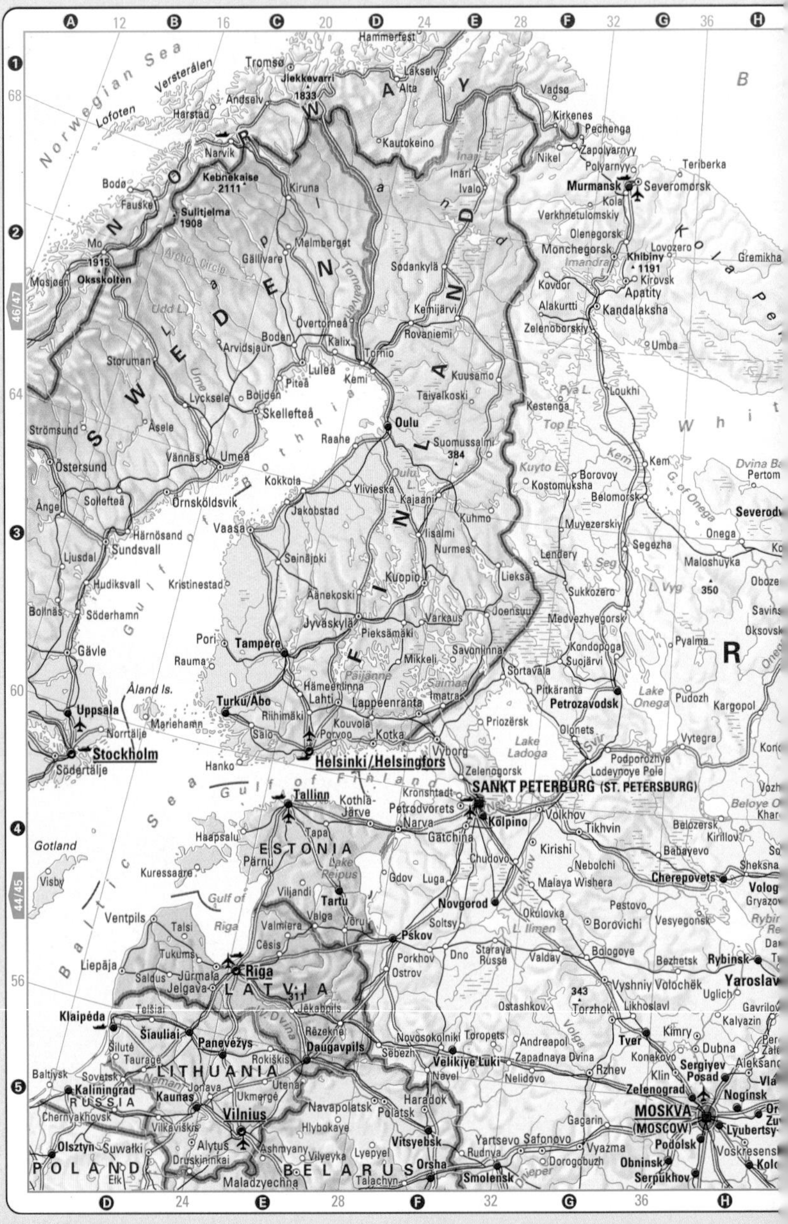

A
12
B
16
C
20
D
24
E
28
F
32
G
36
H
1
2
3
4
5
68
64
60
56
46/47
44/45
Norwegian Sea
Lofoten
Versterålen
Tromsø
Hammerfest
Lakselv
Alta
Jiekkevarri
1833
Andselv
Harstad
Narvik
Vadsø
Kirkenes
Pechenga
Zapolyarnyy
Nikel
Polyarnyy
Teriberka
Murmansk
Severomorsk
Kola
Verkhnetulomskiy
Olenegorsk
Monchegorsk
Lovozero
Imandra
Khibiny
1191
Kirovsk
Apatity
Gremikha
Kovdor
Alakurtti
Kandalaksha
Zelenoborskiy
Umba
Kola Pen.
B
Kautokeino
Inari L.
Inari
Ivalo
Bodø
Fauske
Kebnekaise
2111
Sulitjelma
1908
Kiruna
Mo
1915
Oksskolten
Mosjøen
Arctic Circle
Malmberget
Gällivare
Sodankylä
Kemijärvi
Rovaniemi
Udd L.
Övertorneå
Boden
Kalix
Arvidsjaur
Tornio
Storuman
Luleå
Kemi
Kuusamo
Piteå
Taivalkoski
Lycksele
Boliden
Skellefteå
Oulu
Pya L.
Loukhi
Kestenga
Top L.
Strömsund
Åsele
Raahe
Suomussalmi
384
White Sea
Vännäs
Umeå
Kem
Kuyto L.
Östersund
Kokkola
Oulu L.
Borovoy
Kostomuksha
Belomorsk
Dvina Bay
Pertom
G. of Onega
Ylivieska
Kajaani
Ånge
Sollefteå
Örnsköldsvik
Jakobstad
Kuhmo
Severodvinsk
Muyezerskiy
Härnösand
Vaasa
Iisalmi
Onega
Sundsvall
Nurmes
Segezha
Ljusdal
Lendery
Seg L.
Maloshuyka
Seinäjoki
Lieksa
Hudiksvall
Kristinestad
Kuopio
Sukkozero
L. Vyg
350
Obozerskiy
Äänekoski
Bollnäs
Söderhamn
Gulf of Bothnia
Joensuu
Medvezhyegorsk
Savinskiy
Jyväskylä
Varkaus
Oksovskiy
Pieksämäki
Pori
Tampere
Kondopoga
Pyalma
Gävle
Savonlinna
Rauma
Mikkeli
Suojärvi
R
Sortavala
Päijänne
Saimaa
Åland Is.
Hämeenlinna
Imatra
Pitkäranta
Lake Onega
Pudozh
Lahti
Turku/Åbo
Lappeenranta
Petrozavodsk
Kargopol
Uppsala
Riihimäki
Kouvola
Priozërsk
Mariehamn
Norrtälje
Salo
Porvoo
Kotka
Olonets
Vytegra
Lake Ladoga
Stockholm
Vyborg
Svir
Hanko
Helsinki/Helsingfors
Podporozhye
Lodeynoye Pole
Södertälje
Zelenogorsk
Gulf of Finland
SANKT PETERBURG (ST. PETERSBURG)
Tallinn
Kothla-Järve
Kronshtadt
Petrodvorets
Volkhov
Beloye O.
Kolpino
Narva
Tikhvin
Belozersk
Tapa
Gatchina
Haapsalu
Kirillov
ESTONIA
Kirishi
Gotland
Pärnu
Chudovo
Babayevo
Lake Peipus
Nebolchi
Sheksna
Kuressaare
Malaya Wishera
Cherepovets
Visby
Gdov
Luga
Vologda
Viljandi
Volkhov
Tartu
Gulf of Riga
Novgorod
Gryazovets
Pestovo
Valga
Ventpils
Talsi
Võru
Okulovka
Borovichi
Vesyegonsk
Valmiera
Soltsy
Rybinsk Res.
L. Ilmen
Pskov
Cēsis
Baltic Sea
Tukums
Staraya Russa
Dno
Valday
Bologoye
Porkhov
Liepāja
Rīga
Rybinsk
Saldus
Jūrmala
Ostrov
Bezhetsk
Jelgava
LATVIA
311
Yaroslavl
343
Vyshniy Volochëk
Uglich
Telšiai
Jēkabpils
Ostashkov
Torzhok
Likhoslavl
Gavrilov
Klaipėda
Kalyazin
Rēzekne
Volga
Šiauliai
Zap. Dvina
Novosokolniki
Toropets
Andreapol
Kimry
Tver
Dubna
Šilutė
Panevėžys
Daugavpils
Tauragė
Sebezh
Velikiye Luki
Zapadnaya Dvina
Rokiškis
Konakovo
Sergiyev Posad
Baltiysk
Sovetsk
LITHUANIA
Rzhev
Klin
Kaliningrad
Jonava
Utena
Nevel
Nelidovo
Zelenograd
RUSSIA
Kaunas
Ukmergė
Haradok
Noginsk
Navapolatsk
Polatsk
Chernyakhovsk
MOSKVA
(MOSCOW)
Vilnius
Gagarin
Vilkaviškis
Lyubertsy
Hlybokaye
Vitsyebsk
Olsztyn
Suwałki
Alytus
Yartsevo
Safonovo
Vyazma
Podolsk
Ashmyany
Lyepyel
Voskresensk
Vilyeyka
Rudnya
Druskininkai
Dorogobuzh
Obninsk
POLAND
Ełk
BELARUS
Orsha
Smolensk
Dnieper
Serpukhov
Kolomna
Maladzyechna
Talachyn
D
24
E
28
F
32
G
36
H

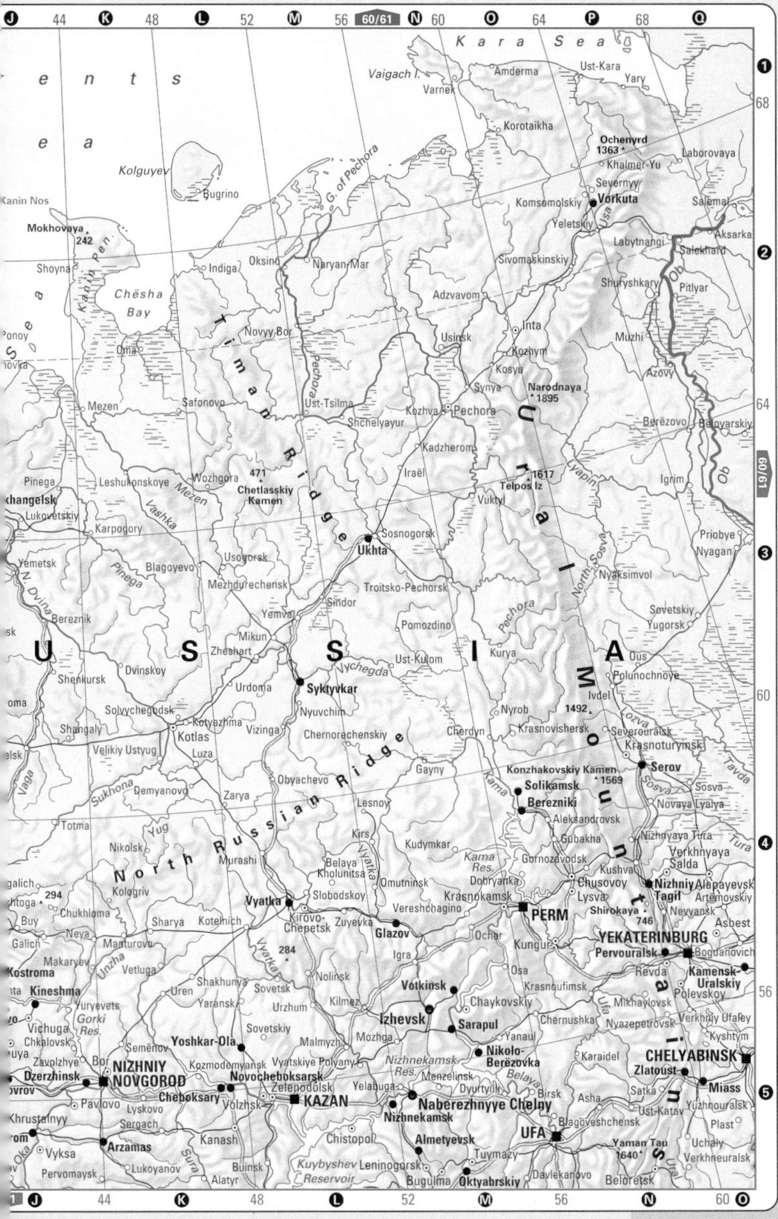
Kara Sea
Barents Sea
Vaigach I.
Varnek
Amderma
Ust-Kara
Yary
Korotaikha
Ochenyrd
1363
Khalmer-Yu
Laborovaya
Kolguyev
Bugrino
G. of Pechora
Severnyy
Vorkuta
Komsomolskiy
Salemal
Kanin Nos
Mokhovaya
242
Kanin Pen.
Yeletskiy
Usa
Aksarka
Labytnangi
Salekhard
Shoyna
Indiga
Oksino
Naryan-Mar
Sivomaskinskiy
Chësha Bay
Shuryshkary
Ob
Pitlyar
Adzvavom
Timan Ridge
Novyy Bor
Ponoy
Inta
Usinsk
Muzhi
Oma
Kozhym
Kosyu
Azovy
Pechora
Synya
Narodnaya
1895
Mezen
Safonovo
Ust-Tsilma
Kozhva
Shchelyayur
Ural Mountains
Berëzovo
Beloyarskiy
Kadzherom
Pinega
Leshukonskoye
Wozhgora
471
Chetlasskiy Kamen
Iraël
1617
Telpos Iz
Lyapin
Igrim
Khangelsk
Lukovetskiy
Vashka
Vuktyl
Karpogory
Sosnogorsk
Priobye
Ukhta
Nyagan
Yemetsk
Usogorsk
North Sosva
Blagoyevo
N. Dvina
Mezhdurechensk
Nyaksimvol
Troitsko-Pechorsk
Sindor
Yemva
Sovetskiy
Yugorsk
Bereznik
Pomozdino
Mikun
RUSSIA
Zheshart
Ust-Kulom
Kurya
Ous
Vychegda
Polunochnoye
Dvinskoy
Shenkursk
Urdoma
Syktyvkar
Ivdel
Nyuvchim
1492
Nyrob
Solvychegodsk
Kotyazhma
Shangaly
Vizinga
Kotlas
Chernorechenskiy
Cherdyn
Krasnovishersk
Lozva
Severouralsk
Krasnoturyinsk
Velikiy Ustyug
Luza
Gayny
Serov
Konzhakovskiy Kamen
1569
Vaga
Obyachevo
Kama
Solikamsk
Sosva
Tavda
Sukhona
Demyanovo
Zarya
Berezniki
Novaya Lyalya
Lesnoy
Aleksandrovsk
North Russian Ridge
Totma
Yug
Kirs
Gubakha
Nizhnyaya Tura
Tura
Kudymkar
Nikolsk
Murashi
Vyatka
Belaya Kholunitsa
Kama Res.
Gornozavodsk
Verkhnyaya Salda
Kushva
Dobryanka
Omutninsk
Chusovoy
Nizhniy Tagil
Alapayevsk
Galich
294
Kologriv
Slobodskoy
Krasnokamsk
Lysva
Artëmovskiy
Chukhloma
Vyatka
Kirovo-Chepetsk
Zuyevka
Vereshchagino
PERM
Shirokaya
746
Nevyansk
Buy
Sharya
Kotelnich
Glazov
Asbest
Neya
Ochër
Kungur
YEKATERINBURG
Galich
Manturovo
284
Igra
Pervouralsk
Bogdanovich
Makaryev
Unzha
Vetluga
Nolinsk
Osa
Revda
Kamensk-Uralskiy
Kostroma
Shakhunya
Sovetsk
Votkinsk
Krasnoufimsk
Polevskoy
Kineshma
Uren
Yaransk
Kilmez
Chaykovskiy
Mikhaylovsk
Yuryevets
Urzhum
Izhevsk
Ufa
Gorki Res.
Vichuga
Sovetskiy
Sarapul
Chernushka
Nyazepetrovsk
Verkhniy Ufaley
Chkalovsk
Yanaul
Kyshtym
Semënov
Yoshkar-Ola
Malmyzh
Mozhga
Bor
Zavolzhye
NIZHNIY NOVGOROD
Kozmodemyansk
Vyatskiye Polyany
Nizhnekamsk Res.
Nikolo-Berëzovka
Karaidel
CHELYABINSK
Dzerzhinsk
Novocheboksarsk
Menzelinsk
Belaya
Zlatoust
Miass
Cheboksary
Zelenodolsk
Yelabuga
Dyurtyuli
Pavlovo
Lyskovo
Volzhsk
KAZAN
Naberezhnyye Chelny
Birsk
Asha
Satka
Yuzhnouralsk
Nizhnekamsk
Ust-Katav
Khrustalnyy
Sergach
Blagoveshchensk
Plast
Arzamas
Kanash
Chistopol
Almetyevsk
UFA
Yaman Tau
1640
Uchaly
Oka
Vyksa
Sura
Tuymazy
Ural
Verkhneuralsk
Pervomaysk
Lukoyanov
Buinsk
Kuybyshev Reservoir
Leninogorsk
Alatyr
Bugulma
Oktyabrskiy
Davlekanovo
Beloretsk
60/61
J 44 K 48 L 52 M 56 N 60 O 64 P 68 Q
J 44 K 48 L 52 M 56 N 60 O
68
64
60
56
1
2
3
4
5

A
B
C
D
E
24
28
32
36
1
2
3
4
5
52
48
44
40
30/31
32/33
34/35
BELARUS
MINSK
Hrodna
Lida
Orsha
Talachyn
Barysaw
Mahilyow
Horki
Dzyarzhynsk
Maryina Horka
Vawkavysk
Slonim
Baranavichy
Krychaw
Kastykovichy
Slutsk
Asipovichy
Salihorsk
Babruysk
Zhlobin
Brest
Kobryn
Drahichyn
Svyetlahorsk
Mikashevichy
Pinsk
Zhytkavichy
Rechytsa
Homyel
Mazyr
Kalinkavichy
Khoyniki
Dnieper
Pripet
Desna
POLAND
WARSZAWA
(WARSAW)
Pruszków
Siedlce
Biała
Ostrołęka
Łomża
Ciechanów
Białystok
Radom
Puławy
Lublin
Chełm
Sandomierz
Zamość
Stalowa Wola
Rzeszów
Przemyśl
Krosno
Vistula
Bug
SL.
H.
UKRAINE
KYYIV
(KIEV)
Kamin-Kashyrskyy
Kovel
Sarny
Novovolynsk
Lutsk
Sokal
Rivne
Novohrad-Volynskyy
Korosten
Ovruch
Chornobyl
Dubno
Lviv
Kremenets
Ternopil
Drohobych
Boryslav
Stryy
471
Uzhhorod
Kalush
Ivano-Frankivsk
Kolomyya
Mukacheve
Khust
Chortkiv
Chernivtsi
Storozhynets
Novoselytsya
Khmelnytskyy
Kamyanets-Podilskyy
Zhmerynka
Vinnytsya
Haysyn
Mohyliv-Podilskyy
Yampil
Uman
Shepetivka
Zhytomyr
Starokostyantyniv
Berdychiv
Malyn
Fastiv
Kozyatyn
Bila Tserkva
Brovary
Boryspil
Kaharlyk
Kaniv
Cherkasy
Smila
Chernihiv
Nosivka
Bakhmach
Nizhyn
Konotop
Romny
Pryluky
Sumy
Hadyach
Hrebinka
Pereyaslav-Khmelnytskyy
Lubny
Okhtyrka
KHARKIV
Merefa
Poltava
Kremenchuk
Svitlovodsk
Oleksandriya
Kirovohrad
Novoukrayinka
Pervomaysk
Balta
Voznesensk
Dniprodzerzhynsk
DNIPROPETROVSK
Novomoskovsk
Pavlohrad
Lozova
Izyum
Slovyansk
Kramatorsk
Krasnoarmiysk
DONETSK
Makiyivka
Horlivka
Lysychansk
Syeverodonetsk
Starobilsk
Kupyansk
Vovchansk
Kryvyy Rih
Zaporizhzhya
Nikopol
Marhanets
Novyy Buh
Mykolayiv
Snihurivka
Kherson
Nova Kakhovka
Kakhovka Res.
Skadovsk
Tokmak
Gulyaypole
324
Melitopol
Berdyansk
Mariupol
Henichesk
ODESA
Illichivsk
Bilhorod-Dnistrovskyy
Izmayil
Kiliya
G. of Karkinitsk
C. Tarkhankut
Crimea
Yevpatoriya
Simferopol
Sevastopol
Roman-Kash
1545
Yalta
C. Sarych
Feodosiya
Kerch
Sea of Azov
Donets
Dniester
Prut
MOLDOVA
Chişinău
Tighina
(Bendery)
Tiraspol
Comrat
Bălţi
Rîbniţa
ROMANIA
BUCUREŞTI
(BUCHAREST)
Satu Mare
Baia Mare
Borşa
2303
Pietrosu
Botoşani
Suceava
Zalău
Bistriţa
Piatra-Neamţ
Cluj-Napoca
Iaşi
Vaslui
Târgu-Mureş
Bacău
Alba Iulia
Sibiu
Sfântu Gheorghe
Moldoveanu
2544
1784
Bârlad
Râmnicu Vâlcea
Braşov
Focşani
Galaţi
Brăila
Târgovişte
Buzău
Piteşti
Ploieşti
Craiova
Slatina
Slobozia
Călăraşi
Alexandria
Giurgiu
Tulcea
Danube
Constanţa
Carpathian Mts.
BULGARIA
Ruse
Razgrad
Pleven
Lovech
Veliko Turnovo
Dobrich
Shumen
Varna
Balkan Mts.
2376
Kazanlŭk
Sliven
Pazardzhik
Plovdiv
Stara Zagora
Burgas
Khaskovo
2191
Kŭrdzhali
Black Sea
GREECE
Komotini
Edirne
Kırklareli
Babaeski
Ergene
Tekirdağ
Çorlu
Keşan
İSTANBUL
Sea of Marmara
Gebze
İzmit
Adapazari
Yalova
Bandırma
Troy
Çanakkale
Düzce
Bolu
Bilecik
BURSA
2543
Sakarya
Edremit
İnegöl
Eskişehir
Lesvos
Mytilíni
Balıkesir
Bergama
Akhisar
Kütahya
Chíos
Manisa
Turgutlu
Simav
Uşak
2309
Çeşme
İZMİR
Salihli
Afyonkarahisar
Ödemiş
Bolvadin
Sámos
1440
Ephesos
Nazilli
Akşehir
Aydın
Denizli
Dinar
Menderes
Mediterranean Sea
Zonguldak
Bartın
Karabük
Kastamonu
İnce Burun
Sinop
Bafra
Samsun
2546
Tosya
Çankırı
İskilip
Merzifon
Çorum
Amasya
Yeşilırmak
ANKARA
Kırıkkale
Hattuşas
Yozgat
Turhal
Tokat
Niksar
Sorgun
Polatlı
Kulu
Lake Tuz
Kırşehir
Nevşehir
Kızılırmak
Aksaray
Kayseri
Erciyeş
3917
Şarkışla
Sivas
Yıldızeli
Ordu
Giresun
2789
Gümüşhane
Şebinkarahisar
Divriği
Kebkan Res.
Euphrates
Tunceli
Elâzığ
Pontine Mts.
Anatolia
TURKEY
RUSSIA
Pochinok
Roslavl
Kirov
Sukhinichi
Kaluga
Serpukhov
Aleksin
Tula
Ryazan
Kozelsk
Shchëkino
Novomoskovsk
Skopin
Zhukovka
Bolkhov
Bryansk
Unecha
Surazh
Klintsy
Novozybkov
Orël
Mtsensk
293
Yefremov
Oka
Zheleznogorsk
Livny
Yelets
Semenivka
Shostka
Lgov
Shchigry
Kursk
Gubkin
Staryy Oskol
Voronezh
Oboyan
Belgorod
Novyy Oskol
Valuyki
Rossosh
Liski
Pavlovsk
Stakhanov
Krasnyy Luch
Novoshakhtinsk
ROSTOV
Taganrog
Yeysk
Primorsko-Akhtarsk
Tikhoretsk
Timashevsk
Slavyansk
Kuban
Krymsk
Anapa
Novorossiysk
Krasnodar
Maykop
Khadyzhensk
Tuapse
Sochi

48/49
64/65
66/67

① North Passage
(Itar Tass, Moscow)

② Aral Sea
(Yamamoto, Osaka)

③ Jordan
(Rother, Schwäbisch Gmünd)

④ Plateau of Tibet and Himalayas
(Rother, Schwäbisch Gmünd)

⑤ Taj Mahal, Agra/India
(Rother, Schwäbisch Gmünd)

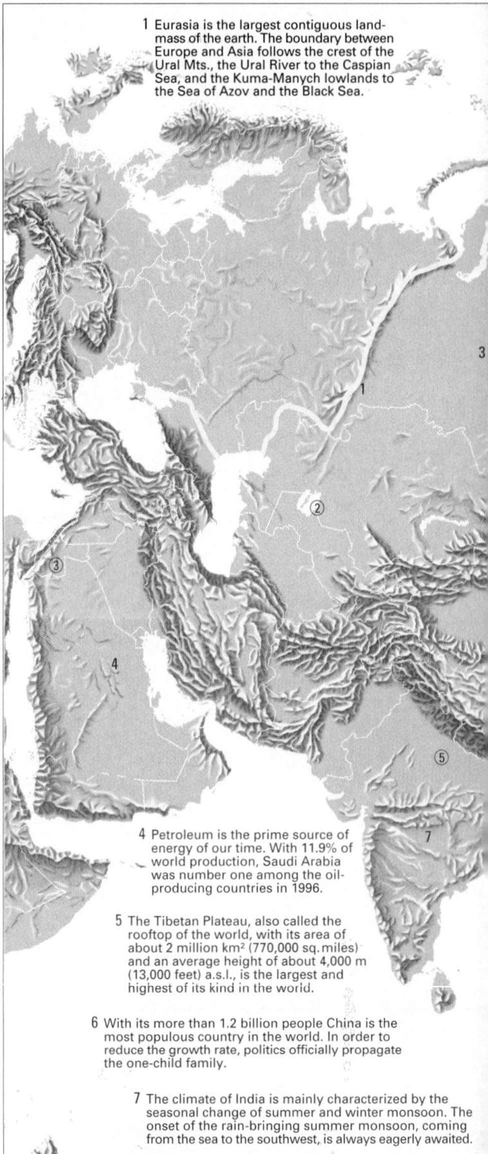

1 Eurasia is the largest contiguous landmass of the earth. The boundary between Europe and Asia follows the crest of the Ural Mts., the Ural River to the Caspian Sea, and the Kuma-Manych lowlands to the Sea of Azov and the Black Sea.

4 Petroleum is the prime source of energy of our time. With 11.9% of world production, Saudi Arabia was number one among the oil-producing countries in 1996.

5 The Tibetan Plateau, also called the rooftop of the world, with its area of about 2 million km² (770,000 sq. miles) and an average height of about 4,000 m (13,000 feet) a.s.l., is the largest and highest of its kind in the world.

6 With its more than 1.2 billion people China is the most populous country in the world. In order to reduce the growth rate, politics officially propagate the one-child family.

7 The climate of India is mainly characterized by the seasonal change of summer and winter monsoon. The onset of the rain-bringing summer monsoon, coming from the sea to the southwest, is always eagerly awaited.

2 Cape Dezhnëv, named after a Russian explorer of the 17th century, is the easternmost point af the Asian mainland (169°40′ W).

Taiga is the name given to the boreal coniferous forest zone of Siberia. The world's largest contiguous forest stretches from the Ural Mts. in the west to the coast mountains of the Pacific Ocean.

8 Japan is part of the circum-pacific belt of high tectonic mobility characterized by frequent volcanic activity and earthquakes. More than 5,000 people died during the disastrous earthquake that hit the city of Kobe in 1995.

9 The Yangtze (Changjiang), with its 5,526 km (3,434 miles), is the longest river of Asia.

rneo (Kalimantan), 6,000 km² 34,000 sq. miles) large, is e largest island of Asia d, trailing Greenland and w Guinea, the third- gest island of the world.

⑥ Gobi
(Rother, Schwäbisch Gmünd)

⑦ Peking
(Rother, Schwäbisch Gmünd)

⑧ Kobe
(Flüchter, Bochum)

⑨ Thailand
(Rother, Schwäbisch Gmünd)

⑩ Malaysia
(Rother, Schwäbisch Gmünd)

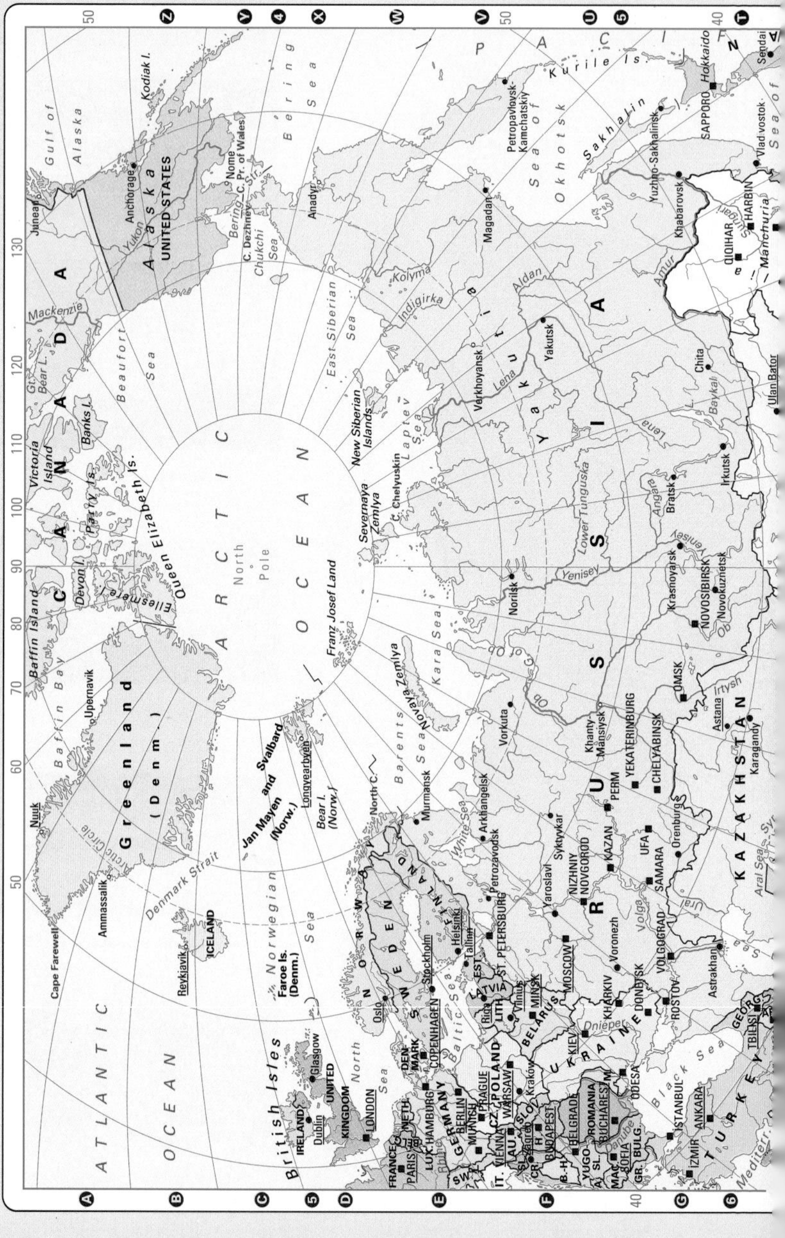
ARCTIC OCEAN
North Pole
ATLANTIC OCEAN
CANADA
Alaska
UNITED STATES
Gulf of Alaska
Kodiak I.
Anchorage
Juneau
Yukon
Mackenzie
Nome
C. Pr. of Wales
Bering Str.
C. Dezhnev
Chukchi Sea
Bering Sea
Anadyr
Beaufort Sea
Gt. Bear L.
Victoria Island
Banks I.
Parry Is.
Queen Elizabeth Is.
Ellesmere I.
Devon I.
Baffin Island
Baffin Bay
Upernavik
Nuuk
Greenland (Denm.)
Arctic Circle
Ammassalik
Cape Farewell
Denmark Strait
ICELAND
Reykjavik
Norwegian Sea
Jan Mayen (Norw.)
Svalbard
Longyearbyen
Bear I. (Norw.)
Faroe Is. (Denm.)
British Isles
IRELAND
Dublin
Glasgow
UNITED KINGDOM
LONDON
North Sea
NORWAY
Oslo
SWEDEN
Stockholm
FINLAND
Helsinki
DENMARK
COPENHAGEN
Baltic Sea
EST.
Tallinn
LATVIA
Riga
LITH.
Vilnius
BELARUS
MINSK
POLAND
WARSAW
Kraków
GERMANY
HAMBURG
BERLIN
MUNICH
NETH.
LUX.
FRANCE
PARIS
SWITZ.
IT.
CZ.
PRAGUE
AU.
VIENNA
SLO.
H.
BUDAPEST
CR.
Zagreb
B.-H.
YUGO.
BELGRADE
A.
MAC.
SL.
ROMANIA
BUCHAREST
M.
BULG.
SOFIA
GR.
UKRAINE
KIEV
Dnieper
KHARKIV
DONETSK
ODESA
Danube
Black Sea
ISTANBUL
ANKARA
IZMIR
TURKEY
Mediterr.
GEORG.
TBILISI
ROSTOV
VOLGOGRAD
Volga
Voronezh
MOSCOW
ST. PETERSBURG
Petrozavodsk
Yaroslavl
NIZHNIY NOVGOROD
KAZAN
SAMARA
UFA
PERM
Syktyvkar
Arkhangelsk
White Sea
Murmansk
North C.
Barents Sea
Novaya Zemlya
Kara Sea
Franz Josef Land
Severnaya Zemlya
C. Chelyuskin
Laptev Sea
New Siberian Islands
East Siberian Sea
Vorkuta
Khanty-Mansiysk
YEKATERINBURG
CHELYABINSK
Orenburg
Ural
Astrakhan
Caspian Sea
Aral Sea
KAZAKHSTAN
Astana
Karagandy
Irtysh
OMSK
Ob
G. of Ob
NOVOSIBIRSK
Novokuznetsk
Krasnoyarsk
Yenisey
Norilsk
Lower Tunguska
Angara
Bratsk
Irkutsk
Baykal
Ulan Bator
Chita
Lena
Yakutsk
Verkhoyansk
Yakutia
Aldan
Indigirka
Kolyma
Magadan
Sea of Okhotsk
Petropavlovsk-Kamchatskiy
Kurile Is.
Sakhalin
Yuzhno-Sakhalinsk
Khabarovsk
Amur
Vladivostok
HARBIN
QIQIHAR
Manchuria
Hokkaido
SAPPORO
Sendai
RUSSIA
PACIFIC

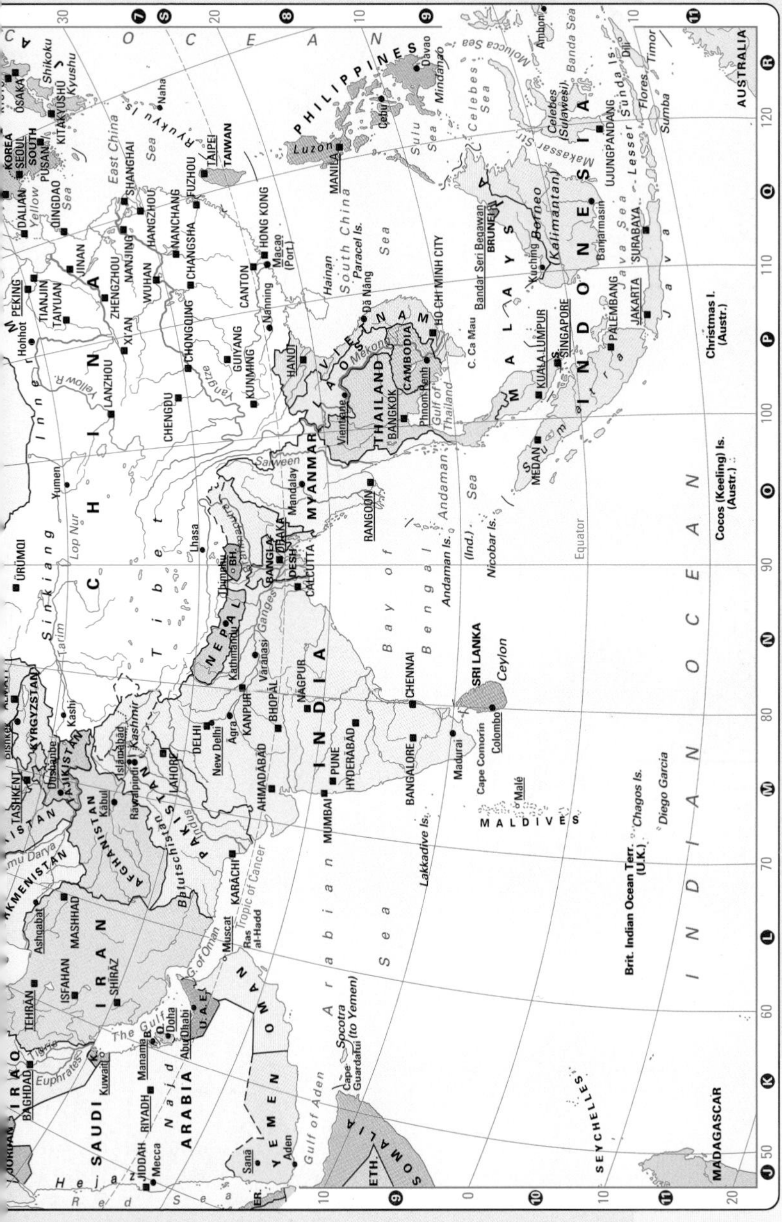
INDIAN OCEAN
CHINA
INDIA
SAUDI ARABIA
IRAN
AFGHANISTAN
PAKISTAN
NEPAL
BANGLADESH
MYANMAR
THAILAND
LAOS
VIETNAM
CAMBODIA
MALAYSIA
INDONESIA
PHILIPPINES
TAIWAN
SRI LANKA
MALDIVES
SEYCHELLES
OMAN
YEMEN
SOMALIA
U.A.E.
TURKMENISTAN
TAJIKISTAN
KYRGYZSTAN
AUSTRALIA
MADAGASCAR
PEKING
SHANGHAI
HONG KONG
DELHI
New Delhi
MUMBAI
CALCUTTA
CHENNAI
BANGKOK
SINGAPORE
JAKARTA
MANILA
RANGOON
KARACHI
TEHRAN
RIYADH
Bay of Bengal
Arabian Sea
South China Sea
Andaman Sea
Tibet
Equator
Tropic of Cancer

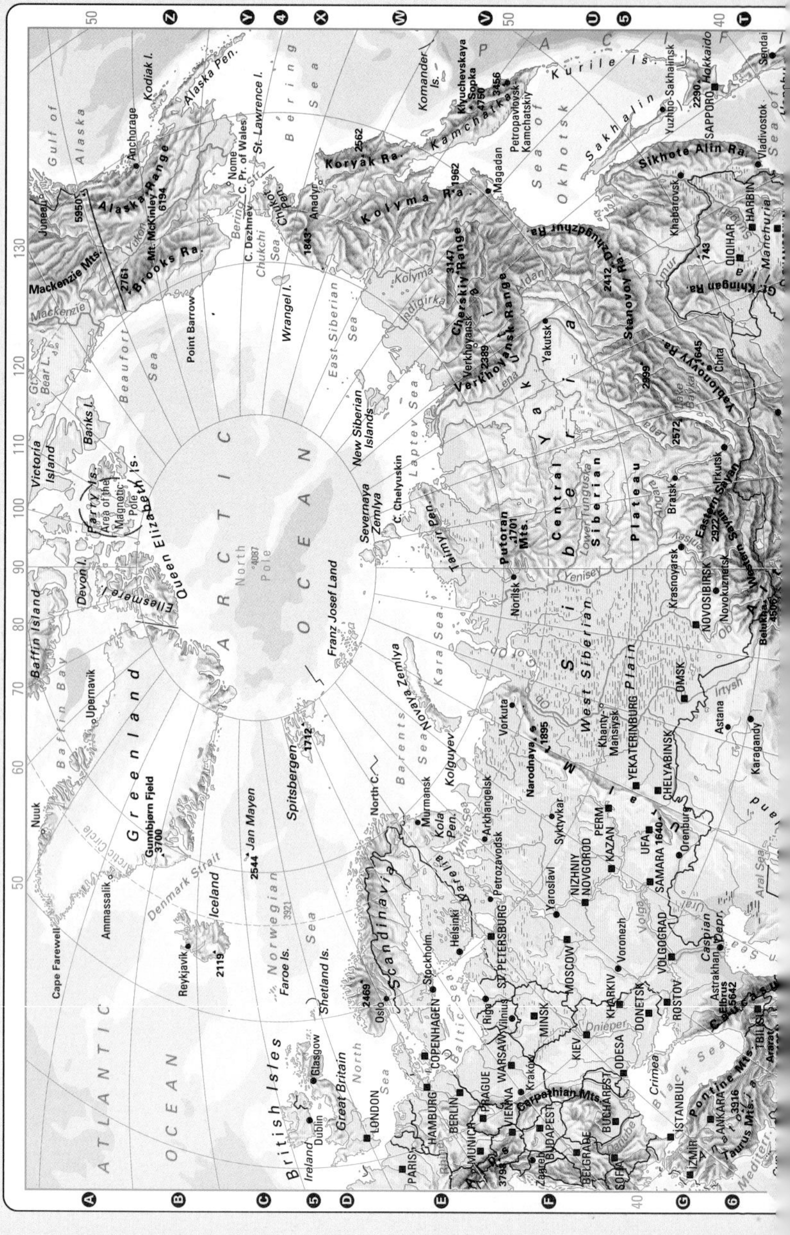

ATLANTIC OCEAN
ARCTIC OCEAN
PACIFIC
Gulf of Alaska
Juneau
Anchorage
Kodiak I.
Alaska Pen.
Alaska Range
Mt. McKinley 6194
5950
Mackenzie Mts.
Mackenzie
Yukon
Brooks Ra.
2761
Point Barrow
Beaufort Sea
Gt. Bear L.
Banks I.
Victoria Island
Parry Is.
Area of the Magnetic Pole
Queen Elizabeth Is.
Devon I.
Ellesmere I.
Baffin Island
Baffin Bay
Upernavik
Greenland
Nuuk
Gunnbjørn Fjeld 3700
Arctic Circle
Cape Farewell
Ammassalik
Denmark Strait
Iceland
Reykjavik
2119
Jan Mayen
2544
Norwegian Sea
3921
Faroe Is.
Shetland Is.
British Isles
Ireland
Dublin
Glasgow
Great Britain
North Sea
LONDON
PARIS
Spitsbergen
1712
North Pole
4087
Franz Josef Land
Severnaya Zemlya
C. Chelyuskin
Taimyr Pen.
Laptev Sea
New Siberian Islands
East Siberian Sea
Wrangel I.
Chukchi Sea
C. Dezhnev
Bering Str.
C. Pr. of Wales
Nome
St. Lawrence I.
Bering Sea
Chukot Pen.
Anadyr
1843
Koryak Ra.
2562
Komander Is.
Klyuchevskaya Sopka 4750
3456
Kamchatka
Petropavlovsk Kamchatskiy
Kurile Is.
Sea of Okhotsk
Sakhalin
Yuzhno-Sakhalinsk
Hokkaido
2290
SAPPORO
Sendai
Vladivostok
Sikhote Alin Ra.
Khabarovsk
HARBIN
QIQIHAR
Manchuria
743
Gt. Khingan Ra.
Amur
Kolyma Ra.
1962
Magadan
Dzhugdzhur Ra.
Kolyma
Indigirka
Cherskiy Range
3147
Verkhoyansk Range
Verkhoyansk
2389
Aldan
2412
Stanovoy Ra.
Yakutsk
Lena
Yablonovyy Ra.
1645
Chita
2999
L. Baikal
Irkutsk
2572
Eastern Sayan
2922
Western Sayan
Central Siberian Plateau
Lower Tunguska
Angara
Bratsk
Putoran Mts.
1701
Norilsk
Yenisey
Krasnoyarsk
NOVOSIBIRSK
Novokuznetsk
Belukha
4506
Altai
Ob
Irtysh
OMSK
Astana
Karagandy
West Siberian Plain
Siberia
Khanty-Mansiysk
Kara Sea
Novaya Zemlya
Barents Sea
Kolguyev
Vorkuta
Narodnaya
1895
Ural Mts.
YEKATERINBURG
CHELYABINSK
North C.
Murmansk
Kola Pen.
White Sea
Arkhangelsk
Syktyvkar
PERM
KAZAN
UFA
1640
Orenburg
SAMARA
NIZHNIY NOVGOROD
Yaroslavl
Petrozavodsk
Karelia
Scandinavia
2469
Oslo
Stockholm
Helsinki
ST. PETERSBURG
MOSCOW
Voronezh
Volga
VOLGOGRAD
Baltic Sea
COPENHAGEN
Riga
Vilnius
MINSK
HAMBURG
BERLIN
PRAGUE
WARSAW
Krakow
KIEV
Dnieper
KHARKIV
DONETSK
ROSTOV
ODESA
Crimea
Black Sea
Carpathian Mts.
VIENNA
BUDAPEST
BUCHAREST
Danube
MUNICH
Alps
3797
Zagreb
BELGRADE
SOFIA
ISTANBUL
IZMIR
ANKARA
Pontine Mts.
Taurus Mts.
3916
Mediterr.
TBILISI
Ararat
Elbrus 5642
Caucasus
Astrakhan
Caspian Depr.
Caspian Sea
Aral Sea
Ural
50
60
70
80
90
100
110
120
130
40

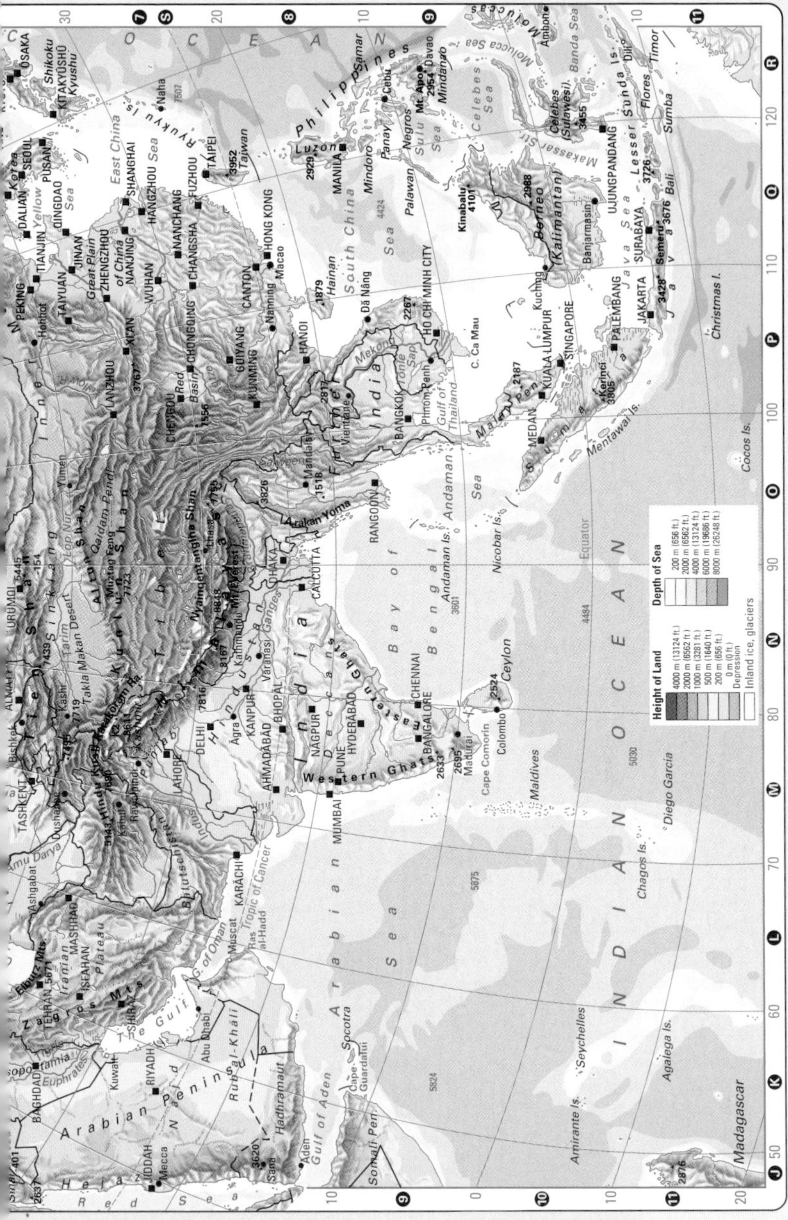
INDIAN OCEAN
Arabian Sea
Bay of Bengal
Andaman Sea
South China Sea
East China Sea
Yellow Sea
Celebes Sea
Sulu Sea
Java Sea
Banda Sea
Molucca Sea
Red Sea
The Gulf
G. of Oman
Gulf of Aden
Gulf of Thailand
Makassar Str.
Arabian Peninsula
Rub al-Khali
Hadhramaut
Iranian Plateau
Zagros Mts.
Elburz Mts.
Hindu Kush
Karakoram Ra.
Tien Shan
Kunlun Shan
Altun Shan
Tarim
Takla Makan Desert
Qaidam Pendi
Tibet
Himalaya
Nyainqentanglha Shan
Mt. Everest
8848
Ganges
Indus
Amu Darya
Hindustan
Deccan
Western Ghats
Eastern Ghats
India
Ceylon
Maldives
Chagos Is.
Diego Garcia
Seychelles
Amirante Is.
Agalega Is.
Madagascar
Socotra
Somali Pen.
Cape Guardafui
Ras al-Hadd
Tropic of Cancer
Equator
Andaman Is.
Nicobar Is.
Arakan Yoma
Salween
Mekong
Tonle Sap
Malay Pen.
Sumatra
Mentawai Is.
Java
Borneo (Kalimantan)
Celebes (Sulawesi)
Lesser Sunda Is.
Bali
Flores
Sumba
Timor
Moluccas
Christmas I.
Cocos Is.
Philippines
Luzon
Mindoro
Panay
Negros
Palawan
Mindanao
Samar
Taiwan
Hainan
Ryukyu Is.
Kyushu
Shikoku
Korea
Red Basin
Great Plain of China
RIYADH
JIDDAH
Mecca
Sana
Aden
BAGHDAD
Kuwait
Abu Dhabi
Muscat
TEHRAN
ISFAHAN
SHIRAZ
MASHHAD
Ashgabat
Dushanbe
TASHKENT
Bishkek
ALMATY
URUMQI
Kashi
Kabul
Rawalpindi
LAHORE
KARACHI
DELHI
Agra
KANPUR
Varanasi
Kathmandu
DHAKA
CALCUTTA
AHMADABAD
BHOPAL
NAGPUR
MUMBAI
PUNE
HYDERABAD
CHENNAI
BANGALORE
Madurai
Colombo
Cape Comorin
RANGOON
Mandalay
BANGKOK
Vientiane
Phnom Penh
HO CHI MINH CITY
C. Ca Mau
HANOI
Da Nang
KUALA LUMPUR
SINGAPORE
MEDAN
PALEMBANG
JAKARTA
SURABAYA
Semeru
Banjarmasin
UJUNGPANDANG
Kuching
Kinabalu
MANILA
Cebu
Davao
Mt. Apo
Ambon
KUNMING
GUIYANG
Nanning
CANTON
HONG KONG
Macao
CHONGQING
CHENGDU
LANZHOU
XI'AN
WUHAN
CHANGSHA
NANCHANG
FUZHOU
TAIPEI
HANGZHOU
SHANGHAI
NANJING
ZHENGZHOU
JINAN
TAIYUAN
PEKING
TIANJIN
Hohhot
QINGDAO
DALIAN
SEOUL
PUSAN
KITAKYUSHU
OSAKA
Naha
Yumen
Lhasa
Lop Nur
Muztag Feng
Height of Land
4000 m (13124 ft.)
2000 m (6562 ft.)
1000 m (3281 ft.)
500 m (1640 ft.)
200 m (656 ft.)
0 m (0 ft.)
Depression
Inland ice, glaciers
Depth of Sea
200 m (656 ft.)
2000 m (6562 ft.)
4000 m (13124 ft.)
6000 m (19686 ft.)
8000 m (26248 ft.)

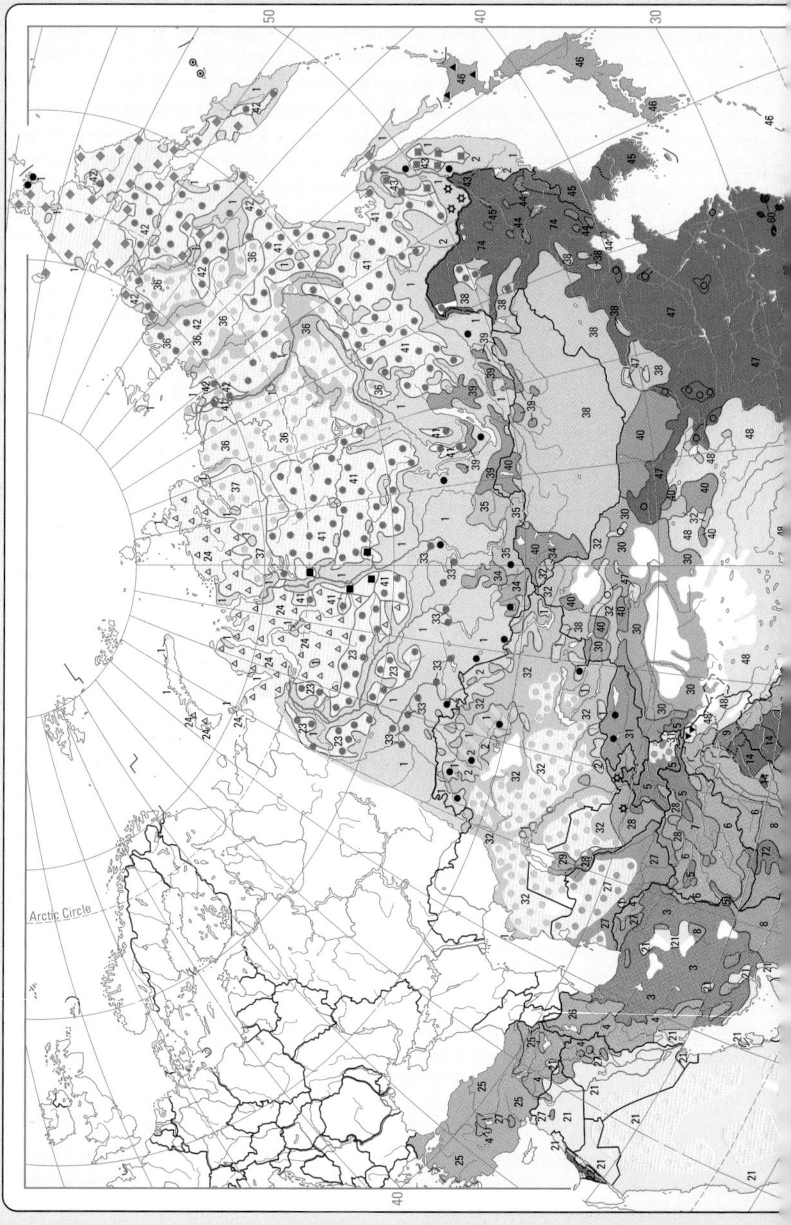
Arctic Circle

1 : 60 000 000

0 500 1000 1500 2000 km
0 500 1000 miles

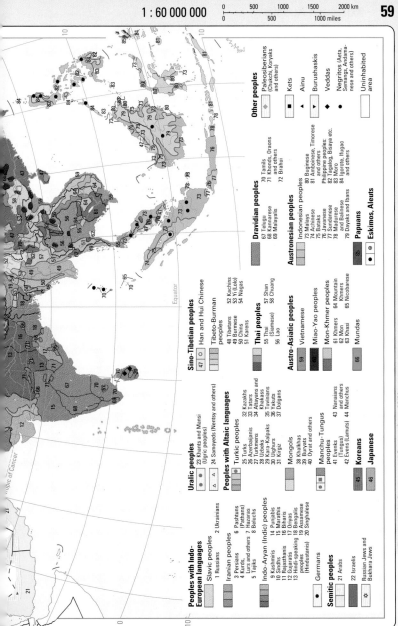

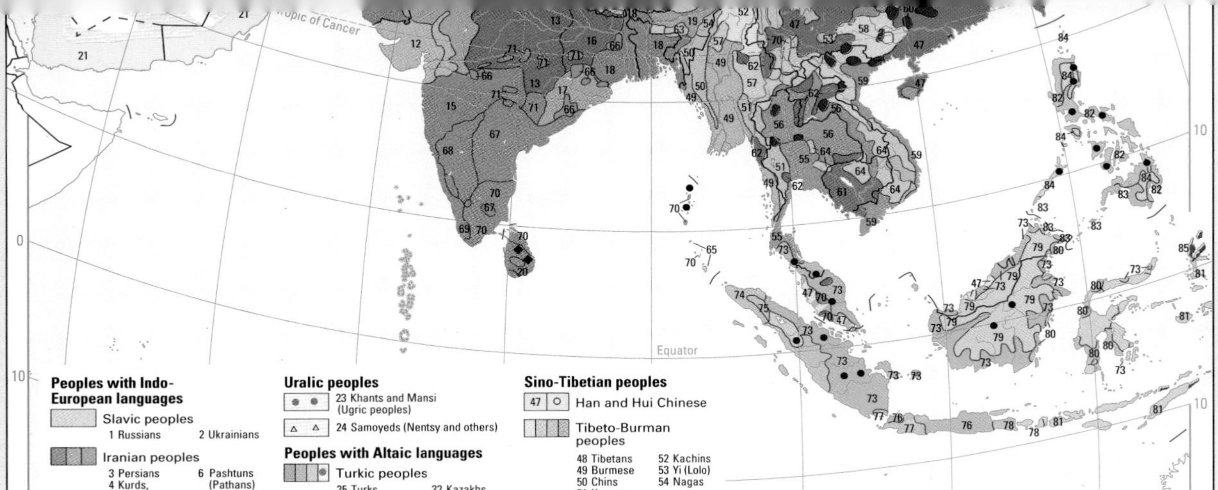

Peoples with Indo-European languages

Slavic peoples
- 1 Russians
- 2 Ukrainians

Iranian peoples
- 3 Persians
- 4 Kurds, Lurs and others
- 5 Tajiks
- 6 Pashtuns (Pathans)
- 7 Hazaras
- 8 Beluchs

Indo-Aryan (Indic) peoples
- 9 Kashmiris
- 10 Sindhs
- 11 Rajasthanis
- 12 Gujaratis
- 13 Hindi-speaking peoples (Hindustanis)
- 14 Punjabis
- 15 Marathis
- 16 Biharis
- 17 Oriyas
- 18 Bengalis
- 19 Assamese
- 20 Singhalese

Germans

Semitic peoples
- 21 Arabs
- 22 Israelis
- Russian Jews and Bukhara Jews

Uralic peoples
- 23 Khants and Mansi (Ugric peoples)
- 24 Samoyeds (Nentsy and others)

Peoples with Altaic languages

Turkic peoples
- 25 Turks
- 26 Azerbaijanis
- 27 Turkmens
- 28 Uzbeks
- 29 Kara-Kalpaks
- 30 Uighurs
- 31 Kirgiz
- 32 Kazakhs
- 33 Tatars
- 34 Altayans and Khakass
- 35 Tuvinians
- 36 Yakuts
- 37 Dolgans

Mongols
- 38 Khalkhas
- 39 Buryats
- 40 Oyrat and others

Manchu-Tungus peoples
- 41 Evenks (Tungus)
- 42 Evens (Lamuts)
- 43 Nanaians and others
- 44 Manchus

45 **Koreans**

46 **Japanese**

Sino-Tibetian peoples

47 Han and Hui Chinese

Tibeto-Burman peoples
- 48 Tibetans
- 49 Burmese
- 50 Chins
- 51 Karens
- 52 Kachins
- 53 Yi (Lolo)
- 54 Nagas

Thai peoples
- 55 Thai (Siamese)
- 56 Lao
- 57 Shan
- 58 Chuang

Austro-Asiatic peoples

59 Vietnamese

60 Miao-Yao peoples

Mon-Khmer peoples
- 61 Khmers
- 62 Mon
- 63 Khasi
- 64 Mountain Khmers
- 65 Nicobarese

66 Mundas

Dravidian peoples
- 67 Telugu
- 68 Kannarese
- 69 Malayalis
- 70 Tamils
- 71 Khonds, Oraons and others
- 72 Brahui

Austronesian peoples

Indonesian peoples
- 73 Malays
- 74 Achinese
- 75 Bataks
- 76 Javanese
- 77 Sundanese
- 78 Madurese and Balinese
- 79 Dayaks and Ibans
- 80 Buginese
- 81 Amboinese, Timorese and others

Philippine peoples:
- 82 Tagalog, Bisaya etc.
- 83 Moro
- 84 Igorote, Ifugao and others

85 **Papuans**

Eskimos, Aleuts

Other peoples
- Paleosiberians (Chukchi, Koryaks and others)
- Kets
- Ainu
- Burushaskis
- Veddas
- Negritos (Aeta, Semangs, Andamanese and others)
- Uninhabited area

Peoples of the Caucasus and Cyprus: see p. 28/29

ARCTIC OCEAN
Bear I. (Norw.)
Spitsbergen (Norw.)
Rudolf I.
George Land
Franz Josef Land
Graham Be
Wilczek Land
Wiese
C. Karlsen
1053
1547
Novaya Zemlya
1292
Kara Sea
White I.
Barents Sea
Tromsø
Narvik
NORWAY
Hammerfest
North Cape
Kiruna
Lakselv
SWEDEN
L. Inari
Vadsø
Kirkenes
Ivalo
Lapland
Nikel
Pechenga
Rovaniemi
FINLAND
Murmansk
Monchegorsk
Severomorsk
Olenegorsk
Imandra L.
1191
Kandalaksha
Kirovsk
Lovozero
Kuusamo
Kola Pen.
C. Kanin Nos
Shoyna
Kanin Pen.
Kolguyev
Kara Strait
Vaigach I.
Drovyanoy
Yamal Pen.
Kem
Belomorsk
White Sea
Ponoy
Chësha Bay
Indiga
G. of Pechora
Amderma
Baydaratskaya Guba
Morrasale
90
Segezha
L. Vyg
L. Seg
Severodvinsk
Mezen
Naryan-Mar
Medvezhyegorsk
350
Onega
Arkhangelsk
Timan Ridge
Pechora
Khalmer-Yu
1363
Ochenyrd
Vorkuta
Yambur
Petrozavodsk
L. Onega
Vytegra
Onega
Plesetsk
N. Dvina
Ust-Tsilma
Usa
Novyy Port
Labytnangi
Yar-Sale
Tazov
Gulf of Ob
Gy
Inta
Nyda
Beloye L.
Konosha
Blagoyevo
471
Pechora
Narodnaya
1895
Salekhard
Novyy Urengo
Belozersk
Velsk
Usogorsk
Ob
Nadym
Cherepovets
Mikun
Ukhta
Sokol
Kotlas
RUSSIA
Vologda
Sukhona
294
Troitsko-Pechorsk
Syktyvkar
Vychegda
Berëzovo
Tarko-Sale
West Siberian Plain
Buy
Kostroma
North Russian Ridge
Pechora
151
Volga
Gorki Res.
Unzha
231
Ivanovo
Mureshi
Ural Mountains
Priobye
Noyabrsk
Kama
Gayny
Kirs
Yugorsk
Kotelnich
Vyatka
Krasnovishersk
Dzerzhynsk
Vyatka
Kama Res.
Solikamsk
Ivdel
Surgut
Oka
NIZHNIY NOVGOROD
Kudymkar
Severouralsk
Nizhnevart
Berezniki
Konzhakovskiy Kamen
1569
Khanty-Mansiysk
Nefteyugansk
Arzamas
Glazov
Serov
Yoshkar-Ola
Gubakha
Strezhevoy
Cheboksary
PERM
Chusovoy
Sosva
Mezhdurechenskiy
Izhevsk
Novaya Lyalya
Tavda
Irtysh
KAZAN
Kama
Demyanskoye
Vyatka
Sarapul
Votkinsk
Kungur
Saransk
Kuybyshev Res.
Nizhnekamsk
Nikolo-Berëzovka
Nizhniy Tagil
Tavda
Vasyu
Chistopol
Pervouralsk
Tobolsk
Simbirsk
Naberezhnyye Chelny
Krasnoufimsk
Irbit
Novy Vasy
Penza
Dimitrovgrad
Belaya
YEKATERINBURG
Tyumen
Ust-Ishim
Volga Heights
Tolyatti
Kamensk-Uralskiy
Tobol
Irtysh
Syzran
Bugulma
Ufa
Ishim
Yalutorovsk
SAMARA
UFA
Zlatoust
Ishim
Tara
Volga
Saratov Res.
Buguruslan
Miass
Engels
Sterlitamak
Yaman Tau
1640
CHELYABINSK
Kurgan
Nazyvayevsk
Tyukalinsk
Buzuluk
Salavat
Troitsk
Kumertau
Belaya
Isilkul
OMSK
Barabin
Petropavl
Oral
Orenburg
Magnitogorsk
Kostanay
Tobol
Tatarsk
Aksay
Ural
Sibay
Ural
KAZAKHSTAN
Rudnyy
Cherlak
KAZAKHSTAN
10
15
20
25
30
35
40
70
A
B
C
D
E
K
L
4
5
6
7
65
60
55
50
46/47
48/49
50/51
F
50
G
55
H
60
J
65
K
70
L
64/65
75
M

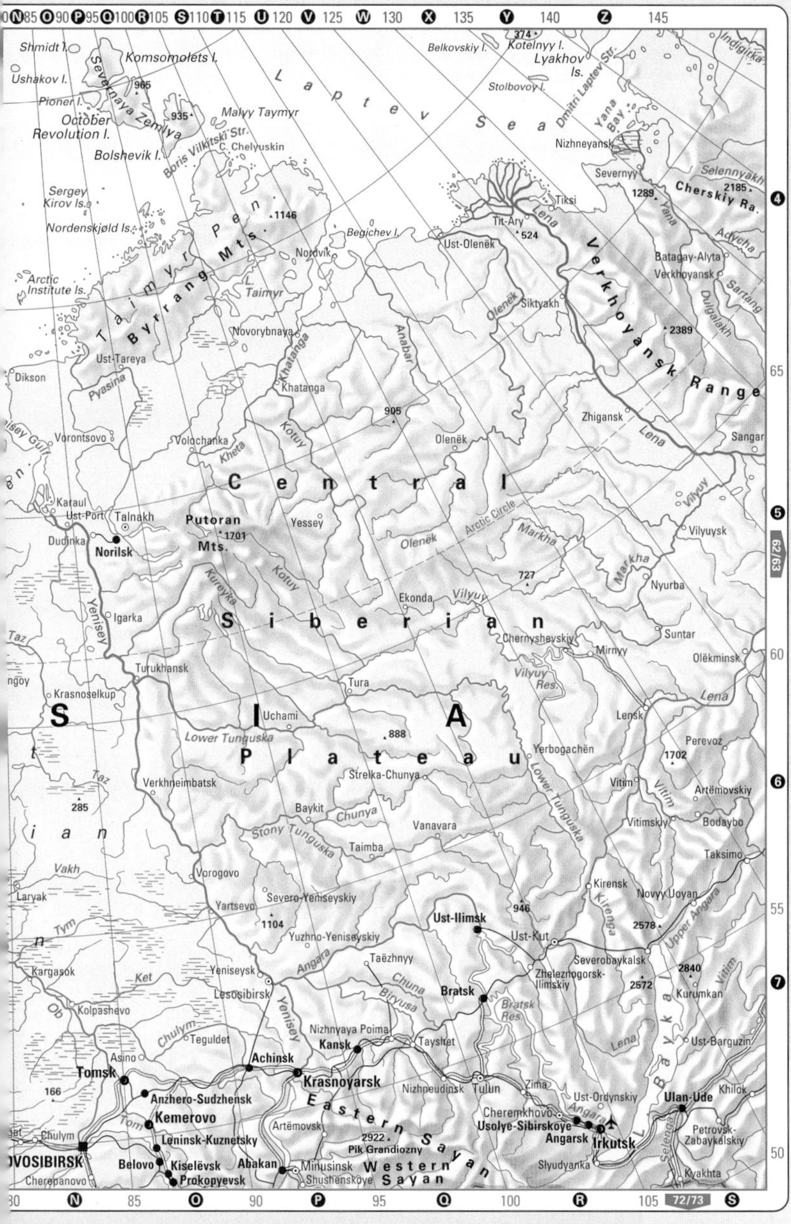
N 85 O 90 P 95 Q 100 R 105 S 110 T 115 U 120 V 125 W 130 X 135 Y 140 Z 145
Laptev Sea
Shmidt I.
Ushakov I.
Komsomolets I.
Severnaya Zemlya
965
Pioneer I.
October Revolution I.
935
Malyy Taymyr
Bolshevik I.
Boris Vilkitski Str.
C. Chelyuskin
Sergey Kirov Is.
Nordenskjøld Is.
Arctic Institute Is.
Taimyr Pen.
Byrrang Mts.
1146
L. Taimyr
Begichev I.
Nordvik
Belkovskiy I.
374
Kotelnyy I.
Lyakhov Is.
Stolbovoy I.
Dmitri Laptev Str.
Yana Bay
Nizhneyansk
Indigirka
Severnyy
Selennyakh
2185
Cherskiy Ra.
1289
Yana
Tiksi
Tit-Ary
524
Ust-Olenëk
Lena
Verkhoyansk Range
Adycha
Batagay-Alyta
Verkhoyansk
Sartang
Dulgalakh
Olenëk
Siktyakh
2389
Novorybnaya
Khatanga
Anabar
Ust-Tareya
Dikson
Pyasina
905
Zhigansk
Sangar
Yenisey Gulf
Vorontsovo
Volochanka
Kheta
Kotuy
Olenëk
Central Siberian Plateau
Karaul
Ust-Port
Talnakh
Putoran Mts.
1701
Yessey
Dudinka
Norilsk
Arctic Circle
Markha
Vilyuy
Vilyuysk
Nyurba
727
Kureyka
Ekonda
Igarka
Yenisey
Taz
Chernyshevskiy
Mirnyy
Suntar
Olëkminsk
Vilyuy Res.
Turukhansk
Tura
Krasnoselkup
Uchami
SIBERIA
Lower Tunguska
888
Lensk
Lena
Perevoz
1702
Yerbogachën
Strelka-Chunya
Vitim
Artëmovskiy
Verkhneimbatsk
285
Baykit
Chunya
Vanavara
Vitimskiy
Bodaybo
Stony Tunguska
Taimba
Taksimo
Vakh
Vorogovo
Kirensk
Novyy Uoyan
Laryak
Severo-Yeniseyskiy
Yartsevo
1104
946
Ust-Ilimsk
Ust-Kut
Upper Angara
2578
Tym
Yuzhno-Yeniseyskiy
Severobaykalsk
Kirenga
Angara
Taëzhnyy
Zheleznogorsk-Ilimskiy
2840
2572
Kargasok
Yeniseysk
Ket
Chuna
Bratsk
Kurumkan
Lesosibirsk
Biryusa
Bratsk Res.
Vitim
Ob
Kolpashevo
Chulym
Teguldet
Nizhnyaya Poima
Kansk
Tayshet
Lena
Ust-Barguzin
L. Baykal
Asino
Achinsk
Tomsk
Krasnoyarsk
Nizhneudinsk
Tulun
Zima
Ust-Ordynskiy
Ulan-Ude
Khilok
166
Anzhero-Sudzhensk
Eastern Sayan
Angara
Kemerovo
Tom
Artëmovsk
Cheremkhovo
Usolye-Sibirskoye
Angarsk
Irkutsk
Petrovsk-Zabaykalskiy
Chulym
2922
Pik Grandiozny
Leninsk-Kuznetsky
Selenga
Novosibirsk
Belovo
Kiselëvsk
Abakan
Minusinsk
Western Sayan
Slyudyanka
Kyakhta
Cherepanovo
Prokopyevsk
Shushenskoye
65
60
55
50
4
5
6
7
62/63
80 N 85 O 90 P 95 Q 100 R 105 72/73 S

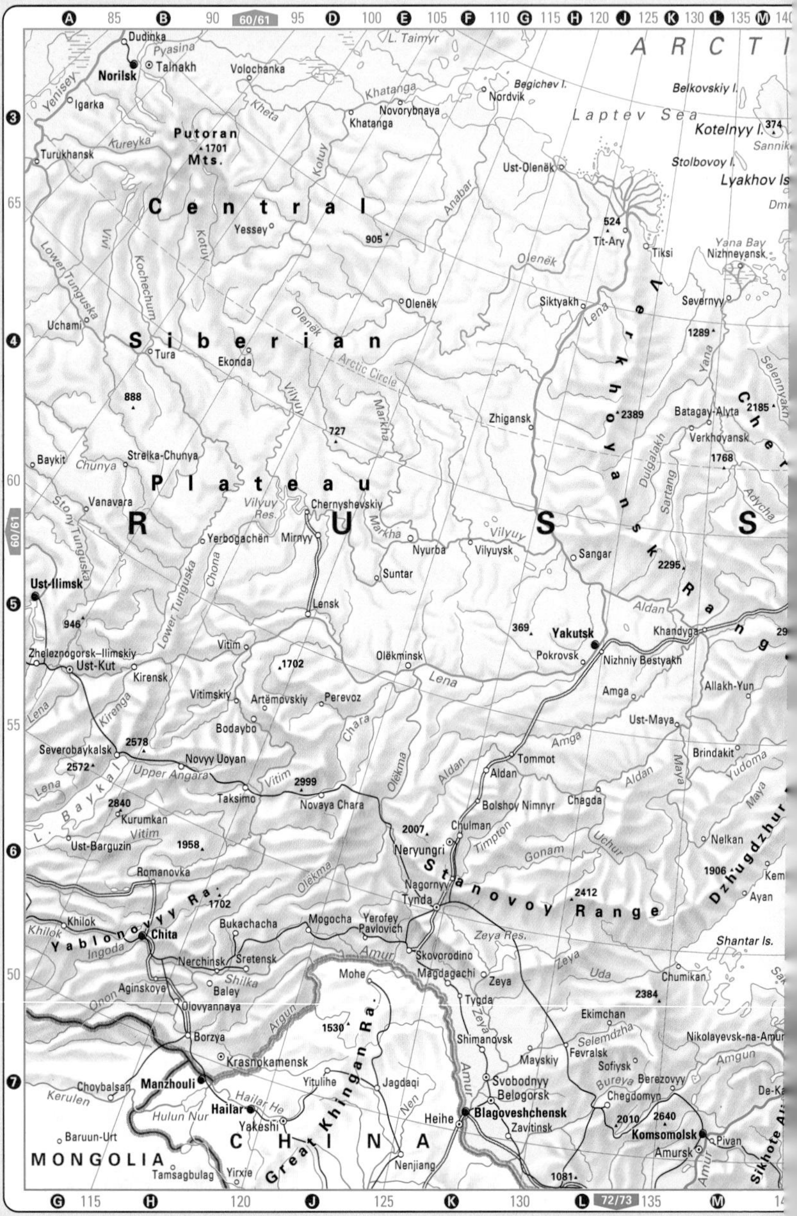

A 85 B 90 60/61 95 D 100 E 105 F 110 G 115 H 120 J 125 K 130 L 135 M 140
3
65
4
60
60/61
5
55
6
50
7
G 115 H 120 J 125 K 130 L 72/73 135 M
ARCTIC
Laptev Sea
Dudinka
Pyasina
Norilsk
Talnakh
Yenisey
Igarka
Volochanka
L. Taimyr
Begichev I.
Nordvik
Belkovskiy I.
Khatanga
Kheta
Novorybnaya
Khatanga
Kotelnyy I.
374
Putoran Mts.
1701
Kureyka
Turukhansk
Kotuy
Anabar
Ust-Olenëk
Stolbovoy I.
Lyakhov Is
Central Siberian Plateau
Yessey
905
524
Tit-Ary
Tiksi
Yana Bay
Nizhneyansk
Vivi
Kotuy
Kochechum
Lower Tunguska
Olenëk
Olenëk
Olenëk
Siktyakh
Severnyy
Uchami
Lena
Verkhoyansk Range
1289
Tura
Ekonda
Arctic Circle
Vilyuy
Yana
888
Markha
727
Zhigansk
2389
Batagay-Alyta
2185
Verkhoyansk
Dulgalakh
Baykit
Chunya
Strelka-Chunya
1768
Sartang
Adycha
Vanavara
Stony Tunguska
Vilyuy Res.
Chernyshevskiy
RUSSIA
Markha
Vilyuy
Yerbogachën
Mirnyy
Nyurba
Vilyuysk
Sangar
2295
Chona
Suntar
Ust-Ilimsk
Lower Tunguska
Lensk
Aldan
946
369
Yakutsk
Khandyga
Zheleznogorsk-Ilimskiy
Vitim
Olëkminsk
Pokrovsk
Nizhniy Bestyakh
Ust-Kut
Kirensk
1702
Lena
Amga
Allakh-Yun
Vitimskiy
Artëmovskiy
Perevoz
Lena
Kirenga
Bodaybo
Chara
Ust-Maya
Amga
Severobaykalsk
2578
Olëkma
Tommot
Brindakit
2572
Novyy Uoyan
Aldan
Maya
Yudoma
Upper Angara
Vitim
2999
Aldan
Aldan
Lena
L. Baykal
Taksimo
Novaya Chara
Bolshoy Nimnyr
Chagda
Maya
2840
Kurumkan
2007
Chulman
Timpton
Uchur
Nelkan
Vitim
Ust-Barguzin
1958
Neryungri
Gonam
Dzhugdzhur
Romanovka
Stanovoy Range
1906
Olëkma
Nagornyy
2412
Ayan
Yablonovyy Ra.
1702
Tynda
Khilok
Khilok
Bukachacha
Mogocha
Yerofey Pavlovich
Zeya Res.
Shantar Is.
Chita
Ingoda
Amur
Skovorodino
Zeya
Nerchinsk
Sretensk
Mohe
Magdagachi
Uda
Chumikan
Shilka
Aginskoye
Baley
Zeya
Onon
Olovyannaya
Tygda
2384
Argun
Zeya
Ekimchan
Borzya
1530
Great Khingan Ra.
Selemdzha
Nikolayevsk-na-Amur
Shimanovsk
Fevralsk
Krasnokamensk
Mayskiy
Amgun
Sofiysk
Manzhouli
Choybalsan
Yitulihe
Jagdaqi
Amur
Svobodnyy
Bureya
Berezovyy
Kerulen
Belogorsk
Chegdomyn
Hailar He
Nen
Hailar
Hulun Nur
Heihe
Blagoveshchensk
2010
2640
Yakeshi
Zavitinsk
Komsomolsk
Pivan
Baruun-Urt
CHINA
Amursk
MONGOLIA
Tamsagbulag
Yirxie
Nenjiang
1081
Amur
Sikhote

145 O 150 P 155 Q 160 R 165 S 170 T 175 U 180 V 175 W 170 X 165 Y
OCEAN
New Siberian Is.
Faddeyev I.
New Siberia
Little Lyakhov I.
Great Lyakhov I.
Laptev Str.
East Siberian Sea
Wrangel I.
1096
Chukchi Sea
De Long Str.
Alaska
UNITED STATES
Kotzebue
Kotzebue Sound
Seward Pen.
Bering Strait
Cape Dezhnev
Uelen
Cape Prince of Wales
Vankarem
Cape Shelagskiy
Ayon I.
Pevek
Bear Is.
Chukot Range
1843
Chukot Pen.
Amguema
1158
Provideniya
Cape Chukotskiy
Saint Lawrence I.
Gulf of Anadyr
Ambarchik
Chokurdakh
Alazeya
Indigirka
Cherskiy
Little Anyuy
Bilibino
1853
Anyuy Ra.
1775
Anadyr
Anadyr
Gt. Anyuy
1797
Belaya Gora
Druzhina
Srednekolymsk
Kolyma
Omolon
Yukagir Plateau
1185
Markovo
Mayn
Velikaya
Beringovskiy
Cape Navarin
2533
Moma
Zyryanka
Kolyma
Pobeda
3147
Ust-Nera
Penzhina
1503
Kamenskoye
Koryak Range
2562
Ledyanaya
Omolon
Kolyma Range
Oymyakon
Seymchan
Susuman
Yagodnoye
2586
Kolyma
Evensk
Merenga
Gizhiga Gulf
Penzhina Gulf
1045
Pakhachi
Korf
Olyutorskiy Bay
Cape Olyutorskiy
1962
Shelekhov Gulf
Ilpyrskiy
Karaginskiy I.
Karaginskiy Bay
Bering Sea
Palana
Motykleyka
Magadan
Cape Tolstoy
Okhotsk
2618
Tigil
Ust-Kamchatsk
Bering I.
Copper I.
Komandor Is.
Aleutian Is.
Attu
Attu I.
Near Is.
UNITED STATES
Kamchatka
Klyuchi
4750
Klyuchevskaya Sopka
Sentral Mts
Milkovo
Sea of Okhotsk
Kirovskiy
Kronotskaya Sopka
3456
Petropavlovsk-Kamchatskiy
PACIFIC OCEAN
Cape Yelizavety
Okha
Oktyabrskiy
Ozernovskiy
First Kurile Str.
2339
Severo-Kurilsk
Paramushir I.
Pogibi
Lazarev
Nogliki
Sakhalin
1609
Aleksandrovsk-Sakhalinskiy
Kurile Is.
Onekotan I.
Smirnykh
Shiashkotan I.
55
60
65
50
110/111
N 145 O 150 P 155 Q 160 R 165 S

A B C D E F G H
35 40 45 50 55 60 65 70
1 2 3 4 5 6
48/49
50/51
66/67
55
50
45
40
35
Vologda
Rybinsk Res.
Rybinsk
Tver
Rzhev
Yaroslavl
Kostroma
Buy
MOSKVA (MOSCOW)
Ivanovo
Vladimir
Serpukhov
Orekhovo-Zuyevo
Kaluga
Kolomna
Dzerzhinsk
NIZHNIY NOVGOROD
Tula
Ryazan
Oka
Arzamas
Cheboksary
Sasovo
Lipetsk
Saransk
Tambov
Simbirsk
Voronezh
Penza
Rtishchevo
Liski
Borisoglebsk
Volga Heights
Syzran
Saratov
Engels
UKR.
Kamyshin
Volgograd Reservoir
VOLGOGRAD
Volzhskiy
Don
Tsimlyansk Res.
Akhtubinsk
Volga
Elista
Astrakhan
Kuma
Nalchik
Vladikavkaz
Groznyy
Makhachkala
Caucasus
GEORGIA
TBILISI
Derbent
ARMENIA
Gancə
L. Sevan
AZERBAIJAN
Xankəndi
BAKI (BAKU)
Aras
TABRĪZ
4811
Kuhhā-ye Sabalān
Ardabīl
Astara
Rasht
Zanjān
Qezel Owzan
Qazvīn
Elburz Mts
Karaj
5671
Demavend
Hamadān
TEHRĀN
Borūjerd
Qom
Arāk
Kāshān
ESFAHĀN (ISFAHAN)
Great Salt Desert
I R A N
Murashi
Kotelnich
Vyatka
Kirs
Kudymkar
Kama
Kama Res.
Glazov
Yoshkar-Ola
Izhevsk
Votkinsk
KAZAN
Sarapul
Chistopol
Kuybyshev Res.
Dimitrovgrad
Naberezhnyye Chelny
Tolyatti
SAMARA
Bugulma
Buguruslan
Buzuluk
Kumertau
Oral
Aksay
Ural
Neftekamsk
Yanaul
UFA
Sterlitamak
Orenburg
Sol-Iletsk
R U S S
Pechora
Gayny
Krasnovishersk
Berezniki
Solikamsk
1569
Kizel
Gubakha
Chusovoy
PERM
Kungur
Pervouralsk
Krasnoufimsk
Zlatoust
Miass
Yaman Tau 1640
Magnitogorsk
Sibay
Orsk
Dombarovskiy
Svetlyy
Aktöbe
Oktyabrsk
Mugodzhary Mts.
Emba
657
Shalkar
Irgiz
Ural Mts
1331
Ivdel
Severouralsk
Serov
Sosva
Verkhoturye
Nizhniy Tagil
Irbit
YEKATERINBURG
Kamensk-Uralskiy
CHELYABINSK
Troitsk
Kostanay
Rudnyy
Tobol
Zhetikara
Kusmuryn
Priobye
231
Ob
Yugorsk
Khanty-Mansiysk
Mezhdurechenskiy
Demyanskoye
Tavda
Tobolsk
Tyumen
Yalutorovsk
Ishim
Kurgan
Petropavl
Kokshetau
Atbasar
Yesil
Tengiz Köl
Arkalyk
Torgay
Karsakpay
Zhezkazgan
K A Z A K
Dossor
Atyrau
Kulsary
Emba
Sor Oli-Kültyk
Beyneu
Fort-Shevchenko
-28
Aktau
-132
340
Caspian Sea
Ustyurt Plateau
Aral Sea
Aral
Zhangakazaly
Baykongyr (Baykonur)
Dzhusaly
Kzylorda
Syr Darya
Karatau
2176
Turkestan
Arys
Shymkent
TOSHKENT (TASHKENT)
Muynoq
Qunghirot
Nukus
Kyzyl Kum
Uchquduq
UZBEKISTAN
Dashhovuz
Urganch
Turtkul
922
Zarafshon
Amu Darya
Bukhoro (Bukhara)
Navoiy
Guliston
Khujand
Kattaqurghon
Samarqand
Qarshi
Kitob
TAJ
Dushanbe
Bekdash
Kara Bogaz Gol
Turkmenbashi
Arlan 1881
Nebitdag
Gyzylarbat
TURKMENISTAN
Kara Kum
Gasan-Kuli
Atrak
Bābol
Sārī
Bandar-e Torkaman
Gorgān
Kopet Dag
Ashgabat
Bojnūrd
Shāhrūd
Semnān
Sabzevār
MASHHAD
Torbat-e Heydarīyeh
Tejen
Mary
Kara Kum Canal
Kerki
Chärjew
Murgab
Gushgy
Termiz
Qurghonteppa
Kulob
Balkh
Sheberghān
Mazār-e Sharīf
Kunduz
Feyzābād
Tāloqān
Meymaneh
Baghlān
Hindu
AFGHANISTAN

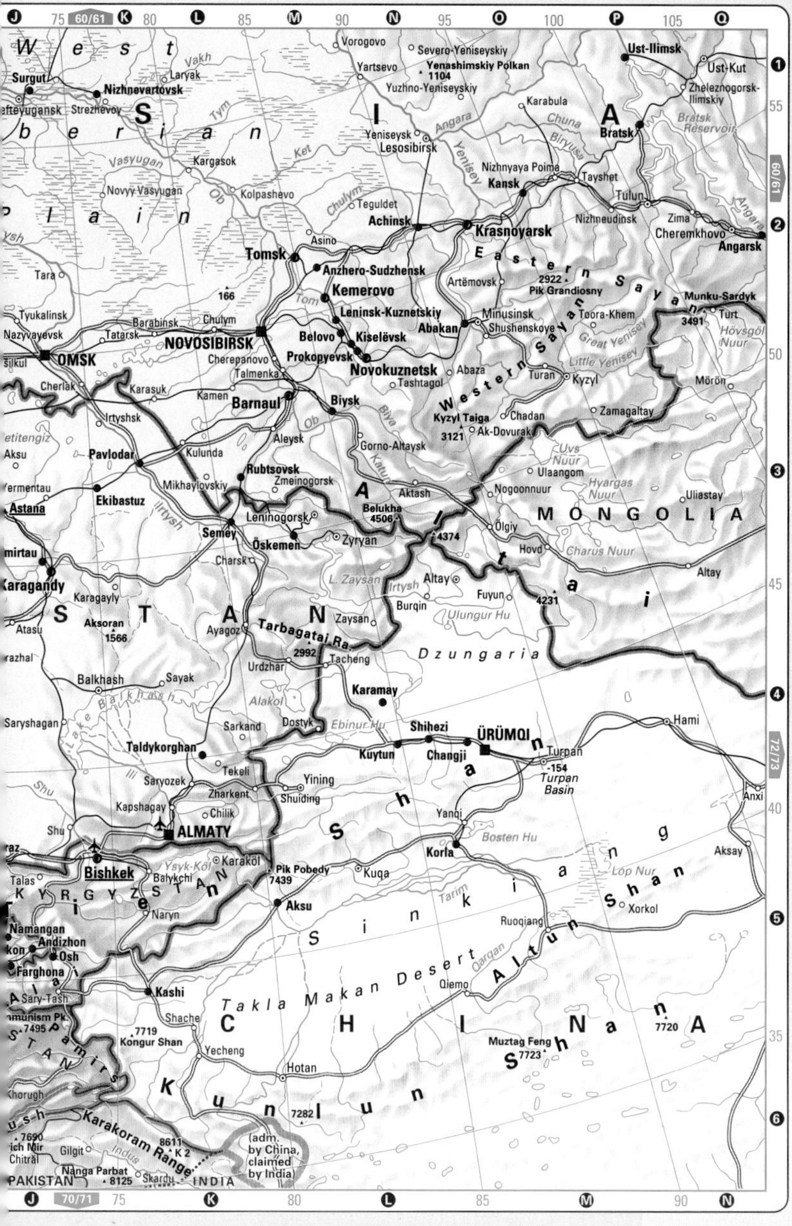
60/61
70/71
72/73
West Siberian Plain
Surgut
Nizhnevartovsk
Nefteyugansk
Strezhevoy
Laryak
Vakh
Tym
Vasyugan
Kargasok
Novyy Vasyugan
Ob
Kolpashevo
Ket
Vorogovo
Severo-Yeniseyskiy
Yartsevo
Yenashimskiy Polkan 1104
Yuzhno-Yeniseyskiy
Yeniseysk
Lesosibirsk
Angara
Yenisey
Karabula
Chuna
Biryusa
Ust-Ilimsk
Ust-Kut
Zheleznogorsk-Ilimskiy
Bratsk
Bratsk Reservoir
Nizhnyaya Poima
Kansk
Tayshet
Tulun
Nizhneudinsk
Zima
Cheremkhovo
Angarsk
Chulym
Teguldet
Achinsk
Krasnoyarsk
Asino
Tomsk
Anzhero-Sudzhensk
Kemerovo
Tom
Leninsk-Kuznetskiy
Belovo
Kiselëvsk
Prokopyevsk
Novokuznetsk
Tara
166
Tyukalinsk
Nazyvayevsk
Barabinsk
Chulym
Tatarsk
NOVOSIBIRSK
OMSK
Isilkul
Cherepanovo
Talmenka
Cherlak
Karasuk
Kamen
Barnaul
Biysk
Irtyshsk
Aleysk
Kulunda
Pavlodar
Aksu
Yermentau
Ekibastuz
Astana
Mikhaylovskiy
Rubtsovsk
Zmeinogorsk
Semey
Irtysh
Leninogorsk
Öskemen
Zyryan
Charsk
Temirtau
Karagandy
Karagayly
Aksoran 1566
Atasu
Ayagoz
Tarbagatai Ra.
2992
Zaysan
L. Zaysan
Urdzhar
Tacheng
Balkhash
Sayak
Lake Balkhash
Alakol
Saryshagan
Sarkand
Dostyk
Ebinur Hu
Taldykorghan
Tekeli
Ili
Saryozek
Zharkent
Yining
Shuiding
Shu
Kapshagay
Chilik
ALMATY
Bishkek
Talas
Ysyk-Köl
Karakol
Balykchy
Naryn
KYRGYZSTAN
Pik Pobedy 7439
Aksu
Namangan
Andizhon
Kokand
Osh
Farghona
Sary-Tash
Kommunism Pk. 7495
TAJIKISTAN
Pamirs
Khorugh
Hindu Kush
7690
Tirich Mir
Chitral
Gilgit
Indus
Karakoram Range
8611 K 2
Nanga Parbat 8125
Skardu
PAKISTAN
INDIA
(adm. by China, claimed by India)
Kashi
Shache
7719 Kongur Shan
Yecheng
Hotan
Kunlun Shan
7282
Takla Makan Desert
Tarim
Sinkiang
Kuqa
Korla
Bosten Hu
Yanqi
Kuytun
Shihezi
Changji
ÜRÜMQI
Turpan
-154
Turpan Basin
Tian Shan
Karamay
Dzungaria
Hami
Anxi
Aksay
Lop Nur
Xorkol
Ruoqiang
Qarqan
Qiemo
Altun Shan
Muztag Feng 7723
7720
CHINA
Eastern Sayan
Western Sayan
Artëmovsk
2922 Pik Grandiosny
Abakan
Minusinsk
Shushenskoye
Abaza
Tashtagol
Toora-Khem
Great Yenisey
Little Yenisey
Turan
Kyzyl
Munku-Sardyk 3491
Turt
Hövsgöl Nuur
Mörön
Zamagaltay
Chadan
Kyzyl Taiga 3121
Ak-Dovurak
Gorno-Altaysk
Biya
Katun
Uvs Nuur
Ulaangom
Hyargas Nuur
Nogoonnuur
Uliastay
Aktash
Belukha 4506
4374
Altai
Ölgiy
MONGOLIA
Hovd
Charus Nuur
Altay
Altay
Fuyun
Burqin
Ulungur Hu
4231
KAZAKHSTAN
RUSSIA

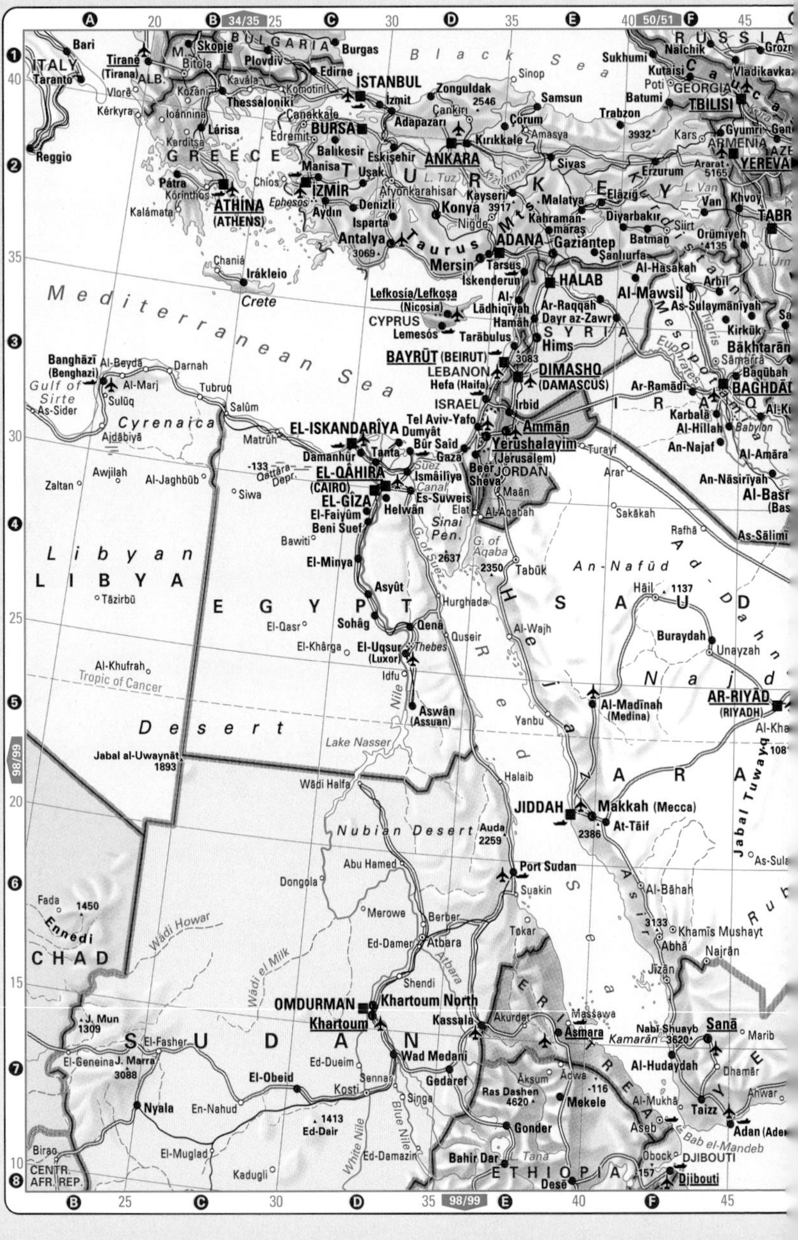

34/35
50/51
98/99
ITALY
Bari
Taranto
Reggio
Tiranë (Tirana)
ALB.
Vlorë
Kérkyra
Skopje
M.
Bitola
BULGARIA
Plovdiv
Burgas
Edirne
Kaválla
Komotini
Kozáni
Thessaloníki
Ioánnina
Lárisa
Karditsa
GREECE
Pátra
Kórinthos
ATHÍNA (ATHENS)
Kalámata
Chios
Chaniá
Irákleio
Crete
Black Sea
İSTANBUL
İzmit
Çanakkale
BURSA
Edremit
Balıkesir
Eskişehir
Manisa
Uşak
İZMİR
Ephesos
Aydın
Denizli
Isparta
Antalya
3069
Zonguldak
2546
Çankırı
Adapazarı
ANKARA
Kırıkkale
L. Tuz
TURKEY
Afyonkarahisar
Konya
Kayseri
3917
Niğde
Taurus Mts.
ADANA
Mersin
Tarsus
İskenderun
Sinop
Samsun
Çorum
Amasya
Kızılırmak
Sivas
Malatya
Kahramanmaraş
Gaziantep
Şanlıurfa
Elâzığ
Erzurum
Trabzon
3932
Diyarbakır
Batman
Siirt
Kurdistan
L. Van
Van
Khvoy
Orūmīyeh
4135
L. Urm
TABR
RUSSIA
Nalchik
Grozn
Vladikavkaz
Sukhumi
Kutaisi
Poti
GEORGIA
Batumi
TBILISI
Caucasus
Kura
Kars
Gyumri
ARMENIA
Ararat
5165
YEREVA
AZE
Mediterranean Sea
Lefkosía/Lefkoşa (Nicosia)
CYPRUS
Lemesós
Al-Lādhiqīyah
Hamāh
Tarābulus
Hims
SYRIA
HALAB
Ar-Raqqah
Dayr az-Zawr
Al-Hasakah
Al-Mawsil
Arbil
As-Sulaymānīyah
Kirkūk
Mesopotamia
Tigris
Euphrates
Bākhtarān
Sāmarrā
Ba'qūbah
BAGHDĀD
Ar-Ramādī
IRAQ
Karbalā
Al-Hillah
Babylon
An-Najaf
Al-Amāra
An-Nāsirīyah
Al-Basr (Bas
Al-K
BAYRŪT (BEIRUT)
3083
LEBANON
DIMASHQ (DAMASCUS)
Hefa (Haifa)
ISRAEL
Irbid
Tel Aviv-Yafo
'Ammān
Yerushalayim (Jerusalem)
Turayf
'Arar
Be'er Sheva
JORDAN
Ma'ān
Elat
Al-'Aqabah
G. of Aqaba
Sakākah
Rafhā
As-Sālimī
Banghāzī (Benghazi)
Al-Beydā
Darnah
Al-Marj
Gulf of Sirte
Sulūq
As-Sider
Tubruq
Salûm
Cyrenaica
Ajdābiyā
Awjilah
Al-Jaghbūb
Zaltan
Siwa
Matrûh
Qattâra Depr.
-133
EL-ISKANDARÎYA
Dumyât
Bûr Saîd
Tanta
Damanhûr
Gaza
EL-QÂHIRA (CAIRO)
Ismâilîya
Suez Canal
Es-Suweis
EL-GÎZA
Helwân
El-Faiyûm
Beni Suef
Sinai Pen.
G. of Suez
2637
2350
Tabūk
Bawiti
El-Minya
Libyan Desert
LIBYA
Tāzirbū
EGYPT
Asyût
Hurghada
Sohâg
Qenâ
El-Qasr
El-Khârga
El-Uqsur (Luxor)
Thebes
Quseir
Idfu
Nile
Aswân (Assuan)
Al-Khufrah
Tropic of Cancer
Lake Nasser
Jabal al-Uwaynāt
1893
Wādī Halfa
Red Sea
Al-Wajh
Yanbu
Halaib
Hejaz
An-Nafūd
Ha'il
1137
SAUDI ARABIA
Buraydah
'Unayzah
Ad-Dahna
Najd
AR-RIYĀD (RIYADH)
Al-Madīnah (Medina)
Al-Kha
108
Jabal Tuwayq
JIDDAH
Makkah (Mecca)
At-Tāif
2386
As-Sul
Nubian Desert
Auda
2259
Abu Hamed
Dongola
Port Sudan
Suakin
Al-Bāhah
Asir
Rub'
Merowe
Berber
Tokar
3133
Khamīs Mushayt
Abhā
Najrān
Jīzān
Ed-Damer
Atbara
Fada
1450
Ennedi
CHAD
Wādi Howar
Wādi el Milk
Shendi
OMDURMAN
Khartoum North
Khartoum
Kassala
Akurdet
Massawa
Asmara
ERITREA
Kamarān
Nabi Shuayb
3620
Sanā
Marib
YEMEN
J. Mun
1309
SUDAN
El-Fasher
El-Geneina
J. Marra
3088
Ed-Dueim
Wad Medani
El-Obeid
Sennar
Gedaref
Kosti
Singa
Aksum
Adwa
-116
Ras Dashen
4620
Mekele
Al-Hudaydah
Dhamār
Al-Mukhā
Ahwar
Taizz
Adan (Aden)
Nyala
En-Nahud
1413
Ed-Dair
Blue Nile
White Nile
Gonder
Aseb
Bab el-Mandeb
Birao
El-Muglad
Ed-Damazin
Bahir Dar
L. Tana
Obock
DJIBOUTI
CENTR. AFR. REP.
Kadugli
ETHIOPIA
Desē
157
Djibouti

KAZAKHSTAN
UZBEKISTAN
Kyzyl Kum
KAZ
Shymkent
Arys
Tien Shan
KYRGYZSTAN
Aksu
TOSHKENT (TASHKENT)
Naryn
Namangan
Andijon
Osh
Quqon
Farghona
Kashi
Khujand
Makhachkala
Derbent
Caspian Sea
Qunghirot
Nukus
Urganch
Turtkul
Dashhovuz
Kara Kum
Zeravshan
Kattaqurghon
Nawoiy
Samarqand
Bukhoro
Amu Darya
Syr Darya
CHINA
Kongur Shan
7719
Shache
Yecheng
Communism Pk.
7495
Dushanbe
TAJIKISTAN
Pamirs
Sumqayit
AZERBAIJAN
BAKI
(BAKU)
Turkmenbashi
TURKMENISTAN
Nebitdag
Gyzylarbat
Chärjew
Qarshi
Qurghonteppa
Khorug
Astara
Ardabil
Kopet Dag
Ashgabat
2942
Mary
Kerki
Termiz
Feyzabad
Taloqan
Jammu
Karakoram Range
K2 8611
Rasht
Gonbad-e Kāvūs
Gorgān
Sabzevār
Sārī
Elburz Mts.
5671
Demavend
Mazār-e Sharīf
Kunduz
Baghlān
Hindu Kush
7690
Chitrāl
Gilgit
Skardu
8125
Nanga Parbat
Asadābād
Leh
Qazvīn
Karaj
TEHRĀN
Shāhrūd
MASHHAD
Gushgy
Meymaneh
Kābul
5143
Jalālābād
Srīnagar
Kashmir
Indus
Qom
Torbat-e Heydarīyeh
Qaleh-ye Now
Peshāwar
Islāmābād
Rāwalpindi
Hamadān
Great Salt Desert
Herāt
Hari Rud
Ghaznī
Gardēz
Bannu
Jhelum
Jammu
Himachal Pradesh
Arāk
Kāshān
Gujrānwāla
Siālkot
Borūjerd
IRAN
Sargodha
Amritsar
6248
Khorramābād
ESFAHĀN (ISFAHAN)
Bīrjand
AFGHANISTAN
Helmand
Kalāt
Dera Ismāīl Khān
LAHORE
Jalandhar
Zard Kūh
4548
Dezfūl
Farāh
Kandahār
FAISALĀBĀD
LUDH.
Shimla
Masjed-e Soleymān
Yazd
Lashkar Gāh
Jhang
Chandīgarh
Hāmūn-e Sāberī
Zaranj
Chaman
Multān
Sāhīwāl
Karnāl
Ahvāz
Zagros Mts.
Dera Ghāzi Kh.
Gangānagar
Hisār
Khorramshahr
Ābādān
Quetta
Bahāwalpur
Sutlej
DELHI
New Delhi
KUWAIT
Al-Kuwayt (Kuwait)
Persepolis
Kermān
Zāhedān
1264
Kalāt
Khānpur
1580
Sīkar
SHĪRĀZ
Sīrjān
Bam
Kūh-e Taftān
4042
2457
Baluchistan
Rahīmyār Khān
Bīkāner
Mina Saud
Bandar-e Būshehr
Fasā
Sukkur
Thar Desert
Phalodi
Rajasthan
Ajmer
JAIPUR
The Gulf
Lār
Furgun
3280
Īrānshahr
Lārkāna
Khairpur
Jodhpur
Tonk
Al-Jubayl
Bandar-e Abbās
Bandar-e Langeh
Zābolī
PAKISTAN
Beāwar
Kota
Ad-Dammām
Al-Manāmah (Manama)
BAHRAIN
Str. of Hormuz
Nawābshāh
Bela
Bārmer
975
INDIA
Dharan
Hyderābād
Mīrpur Khas
(to Oman)
Sharjah
QATAR
Ad-Dawhah (Doha)
Dubai
Al-Hufūf
KARĀCHI
Gwādar
Pātan
Udaipur
Gujarat
Gāndhīnagar
Ratlām
Ujjain
Abu Dhabi
Suhār
Gulf of Oman
AHMADĀBĀD
INDORE
M. Pr.
Haradh
UNITED ARAB EMIRATES
Masqat (Muscat)
Bhuj
Kandla
Rājkot
Godhra
2980
Gulf of Kutch
Jāmnagar
Bharūch
VADODARA
Kathiawar
Nizwa
Sūr
Ras al-Hadd
Porbandar
Bhāvnagar
Jalgaon
Jūnāgadh
1117
SŪRAT
Mālegaon
SAUDI ARABIA
Rub al-Khālī
Daman
Diu
Silvassa
Daman and Diu
D. & N.H.
KALYAN
1646
OMAN
Masīrah
MUMBAI (BOMBAY)
PUNE
Sātāra
Mahārāshtra
Sāngli
Ratnāgiri
Kolhāpur
YEMEN
Dhofar
1463
Kuria Muria Is.
Arabian Sea
Salālah
Goa
Panaji
Sayūn
Hadhramaut
Al-Ghaydah
Kartnātaka
Al-Mukallā
Gulf of Aden
Amīndīvi Is.
Lakshadweep
Laccadive Islands
Kavaratti
Qādib
Socotra
Bosaaso
C. Guardafui
SOMALIA
64/65
70/71
50 55 60 65 70 75 80
H J K L M N
40 35 30 25 20 15 10
1 2 3 4 5 6 7 8

A
34/35
32
B
36
1
2
3
TURKEY
Taurus Mts.
Perge
Aspendos
Side
Serik
Antalya
Manavgat
Elmalı
3069
Bey Dağları
Gulf of Antalya
Kumluca
Kaş
Finike
Yardımcı Burnu
Kastellórizo
GREECE
Hadım
Akdağ 2720
Ermenek
Göksu
Mut
Alanya
Gazipaşa
Anamur
Cape Anamur
Silifke
İncekum Burnu
Tarsus
Mersin
ADANA
Seyhan
Ceyhan
Erdemli
İskenderun
Karataş
G. of İskenderun
Kırıkhan
Amik Ovası
Afrīn
Antakya
Samandağı
Orontes
Idlib
Islâhiye
Jisr ash-Shaghur
Arīhā
Jabal as-Sāhilīyah
Al-Lādhiqīyah (Latakia)
Maarrat an-Numān
Suqaylibīya
Jablah
Bāniyās
1385
Masyāf
Ar-Rastān
Tartūs
Safita
Tall Kalakh
Al-Qusayr
C. Andreas
Dipkarpaz
C. Kormakíti
Girne
Lefkosia/Lefkoşa (Nicosia)
Güzelyurt
C. Arnauti
Pólis
Troódos
Ólympos 1953
Gazimağusa (Famagusta)
C. Greco
Lárnaka
Páfos
CYPRUS
Lemesós (Limassol)
C. Gata
Mediterranean Sea
Tarābulus (Tripoli)
Lebanon Mts.
3083
LEBANON
Balabakk
Anti-Lebanon
Jūniyah
BAYRŪT (BEIRUT)
Zahlah
Az-Zabdānī
Al-Qutayfah
Saydā (Sidon)
DIMASHQ (DAMASCUS)
Dūmā
Mt. Hermon 2814
Qatanā
Lītānī
Sūr
Al-Qunaytirah
Akko
Hefa (Haifa)
Teverya
Tiberias
Izra
Shahbā
As-Suwaydā
Ar-Ramthā
Darā
Nazerat (Nazareth)
Jordan
Irbid
Salkhad
Netanya
Jenin
Nāblus
Al-Mafraq
Jarash
ISRAEL
Tel Aviv-Yafo
Petah Tiqwa
As-Salt
Az-Zarqā
Holon
Arīha (Jericho)
Ammān
Ramla
Ashdod
Yerushalayim (Jerusalem)
Ashqelon
Bet Lehem
Madabā
Gaza
Al-Khalīl (Hebron)
Dead Sea
Khân Yûnis
-401
981
Al-Qatrānah
Beér Sheva (Beersheba)
Al-Karak
Dimona
Negev
At-Tafilah
1082
1736
1035
Petra
Wādī Mūsā
Maān
Al-Jafr
Qā al-Jafr
Ras an-Naqb
JORDAN
Elat
Tâba
Al-Aqabah
Jabal Ramm 1754
G. of Aqaba
Al-Mudawwarah
Haql
Baltîm
Rashîd (Rosetta)
L. Burullus
Dumyât (Damietta)
Abû Qir
EL-ISKANDARIYA (ALEXANDRIA)
Shirbîn
El-Manzala
Bûr Saîd (Port Said)
Disûq
Kafr el-Sheikh
Kafr el-Dauwâr
Damanhûr
El-Mansûra
Suez
Hôsh Isa
El-Mahalla el-Kubra
Români
El-Arîsh
Kafr el-Zaiyât
El-Simbillâwein
El-Qantara
Tanta
Zifta
Fâqûs
Nasr
Zagazig
Ismâilîya
Shibîn el-Kôm
Benha
Canal
Wâdi el-Arîsh
Bilbeis
Fâyid
Great Bitter L.
1094
Shubrâ el-Khayma
Shibîn el-Qanâtir
EGYPT
EL-GÎZA
EL-QÂHIRA (CAIRO)
Desert el-Tih
Pyramides
El-Suweis (Suez)
Nakhl
Saqqâra
Helwân
Eastern Desert
Gulf of Suez
El-Aiyat
Sudr
L. Qarun
El-Saff
Nile
Sinnûris
Sinai Pen.
Ibshawâî
El-Faiyûm
El-Wasta
98/99

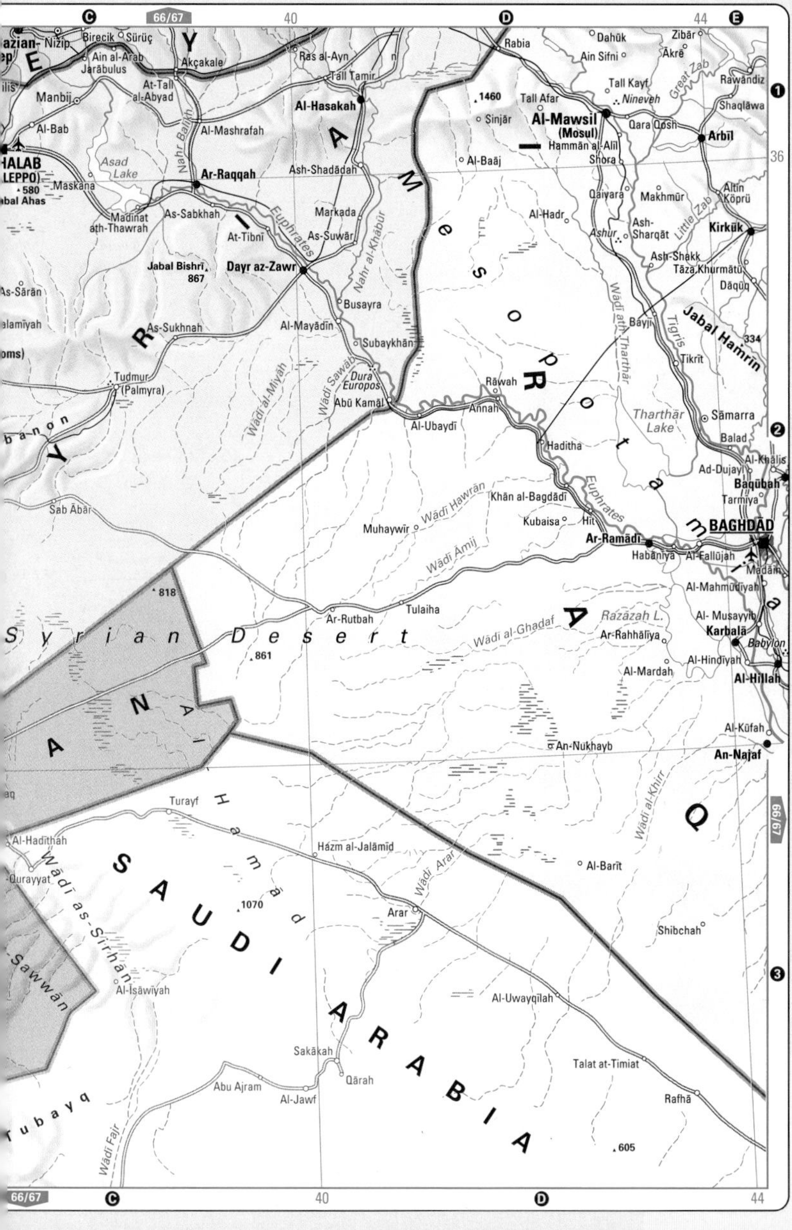
66/67
C
40
D
44
E
1
2
3
36
Birecik
Sürüç
Nizip
Ain al-Arab
Jarābulus
Akçakale
Ras al-Ayn
Tall Tamir
At-Tall al-Abyad
Manbij
Al-Bab
HALAB
(ALEPPO)
580
Jabal Ahas
Maskana
Asad Lake
Nahr Balikh
Al-Mashrafah
Al-Hasakah
Ar-Raqqah
Ash-Shadādah
Madinat ath-Thawrah
As-Sabkhah
Euphrates
Markada
As-Suwār
At-Tibnī
Jabal Bishrī
867
Dayr az-Zawr
Nahr al-Khābūr
Busayra
As-Sārān
Salamīyah
Homs)
As-Sukhnah
Al-Mayādīn
Subaykhān
Tudmur
(Palmyra)
Wādī al-Miyāh
Wādī Sawāb
Dura Europos
Abū Kamāl
Lebanon
Y
R
I
A
M
Rabia
Dahūk
Ain Sifni
Zibār
Ākrē
Great Zab
Rawāndiz
Tall Kayf
Nineveh
1460
Sinjār
Tall Afar
Al-Mawsil
(Mosul)
Hammān al-Alīl
Shora
Qara Qosh
Arbīl
Shaqlāwa
Al-Baāj
Qaiyara
Makhmūr
Altin Köprü
Al-Hadr
Ashur
Ash-Sharqāt
Little Zab
Kirkūk
Ash-Shakk
Tāza Khurmātū
Dāqūq
Wādī ath-Tharthār
Bayjī
Tigris
Jabal Hamrin
334
Tikrīt
Rāwah
Annah
Al-Ubaydī
Haditha
Tharthār Lake
Sāmarra
Balad
Al-Khālis
Ad-Dujayl
Baqūbah
Tarmiya
Khān al-Bagdādī
Wādī Hawrān
Muhaywīr
Kubaisa
Hit
Euphrates
Ar-Ramādī
BAGHDĀD
Habāniya
Al-Fallūjah
Madāin
Wādī Āmij
Al-Mahmūdiyah
Al-Musayyib
Karbalā
Babylon
Al-Hindīyah
Al-Hillah
Tulaiha
Ar-Rutbah
818
Syrian Desert
861
Wādī al-Ghadaf
Razāzah L.
Ar-Rahhālīya
Al-Mardah
Mesopotamia
IRAQ
Al-Kūfah
An-Najaf
An-Nukhayb
JORDAN
Turayf
Hamād
Hazm al-Jalāmīd
Wādī al-Khirr
Al-Barīt
Al-Hadīthah
Qurayyat
Wādī as-Sirhān
Wādī Arar
1070
Arar
Shibchah
Sawwān
Al-Īsāwīyah
SAUDI ARABIA
Al-Uwayqīlah
Sakākah
Qārah
Talat at-Timiat
Abu Ajram
Al-Jawf
Rafhā
Tubayq
Wādī Fajr
605

Sanandaj
Hamadān
TEHRĀN
Qom
Bākhtarān
Arāk
Borūjerd
Kāshān
Khorramābād
Dezfūl
ESFAHĀN
(ISFAHAN)
Zard Kūh
4548
Al-Amārah
An-Nāsirīyah
Masjed-e Soleymān
Ahvāz
Al-Basrah
Khorramshahr
Ābādān
Al-Kuwayt
(Kuwait)
As-Sālimīyah
KUWAIT
Mina Saud
Sabzevār
MASHHAD
Torbat-e Heydarīyeh
Great Salt Desert
Bīrjand
Yazd
I R A N
Kermān
Persepolis
SHĪRĀZ
Bandar-e Būshehr
Fasā
Sīrjān
Bam
Zāhedān
Kūh-e Taftān
4042
2457
Lār
Furgun
3280
Bandar-e Abbās
Al-Jubayl
Ad-Dammām
Dharan
Al-Manāmah
(Manama)
BAHRAIN
Bandar-e Langeh
Al-Hufūf
QATAR
Ad-Dawhah
(Doha)
(to Oman)
Dubai
Sharjah
Abu Dhabi
Str. of Hormuz
Haradh
Tropic of Cancer
UNITED ARAB EMIRATES
Suhār
Gulf of Oman
Masqat
(Muscat)
2980
Nizwa
Sūr
Ras al-Hadd
SAUDI ARABIA
Rub al-Khālī
OMAN
Masirah
Dhofar
1463
Salālah
Kuria Muria Is.
YEMEN
Hadhramaut
Al-Ghaydah
Gulf of Aden
Qādib
Socotra
C. Guardafui
SOMALIA
TURKMENISTAN
Gushgy
Mazār-e Sharīf
Kunduz
Tāloqān
Baghlān
Meymaneh
Qaleh-ye Now
Herāt
Hari Rud
Hindu Kush
5143
Kābul
Jalālābād
Asadābād
Gardēz
Ghaznī
Farāh
Helmand
Kalāt
Lashkar Gāh
Kandahār
Hāmūn-e Sāberī
AFGHANISTAN
Chaman
Quetta
Baluchistan
Kalāt
Īrānshahr
Zāboli
Gwādar
Bela
KARĀCHI
Jammu
7690
Chitrāl
Gilgit
Skardu
8126
Nanga Parbat
Islāmābād
Srinagar
Rawalpindi
Peshāwar
Jhelum
Jammu
Bannu
Sialkot
Dera Ismāīl Khān
Sargodha
Gujrāt
Faisalābād
LAHORE
Jhang
Sāhīwal
Multān
LUDHIANA
Dera Ghāzi Khān
Bahāwalpur
1264
Sutlej
Indus
Khānpur
158
Rahīmyār Khān
Sukkur
Lārkāna
Khairpur
Nawābshāh
Mīrpur Khās
Hyderābād
PAKISTAN
Thar Desert
Rājasthān
Bīkāner
Sīkar
Phalodi
Jodhpur
JAIPUR
Ajmer
Beāwar
Tonk
Bārmer
975
Kota
Pātan
Udaipur
Gāndhīnagar
Ratlām
Gujarāt
Bhuj
Kandla
AHMADĀBĀD
INDORE
Gulf of Kutch
Jāmnagar
Rājkot
Godhra
VADODARA
Kathiawar
Porbandar
Jūnāgadh
1117
Bharūch
Bhāvnagar
Bhusāwal
SŪRAT
Jalgaon
Diu
Daman
Daman and Diu
Dādra and Nagar Haveli
Silvassa
Nāshik
1646
KALYĀN
MUMBAI
(BOMBAY)
PUNE
Ahmadnagar
Sātāra
Western Ghats
Ratnāgiri
Sāngli
Solāpur
Kolhāpur
Belgaum
Goa
Panaji
Hubli-Dhārwād
Sāgar
Bhadrāvati
Mangalore
Karnataka
Amīndīvi Is.
Lakshadweep
Pond. Mahe
Kozhikode
Laccadive Islands
Kavaratti
Kochi
Alappuzha
Thiruvananthapuram
(Trivandrum)
Minicoy I.
MALDIVES
Malé
Arabian Sea
INDIAN
64/65
66/67
98/99

72/73
74/75
Kunlun Shan
Muztag Feng 7723
Hotan
Golmud
5730
Madoi
Linxia
5020
Baoji
Tianshui
Min Xian
Hanzhong
Wudu
Zoigê
Guangyuan
Ngoring Hu
Yellow River
Jialing Jiang
Tuotuoheyan
6800
Yangtze
Yalong Jiang
4720
Bazhong
CHINA
Tibet
Yushu
Mianyang
Nanchong
Suining
Indus
Kashmir
Nganglong Kangri 6596
Gêrzê
6300
6230
Nagqu
Garzê
CHENGDU
Gar
Qamdo
Hechuan
Neijiang
Himalaya
Kangrinboqê (Kailash) 6714
Salween
Mekong
Batang
Kangding
Ya'an
Leshan
Zigong
Yibin
Luzhou
7556
Gongga Shan
6355
7111
Nyainqêntanglha Shan
7755
Chandigarh
Shimla
Dehra Dūn
Sahāranpur
Paryang
Lhasa
Nyingchi
Jiunlian
Karnāl
Saga
Xigazê
Mustang
Brahmaputra
Zhongdian
Xichang
Zhaotong
Morādābād
Rāmpur
Dhaulagiri 8167
Gyangzê
Arunachal Pradesh
New Delhi
Bareilly
Pokhara
Mt. Everest 8848
Punakha
Tinsukia
Putao
4816
Lijiang
Panzhihua
Uttar Pradesh
Ganges
Shāhjahānpur
Sītāpur
NEPAL
Kathmandu
Gangtok
Sikkim
BHUTAN
Thimphu
Itānagar
Dibrugarh
Panxian
Aligarh
LUCKNOW
Faizābād
Biratnagar
Jorhāt
Jianchuan
Qujing
Xingyi
KANPUR
Gorakhpur
Darbhanga
Shiliguri
Guwāhāti
Tezpur
Nāgāland
Singkaling Hkamti
Dali
KUNMING
Gwalior
Jaunpur
Muzaffarpur
Katihār
Rangpur
Dispur
Assam
Shillong
Meghālaya
Kohima
Imphāl
Myitkyina
Chuxiong
Yiliang
Munger
Baoshan
Yuxi
Jhānsi
Allahābād
Ara
Patna
Bhāgalpur
Sylhet
Lincang
Shiping
Kaiyuan
Mirzapur
Vārānasi (Benares)
Gaya
Rajshāhi
Mymensingh
Manipur
Bhamo
Katha
Bihār
BANGLADESH
Tripura
Aizawl
Yuanjiang
Gejiu
Mengzi
Murwāra
INDIA
Baharampur
Dhanbād
Āsansol
DHAKA
Agartala
Kalemyo
Lashio
Simao
Lao Cai
Sāgar
Jabalpur
West Bengal
Comilla
Mizoram
Falam
Ye-u
Shwebo
3143
VIETNAM
Rānchi
Barddhamān
Phôngsali
Điên Biên
BHOPĀL
Jamshedpur
Khulna
Monywa
Mandalay
Shahdol
CHITTAGONG
Keng Tung
Madhya Pradesh
Raurkela
Kharagpur
CALCUTTA
Arakan Yoma
Myingyan
2604
Bilāspur
MYANMAR
Xam Nua
Cox's Bazar
Taunggyi
LAOS
Gondia
Raipur
Sambalpur
Bāleshwar
Mekong
Nāgpur
Bhilainagar
Loi-Kaw
Chiang Rai
Louangphrabang
Akola
Wardha
Orissa
Cuttack
Sittwe
Pyinmana
Phayao
Phou Bia
Bhubaneshwar
Kyaukpyu
Toungoo
Chiang Mai
Viangchan (Vientiane)
2817
Chandrapur
Puri
Ramree
Irrawaddy
Salween
Hot
Lampang
Nong Khai
Nānded
Jagdalpur
Brahmapur
Cheduba
Sandoway
Prome
Udon Thani
Tanen Range
2012
Phitsanulok
Nizāmābād
Devodi Munda
Henzada
Pegu
Thaton
Tak
Khon Kaen
Warangal
Godāvari
1680
Vizianagaram
Bassein
THAILAND
HYDERABAD
Visākhapatnam
YANGON (RANGOON)
Moulmein
Nakhon Sawan
Bua Yai
Eastern Ghats
Rājahmundry
Nakhon Ratchasima
Gulbarga
Yanam Pondicherry
G. of Martaban
Ye
Chao Phraya
Andhra Pradesh
Vijayawāda
C. Negrais
Krishna
Guntūr
Machilīpatnam
Bay of Bengal
KRUNG THEP (BANGKOK)
Sara Buri
Kurnool
Tavoy
Proddatūr
Phetchaburi
1679
Bellary
Nellore
Mergui
Chanthaburi
732
Andaman Sea
Mergui Archipelago
Chang
CHENNAI (MADRAS)
Prachuap Khiri Khan
Kolar
Andaman Islands
BANGALORE
Vellore
Gulf of Thailand
Port Blair
Mysore
Pondicherry Pondicherry
Salem
Tamil Nadu
Chumphon
Phangan
Samui
Kāraikāl Pondicherry
Thanjāvūr
Surat Thani
Tiruchchirāppalli
Palk Str.
Andaman and Nicobar Is.
Nakhon Si Thammarat
Madurai
Jaffna
Trang
Phuket
G. of Mannar
Trincomalee
Tuticorin
Katchall I.
Nicobar Islands
Hat Yai
Pattani
Anuradhapura
Kangar
Batticaloa
Kandy
Alor Setar
SRI LANKA
Negombo
2524
Pidurutalagala
Great Nicobar
George Town
MALAYSIA
Colombo
Sri Jayawardenepura
Sigli
Taiping
Bandaaceh
Ipoh
Galle
Ceylon
Langsa
Strait of Malacca
Dondra Head
Matara
INDONESIA
Sumatra
MEDAN
Meulaboh
Leuser 3404
OCEAN
G H J K L M N
80 85 90 95 100 105
30 25 20 15 10 5
2 3 4 5 6 7 8

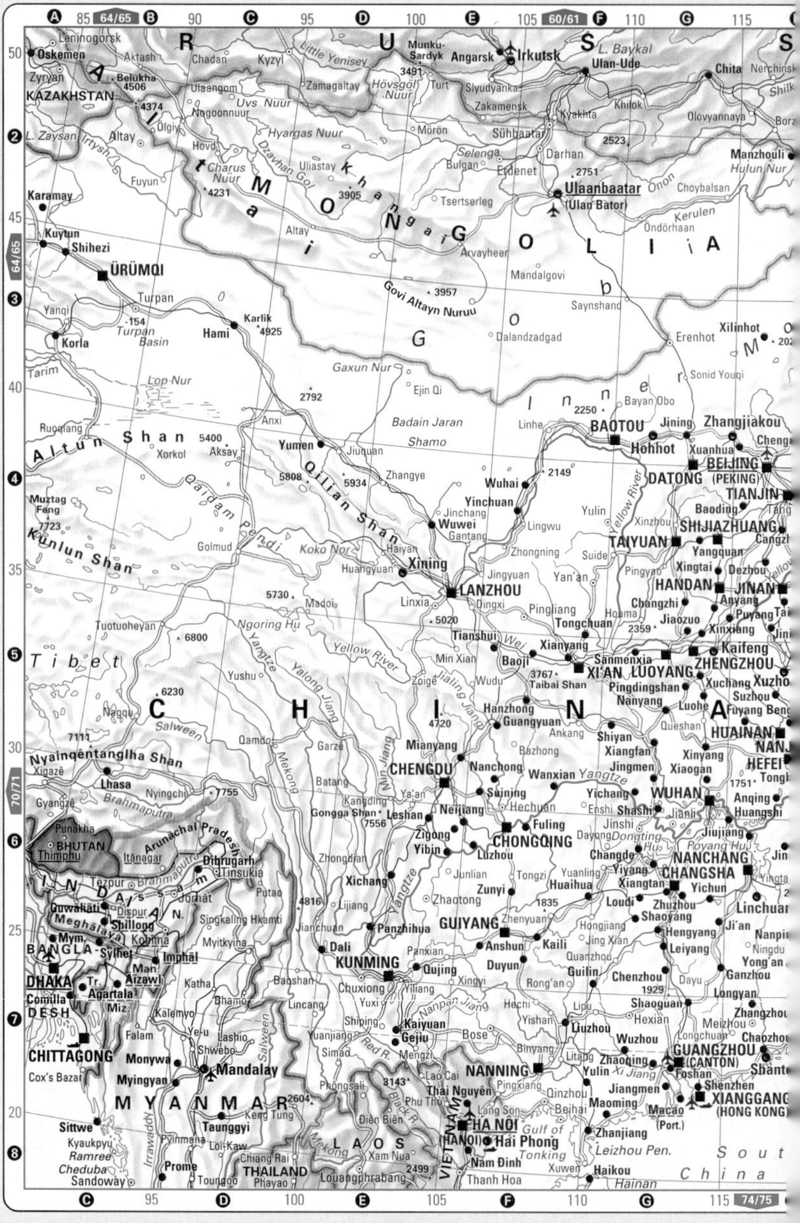

64/65
60/61
74/75
70/71
Leninogorsk
Öskemen
Zyryan
KAZAKHSTAN
Aktash
Belukha 4506
4374
L. Zaysan
Irtysh
Altay
Chadan
Kyzyl
Little Yenisey
Munku-Sardyk 3491
Angarsk
Irkutsk
L. Baykal
Ulan-Ude
Chita
Nerchinsk
Shilka
Ulaangom
Uvs Nuur
Nogoonnuur
Ölgiy
Hovd
Zamagaltay
Hövsgöl Nuur
Turt
Slyudyanka
Zakamensk
Kyakhta
Khilok
Olovyannaya
Hyargas Nuur
Mörön
Sühbaatar
2523
Manzhouli
Hulun Nur
Charus Nuur
Dzavhan Gol
Uliastay
Selenga
Bulgan
Erdenet
Darhan
2751
Fuyun
4231
3905
Tsertserleg
Ulaanbaatar
(Ulan Bator)
Onon
Choybalsan
Kerulen
Öndörhaan
Karamay
Kuytun
Shihezi
ÜRÜMQI
Altay
Arvayheer
MONGOLIA
Mandalgovi
Govi Altayn Nuruu
3957
Saynshand
Gobi
Turpan
Yanqi
-154
Turpan Basin
Hami
Karlik 4925
Korla
Dalandzadgad
Erenhot
Xilinhot
Tarim
Lop Nur
Gaxun Nur
Ejin Qi
Sonid Youqi
2792
Inner Mongolia
Bayan Obo
2250
Ruoqiang
Anxi
Badain Jaran Shamo
Linhe
BAOTOU
Jining
Zhangjiakou
Chengde
Altun Shan
5400
Xorkol
Aksay
Yumen
Jiuquan
Hohhot
Xuanhua
BEIJING
(PEKING)
5808
5934
Zhangye
Wuhai
2149
DATONG
TIANJIN
Qilian Shan
Qaidam Pendi
Muztag Feng 7723
Yinchuan
Jinchang
Wuwei
Gantang
Yulin
Lingwu
Yellow River
Xinzhou
Baoding
SHIJIAZHUANG
Cangzhou
Kunlun Shan
Golmud
Koko Nor
Haiyan
Xining
Huangyuan
Zhongning
Suide
TAIYUAN
Yangquan
Jingyuan
Yan'an
Pingyao
Xingtai
Dezhou
HANDAN
JINAN
5730
Madoi
LANZHOU
Linxia
Dingxi
Pingliang
Changzhi
Anyang
Houma
Tongchuan
2359
Jiaozuo
Puyang
Xinxiang
Tuotuoheyan
6800
Ngoring Hu
5020
Tianshui
Wei
Xianyang
Sanmenxia
Kaifeng
Tibet
Yellow River
Min Xian
Baoji
3767
Taibai Shan
XI'AN
LUOYANG
ZHENGZHOU
Yushu
Yangtze
Yalong Jiang
Zoigê
Jialing Jiang
Wudu
Pingdingshan
Xuchang
Xuzhou
6230
Nanyang
Suzhou
Nagqu
CHINA
4720
Hanzhong
Guangyuan
Ankang
Luohe
Fuyang
Bengbu
Salween
Queshan
HUAINAN
7111
Qamdo
Garzê
Mekong
Mianyang
Shiyan
Xiangfan
NANJING
Nyainqêntanglha Shan
Bazhong
Xinyang
HEFEI
Xigazê
CHENGDU
Nanchong
Jingmen
Xiaogan
Lhasa
Batang
Min Jiang
Wanxian
Yangtze
1751
Tongling
Nyingchi
7755
Ya'an
Suining
Yichang
WUHAN
Anqing
Brahmaputra
Kangding
Hechuan
Enshi
Shashi
Jianli
Huangshi
Gyangzê
Gongga Shan 7556
Leshan
Neijiang
Jinshi
Punakha
BHUTAN
Thimphu
Arunachal Pradesh
Zigong
CHONGQING
Fuling
Dongting Hu
Jiujiang
Yibin
Luzhou
Dayong
Changde
Poyang Hu
Itanagar
Zhongdian
Changde
NANCHANG
Dibrugarh
Tinsukia
Brahmaputra
Junlian
Tongzi
Yuanling
Yiyang
CHANGSHA
Yingtan
INDIA
Tezpur
Assam
Jorhat
Putao
Xichang
Huaihua
Xiangtan
Yichun
Zunyi
Guwahati
Dispur
Nagaland
Lijiang
Zhaotong
1835
Loudi
Zhuzhou
Linchuan
Meghalaya
Shillong
Kohima
Singkaling Hkamti
4816
Jianchuan
GUIYANG
Zhenyuan
Hongjiang
Shaoyang
Ji'an
Nanping
Mym.
Panzhihua
Kaili
Jing Xian
Hengyang
Ningdu
BANGLADESH
Sylhet
Imphal
Myitkyina
Dali
Panxian
Anshun
Leiyang
Yong'an
Manipur
Aizawl
KUNMING
Qujing
Duyun
Quanzhou
Guilin
Chenzhou
Ganzhou
DHAKA
Tr.
Agartala
Katha
Baoshan
Chuxiong
Yiliang
Xingyi
Rong'an
Dayu
Comilla
Miz.
Bhamo
Lincang
Yuxi
Nanpan Jiang
Hechi
Lipu
1929
Longyan
Kalemyo
Salween
Shiping
Kaiyuan
Yishan
Shaoguan
Hexian
Zhangzhou
Falam
Ye-u
Lashio
Yuanjiang
Gejiu
Bose
Liuzhou
Meizhou
Shwebo
Simao
Red R.
Mengzi
Wuzhou
Longchuan
Chaozhou
CHITTAGONG
Monywa
Mandalay
Binyang
GUANGZHOU
(CANTON)
Shantou
Cox's Bazar
Myingyan
Phongsali
3143
Lao Cai
NANNING
Litang
Zhaoqing
Foshan
Shenzhen
MYANMAR
2604
Black R.
Thai Nguyên
Pingxiang
Qinzhou
Yulin
Xi Jiang
Jiangmen
XIANGGANG
(HONG KONG)
Irrawaddy
Keng Tung
Phu Tho
Lang Son
Beihai
Maoming
Macao
(Port.)
Sittwe
Taunggyi
Điên Biên
HA NOI
(HANOI)
Gulf of Tonking
Kyaukpyu
Ramree
Pyinmana
Loi-Kaw
Mekong
LAOS
Hai Phong
Zhanjiang
Cheduba
Chiang Rai
Xam Nua
Nam Đinh
Leizhou Pen.
South China Sea
Sandoway
Prome
THAILAND
Toungoo
Phayao
Louangphrabang
2499
VIETNAM
Thanh Hoa
Xuwen
Haikou
Hainan

120
125
130
62/63
135
140
145
150
J
K
L
M
N
O
P
I
A
Sea of
Okhotsk
Sakhalin
Onekotan I.
Nogliki
De Kastri
Sofiysk
Selemdzha
Amur
Chegdomyn
2010
Komsomolsk
Aleksandrovsk-Sakhalinskiy
1530
Svobodnyy
Belogorsk
Yitulihe
Jagdaqi
Blagoveshchensk
Heihe
Zavitinsk
Birobidzhan
2077
Sovetskaya Gavan
Tatar Str.
Poronaysk
Makarov
Ilyinskiy
Sikhote Alin Range
Kuril Islands
Simushir I.
Urup I.
Yakeshi
Nenjiang
Wuyiling
Bei'an
Khabarovsk
Kholmsk
Yuzhno-Sakhalinsk
Korsakov
Gornozavodsk
Svetlaya
Great Khingan Range
Zalantun
Yichun
1047
Hegang
QIQIHAR
Hailun
Daqing
Tangyuan
Fujin
Bikin
C. Crillon
La Pérouse Strait
Wakkanai
Iturup I.
Kurilsk
Yirxie
1749
Anda
Suihua
Jiamusi
Shuangyashan
Ulanhot
Sungari
HARBIN
Jixi
Lesozavodsk
Hokkaido
Abashiri
Kunashir I.
Yuzhno-Kurilsk
Baicheng
Manchuria
L. Khanka
Spassk-Dalniy
Dalnegorsk
Rudnaya Pristan
Tongyu
Mudanjiang
Asahikawa
2290
Nemuro
CHANGCHUN
JILIN
Ussuriysk
1855
Otaru
Ebetsu
Kushiro
Kailu
Tongliao
Shuangliao
Vladivostok
SAPPORO
Obihiro
Siping
Yanji
Nakhodka
C. Povorotnyy
Okushiri
Muroran
C. Erimo
SHENYANG
Liaoyuan
Hakodate
Tsugaru Str.
Fuxin
FUSHUN
Baitou Shan 2744
Najin
Ch'ongjin
Aomori
Chaoyang
Tonghua
Hyesan
Sea of Japan
Benxi
Kanggye
Kimch'aek
Morioka
Akita
Chokai-san 2230
ANSHAN
Yingkou
Dandong
Huich'on
Sinuiju
Hamhung
Anju
NORTH KOREA
P'YONGYANG
Wonsan
Yamagata
Sendai
Namp'o
Sado
Fukushima
Kaesong
C.Suzu
Niigata
Aizu-Wakamatsu
DALIAN
Haeju
Ch'unch'on
Kangnung
SOUL (SEOUL)
Nagano
Utsunomiya
Yantai
Weihai
Ullung
Toyama
Mito
INCH'ON
Suwon
Ch'ungju
Kanazawa
Maebashi
Ch'onan
Oki Is.
Fukui
Chiba
Yellow
TAEJON
SOUTH KOREA
Gifu
TOKYO
TAEGU
Tottori
Mt. Fuji 3776
YOKOHAMA
QINGDAO
Kunsan
Ulsan
Matsue
KYOTO
Masan
NAGOYA
Honshu
KWANGJU
1915
KOBE
OSAKA
PUSAN
Okayama
Mokp'o
Sea
Lianyungang
Yosu
Shimonoseki
HIROSHIMA
Wakayama
Izu Islands
KITAKYUSHU
Tokushima
PACIFIC OCEAN
FUKUOKA
Uwajima
Kochi
C. Shiono
Cheju
Saga
1788
Oita
Shikoku
Yancheng
Cheju I.
Nagasaki
Kumamoto
Taizhou
Goto Is.
Kyushu
Nantong
Miyazaki
Wuxi
Kagoshima
Suzhou
SHANGHAI
C. Sata
East China Sea
Jiaxing
Osumi Is.
HANGZHOU
NINGBO
Ryukyu Islands
Bonin Is. (Jap.)
Ninghai
Jinhua
Naze
Lishui
Amami
Wenzhou
Fuding
Volcano Is. (Jap.)
498
Okinawa
Naha
Daito Is. (Jap.)
FUZHOU
Chilung
Miyako
Tropic of Cancer
T'AIPEI
Ishigaki
Iriomote
T'aichung
3952
TAIWAN
T'aitung
Taiwan
C. Garan
Okino Tori (Jap.)
Northern Mariana Islands (U.S.)
Mariana Is.
Batan Is.
Luzon Strait
45
40
35
30
25
20
2
3
4
5
6
7
8

A
B
C
D
E
F
95
100
105
110
115
72/73
70/71
2
3
4
5
6
7
8
15
10
5
0
5
10
MYANMAR
Kyaukpyu
Ramree
Cheduba
Sandoway
Pyinmana
Irrawaddy
Loi-Kaw
Toungoo
Prome
Henzada
Pegu
Bassein
Salween
YANGON
(RANGOON)
C. Negrais
Thaton
G. of
Martaban
Moulmein
Ye
Tavoy
Tan'en Range
Hot
2012
Chiang Rai
Phayao
Chiang Mai
Lampang
Mekong
Phitsanulok
Tak
Udon Thani
Nong Khai
THAILAND
Khon Kaen
Nakhon Sawan
Chao Phraya
Bua Yai
KRUNG THEP
(BANGKOK)
Sara Buri
Nakhon Ratchasima
Ubon Ratchathani
Phetchaburi
Mergui Archipelago
Mergui
Chanthaburi
Prachuap Khiri Khan
Gulf of Thailand
Chumphon
Phangan
Samui
Surat Thani
Nakhon Si Thammarat
Phuket
Trang
Hat Yai
Pattani
Kangar
Alor Setar
George Town
Pinang
Kota Baharu
Malay Peninsula
Taiping
Kuala Terengganu
Ipoh
Tahan
2187
Kuantan
KUALA LUMPUR
Kelang
Seremban
Melaka
Johor Baharu
Riau Arch.
SINGAPORE
SINGAPORE
Strait of Malacca
Xam Nua
HA NOI
(HANOI)
Louangphrabang
2499
Phou Bia
2817
Viangchan
(Vientiane)
Nakhon Phanom
LAOS
Khanthabouli
Pakxé
Phumi Sâmraông
Angkor
Siĕmréab
Bătdâmbâng
Tônlé Sap
Stoeng Trêng
1679
CAMBODIA
Krâchéh
1813
Pouthisăt
Chang
Phnum Penh
(Phnom Penh)
Kâmpôt
Kâmpóng Saôm
Long Xuyên
Rach Gia
Cân Thơ
My Tho
Tra Vinh
Ca Mau
C. Ca Mau
Côn Đao
HO CHI MINH CITY
(SAIGON)
Biên Hoa
Phan Thiêt
Cam Ranh
Nha Trang
Đa Lat
Buôn Ma Thuôt
Sông Câu
Quy Nhơn
Quang Ngai
Ngoc Linh
2598
Đă Nâng
Huê
Đông Hơi
Truong Son
Vinh
Thanh Hoa
Nam Đinh
Hai Phong
VIETNAM
Gulf of Tonking
Xuwen
Zhanjiang
Leizhou Pen.
CHINA
Haikou
Hainan
Dongfang
Wuzhi Shan
1867
Wanning
Sanya
Paracel Islands
(China)
South China Sea
Calamian
Puerto Princesa
Palawan
2085
C. Buliluyan
Balabac
Banggi
C. Sempang Mangayau
Kota Kinabalu
Kinabalu
4101
Labuan
Bandar Seri Begawan
BRUNEI
Miri
Sapulut
Tawan
Bintulu
Sibu
Kuching
Rajang
Iran Ra.
Tanjungredeb
2988
Borneo
(Kalimantan)
Samarinda
Balikpapan
Mahakam
Bukit Raya
2278
Nangapinoh
Sukadana
Muarateweh
Ketapang
Palangkaraya
Tanjung
Sampit
1892
Kotabaru
Banjarmasin
Cape Selatan
Laut
Makassar
Pontianak
Singkawang
MALAYSIA
Natuna Besar
Natuna Is.
Subi Besar
Anambas Is.
Tambelan Is.
INDIA
Andaman Islands
732
Andaman Sea
Katchall I.
Nicobar Islands
Bandaaceh
Sigli
Meulaboh
Langsa
Leuser
3404
MEDAN
Pematangsiantar
Simeulue
Banyak Is.
Toba L.
Rantauprapat
Sibolga
Nias
Sumatra
Pini
Tanahmasa
Batu Is.
Tanahbala
Pekanbaru
Bengkalis
Bukittinggi
Padang
Siberut
Muarasiberut
Solok
Rengat
Indragiri
Kelume
Lingga Arch.
Kerinci
3805
Jambi
Sipora
Pagai Utara
Pagai Selatan
Mentawai Is.
Barisan
Bangka
Pangkalpinang
Karimata Is.
Karimata Str.
Tanjungpandan
Belitung
Cape Sambar
PALEMBANG
Bengkulu
Tebingtinggi
Baturaja
Manna
Enggano
Krui
INDONESIA
Bandarlampung
C. Cina
813
Merak
Rakata (Krakatau)
C. Cangkuang
JAKARTA
Bogor
Cirebon
Sukabumi
BANDUNG
Tegal
Cilacap
3428
Peka-
longan
Karimunjawa Is.
Bawean
SEMARANG
Surakarta
Magelang
Yogyakarta
Madiun
Kediri
Malang
Semeru
3676
SURABAYA
Probolinggo
Madura
Sumenep
Banyuwangi
Bali
Denpasar
Java Sea
Java
Masalembo Besar
UJUNGPANDANG
Kangean Is.
Sabalana
Sumbawa
3726
Mataram
Lombok
Cocos (Keeling) Islands
(Austr.)
Christmas Island
(Austr.)
INDIAN OCEAN

G
125
H
130
J
135
K
140
L
145
M
Okino Tori (Jap.)
Batan Islands
Luzon Strait
Babuyan I.
Calayan
Babuyan Is.
Escarpada Point
Tuguegarao
Luzon
Ilagan
Mt. Pulog 2929
Bayombong
Baguio
Dagupan
Cabanatuan
Polillo Is.
San Fernando
MANILA
Lucena
Catanduanes
Naga
2462
Legaspi
Burias
Masbate
Calbayog
Tablas
Masbate
Samar
Roxas
Culion
Panay
Ormoc
Tacloban
Iloilo
Cadiz
Leyte
Dumaran
Bacolod
Cebu
Cebu
Dinagat
Bohol
Surigao
Bayawan
Tagbilaran
Negros
Butuan
Siquijor
Dipolog
Cagayan de Oro
Bislig
Iligan
DAVAO
Cotabato
Mindanao
2954
Mount Apo
Lamitan
Basilan
Jolo
Moro Gulf
Cape San Agustin
General Santos
Jolo
Tawitawi Group
PHILIPPINES
Philippine Sea
Agrihan
Pagan
Northern Mariana Is. (U. S.)
Mariana Is.
Anatahan
Saipan
Tinian
Rota
Guam (U. S.)
Agaña
PACIFIC OCEAN
Ulithi Atoll
Yap Is.
Fais
Colonia
MICRONESIA
Sorol
Ngulu Atoll
Caroline Islands
Ngcheangel
Babeldaob
Oreor (Koror)
PALAU
Pulo Anna
Talaud Is.
Karakelong
Tobi
Helen Reef
Sangihe
Sangir Is.
Celebes Sea
Morotai
C. Lelai
Equator
Manado
1635
Ternate
Halmahera
2913
Gorontalo
Kotamobagu
Waigeo
Gulf of Tomini
Togian Is.
Kasiruta
Molucca Sea
Sorong
Manokwari
Biak
Biak
D'Urville C.
2970
Yapen
Doberai Pen.
Jayapura
Vanimo
Luwuk
Peleng
Bacan
Salawati
Misool
Serui
Sarera Bay
Mamberamo
Poso
Mangole
Obi
Maniwori
Sanana
Sanana
Seram Sea
Taliabu
Nabire
Saroako
Namlea
Binaiya 3019
Fakfak
1490
Kaimana
Maoke Range
Malamala
2799
2736
Amahai
Seram
Enarotali
5030
Puncak Jaya
Oksibil
Rantekombola
Kendari
Ambon
Buru
Adi
PAPUA NEW GUINEA
Watampone
Wowoni
Bandanaira
Amamapare
Muna
Tual
Wokam
Kai Is.
Dobo
Kobroor
NEW GUINEA
INDONESIA
Kabaena
Buton
Banda Sea
Trangan
Aru Is.
Benteng
Damar Is.
Digul
Yamdena
Yos Sudarso
Tanahjampea
Fly
Wetar
Saumlaki
Babar
Tanimbar Is.
Alor
Huaki
Leti Is.
Selaru
Merauke
Dili
2400
Maumere
Tutuala
Flores
Endeh
Lomblen
2980
Ramelau
Timor
Arafura Sea
Kefamenanu
Savu Sea
1225
Cape Wessel
Kupang
Timor Sea
Croker I.
Wessel Is.
Sawu
Roti
Melville I.
Cape Arnhem
Bathurst I.
Darwin
AUSTRALIA
15
10
5
0
86/87
84/85

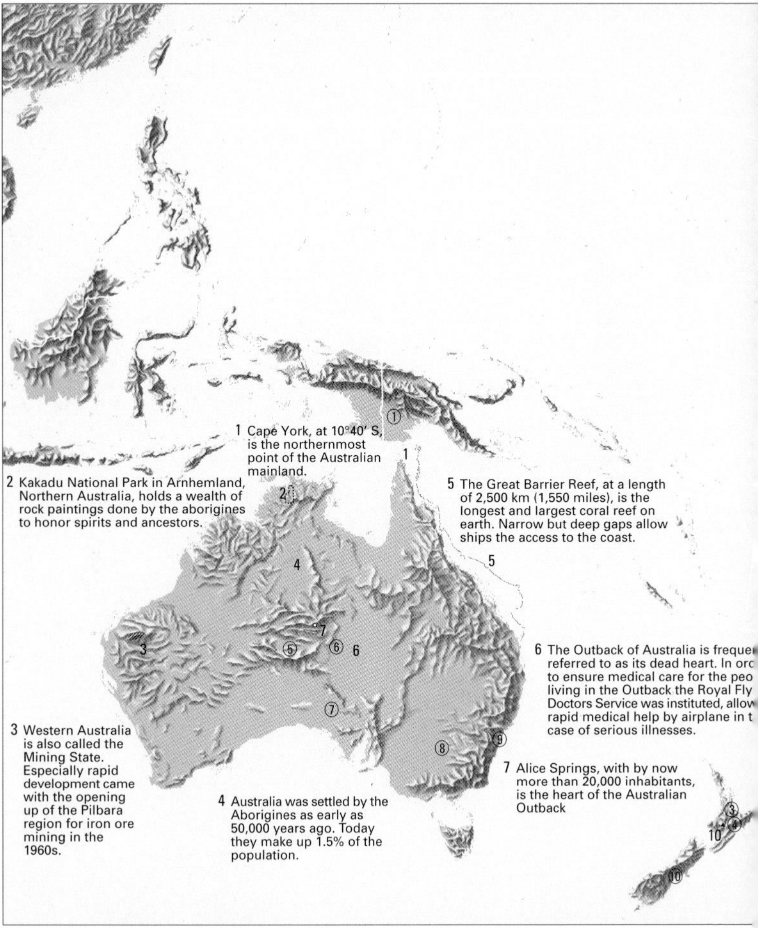
1 Cape York, at 10°40′ S, is the northernmost point of the Australian mainland.
2 Kakadu National Park in Arnhemland, Northern Australia, holds a wealth of rock paintings done by the aborigines to honor spirits and ancestors.
5 The Great Barrier Reef, at a length of 2,500 km (1,550 miles), is the longest and largest coral reef on earth. Narrow but deep gaps allow ships the access to the coast.
6 The Outback of Australia is freque referred to as its dead heart. In orc to ensure medical care for the peo living in the Outback the Royal Fly Doctors Service was instituted, allov rapid medical help by airplane in t case of serious illnesses.
3 Western Australia is also called the Mining State. Especially rapid development came with the opening up of the Pilbara region for iron ore mining in the 1960s.
4 Australia was settled by the Aborigines as early as 50,000 years ago. Today they make up 1.5% of the population.
7 Alice Springs, with by now more than 20,000 inhabitants, is the heart of the Australian Outback

⑤ Ayers Rock
(Rother, Schwäbisch Gmünd)

⑥ Central Australia
(Rother, Schwäbisch Gmünd)

⑦ Kangaroo
(Rother, Schwäbisch Gmünd)

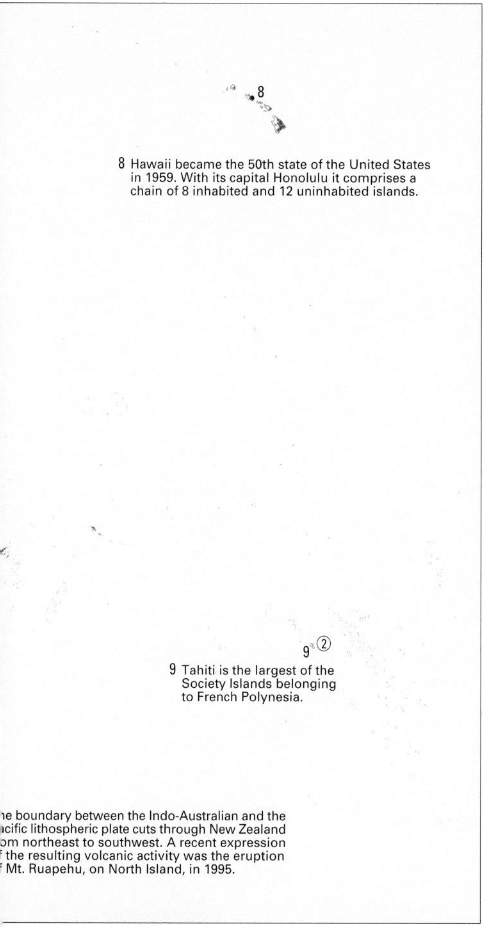

8 Hawaii became the 50th state of the United States in 1959. With its capital Honolulu it comprises a chain of 8 inhabited and 12 uninhabited islands.

9 Tahiti is the largest of the Society Islands belonging to French Polynesia.

ıe boundary between the Indo-Australian and the ıcific lithospheric plate cuts through New Zealand om northeast to southwest. A recent expression f the resulting volcanic activity was the eruption f Mt. Ruapehu, on North Island, in 1995.

① Rain Forest
(PhotoDisc)

② Tahiti
(Rother, Schwäbisch Gmünd)

③ Maori Marae, Rotorua
(Maresch, Rutesheim)

④ Weirakei Geothermal Field
(Maresch, Rutesheim)

Sheep Station
Rother, Schwäbisch Gmünd)

⑨ Sydney
(Rother, Schwäbisch Gmünd)

⑩ Canterbury Plain
(Rother, Schwäbisch Gmünd)

CHINA
FUZHOU
TAIPEI
Naha
Ryukyu Is.
JAPAN
Daito Is. (Jap.)
Bonin Is.
Volcano Is.
(Jap.)
Marcus I. (Jap.)
Xi Jiang
Shantou
Taiwan Str.
TAIWAN
CANTON
HONG KONG
Macao (Port.)
Okino Tori (Jap.)
Northern Mariana Is. (U.S.)
Hainan
Philippine Sea
Luzon
Paracel Is. (China)
Saipan
MANILA
Agaña
Guam (U.S.)
Micronesia
Polynesia
MARS
Enew Atc
PHILIPPINES
Mindoro
Samar
South China Sea
Panay
Cebu
Palawan
Yap Is.
Negros
Palau Is.
Koror
Weno
Chuuk Is.
Pohnpei
Palikir
Sulu Sea
Zamboanga
Davao
Mindanao
PALAU
Caroline Is.
Kosra
Bandar Seri Begawan
BRUNEI
MALAYSIA
Sulu Arch.
MICRONESIA
Sangir Is.
Melanesia
Manado
Molucca Sea
Halmahera
Biak
Borneo
Samarinda
Makassar Str.
Moluccas
Jayapura
Admiralty Is.
Bismarck Arch.
Rabaul
New Ireland
(Kalimantan)
Celebes (Sulawesi)
Seram
Ambon
Buru
New Guinea (Irian)
Sepik
Banjarmasin
INDONESIA
PAPUA NEW GUINEA
New Britain
Bougainville I.
Choiseul
SOLO
Kai Is.
Aru Is.
Lae
UJUNGPANDANG
Banda Sea
Solomon Sea
Santa
Java Sea
Tanimbar Is.
Fly
Port Moresby
Solomon Is.
Honiara
Ma
SEMARANG
Madura
SURABAYA
Lesser Sunda Is.
Yos Sudarso
Arafura Sea
Guadalcanal
Dili
Timor
Flores
Torres Str.
C. York
Java
Bali
Denpasar
Sumba
Melville I.
Louisiade Arch.
Ashmore (Austr.)
Cartier
Darwin
C. Arnhem
Timor Sea
Gulf of Carpentaria
Cape York Pen.
Coral Sea
Es
Cairns
Coral Sea Is. (Austr.)
Derby
Fitzroy
Flinders
Townsville
Chesterfield Is.
Mount Isa
Mackay
New Caled
Port Hedland
Rockhampton
North West Cape
Alice Springs
Fraser I.
AUSTRALIA
Cooper
BRISBANE
Gold Coast
Carnarvon
INDIAN OCEAN
Lord Howe I. (Austr.)
Broken Hill
Darling
Geraldton
Ceduna
Port Augusta
Newcastle
SYDNEY
Wollongong
Great Australian Bight
Murray
PERTH
ADELAIDE
Canberra
Kangaroo I.
Cape Leeuwin
Albany
Geelong
MELBOURNE
Tasman
King I.
Bass Str.
Tasmania
Hobart
South East Cape
Stewart
South West Cap
Au
110 120 130 150 160
100 110 120 130 140 150 160
20 10 0 10 20 30 40
A B C D E F G
1 2 3 4 5 6 7 8

0 500 1000 1500 2000 km
0 500 1000 miles

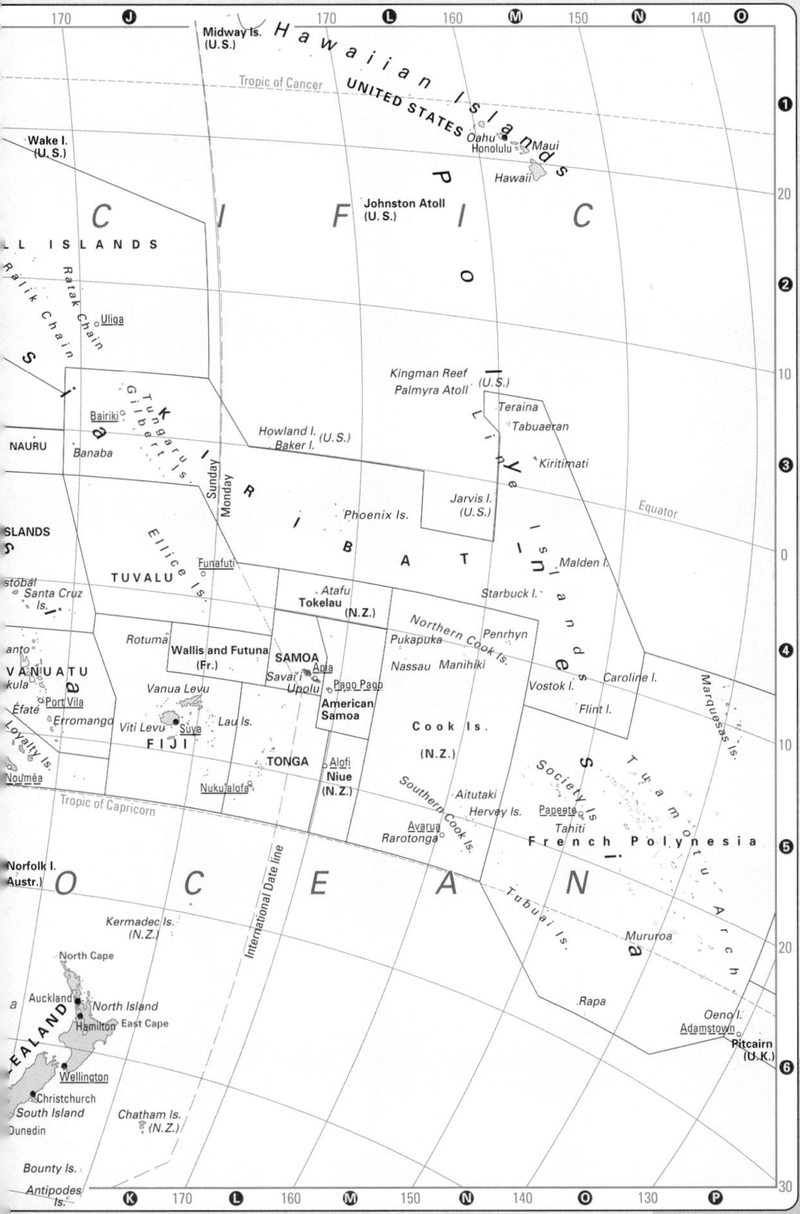

Midway Is. (U.S.)
Hawaiian Islands
Tropic of Cancer
UNITED STATES
Oahu
Honolulu
Maui
Hawaii
Wake I. (U.S.)
Johnston Atoll (U.S.)
PACIFIC OCEAN
MARSHALL ISLANDS
Ralik Chain
Ratak Chain
Uliga
Kingman Reef
Palmyra Atoll (U.S.)
Teraina
Tabuaeran
Kiritimati
Line Islands
Bairiki
Tungaru
Gilbert Is.
KIRIBATI
Howland I.
Baker I. (U.S.)
NAURU
Banaba
Sunday
Monday
Jarvis I. (U.S.)
Phoenix Is.
Equator
SOLOMON ISLANDS
Ellice Is.
Funafuti
TUVALU
Malden I.
Starbuck I.
Santa Cruz Is.
Atafu
Tokelau (N.Z.)
Northern Cook Is.
Penrhyn
Pukapuka
Nassau
Manihiki
Rotuma
Wallis and Futuna (Fr.)
SAMOA
Apia
Savai'i
Upolu
Pago Pago
American Samoa
VANUATU
Port Vila
Éfaté
Erromango
Vanua Levu
Viti Levu
Suva
FIJI
Lau Is.
Vostok I.
Caroline I.
Flint I.
Marquesas Is.
Loyalty Is.
Nouméa
TONGA
Nuku'alofa
Alofi
Niue (N.Z.)
Cook Is. (N.Z.)
Society Is.
Tuamotu Archipelago
Southern Cook Is.
Aitutaki
Hervey Is.
Papeete
Tahiti
Avarua
Rarotonga
French Polynesia
Tropic of Capricorn
Norfolk I. (Austr.)
International Date line
Tubuai Is.
Kermadec Is. (N.Z.)
Mururoa
North Cape
Auckland
North Island
Hamilton
East Cape
NEW ZEALAND
Wellington
Christchurch
South Island
Dunedin
Chatham Is. (N.Z.)
Bounty Is.
Antipodes Is.
Rapa
Oeno I.
Adamstown
Pitcairn (U.K.)

FUZHOU
Naha
TAIPEI
Ryukyu Is.
Daito Is.
Bonin Is.
Volcano Is.
Marcus I.
Shantou
Xi Jiang
CANTON
HONG KONG
Macao
Taiwan Str.
3952
Taiwan
Okino Tori
Mariana Is.
Hainan
1879
South China Sea
Philippine Sea
Luzon
2929
Philippines
Saipan
Paracel Is.
MANILA
Guam
Micronesia
5559
Mindoro
Challenger Deep
11022
Enewetak Atoll
Samar
Panay
Cebu
10497
Palawan
Negros
Yap Is.
Palau Is.
Sulu Sea
Zamboanga
Mt. Apo
2954
Davao
Mindanao
Chuuk Is.
Pohnpei
Caroline Is.
Kinabalu
4101
Bandar Seri Begawan
Sulu Arch.
Kosrae
Sangir Is.
Melanesia
Manado
Molucca Sea
Halmahera
2988
Makassar Str.
Biak
Admiralty Is.
Borneo
2278
Samarinda
3311
Jayapura
(Kalimantan)
Moluccas
Bismarck Arch.
Rabaul
New Ireland
Celebes
(Sulawesi)
Seram
New Guinea
Maoke Range
Sepik
Banjarmasin
Buru
Ambon
Puncak Jaya
5030
(Irian Jaya)
Mt. Wilhelm
4509
3455
Butung
2685
Bougainville I.
Kai Is.
Aru Is.
New Britain
9140
Choiseul
UJUNGPANDANG
Banda Sea
Lae
Solomon Sea
Santa Isabel
Java Sea
Tanimbar Is.
Mt. Victoria
4073
Solomon Is.
Malaita
SEMARANG
Madura
Lesser Sunda Is.
Yos Sudarso
Fly
Port Moresby
SURABAYA
2851
Arafura Sea
Guadalcanal
2331
San C
Semeru
3726
Flores
Timor
Torres Str.
C. York
Java
3676
Bali
Denpasar
Kupang
Melville I.
Louisiade Arch.
Sumba
C. Arnhem
Darwin
Arnhem Land
Gulf of Carpentaria
Cape York Pen.
Timor Sea
Great Barrier Reef
Coral Sea
Espírit
Cairns
1622
Derby
Fitzroy
Flinders
Townsville
Chesterfield Is.
Mount Isa
Mackay
1628
Port Hedland
Great Dividing Range
Rockhampton
New Caledoni
North West Cape
1611
Macdonnell Ra.
Alice Springs
Fraser I.
1251
Ayers Rock
860
Cooper
Australia
BRISBANE
1515
Gold Coast
Carnarvon
L. Eyre
-12
Gt. Victoria Desert
1615
Broken Hill
1189
Darling
Lord Howe I.
Nullarbor Plain
Geraldton
Port Augusta
Ceduna
Newcastle
Great Australian Bight
SYDNEY
PERTH
ADELAIDE
Murray
Canberra
Wollongong
Mt. Kosciusko
2228
Austral Alps
Kangaroo I.
Cape Leeuwin
Albany
Geelong
MELBOURNE
Tasman Sea
INDIAN OCEAN
5671
King I.
Bass Str.
5267
1617
Tasmania
Hobart
South East Cape
Stewart I.
South West Cape
Auckla

Hawaiian Islands
Midway Is.
7686
Tropic of Cancer
Wake I.
Oahu
Honolulu
Maui
Mauna Kea
4205
Hawaii
Johnston Atoll
PACIFIC OCEAN
Bikini Atoll
Ralik Chain
Ratak Chain
Marshall Islands
Majuro Atoll
6325
Kingman Reef
Palmyra Atoll
Teraina
Tabuaeran
Line Islands
Kiritimati
Jarvis I.
Gilbert Is.
Banaba
Howland I.
Baker I.
Sunday
Monday
Kanton
7316
Phoenix Is.
Equator
Ellice Is.
Malden I.
Funafuti Atoll
Atafu
Tokelau Is.
Starbuck I.
Santa Cruz Is.
Northern Cook Is.
Penrhyn
Pukapuka
Rotuma
Wallis Is.
Futuna
1858
Samoa Is.
Savai'i
Upolu
Tutuila
Nassau
Manihiki
Vostok I.
Caroline I.
Marquesas Is.
New Hebrides
Vanua Levu
Fiji Is.
Viti Levu
Suva
Lau Is.
Suwarrow
Flint I.
Erromango
Éfate
Loyalty Is.
Nouméa
Tonga Is.
Niue
Southern Cook Is.
Aitutaki
Hervey Is.
Society Is.
Papeete
2241
Tahiti
Tuamotu Archipelago
Tropic of Capricorn
5303
10882
Rarotonga
Norfolk I.
International Date line
6041
Tubuai Is.
Kermadec Is.
Mururoa
North Cape
10047
Auckland
North Island
Hamilton
East Cape
New Zealand
Mt. Ruapehu
2797
1088
Rapa
Oeno I.
Pitcairn I.
Wellington
Christchurch
South Island
Chatham Is.
Maria Theresa Reef
Dunedin
Bounty Is.
Antipodes Is.
Height of Land
4000 m (13124 ft.)
2000 m (6562 ft.)
1000 m (3281 ft.)
500 m (1640 ft.)
200 m (656 ft.)
0 m (0 ft.)
Depression
Depth of Sea
200 m (656 ft.)
2000 m (6562 ft.)
4000 m (13124 ft.)
6000 m (19686 ft.)
8000 m (26248 ft.)
Reef

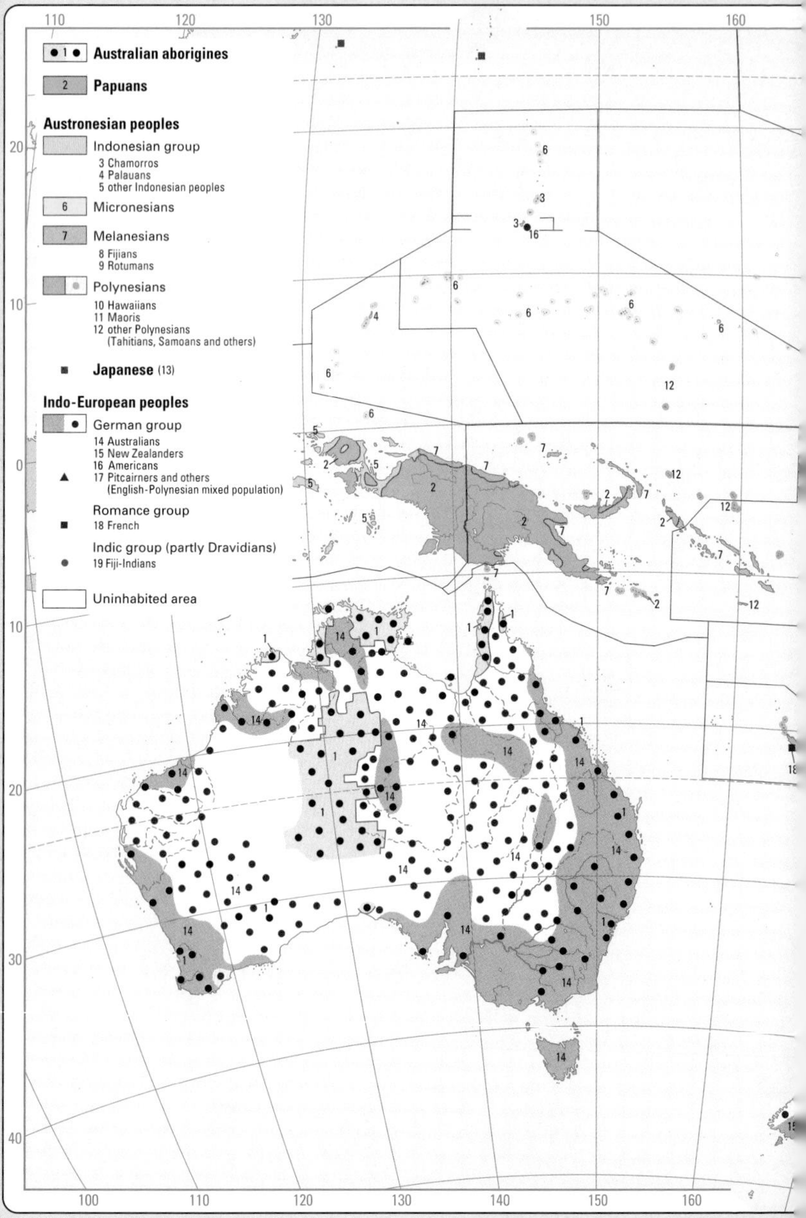

Australian aborigines
Papuans
Austronesian peoples
Indonesian group
3 Chamorros
4 Palauans
5 other Indonesian peoples
Micronesians
Melanesians
8 Fijians
9 Rotumans
Polynesians
10 Hawaiians
11 Maoris
12 other Polynesians (Tahitians, Samoans and others)
Japanese (13)
Indo-European peoples
German group
14 Australians
15 New Zealanders
16 Americans
17 Pitcairners and others (English-Polynesian mixed population)
Romance group
18 French
Indic group (partly Dravidians)
19 Fiji-Indians
Uninhabited area

1 : 55 000 000

0 500 1000 1500 2000 km
0 500 1000 miles
Tropic of Cancer
Equator
Tropic of Capricorn
170
160
150
140
130
20
10
0
30
16
13
10
6
12
9
7
8
19
18
17
15
11

74/75
INDONESIA
Sumba
Sawu
Roti
Timor
Kupang
Ashmore, Cartier (Austr.)
Ashmore Reef
Timor Sea
Melville I.
Bathurst I.
Darwin
366
Cape Londonderry
Joseph Bonaparte Gulf
Pine Creek
Katherine
Victoria
Wyndham
Cape Lévêque
Kimberley
Mount Wells
970
Derby
Halls Creek
Broome
Fitzroy
Wave
No
Tanami
Port Hedland
Great Sandy Desert
Dampier
Marble Bar
Yuendumu
Barrow Island
Roebourne
Lake Mackay
Onslow
Macdonnell
North West Cape
Western
Te
Hamersley Range
1251
Ashburton
Newman
Gibson Desert
Tropic of Capricorn
AUST
Ayers Rock (Uluru)
867
Musgrave
1440
Carnarvon
Gascoyne
Lake Carnegie
Cape Inscription
Denham
Wiluna
661
Meekatharra
Murchison
Australia
Mount Magnet
Laverton
Mullewa
Lake Barlee
Leonara
Great Victoria Desert
Geraldton
Dongara
Menzies
Nullarbor Plain
Lake Moore
Coolgardie
Kalgoorlie
Rawlinna
Cook
Moora
Eucla
PERTH
Meeredin
Northam
Norseman
Great Australian Bight
Narrogin
Collie
Bunbury
Esperance
Katanning
1110
Augusta
Cranbrook
Cape Leeuwin
Albany
INDIAN OCEAN
110
115
120
125
130
105
10
15
20
25
30
35
40

86/87
New Guinea
PAPUA NEW GUINEA
Woodlark I.
Esa'ala
D'Entrecasteaux Is.
Abau
Alotau
Samarai
Louisiade Arch.
Wessel Islands
Cape Wessel
Prince of Wales I.
Moa
Cape York
Bamaga
Cape York Pen.
Jabiru
Cape Arnhem
Gulf of Carpentaria
Groote Eylandt
Coen
Coral Sea Islands
(Austr.)
Coral Sea
Larrimah
Daly Waters
Wellesley Islands
Cooktown
Mossman
Mareeba
Cairns
Bartle Frere 1622
Innisfail
Normanton
Croydon
Burketown
Forsayth
Ingham
Townsville
Bowen
Camooweal
Kajabbi
Charters Towers
Mount Isa
Cloncurry
Richmond
Hughenden
Dajarra
1259
Mackay
Flinders
Great Dividing Range
Queensland
Winton
Georgina
Diamantina
Alice Springs
Clermont
Longreach
Barcaldine
232
Rockhampton
Blackall
Emerald
Gladstone
Kulgera Roadhouse
Yaraka
Windorah
Tambo
Theodore
Bundaberg
Sandy Cape
Monto
Birdsville
Great Artesian Basin
Injune
Fraser I.
Charleville
Quilpie
Gayndah
Maryborough
Gympie
Roma
Miles
Oodnadatta
Cooper Creek
Innamincka
Thargomindah
Murgon
1143
Nambour
Dalby
Toowoomba
BRISBANE
Cunnamulla
Warrego
Dirranbandi
Goondiwindi
Warwick
Gold Coast
Lake Eyre -12
Marree
83
Milparinka
Lismore
Moree
Leigh Creek
34
Walgett
Kingoonya
Lake Torrens
Lake Frome
Bourke
Grafton
Narrabri
Armidale
Lake Gairdner
Ceduna
Broken Hill
New South Wales
Coonamble
1608
Port Augusta
Cobar
Nyngan
Tamworth
Darling
Whyalla
Peterborough
Ivanhoe
Dubbo
Kimba
Port Pirie
Spencer Gulf
Wallaroo
Parkes
Taree
Lord Howe I.
Mount Hope
Renmark
Wentworth
Mildura
Orange
Cessnock
Lithgow
Newcastle
Port Lincoln
ADELAIDE
Balranald
Griffith
Katoomba
1402
Murray
Narrandera
Wagga Wagga
SYDNEY
Victor Harbour
Murray Bridge
Goulburn
Wollongong
Kangaroo Island
Kingscote
Swan Hill
Canberra
Albury
Australian Alps
Shepparton
Horsham
Mt. Kosciusko 2228
Bendigo
Wangaratta
Naracoorte
Bega
Victoria
Hamilton
Bombala
Mount Gambier
MELBOURNE
Ballarat
Orbost
Cape Howe
Portland
Geelong
Bairnsdale
Warrnambool
Moe
Wonthaggi
PACIFIC OCEAN
King Island
Bass Strait
Tasman Sea
Currie
Furneaux Is.
Cape Grim
Stanley
Devonport
Burnie
Mt. Ossa 1617
Launceston
Queenstown
Tasmania
Hobart
South East Cape

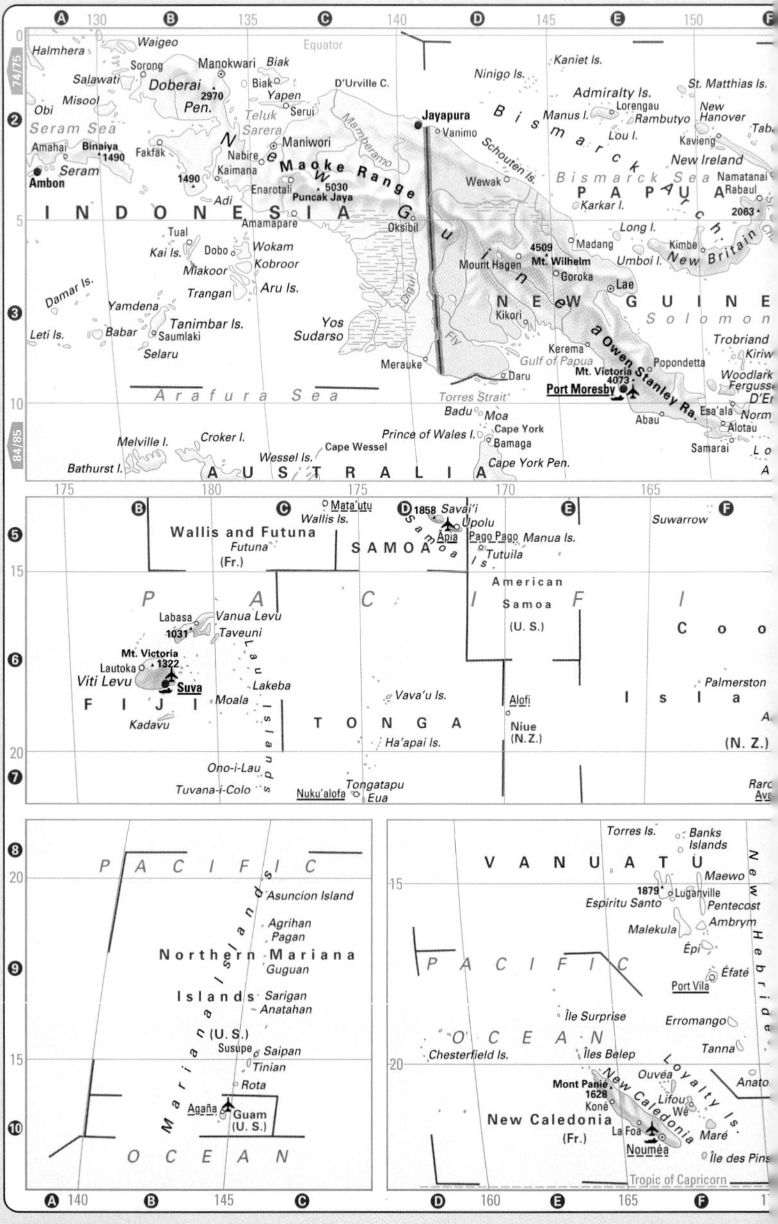

74/75
84/85
Equator
Halmhera
Waigeo
Sorong
Manokwari
Biak
Salawati
Doberai
2970
Pen.
Misool
Obi
Yapen
Serui
D'Urville C.
Seram Sea
Teluk
Sarera
Amahai
Binaiya
1490
Fakfak
Nabire
Maniwori
Seram
Ambon
1490
Kaimana
Maoke Range
Enarotali
5030
Puncak Jaya
Adi
Mamberamo
Jayapura
Vanimo
Schouten Is.
Ninigo Is.
Kaniet Is.
Admiralty Is.
Lorengau
Manus I.
Rambutyo
Lou I.
St. Matthias Is.
New Hanover
Kavieng
New Ireland
Bismarck Sea
Bismarck Arch.
Namatanai
Rabaul
Wewak
PAPUA
Karkar I.
2063
INDONESIA
New Guinea
Amamapare
Oksibil
Tual
Kai Is.
Dobo
Wokam
Kobroor
Miakoor
Aru Is.
Trangan
Damar Is.
Yamdena
Tanimbar Is.
Leti Is.
Babar
Saumlaki
Selaru
Yos Sudarso
Digul
Fly
Long I.
Madang
4509
Mt. Wilhelm
Mount Hagen
Goroka
Kimbe
Umboi I.
New Britain
Lae
NEW GUINEA
Solomon
Kikori
Trobriand
Kerema
Gulf of Papua
Popondetta
Owen Stanley Ra.
Mt. Victoria
4073
Port Moresby
Merauke
Daru
Torres Strait
Woodlark
Fergusson
D'Entrecasteaux
Esa'ala
Normanby
Arafura Sea
Badu
Moa
Cape York
Bamaga
Prince of Wales I.
Abau
Alotau
Samarai
Melville I.
Croker I.
Cape Wessel
Wessel Is.
Bathurst I.
Cape York Pen.
AUSTRALIA
Mata'utu
Wallis Is.
Wallis and Futuna
Futuna
(Fr.)
1858
Savai'i
Upolu
Apia
Samoa Is.
SAMOA
Pago Pago
Tutuila
Manua Is.
Suwarrow
American Samoa
(U. S.)
PACIFIC
Labasa
Vanua Levu
1031
Taveuni
Mt. Victoria
1322
Lautoka
Viti Levu
Suva
Lau Islands
Lakeba
Moala
FIJI
Kadavu
Vava'u Is.
TONGA
Ha'apai Is.
Alofi
Niue
(N.Z.)
Palmerston
Cook Islands
(N. Z.)
Ono-i-Lau
Tuvana-i-Colo
Nuku'alofa
Tongatapu
Eua
PACIFIC OCEAN
Asuncion Island
Agrihan
Pagan
Northern Mariana Islands
(U. S.)
Guguan
Sarigan
Anatahan
Mariana Islands
Susupe
Saipan
Tinian
Rota
Agaña
Guam
(U. S.)
Torres Is.
Banks Islands
VANUATU
Maewo
1879
Luganville
Espiritu Santo
Pentecost
Ambrym
Malekula
Épi
Éfaté
Port Vila
New Hebrides
PACIFIC OCEAN
Île Surprise
Erromango
Tanna
Chesterfield Is.
Îles Belep
Loyalty Is.
Ouvéa
Mont Panié
1628
Koné
New Caledonia
Lifou
Wé
Anatom
New Caledonia
(Fr.)
La Foa
Nouméa
Maré
Île des Pins
Tropic of Capricorn

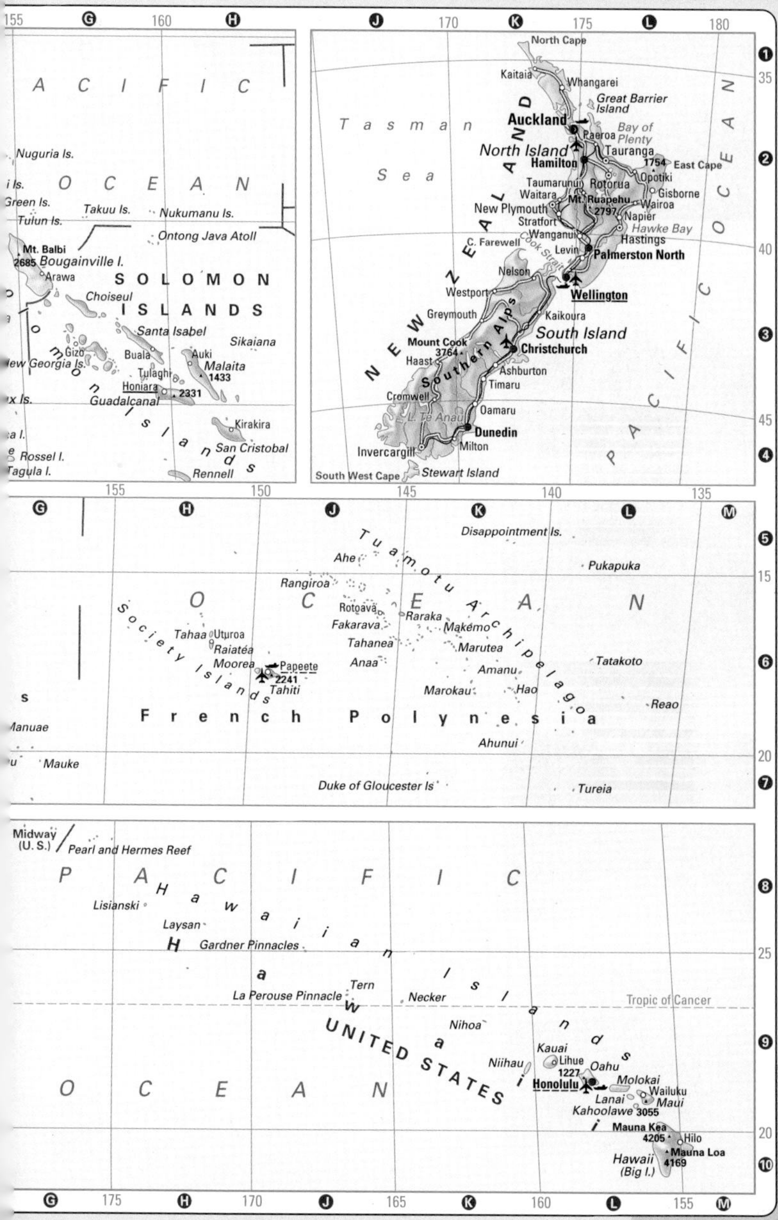
North Cape
Kaitaia
Whangarei
Great Barrier Island
Auckland
Paeroa
Bay of Plenty
North Island
Hamilton
Tauranga
1754
East Cape
Opotiki
Taumarunui
Rotorua
Waitara
Mt. Ruapehu
2797
Gisborne
New Plymouth
Wairoa
Napier
Stratfort
Hawke Bay
Wanganui
Hastings
C. Farewell
Cook Strait
Levin
Palmerston North
Nelson
Westport
Wellington
Greymouth
Kaikoura
South Island
Mount Cook
3764
Christchurch
Haast
Southern Alps
Ashburton
Timaru
Cromwell
Oamaru
L. Te Anau
Dunedin
Invercargill
Milton
South West Cape
Stewart Island
NEW ZEALAND
Tasman Sea
PACIFIC OCEAN
Nuguria Is.
Green Is.
Takuu Is.
Nukumanu Is.
Tulun Is.
Ontong Java Atoll
Mt. Balbi
2685
Bougainville I.
Arawa
SOLOMON ISLANDS
Choiseul
Santa Isabel
Sikaiana
Gizo
Buala
Auki
New Georgia Is.
Malaita
1433
Tulaghi
Honiara
2331
Guadalcanal
Kirakira
San Cristobal
Rossel I.
Tagula I.
Rennell
Solomon Islands
Disappointment Is.
Tuamotu Archipelago
Ahe
Pukapuka
Rangiroa
OCEAN
Society Islands
Rotoava
Raraka
Fakarava
Makemo
Tahaa
Uturoa
Raiatea
Tahanea
Marutea
Moorea
Papeete
Anaa
Tatakoto
Amanu
2241
Tahiti
Marokau
Hao
Reao
French Polynesia
Manuae
Ahunui
Mauke
Duke of Gloucester Is
Tureia
Midway (U. S.)
Pearl and Hermes Reef
PACIFIC OCEAN
Hawaiian Islands
Lisianski
Laysan
Gardner Pinnacles
Tern
La Perouse Pinnacle
Necker
Tropic of Cancer
Nihoa
UNITED STATES
Kauai
Niihau
Lihue
1227
Oahu
Molokai
Honolulu
Wailuku
Lanai
Maui
Kahoolawe
3055
Mauna Kea
4205
Hilo
Mauna Loa
4169
Hawaii (Big I.)

① Tinerhir Oasis, Morocco
(Hokenmaier, Wäschenbeuren)

② Ahaggar
(Geiger, Sonthofen)

③ Thornbush Savanna
(Rother, Tübingen)

④ Tropical Rain Forest
(Rother, Schwäbisch Gmünd)

⑤ Namib Desert
(Rother, Tübingen)

1 Cape Verde, at 17°30′ W, is the westernmost point of the African continent.

2 The Sahara is the largest desert of the world and the best known by name. It covers about one quarter of the African continent. Hyperarid today and several times in the past, it was a more humid region dominated by lakes and swamps between at least about 10,000 and 7,000 years ago, and the realm of Neolithic cattlemen until about 4,000 years ago.

3 The transition zone between the Saharan Desert and the savannas to the south is called Sahel, Arabic for shore. Extended periods of below-average rainfalls in combination with man-induced over-use of the land have led to desertification and repeated drought catastrophies in our century.

4 Lake Victoria, shared by Uganda, Kenya and Tanzania, covers an area of 69,484 km² (26,828 sq. miles), making it the largest lake on the African continent. In contrast to the long, narrow and deep rift valley lakes of East Africa its average depth is a mere 40 m (131 ft.).

5 At the Victoria Falls the waters of the Zambezi River plunge down 110 m (360 ft.) with a deafening noise, creating one of the grandest natural spectacles of the earth.

6 South of Cape Town the Cape of Good Hope rises as a promontory 620 m (2,034 ft.) high. The southernmost point of Africa, however, is Cape Agulhas (Needle Cape), at 34°50′ S, about 150 km (90 miles) east of the Cape of Good Hope.

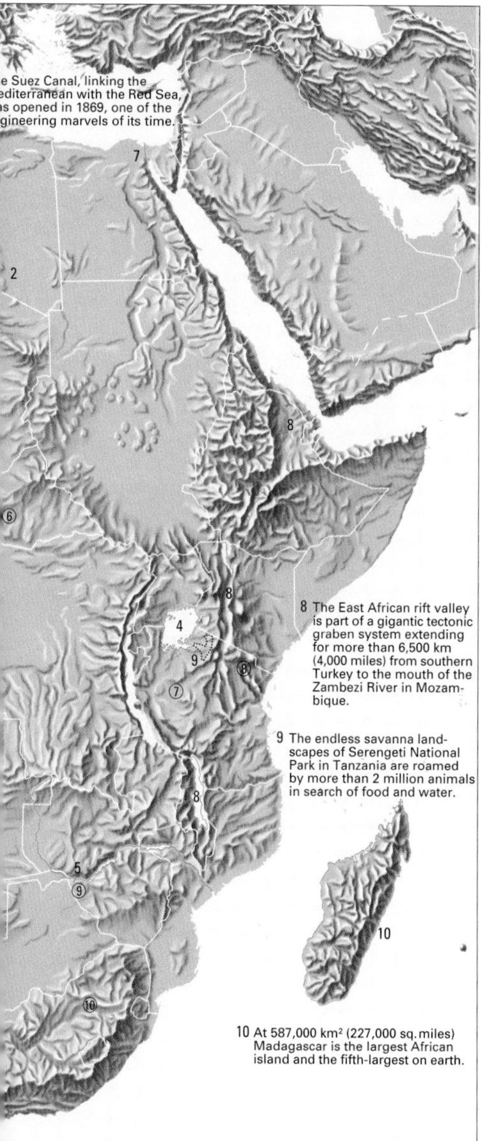
e Suez Canal, linking the
editerranean with the Red Sea,
as opened in 1869, one of the
gineering marvels of its time.
8 The East African rift valley is part of a gigantic tectonic graben system extending for more than 6,500 km (4,000 miles) from southern Turkey to the mouth of the Zambezi River in Mozambique.
9 The endless savanna landscapes of Serengeti National Park in Tanzania are roamed by more than 2 million animals in search of food and water.
10 At 587,000 km² (227,000 sq. miles) Madagascar is the largest African island and the fifth-largest on earth.

⑥ Humid Savanna
(Rother, Schwäbisch Gmünd)

⑦ Dry Savanna
(Rother, Schwäbisch Gmünd)

⑧ Kilimanjaro (on the left)
(Bonatz, Lüneburg)

⑨ Victoria Falls
(Rother, Schwäbisch Gmünd)

⑩ Johannesburg
(Newig, Flintbek)

ATLANTIC OCEAN
Mediterranean Sea
Black Sea
Caspian Sea
Red Sea
North Sea
Bay of Biscay
Aegean Sea
Adriatic Sea
Gulf of Aden
The Gulf
Str. of Gibraltar
Tropic of Cancer
RUSSIA
KAZAKHSTAN
UZBEKISTAN
TURKMENISTAN
UKRAINE
BELARUS
POLAND
GERMANY
FRANCE
SPAIN
PORTUGAL
ITALY
ROMANIA
BULGARIA
GREECE
TURKEY
SYRIA
IRAQ
IRAN
JORDAN
SAUDI ARABIA
YEMEN
OMAN
EGYPT
LIBYA
TUNISIA
ALGERIA
MOROCCO
MAURITANIA
MALI
NIGER
CHAD
SUDAN
ETHIOPIA
ERITREA
DJIBOUTI
NIGERIA
BURKINA FASO
SENEGAL
GAMBIA
GUINEA
GUINEA-BISSAU
SIERRA LEONE
CYPRUS
MALTA
UNITED KINGDOM
IRELAND
Western Sahara
LONDON
PARIS
MADRID
LISBON
ROME
BERLIN
WARSAW
KIEV
ATHENS
ANKARA
DAMASCUS
BAGHDAD
TEHRĀN
RIYADH
CAIRO
TRIPOLI
ALGIERS
TUNIS
RABAT
KHARTOUM
ADDIS ABABA
N'DJAMENA
DAKAR
BAMAKO
NIAMEY
Ouagadougou
Nouakchott
Abuja
Canary Is. (Sp.)
Madeira (Port.)
Azores (Port.)

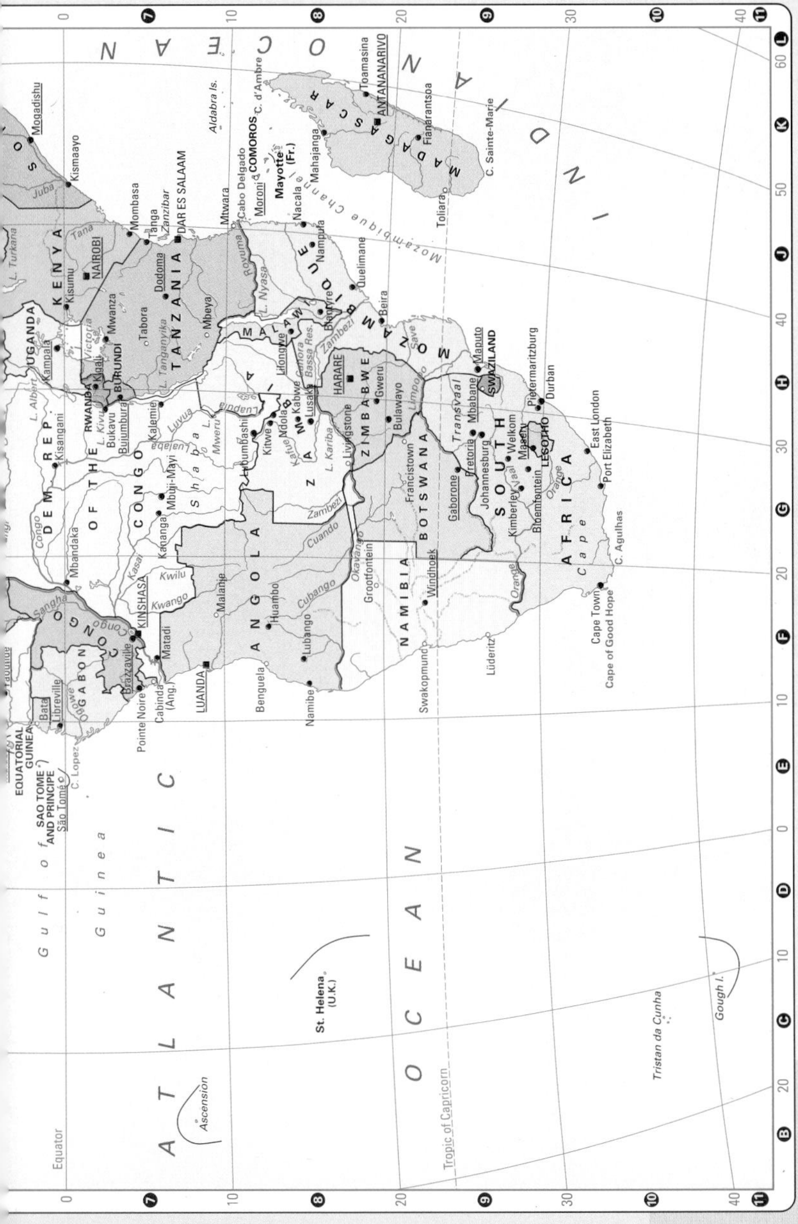
ATLANTIC OCEAN
INDIAN OCEAN
Gulf of Guinea
Equator
Tropic of Capricorn
DEM. REP. OF THE CONGO
CONGO
GABON
EQUATORIAL GUINEA
SAO TOME AND PRINCIPE
São Tomé
ANGOLA
NAMIBIA
BOTSWANA
ZIMBABWE
ZAMBIA
MALAWI
MOZAMBIQUE
TANZANIA
KENYA
UGANDA
RWANDA
BURUNDI
SOUTH AFRICA
LESOTHO
SWAZILAND
MADAGASCAR
COMOROS
Mayotte (Fr.)
Mogadishu
Kismaayo
Juba
L. Turkana
Tana
NAIROBI
Kisumu
Mombasa
Tanga
Zanzibar
DAR ES SALAAM
Dodoma
Tabora
Mwanza
L. Victoria
Kampala
L. Albert
Kigali
Bujumbura
Bukavu
L. Kivu
L. Tanganyika
Kalemie
Kisangani
Mbandaka
Congo
Sangha
Libreville
Bata
Ogooué
C. Lopez
Pointe Noire
Cabinda (Ang.)
Brazzaville
KINSHASA
Matadi
Kasai
Kwilu
Kwango
Kananga
Mbuji-Mayi
Lualaba
Shaba
L. Mweru
Luvua
Luapula
Lubumbashi
Kitwe
Ndola
Kabwe
Lusaka
Kafue
Lilongwe
L. Kariba
Livingstone
Zambezi
Cuando
Cubango
Okavango
LUANDA
Malanje
Huambo
Benguela
Lubango
Namibe
Grootfontein
Windhoek
Swakopmund
Lüderitz
Francistown
Gaborone
Bulawayo
Gweru
HARARE
Limpopo
Save
Cahora Bassa Res.
Blantyre
L. Nyasa
Mbeya
Rovuma
Mtwara
Cabo Delgado
Moroni
Nacala
Nampula
Quelimane
Beira
Maputo
Mbabane
Pretoria
Johannesburg
Transvaal
Welkom
Maseru
Kimberley
Vaal
Bloemfontein
Orange
Pietermaritzburg
Durban
East London
Port Elizabeth
Cape
C. Agulhas
Cape Town
Cape of Good Hope
Mozambique Channel
Aldabra Is.
C. d'Ambre
Mahajanga
Toamasina
ANTANANARIVO
Fianarantsoa
Toliara
C. Sainte-Marie
St. Helena (U.K.)
Ascension
Tristan da Cunha
Gough I.

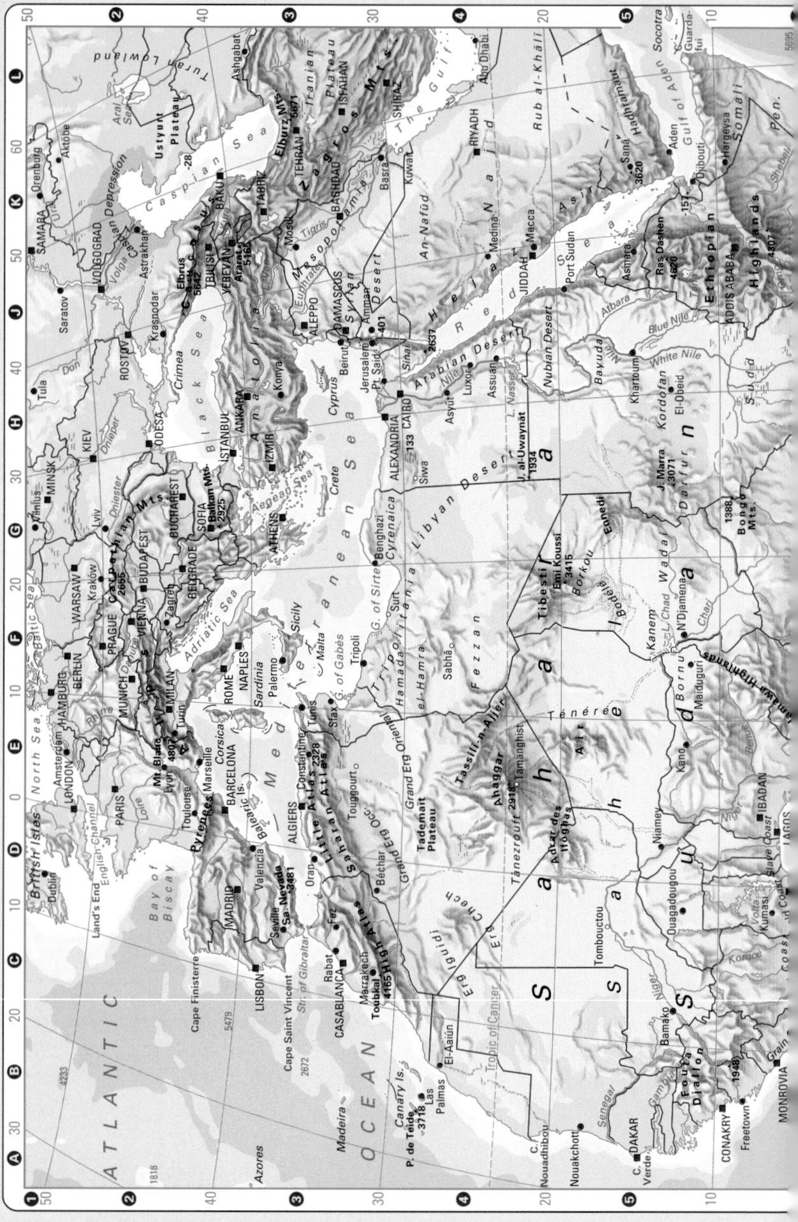
ATLANTIC
OCEAN
Azores
Madeira
Canary Is.
P. de Teide 3718
Las Palmas
Bay of Biscay
British Isles
Dublin
LONDON
PARIS
Land's End
English Channel
North Sea
Baltic Sea
Amsterdam
HAMBURG
BERLIN
WARSAW
PRAGUE
VIENNA
MUNICH
Mt. Blanc 4807
MILAN
Turin
Lyon
Marseille
Toulouse
Pyrenees
MADRID
LISBON
BARCELONA
Balearic Is.
Valencia
Seville
Sa. Nevada 3481
Cape Finisterre
Cape Saint Vincent
Str. of Gibraltar
Corsica
Sardinia
Sicily
Malta
ROME
NAPLES
Palermo
Adriatic Sea
Zagreb
BUDAPEST
BELGRADE
BUCHAREST
SOFIA
Balkan Mts. 2925
Carpathian Mts.
Kraków
Lviv
MINSK
Vilnius
KIEV
ODESA
Dnieper
Dniester
ROSTOV
Don
Tula
Saratov
VOLGOGRAD
SAMARA
Orenburg
Aktöbe
Astrakhan
Krasnodar
Crimea
Black Sea
Caspian Sea
Caspian Depression
Aral Sea
Ustyurt Plateau
Turan Lowland
Ashgabat
Elbrus 5642
Caucasus
TBILISI
YEREVAN
Ararat 5165
BAKU
TABRIZ
TEHRAN
Elburz Mts. 5671
ISFAHAN
SHIRAZ
Iranian Plateau
Zagros Mts.
ISTANBUL
ANKARA
IZMIR
Konya
Anatolia
Aegean Sea
ATHENS
Crete
Cyprus
Mediterranean Sea
ALEPPO
DAMASCUS
Beirut
Jerusalem
Amman
Syrian Desert
Mosul
Tigris
Euphrates
BAGHDAD
Mesopotamia
Basra
Kuwait
The Gulf
Abu Dhabi
RIYADH
Najd
An-Nafūd
Rub al-Khālī
Medina
Mecca
JIDDAH
Hejaz
Red Sea
Sinai
Pt. Said
CAIRO
ALEXANDRIA
Siwa
Asyūt
Luxor
Assuan
L. Nasser
Nile
Arabian Desert
Nubian Desert
Libyan Desert
J. al-'Uwaynāt 1934
Port Sudan
Asmara
Ras Dashen 4620
ADDIS ABABA
Ethiopian Highlands
Blue Nile
White Nile
Atbara
Khartoum
Bayuda
Kordofan
El-Obeid
Darfur
J. Marra 3071
Bongo Mts.
Sudd
Sana 3620
Aden
Gulf of Aden
Hadhramaut
Socotra
Djibouti
Hargeysa
Somali Pen.
C. Guardafui
Benghazi
Cyrenaica
G. of Sirte
Surt
Tripoli
Tripolitania
Hamada el-Hamra
Sabhā
Fezzan
Tibesti
Emi Koussi 3415
Borkou
Ennedi
Bodélé
Wadai
L. Chad
N'Djamena
Kanem
Chari
Bornu
Maiduguri
Ténéré
Aïr
Tassili-n-Ajjer
Ahaggar
Tamanghist
2918
Tanezrouft
Adrar des Iforas
Tademait Plateau
Touggourt
Grand Erg Oriental
Grand Erg Occ.
Béchar
Erg Chech
Erg Iguidi
ALGIERS
Oran
Constantine
Tunis
Sfax
G. of Gabès
Little Atlas
Saharan Atlas
Atlas 2328
High Atlas
Toubkal 4165
Marrakech
Rabat
CASABLANCA
Fez
El-Aaiún
Tropic of Cancer
C. Nouadhibou
Nouakchott
Senegal
DAKAR
C. Verde
Gambia
Fouta Djallon
1948
CONAKRY
Freetown
MONROVIA
Grain Coast
Bamako
Niger
Tombouctou
Ouagadougou
Niamey
Kano
Benue
IBADAN
LAGOS
Slave Coast
Kumasi
Volta
Komoé
Adamawa Highlands
Sahara
Sudan
Sahel

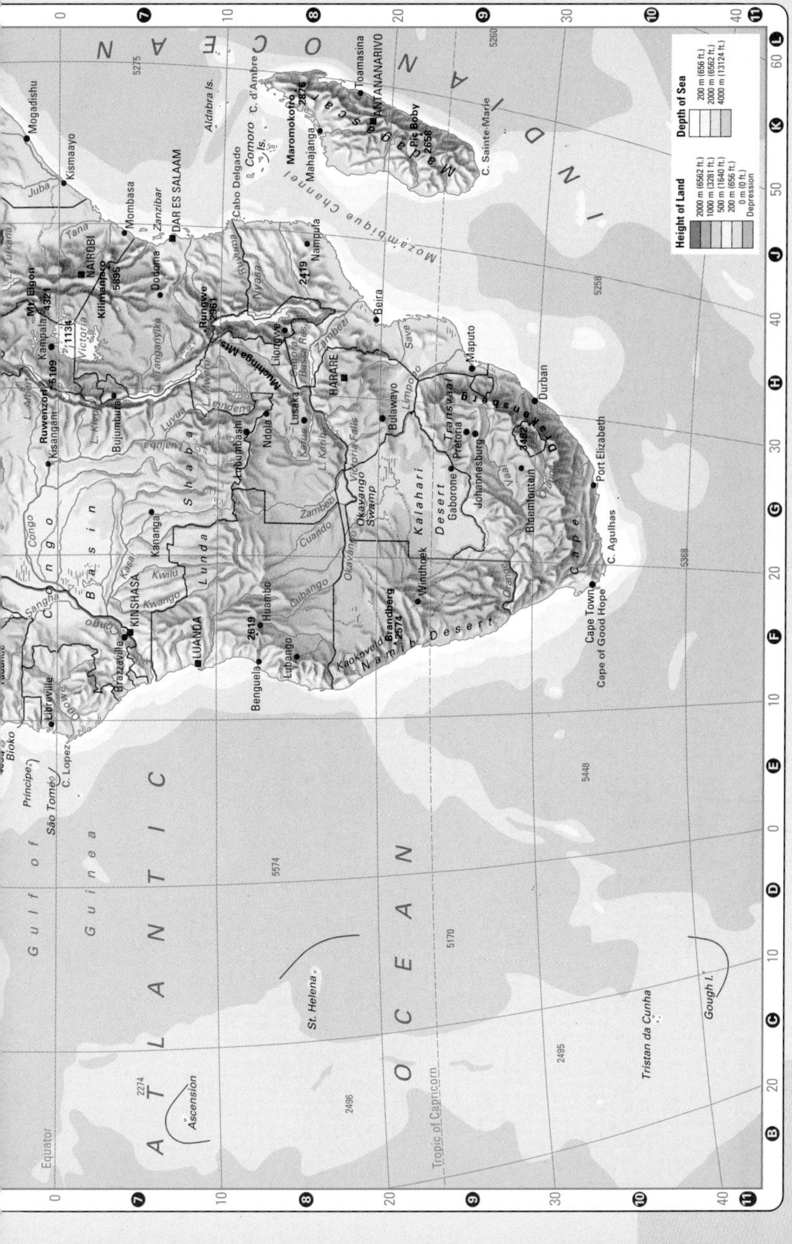

ATLANTIC OCEAN
INDIAN OCEAN
Gulf of Guinea
Equator
Tropic of Capricorn
Height of Land
2000 m (6562 ft.)
1000 m (3281 ft.)
500 m (1640 ft.)
200 m (656 ft.)
0 m (0 ft.)
Depression
Depth of Sea
200 m (656 ft.)
2000 m (6562 ft.)
4000 m (13124 ft.)
Congo Basin
Kalahari Desert
Namib Desert
Lunda
Shaba
Madagascar
Drakensberg
Mozambique Channel
Muchinga Mts.
Mogadishu
Kismaayo
Juba
Mombasa
Zanzibar
DAR ES SALAAM
NAIROBI
Kilimanjaro 5895
Mt. Elgon 4321
Kampala
Ruwenzori 5109
Kisangani
Bujumbura
Dodoma
Rungwe 2961
Lilongwe
HARARE
Lusaka
Ndola
Lubumbashi
Kananga
KINSHASA
Brazzaville
LUANDA
Libreville
Huambo 2619
Benguela
Lubango
Brandberg 2574
Windhoek
Kaokoveld
Okavango Swamp
Victoria Falls
Bulawayo
Gaborone
Pretoria
Johannesburg
Transvaal
Maputo
Durban
Bloemfontein
3482
Port Elizabeth
Cape Town
Cape of Good Hope
C. Agulhas
Beira
Nampula 2419
Cabo Delgado
Comoro Is.
Aldabra Is.
C. d'Ambre
Maromokotro 2876
Mahajanga
Toamasina
ANTANANARIVO
Pic Boby 2658
C. Sainte-Marie
Bioko
Príncipe
São Tomé
C. Lopez
St. Helena
Ascension
Tristan da Cunha
Gough I.
Zambezi
Limpopo
Orange
Vaal
Save
Cuando
Cubango
Okavango
Kasai
Kwango
Kwilu
Congo
Sangha
Ogowe
L. Victoria
L. Tanganyika
L. Nyasa
L. Kariba
L. Tana
Kafue
Luvua
Mweru
Lualaba
Cahora Bassa Res.
Ruvuma
5275
5260
5258
5574
5448
5368
5170
2496
2495
2274
1134

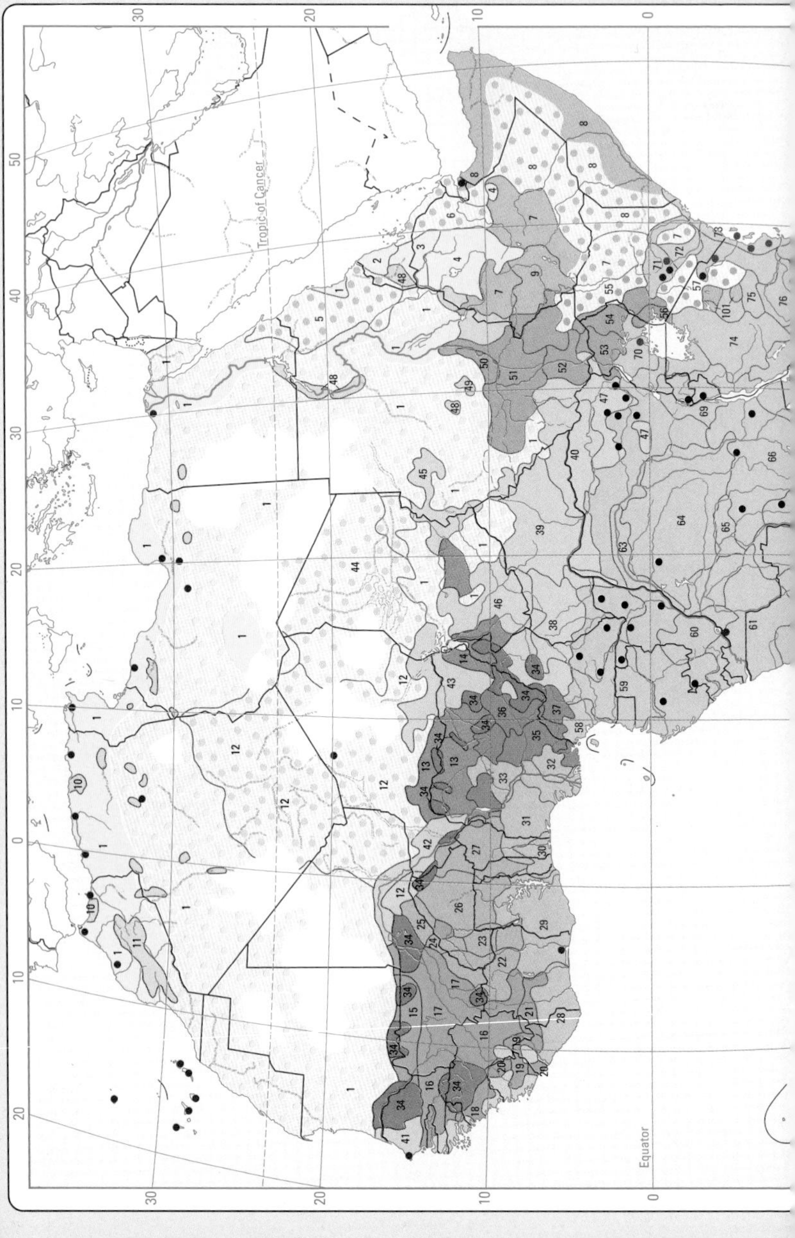
Tropic of Cancer
Equator

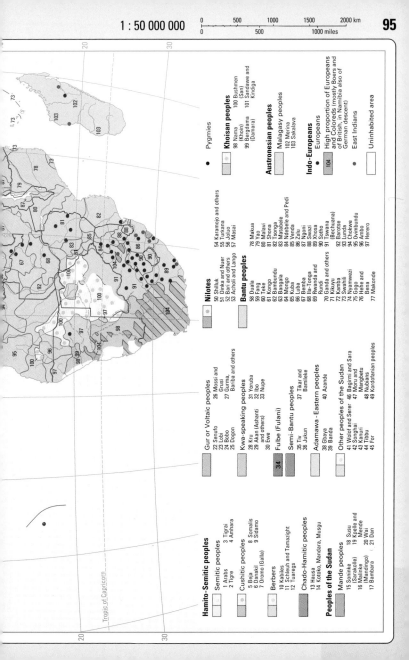

Hamito-Semitic peoples

Semitic peoples
1 Arabs
2 Tigre
3 Tigrai
4 Amhara

Cushitic peoples
5 Beja
6 Danakil
7 Oromo (Galla)
8 Somalis
9 Sidamo

Berbers
10 Kabiles
11 Schleuh and Tamazight
12 Tuaregs

Chado-Hamitic peoples
13 Hausa
14 Kotoko, Mandara, Musgu

Peoples of the Sudan

Mande peoples
15 Soninke (Sarakolle)
16 Malinke (Mandingo)
17 Bambara
18 Susu
19 Kpelle and Mende
20 Wai
21 Dan

Gur or Voltaic peoples
22 Senufo
23 Lobi
24 Bobo
25 Dogon
26 Mossi and Grusi
27 Gurma, Bariba and others

Kwa-speaking peoples
28 Kru
29 Akan (Ashanti and others)
30 Ewe
31 Yoruba
32 Ibo
33 Nupe

34 Fulbe (Fulani)

Semi-Bantu peoples
35 Tiv
36 Jukun
37 Tikar and Bamileke

Adamawa - Eastern peoples
38 Gbaya
39 Banda
40 Azande

Other peoples of the Sudan
41 Wolof and Serer
42 Songhai
43 Kanuri
44 Tibbu
45 For
46 Bagirmi and Sara
47 Moru and Mangbetu
48 Nubians
49 Kordofanian peoples

Nilotes
50 Shilluk
51 Dinka and Nuer
52 Bari and others
53 Acholi and Lango
54 Karamojo and others
55 Turkana
56 Joluo
57 Masai

Bantu peoples
58 Duala
59 Fang
60 Teke
61 Kongo
62 Bambundu
63 Bangala
64 Mongo
65 Kuba
66 Luba
67 Bemba
68 Ila-Tonga
69 Rwanda and Rundi
70 Ganda and others
71 Kikuyu
72 Kamba
73 Swahili
74 Nyamwezi
75 Gogo
76 Hehe and Bena
77 Makonde
78 Makua
79 Yao
80 Malavi
81 Shona
82 Tsonga
83 Matabele
84 Ndebele and Pedi
85 Venda
86 Zulu
87 Ngoni
88 Swazi
89 Xhosa
90 Sotho
91 Tswana (Bechuana)
92 Barotse
93 Lunda
94 Chokwe
95 Ovimbundu
96 Ambo
97 Herero

● Pygmies

Khoisan peoples
98 Nama (Khoin)
99 Bergdama (Damara)
100 Bushmen (San)
101 Sandawe and Kindiga

Austronesian peoples

Malagasy peoples
102 Merina
103 Sakalava

Indo-Europeans
● Europeans
104 High proportion of Europeans and Coloreds (mostly Boers and of British, in Namibia also of German descent)
● East Indians
Uninhabited area

PORTUGAL
Sevilla
Cádiz
Strait of Gibraltar
Tanger
Tétouan
El-Ksar el-Kbir
Kénitra
Rabat
DAR AL-BEIDA
(CASABLANCA)
Meknès
Khouribga
Safi
Essaouira
Beni-Mellal
Marrakech
4165
High Atlas
Cap Rhir
Agadir
Ouarzazate
2531
Anti Atlas
Ifni
Dra
MOROCCO
1847
Porto Santo
Madeira
(Port.)
Selvagens
(Port.)
Santa Cruz
de la Palma
La Palma
Canary Islands
(Sp.)
Santa Cruz
de T.
3718
Pico de Teide
Arrecife
Lanzarote
Fuerte-
ventura
Hierro
Tenerife
Las Palmas
Tarfaya
Gran Canaria
Laâyoune
(El-Aaiún)
Smara
Tindouf
Erg Iguidi
Western Sahara
Ad-Dakhla
Tropic of Cancer
Zouérat
Taoudenni
Cape Nouadhibou
Nouâdhibou
Atâr
Cape Timirist
Akjoujt
Tidjikja
Nouakchott
MAURITANIA
SAHARA
ATLANTIC OCEAN
Santo Antão
Mindelo
São Nicolau
Boa Vista
Cape Verde Is.
Santiago
Fogo
2829
Praia
CAPE VERDE
Rosso
Senegal
Kiffa
Ayoûn el-Atroûs
Tombouctou
Saint-Louis
Kaédi
Néma
Linguère
Thiès
Cape Verde
DAKAR
Diourbel
Kaolack
SENEGAL
Nioro
Kayes
Mopti
Banjul
GAMBIA
Tambacounda
Gambia
Kita
Ségou
Bani
Ziguinchor
Bamako
Koulikoro
San
Ouagadougou
GUINEA-
BISSAU
1538
Fouta Djallon
Koudougou
Bissau
Labé
Siguiri
Sikasso
FASO
BURKINA
MALI
Bissagos
Is.
GUINEA
Niger
Bobo-Dioulasso
Bolgata
Kindia
Kankan
Odienné
Black Volta
CONAKRY
Bintimani
1948
Makeni
Koidu
Korhogo
SIERRA
LEONE
Freetown
Beyla
CÔTE D'IVOIRE
Katiola
Bo
Kenema
Nimba Mts.
1752
Nzérékoré
Bouaké
Sunyani
Sanniquellie
Daloa
Abengourou
Tubmanburg
Yamoussoukro
MONROVIA
LIBERIA
Gagnoa
Asamankese
Buchanan
ABIDJAN
Cape Coast
Grand-Bassam
Greenville
Sassandra
C. Three Points
Harper
C. Palmas
30
25
20
15
10
5

38/39
36/37
34/35
66/98
100/101
SPAIN
AL-JAZA'IR
(ALGIERS)
Almería
Ouahran
(Oran)
Mostaganem
Béjaïa
Skikda
Annaba
Binzert
Carthage
Cap Bon
Tunis
Sousse
Mahdia
Palermo
ITALY
Catania
Siracusa
Ragusa
Sicily
Valletta
MALTA
Pátrai (Patras)
Kórinthos
Kalamata
ATHINA
(ATHENS)
GREECE
Chaniá
Crete
Mediterranean Sea
Oujda
Sidi bel Abbès
Tilimsan (Tlemcen)
Little Atlas
1985
Qacentina
(Constantine)
Sétif
Batna
Kairouan
Béja
Dj. Chelia
2328
Djelfa
Chott ech-Chergui
Chott Melghir
Biskra
-40
Gafsa
Sfax
Tozeur
Gabès
Gulf of Gabès
Jerba
Chott-el-Jerid
El-Oued
Laghouat
Saharan Atlas
Aïn Sefra
2236
Figuig
Béchar
Ghardaïa
Touggourt
Médenine
Zuwārah
Tarābulus (Tripoli)
Al-Khums
Misrātah
Az-Zāwiyah
723
Gharyān
Jabal Nefusa
Banghāzi
(Benghazi)
Al-Bayḍā
Darnah
Al-Marj
Suluq
Tubruq
Cyrenaica
Gulf of Sirte
Surt
As-Sider
Adjdābiyā
Tripolitania
Abadla
Grand Erg Occidental
Ouargla
Hassi Messaoud
El-Goléa
Beni Abbès
Timimoun
Grand Erg Oriental
Ghadāmis
TUNISIA
ALGERIA
Adrar
Bordj Omar Driss
Edjeleh
In Salah
Reggane
Sebkha Mekerrhane
Illizi
Hun
804
Jabal as-Sawdā
Zaltan
Awjilah
Zillah
LIBYA
Sabhā
Awbārī
Fezzan
Murzuq
Tāzirbū
Wāw al-Kabīr
Ghāt
Al-Qatrūn
Djanet
Al-Khufrah
Sahara
Libyan Desert
Ahaggar
2918
Tamanghist
Tanezrouft
Ténéré
Madama
Tibesti
3265
Bardaï
Zouar
3415
Emi Koussi
Tessalit
Adrar des Ifôghas
853
Kidal
Iférouane
1800
Aïr
Arlit
Bilma
NIGER
Agadèz
Faya
Fada
1450
Ennedi
Gao
Ménaka
Koro-Toro
CHAD
Tillabéri
Téra
Niamey
Tahoua
Nguigmi
Lake Chad
Mao
Maradi
Zinder
Diffa
Abéché
J. Mun
1309
SUDAN
Ati
El-Geneina
Dosso
Sokoto
Katsina
Nguru
Gusau
Kano
Hadejia
Bornu
N'Djamena
Mongo
Fada-Ngourma
Zaria
Maiduguri
Dapaong
Kandi
Natitingou
Kainji Res.
Jos
Bauchi
NIGERIA
Maroua
Chari
Bousso
Am-Timan
Djougou
Kaduna
Birao
Parakou
Sokodé
Minna
Jos Plateau
Shere Hill
1780
Kumo
Garoua
Bongor
Pala
Laï
Logone
J. Ngaja
1388
Yola
Sarh
Moundou
Doba
TOGO
BENIN
Ilorin
Abuja
Niger
Dimlang
2042
Ndélé
Ogbomosho
Iwo
Oshogbo
Ife
Benue
Abomey
Abeokuta
Akure
Makurdi
Adamawa Highlands
Kaga Bandoro
Porto-Novo
IBADAN
Enugu
Ngaoundéré
CENTRAL AFRICAN REP.
Tema
Lomé
Coto-nou
LAGOS
Benin City
Onitsha
Bamenda
2740
Bafoussam
Bossangoa
Bria
Bouar
ACCRA
Bight of Benin
Aba
Calabar
CAMEROON
Nkongsamba
Sibut
Bambari
Bangassou
Port Harcourt
Cameroon Mtn.
4095
Buea
DOUALA
Sanaga
Bertoua
Berbérati
Ubangi
Bangui
Gulf of Guinea
Bight of Biafra
Bioko
EQU. GUINEA
3008
Malabo
Edéa
Yaoundé
CONGO
DEM. REP. OF THE CONGO
Bondo

Mediterranean Sea
Touggourt
El Oued
Chott el-Jerid
Ghardaïa
Médenine
TUNISIA
Zuwārah
Tarābulus (Tripoli)
Al-Khums
Az-Zāwiyah
Misrātah
723
Gharyān
Jabal Nefusa
Ouargla
Hassi Messaoud
Banghāzī (Benghazi)
Al-Baydā
Darnah
Al-Marj
Tubruq
Sulūq
Gulf of Sirte
Cyrenaica
Ajdābiyā
Surt
As-Sider
Tripolitania
Ghadāmis
Grand Erg Oriental
Salûm
EL-ISKANDARÎYA (ALEXANDRIA)
Matrûh
Damanhûr
Qattâra Depr.
-133
EL-QÂHIRA
Siwa
Al-Jaghbūb
Hūn
840
Jabal as-Sawdā
Zaltan
Awjilah
Zillah
Bordj Omar Driss
Edjeleh
Bawiti
El-Faiyûm
El-Minya
LIBYA
EGYPT
Illizi
Awbārī
Sabhā
Fezzan
Murzuq
Tāzirbū
El-Qasr
El-Khârga
Ghāt
Al-Qatrūn
Wāw al-Kabīr
Djanet
Sahara
Al-Khufrah
Libyan Desert
ALGERIA
Ahaggar
2918
Tamanghist
Tropic of Cancer
Ténéré
Madama
Tibesti
3265
Bardaï
Zouar
Jabal al-Uwaynāt 1893
3415 Emi Koussi
Iférouane
1800
Aïr
Arlit
Bilma
Faya
NIGER
Agadèz
Fada
1450
Ennedi
Wādī Howar
Wādī el-Milk
Koro-Toro
CHAD
Tahoua
Nguigmi
Mao
Lake Chad
J. Mun 1309
Abéché
El-Fasher
Maradi
Zinder
Diffa
Sokoto
Ati
El-Geneina
Jebel Marra 3071
El-Obeid
Katsina
Nguru
Gusau
Kano
Hadejia
Bornu
Maiduguri
N'Djamena
Mongo
SUDAN
Nyala
En-Nahud
Kaduna
Zaria
Jos
Bauchi
Am Timan
El-Muglad
Kadugli
NIGERIA
Maroua
Chari
Bousso
Birao
Jos Plateau
Shere Hill 1780
Kumo
Garoua
Bongor
Jebel Ngaja 1388
Minna
Abuja
Yola
Pala
Laï
Logone
Sarh
Bahr el-Arab
Buru
Niger
Benue
Dimlang 2042
Moundou
Doba
Ndélé
Makurdi
Adamawa Highlands
Ngaoundéré
Wau
Kaga Bandoro
Enugu
CENTRAL AFRICAN REP.
Bria
Sue
Rumbek
Benin C.
Onitsha
Bamenda
2740
Bafoussam
Bouar
Bossangoa
Sibut
Aba
Calabar
CAMEROON
Bambari
Bangassou
Obo
Port Harcourt
Nkongsamba
Bangui
Yambio
Cameroon Mtn. 4095
Buea
DOUALA
Sanaga
Bertoua
Ubangi
Bomu
Uele
Gulf of Guinea
3008
Malabo
Bioko
Edéa
Yaoundé
Berbérati
Bondo
Ebolowa
Aketi
Buta
Titule
Mungbere
EQUATORIAL GUINEA
Bata
Oyem
Lisala
Bumba
Isiro
Congo
Aruwimi
SAO TOME AND PRINCIPE
São Tomé
Ouésso
Sangha
CONGO
DEM. REP. OF THE CONGO
Makokou
Yangambi
Kisangani
Libreville
Port-Gentil
GABON
Lambaréné
Owando
Mbandaka
Tshuapa
Lomami
Ubundu
Lualaba
Butembo
ATLANTIC OCEAN

96/97
100/101

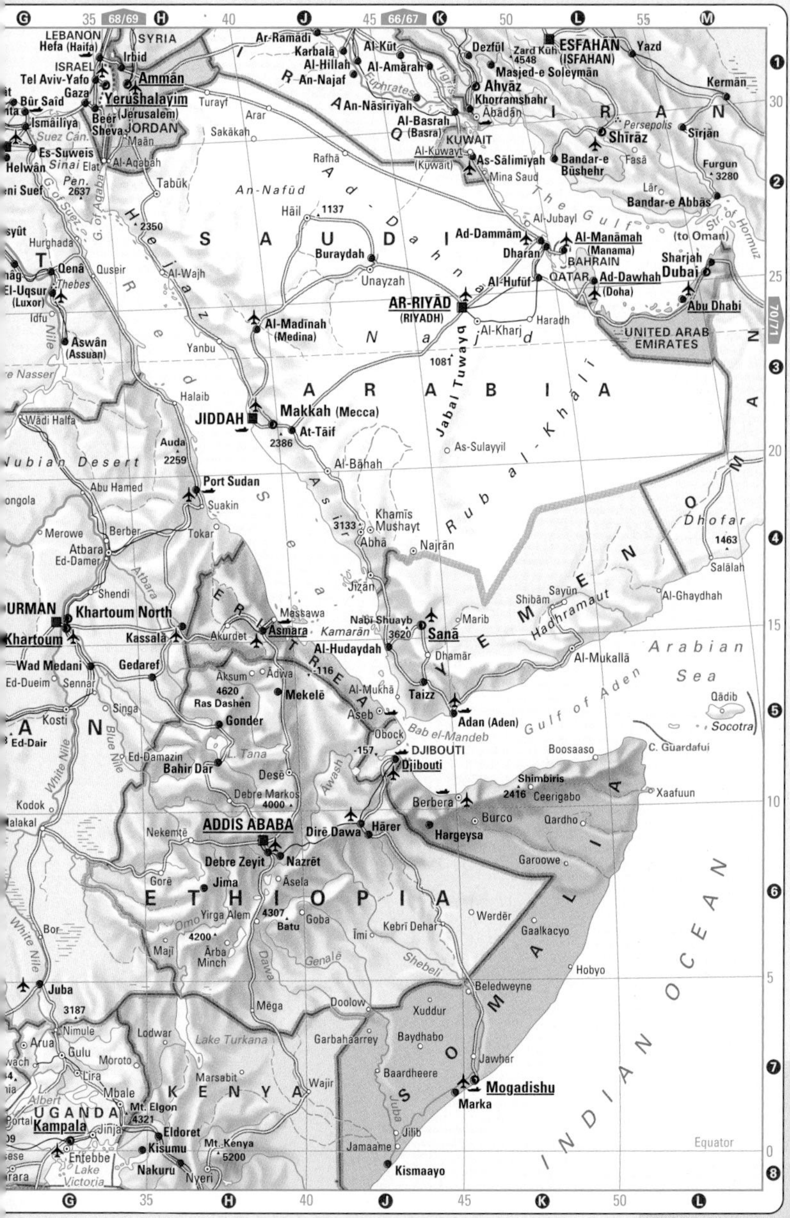
68/69
66/67
70/71
LEBANON
SYRIA
Hefa (Haifa)
Irbid
ISRAEL
Tel Aviv-Yafo
Ammān
Gaza
Bûr Saîd
Yerushalayim
(Jerusalem)
Ismâilîya
Beer Sheva
JORDAN
Suez Can.
Maān
Es-Suweis
Helwân
Sinai Pen.
Elat
Al-Aqabah
2637
G. of Aqaba
G. of Suez
Tabūk
Turayf
Arar
Sakākah
Ar-Ramādī
Karbalā
Al-Hillah
An-Najaf
Al-Kūt
Al-Amārah
Euphrates
Tigris
An-Nāsirīyah
Al-Basrah (Basra)
IRAQ
KUWAIT
Al-Kuwayt (Kuwait)
As-Sālimīyah
Mina Saud
Dezfūl
Zard Kūh 4548
ESFAHĀN (ISFAHAN)
Yazd
Masjed-e Soleymān
Ahvāz
Khorramshahr
Ābādān
IRAN
Persepolis
Shīrāz
Kermān
Sīrjān
Bandar-e Būshehr
Fasā
Furgun 3280
Lār
Bandar-e Abbās
Str. of Hormuz
(to Oman)
The Gulf
Al-Jubayl
Ad-Dammām
Dharan
Al-Manāmah (Manama)
BAHRAIN
QATAR
Ad-Dawhah (Doha)
Sharjah
Dubai
Abu Dhabi
UNITED ARAB EMIRATES
Rafhā
An-Nafūd
Ad-Dahnā
Hāil
1137
SAUDI ARABIA
Buraydah
Unayzah
Al-Hufūf
AR-RIYĀD (RIYADH)
Al-Kharj
Haradh
Najd
Al-Madīnah (Medina)
Yanbu
Al-Wajh
Hejaz
2350
1081
Jabal Tuwayq
Rub al-Khālī
As-Sulayyil
Halaib
Red Sea
JIDDAH
Makkah (Mecca)
At-Tāif
2386
Al-Bāhah
Asīr
3133
Khamīs Mushayt
Abhā
Najrān
Jīzān
OMAN
Dhofar
1463
Salālah
Al-Ghaydhah
Hadhramaut
Sayūn
Shibām
YEMEN
Marib
Nabī Shuayb 3620
Sanā
Dhamār
Al-Hudaydah
Kamarān
Al-Mukallā
Taizz
Al-Mukhā
Adan (Aden)
Arabian Sea
Qādib
Socotra
Gulf of Aden
Bab el-Mandeb
Hurghada
Qusêir
Qenâ
Thebes
El-Uqsur (Luxor)
Idfu
Nile
Aswân (Assuan)
Lake Nasser
Wâdi Halfa
Nubian Desert
Auda 2259
Port Sudan
Suakin
Abu Hamed
Dongola
Merowe
Berber
Tokar
Atbara
Ed-Damer
Shendi
OMDURMAN
Khartoum North
Khartoum
Kassalā
Akurdet
Massawa
Asmara
ERITREA
-116
Wad Medani
Gedaref
Ed-Dueim
Sennar
Singa
Aksum
Ādwa
Mekelē
4620
Ras Dashen
Gonder
Aseb
Kosti
SUDAN
Ed-Dair
Blue Nile
White Nile
Ed-Damazin
L. Tana
Bahir Dar
Desē
Debre Markos 4000
Obock
-157
DJIBOUTI
Djibouti
Awash
Boosaaso
C. Guardafui
Shimbiris 2416
Ceerigaabo
Xaafuun
Berbera
Burco
Hargeysa
Qardho
Kodok
Malakal
Nekemtē
ADDIS ABABA
Dirē Dawa
Hārer
Debre Zeyit
Nazrēt
Āsela
Gorē
Jīma
ETHIOPIA
Garoowe
Omo
Yirga Alem
4307 Batu
Goba
Werdēr
Kebrī Dehar
Gaalkacyo
Bor
4200
Majī
Ārba Minch
Īmi
Genalē
Shebeli
Dawa
Hobyo
SOMALIA
Juba
3187
Mēga
Dolow
Beledweyne
Xuddur
Lodwar
Lake Turkana
Nimule
Arua
Gulu
Moroto
Lira
Garbahaarrey
Baydhabo
Jawhar
Baardheere
Marsabit
Wajir
Mogadishu
Marka
Albert
Mbale
Mt. Elgon 4321
UGANDA
KENYA
Kampala
Jinja
Eldoret
Kisumu
Mt. Kenya 5200
Entebbe
Lake Victoria
Nakuru
Nyeri
Jilib
Jamaame
Kismaayo
INDIAN OCEAN
Equator
G H J K L M
35 40 45 50 55
30 25 20 15 10 5 0

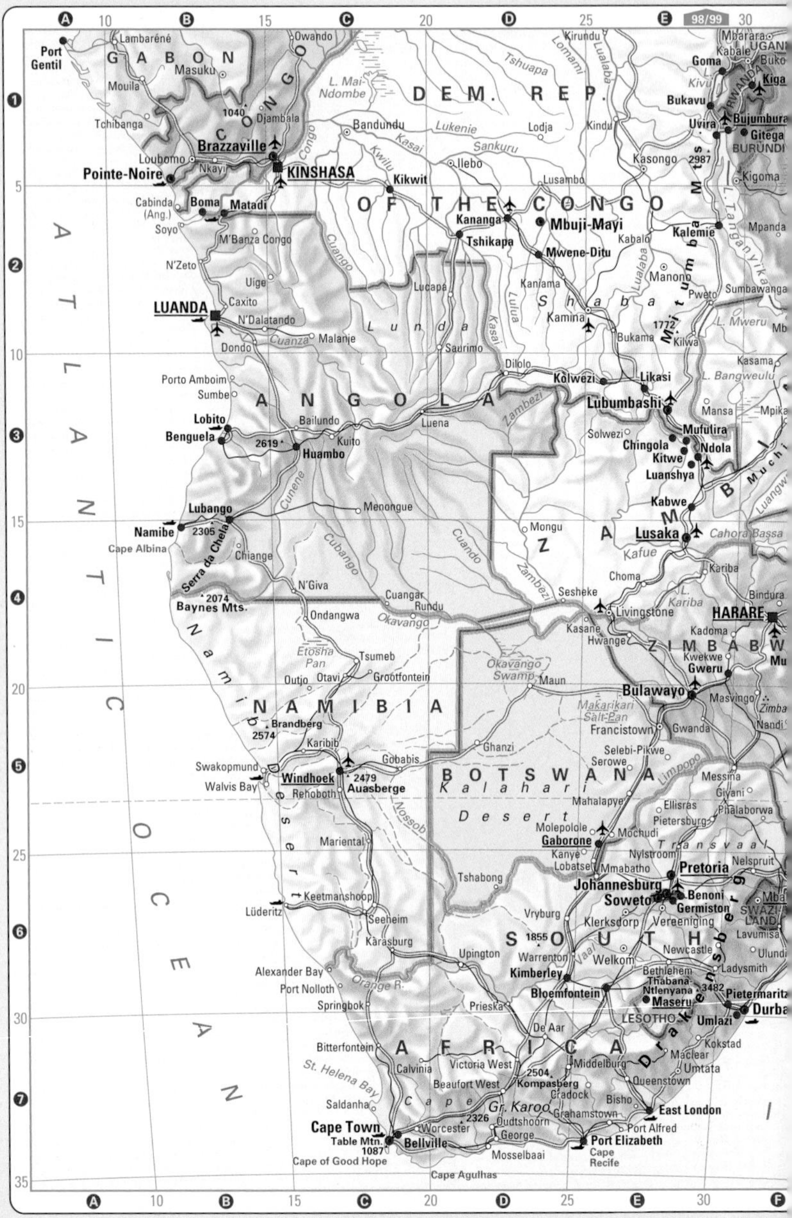
A
10
B
15
C
20
D
25
E
98/99
30
Port Gentil
Lambaréné
GABON
Masuku
Mouila
CONGO
1040
Djambala
Owando
L. Mai-Ndombe
DEM. REP.
OF THE CONGO
Tshuapa
Lomami
Lualaba
Kirundu
Mbarara
Kabale
UGAN
Goma
Buko
Kivu
RWANDA
Kiga
Bukavu
Uvira
Bujumbura
Gitega
BURUNDI
Tchibanga
Brazzaville
Bandundu
Lukenie
Lodja
Kindu
Sankuru
Kasai
Kwilu
Congo
Loubomo
Nkayi
Pointe-Noire
KINSHASA
Ilebo
Kasongo
2987
Kigoma
Kikwit
Lusambo
Cabinda (Ang.)
Boma
Matadi
Kananga
Mbuji-Mayi
Tshikapa
Mwene-Ditu
Kabalo
Kalemie
Mpanda
L. Tanganyika
Soyo
M'Banza Congo
Cuango
N'Zeto
Uige
Lucapa
Kaniama
Manono
Pweto
Sumbawanga
Lulua
Shaba
Mitumba Mts.
LUANDA
Caxito
N'Dalatando
Kamina
1772
L. Mweru
Cuanza
Malanje
Lunda
Kasai
Bukama
Kilwa
Dondo
Saurimo
Kasama
Dilolo
Kolwezi
Likasi
L. Bangweulu
Porto Amboim
Sumbe
ANGOLA
Zambezi
Lubumbashi
Mansa
Mpika
Lobito
Bailundo
Luena
Benguela
2619
Kuito
Huambo
Solwezi
Mufulira
Chingola
Ndola
Kitwe
Luanshya
Muchinga
Cunene
Lubango
Menongue
Kabwe
Namibe
2305
Mongu
ZAMBIA
Lusaka
Cahora Bassa
Cape Albina
Serra da Chela
Chiange
Cubango
Cuando
Kafue
Choma
Kariba
N'Giva
Zambezi
Sesheke
L. Kariba
Bindura
2074
Baynes Mts.
Cuangar
Rundu
Livingstone
HARARE
Ondangwa
Okavango
Kasane
Hwange
Kadoma
Namib
Etosha Pan
Tsumeb
ZIMBABWE
Kwekwe
Gweru
Okavango Swamp
Maun
Outjo
Otavi
Grootfontein
Bulawayo
Masvingo
NAMIBIA
Makarikari Salt Pan
Zimba
Brandberg
2574
Francistown
Gwanda
Nandi
Karibib
Ghanzi
Selebi-Pikwe
Swakopmund
Gobabis
Serowe
Windhoek
2479
Auasberge
BOTSWANA
Limpopo
Messina
Walvis Bay
Rehoboth
Kalahari
Mahalapye
Giyani
Desert
Nossob
Ellisras
Phalaborwa
Molepolole
Pietersburg
Mochudi
Gaborone
Transvaal
Mariental
Kanye
Nylstroom
Nelspruit
Lobatse
Mmabatho
Pretoria
Tshabong
Johannesburg
Benoni
Soweto
Germiston
Keetmanshoop
Lüderitz
Vryburg
Klerksdorp
Vereeniging
SWAZILAND
Mbabane
Seeheim
Lavumisa
1855
SOUTH AFRICA
Karasburg
Newcastle
Ulundi
Upington
Warrenton
Vaal
Welkom
Alexander Bay
Kimberley
Bethlehem
Ladysmith
Port Nolloth
Orange R.
Thabana-Ntlenyana
3482
Bloemfontein
Maseru
Pietermaritzburg
Springbok
Prieska
LESOTHO
Durban
Umlazi
De Aar
Drakensberg
Kokstad
Bitterfontein
Maclear
Calvinia
Victoria West
Middelburg
Umtata
St. Helena Bay
2504
Kompasberg
Beaufort West
Queenstown
Cradock
Saldanha
Cape
Gr. Karoo
Bisho
2326
Grahamstown
East London
Cape Town
Worcester
Oudtshoorn
Port Alfred
Table Mtn. 1087
Bellville
George
Port Elizabeth
Cape of Good Hope
Mosselbaai
Cape Recife
Cape Agulhas
ATLANTIC OCEAN
1
2
3
4
5
6
7
5
10
15
20
25
30
35
A
10
B
15
C
20
D
25
E
30
F

KENYA
SOMALIA
Nakuru
Nyeri
Kismaayo
NAIROBI
Machakos
Lake Victoria
Musoma
L. Natron
Lamu
Mwanza
Serengeti Plain
Kilimanjaro
5895
L. Eyasi
Arusha
Voi
Malindi
Moshi
Shinyanga
Hanang
3417
Mombasa
Singida
Tanga
Tabora
Pemba
Chake Chake
Zanzibar
Zanzibar
Dodoma
Morogoro
TANZANIA
DAR ES SALAAM
2646
Mafia
L. Rukwa
Iringa
Rufiji
Rungwe
2961
Kilwa Kivinje
Ndjombe
Lindi
Mtwara
Karonga
C. Delgado
Songea
Ruvuma
Mzuzu
Lake Nyasa
MALAWI
Mocímboa da Praia
2361
Ngazidja
Moroni
COMOROS
Mwali
Nzwani
Mayotte (Fr.)
Mamoudzou
Lichinga
Pemba
Salima
Lilongwe
Mangochi
MOZAMBIQUE
Nacala
Zomba
Blantyre
3002
Lumbo
Nampula
Angoche
Juan de Nova (Fr.)
Zambezi
Mocuba
Caia
Quelimane
Marromeu
Chinde
Chimoio
Beira
Machanga
Save
Vilankulo
Bassas da India (Fr.)
Europa (Fr.)
Mozambique Channel
Ponta da Barra
Inhambane
Inharrime
Xai-Xai
Maputo
Seychelle Is.
Victoria
Mahé
Amirante Is.
Coëtivy
SEYCHELLES
Aldabra Is.
Cosmoledo Is.
Cerf
Farquhar Is.
Agalega Is.
Îles Glorieuses (Fr.)
C. d'Ambre
Antsirañana
Nosy Be
2876
Maromokotro
Antalaha
Mahajanga
Marovoay
Tromelin
Nosy Sainte Marie
Ambatondrazaka
Maintirano
Toamasina
ANTANANARIVO
MADAGASCAR
Antsirabe
Morondava
Madagascar
Mananjary
Morombe
Mangoky
Fianarantsoa
Pic Boby
2658
Manakara
Farafangana
Toliara
Tropic of Capricorn
Tôlañaro
Cape Sainte Marie
Port Louis
St-Denis
Réunion (Fr.)
MAURITIUS
Piton des Neiges
3069
INDIAN OCEAN

North America at a Glimpse

① St. Elias Mountains
(Rother, Schwäbisch Gmünd)

② Rocky Mountains near Banff
(Heinrich, Aalen)

③ Vancouver
(Kraus, Wäschenbeuren)

④ Yosemite National Park
(Leicht, Mutlangen)

⑤ Mexican Plateau
(Rother, Schwäbisch Gmünd)

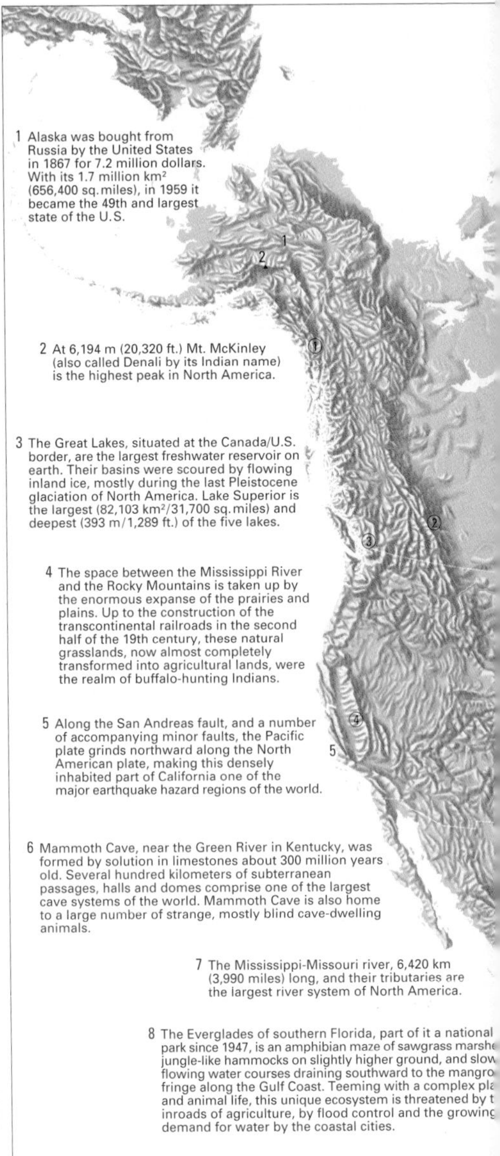

1 Alaska was bought from Russia by the United States in 1867 for 7.2 million dollars. With its 1.7 million km² (656,400 sq. miles), in 1959 it became the 49th and largest state of the U.S.

2 At 6,194 m (20,320 ft.) Mt. McKinley (also called Denali by its Indian name) is the highest peak in North America.

3 The Great Lakes, situated at the Canada/U.S. border, are the largest freshwater reservoir on earth. Their basins were scoured by flowing inland ice, mostly during the last Pleistocene glaciation of North America. Lake Superior is the largest (82,103 km²/31,700 sq. miles) and deepest (393 m/1,289 ft.) of the five lakes.

4 The space between the Mississippi River and the Rocky Mountains is taken up by the enormous expanse of the prairies and plains. Up to the construction of the transcontinental railroads in the second half of the 19th century, these natural grasslands, now almost completely transformed into agricultural lands, were the realm of buffalo-hunting Indians.

5 Along the San Andreas fault, and a number of accompanying minor faults, the Pacific plate grinds northward along the North American plate, making this densely inhabited part of California one of the major earthquake hazard regions of the world.

6 Mammoth Cave, near the Green River in Kentucky, was formed by solution in limestones about 300 million years old. Several hundred kilometers of subterranean passages, halls and domes comprise one of the largest cave systems of the world. Mammoth Cave is also home to a large number of strange, mostly blind cave-dwelling animals.

7 The Mississippi-Missouri river, 6,420 km (3,990 miles) long, and their tributaries are the largest river system of North America.

8 The Everglades of southern Florida, part of it a national park since 1947, is an amphibian maze of sawgrass marshe jungle-like hammocks on slightly higher ground, and slow flowing water courses draining southward to the mangro fringe along the Gulf Coast. Teeming with a complex pla and animal life, this unique ecosystem is threatened by t inroads of agriculture, by flood control and the growing demand for water by the coastal cities.

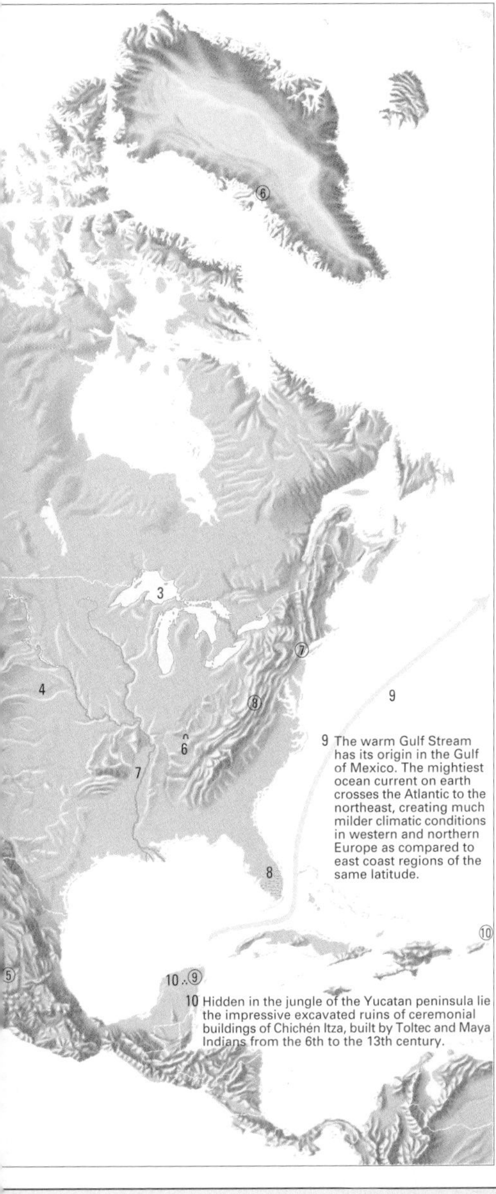

9 The warm Gulf Stream has its origin in the Gulf of Mexico. The mightiest ocean current on earth crosses the Atlantic to the northeast, creating much milder climatic conditions in western and northern Europe as compared to east coast regions of the same latitude.

10 Hidden in the jungle of the Yucatan peninsula lie the impressive excavated ruins of ceremonial buildings of Chichén Itza, built by Toltec and Maya Indians from the 6th to the 13th century.

⑥ Ilulissat, Greenland
(Pott, Stuttgart)

⑦ New York
(PhotoDisc)

⑧ Appalachian Mountains
(Krauter, Esslingen)

⑨ Maya Pyramid, Chichén Itza
(Rother, Schwäbisch Gmünd)

⑩ Tropical Beach, Virgin Islands
(PhotoDisc)

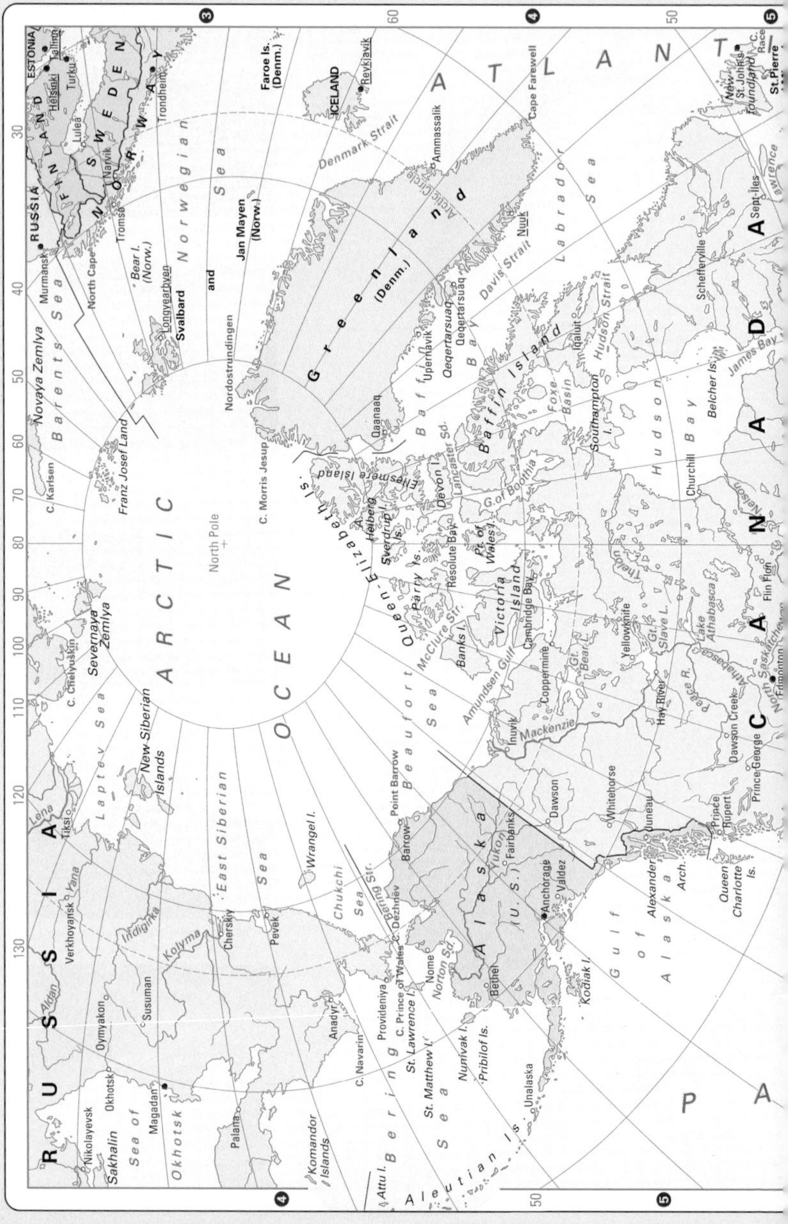
ARCTIC OCEAN
North Pole
ATLANTIC
PACIFIC
RUSSIA
CANADA
ESTONIA
FINLAND
SWEDEN
NORWAY
ICELAND
Greenland (Denm.)
Alaska (U.S.)
Tallinn
Helsinki
Turku
Lulea
Narvik
Trondheim
Tromsø
Murmansk
North Cape
Faroe Is. (Denm.)
Reykjavik
Jan Mayen (Norw.)
Bear I. (Norw.)
Svalbard and Jan Mayen
Longyearbyen
Norwegian Sea
Barents Sea
Novaya Zemlya
Franz Josef Land
C. Karlsen
Severnaya Zemlya
C. Chelyuskin
Laptev Sea
New Siberian Islands
East Siberian Sea
Wrangel I.
Chukchi Sea
Bering Str.
Bering Sea
Sea of Okhotsk
Sakhalin
Nikolayevsk
Okhotsk
Magadan
Oymyakon
Susuman
Verkhoyansk
Tiksi
Lena
Yana
Indigirka
Kolyma
Aldan
Cherskiy
Pevek
Anadyr
Provideniya
C. Navarin
Palana
Komandor Islands
Attu I.
Aleutian Is.
Unalaska
Pribilof Is.
Nunivak I.
St. Matthew I.
St. Lawrence I.
C. Prince of Wales
C. Dezhnev
Nome
Norton Sd.
Bethel
Kodiak I.
Anchorage
Valdez
Fairbanks
Yukon
Barrow
Point Barrow
Beaufort Sea
Gulf of Alaska
Alexander Arch.
Queen Charlotte Is.
Juneau
Prince Rupert
Prince George
Dawson Creek
Whitehorse
Dawson
Inuvik
Mackenzie
Coppermine
Amundsen Gulf
Banks I.
McClure Str.
Victoria Island
Cambridge Bay
Gt. Bear L.
Gt. Slave L.
Yellowknife
Hay River
Peace R.
Athabasca
Lake Athabasca
North Saskatchewan
Edmonton
Flin Flon
Thelon
Nelson
Churchill
Hudson Bay
Belcher Is.
James Bay
Southampton I.
Foxe Basin
Hudson Strait
Iqaluit
Baffin Island
Baffin Bay
Davis Strait
Labrador Sea
Nuuk
Cape Farewell
Ammassalik
Denmark Strait
Arctic Circle
Upernavik
Qeqertarsuaq
Qaanaaq
Nordostrundingen
C. Morris Jesup
Ellesmere Island
Queen Elizabeth Is.
Axel Heiberg I.
Sverdrup Is.
Parry Is.
Devon I.
Lancaster Sd.
Resolute Bay
Pt. of Wales I.
G. of Boothia
Schefferville
Sept-Iles
St. Lawrence
Newfoundland
St. John's
C. Race
St. Pierre
30
40
50
60
70
80
90
100
110
120
130

O C E A N
P A C I F I C O C E A N
U N I T E D S T A T E S
M E X I C O
C U B A
B A H A M A S
Gulf of Mexico
Caribbean Sea
Gulf of California
Bay of Campeche
Gulf of Honduras
Yucatan Channel
Str. of Florida
Tropic of Cancer
Equator
Bermuda (U.K.)
Turks and Caicos Is. (U.K.)
Puerto Rico (U.S.)
San Juan
DOMINICAN REP.
SANTO DOMINGO
HAITI
Port-au-Prince
Hispaniola
Neth. Antilles
Navassa (U.S.)
JAMAICA
Kingston
Cayman Is. (U.K.)
HAVANA
Santiago
Nassau
Miami
VENEZUELA
MARACAIBO
San Cristóbal
COLOMBIA
BOGOTÁ
MEDELLÍN
CALI
Pasto
Buenaventura
Buc.
Magdalena
Caquetá
ECUADOR
Malpelo (Col.)
Punta Gallinas
BARRANQUILLA
Cartagena
Providencia
San Andrés (Col.)
PANAMA
Panamá City
Colón
G. of Panamá
Panama Can.
COSTA RICA
San José
NICARAGUA
Managua
L. Nicaragua
HONDURAS
Tegucigalpa
EL SALVADOR
San Salvador
GUATEMALA
GUATEMALA CITY
BELIZE
Belmopan
Cocos I. (C.R.)
Clipperton (Fr.)
Revillagigedo Is. (Mex.)
Guadalupe (Mex.)
MEXICO CITY
PUEBLA
Veracruz
Tampico
Tehuantepec
Acapulco
GUADALAJARA
LEÓN
San Luis Potosí
MONTERREY
Torreón
Durango
Culiacán
Chihuahua
Hermosillo
CD. JUÁREZ
La Paz
Cape San Lucas
Mexicali
Mérida
C. Catoche
Halifax
Fredericton
Cape Sable
Cape Cod
Portland
Boston
Providence
NEW YORK
PHILADELPHIA
Baltimore
Washington
Norfolk
Cape Hatteras
Albany
Québec
MONTRÉAL
Ottawa
Toronto
Buffalo
Cleveland
Pittsburgh
Columbus
Cincinnati
Richmond
Raleigh
Charlotte
Columbia
Charleston
Jacksonville
C. Canaveral
Tampa
Atlanta
Columbus
Montgomery
Birmingham
Jackson
New Orleans
Baton Rouge
HOUSTON
Corpus Christi
SAN ANTONIO
Austin
DALLAS
Fort Worth
Red R.
Little Rock
Memphis
Mississippi
Nashville
Louisville
Ohio
St. Louis
Indianapolis
CHICAGO
DETROIT
Toledo
Erie
Huron
Michigan
Superior
Sudbury
Milwaukee
Thunder Bay
Duluth
St. Paul
Minneapolis
Sioux Falls
Des Moines
Lincoln
Kansas City
Platte
Wichita
Arkansas
Oklahoma City
Amarillo
Winnipeg
Bismarck
Pierre
Regina
Cheyenne
Denver
Pueblo
Albuquerque
Rio Grande
El Paso
Tucson
PHOENIX
Colorado
Salt Lake City
Gt. Salt L.
Helena
Missouri
Boise
Spokane
Seattle
Victoria
Portland
Reno
Las Vegas
Sacramento
San Francisco
Cape Mendocino
Point Conception
LOS ANGELES
SAN DIEGO
0 10 20 30 40 80 90 100 110 120 130

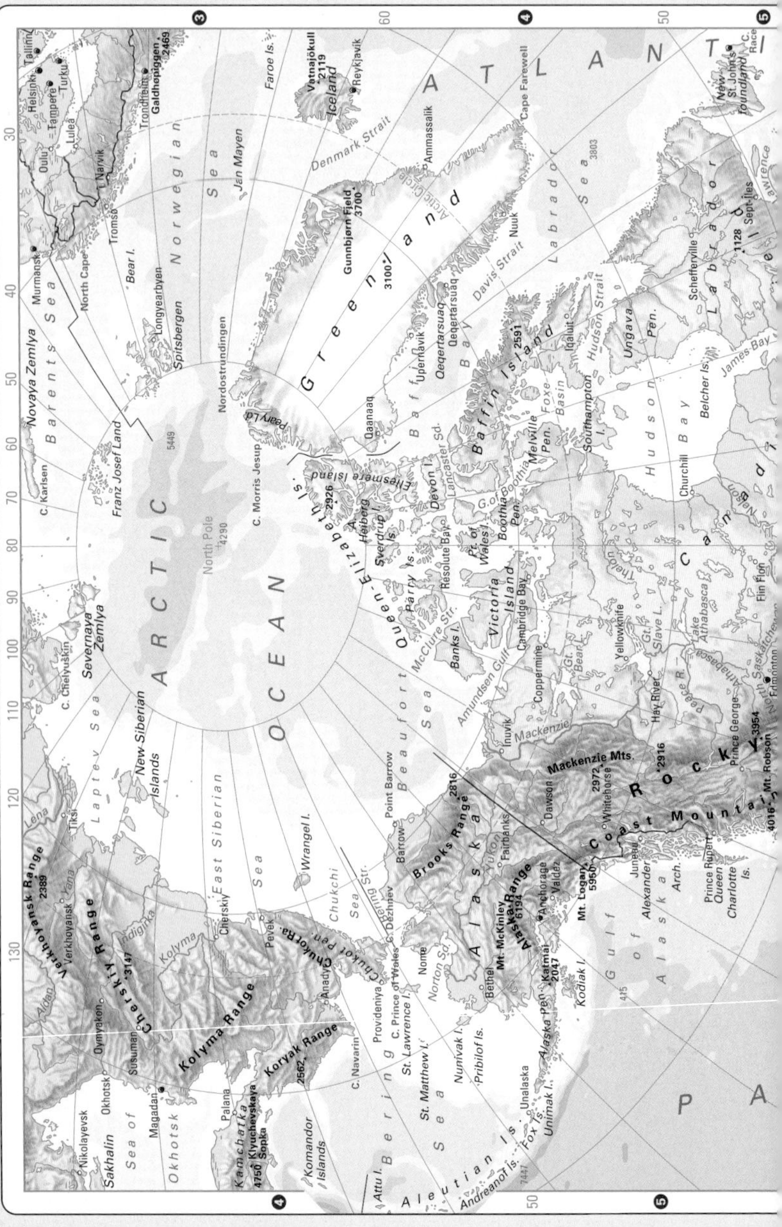
ARCTIC OCEAN
North Pole
4290
5449
Greenland
Gunnbjørn Field
3700
3100
ATLANTIC
Norwegian Sea
Barents Sea
Laptev Sea
East Siberian Sea
Chukchi Sea
Beaufort Sea
Bering Sea
Sea of Okhotsk
Gulf of Alaska
Baffin Bay
Baffin Island
2591
Labrador Sea
Hudson Bay
Hudson Strait
James Bay
Davis Strait
Denmark Strait
Iceland
Vatnajökull
2119
Reykjavík
Faroe Is.
Jan Mayen
Spitsbergen
Longyearbyen
Bear I.
Franz Josef Land
Novaya Zemlya
Severnaya Zemlya
New Siberian Islands
Wrangel I.
Ellesmere Island
Queen Elizabeth Is.
2926
Axel Heiberg
Sverdrup Is.
Parry Is.
Devon I.
Victoria Island
Banks I.
Southampton I.
Melville Pen.
Boothia Pen.
Ungava Pen.
Labrador
Newfoundland
St. John's
C. Race
Canada
Alaska
Brooks Range
2816
Alaska Range
Mt. McKinley
6194
Mt. Logan
5950
Mackenzie Mts.
2972
Rocky Mountains
Mt. Robson
3954
4016
2916
Coast Mountains
Kodiak I.
Katmai
2047
Alaska Pen.
Aleutian Is.
Fox Is.
Andreanof Is.
Unimak I.
Attu I.
Komandor Islands
Kamchatka
Klyuchevskaya Sopka
4750
Koryak Range
2562
Kolyma Range
Cherskiy Range
3147
Verkhoyansk Range
2389
Chukotka Ra.
Chukot Pen.
Sakhalin
Murmansk
Tromsø
Narvik
North Cape
Helsinki
Tallinn
Turku
Tampere
Oulu
Luleå
Trondheim
Galdhøpiggen
2469
Nuuk
Ammassalik
Cape Farewell
Upernavik
Qaanaaq
Iqaluit
Churchill
Schefferville
Sept-Îles
1128
Yellowknife
Hay River
Inuvik
Coppermine
Cambridge Bay
Resolute Bay
Dawson
Whitehorse
Fairbanks
Anchorage
Valdez
Juneau
Prince Rupert
Prince George
Edmonton
Flin Flon
Barrow
Point Barrow
Nome
Bethel
Unalaska
Magadan
Okhotsk
Oymyakon
Susuman
Verkhoyansk
Tiksi
Cherskiy
Pevek
Anadyr
Provideniya
Palana
Nikolayevsk
Great Bear L.
Great Slave L.
Lake Athabasca
Mackenzie
Yukon
Lena
Kolyma
Indigirka
Aldan
Yana
Nelson
Thelon
Peace R.
Athabasca
North Saskatchewan
Pacific
415
7447
3803

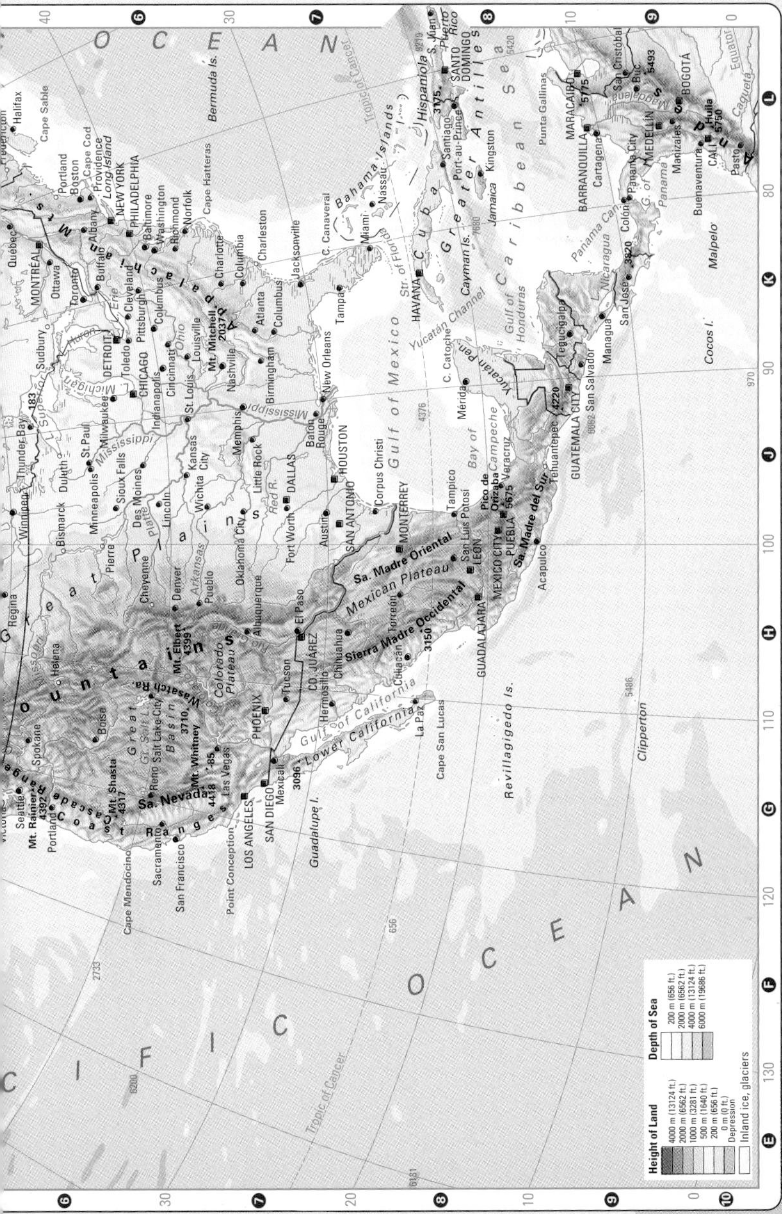
Height of Land
4000 m (13124 ft.)
2000 m (6562 ft.)
1000 m (3281 ft.)
500 m (1640 ft.)
200 m (656 ft.)
0 m (0 ft.)
Depression
Inland ice, glaciers
Depth of Sea
200 m (656 ft.)
2000 m (6562 ft.)
4000 m (13124 ft.)
6000 m (19686 ft.)
P A C I F I C O C E A N
O C E A N
Gulf of Mexico
Caribbean Sea
Greater Antilles
Bahama Islands
Cuba
Hispaniola
Puerto Rico
Jamaica
Cayman Is.
Bermuda Is.
Gulf of California
Lower California
Yucatan Pen.
Bay of Campeche
Gulf of Honduras
Yucatán Channel
Str. of Florida
Great Plains
Rocky Mountains
Appalachian Mts.
Sa. Nevada
Cascade Range
Coast Ranges
Great Basin
Colorado Plateau
Mexican Plateau
Sa. Madre Oriental
Sierra Madre Occidental
Sa. Madre del Sur
Tropic of Cancer
Equator
NEW YORK
PHILADELPHIA
CHICAGO
DETROIT
MONTRÉAL
LOS ANGELES
SAN DIEGO
PHOENIX
HOUSTON
DALLAS
SAN ANTONIO
MONTERREY
GUADALAJARA
MEXICO CITY
PUEBLA
LEÓN
GUATEMALA CITY
HAVANA
SANTO DOMINGO
BARRANQUILLA
MARACAIBO
MEDELLÍN
BOGOTÁ
CALI
CD. JUÁREZ
Washington
Boston
Toronto
Ottawa
Québec
Halifax
Seattle
Portland
San Francisco
Sacramento
Las Vegas
Denver
Albuquerque
El Paso
Tucson
Miami
New Orleans
Atlanta
St. Louis
Memphis
Minneapolis
Winnipeg
Mt. Whitney 4418
Mt. Elbert 4399
Mt. Mitchell 2037
Mt. Rainier 4392
Mt. Shasta 4317
Pico de Orizaba 5675
Cocos I.
Clipperton
Revillagigedo Is.
Guadalupe I.

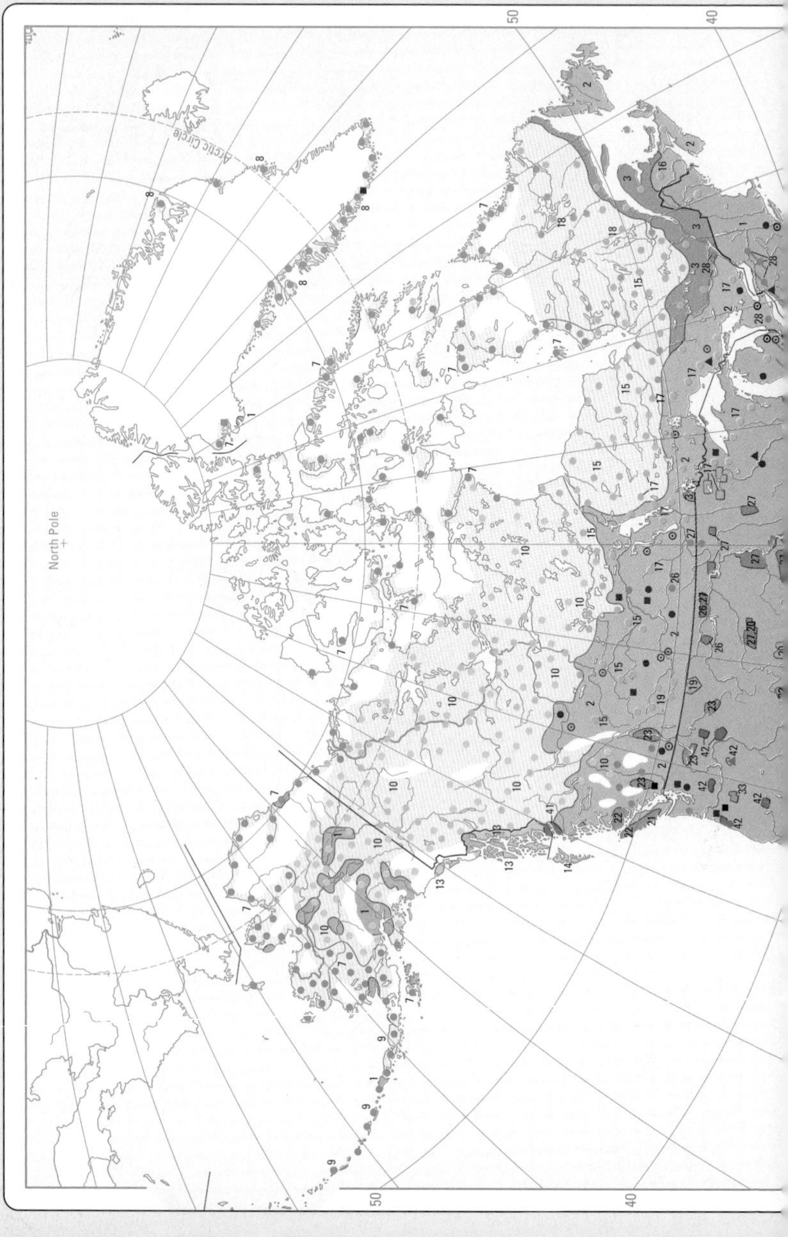
Arctic Circle
North Pole
50
40

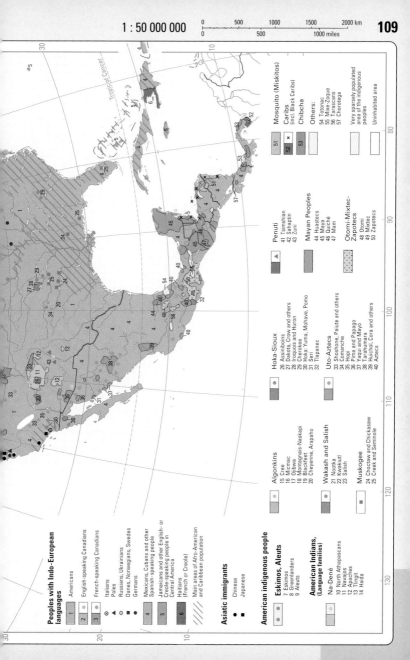

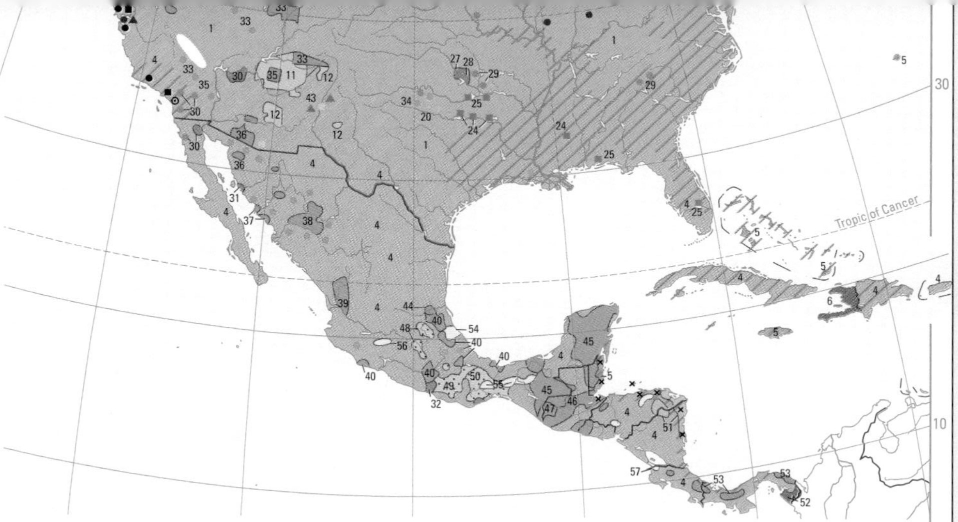

Peoples with Indo-European languages

- 1 Americans
- 2 English-speaking Canadians
- 3 French-speaking Canadians
- ⊙ Italians
- ▲ Poles
- ⊙ Russians, Ukrainians
- ■ Danes, Norwegians, Swedes
- ● Germans
- 4 Mexicans, Cubans and other Spanish-speaking people
- 5 Jamaicans and other English- or Creole-speaking people in Central America
- 6 Haitians (French or Creole)
- //// Main areas of Afro-American and Caribbean population

Asiatic immigrants

- ● Chinese
- ■ Japanese

American indigenous people

Eskimos, Aleuts

7 Eskimos
8 Greenlanders
9 Aleuts

American Indians, (Language families)

Na-Dené

10 North Athapascans
11 Navajos
12 Apaches
13 Tlingit
14 Haida

Algonkins

15 Cree
16 Micmac
17 Ojibwa
18 Montagnais-Naskapi
19 Blackfeet
20 Cheyenne, Arapaho

Wakash and Salish

21 Nootka
22 Kwakiutl
23 Salish

Muskogee

24 Choctaw and Chickasaw
25 Creek and Seminole

Hoka-Sioux

26 Assiniboins
27 Dakota, Crow and others
28 Iroquois and Huron
29 Cherokee
30 Hoka: Yuma, Mohave, Pomo
31 Seri
32 Tlapanec

Uto-Aztecs

33 Shoshone, Paiute and others
34 Comanche
35 Hopi
36 Pima and Papago
37 Yaqui and Mayo
38 Tarahumara
39 Huichol, Cora and others
40 Aztecs

Penuti

41 Tsimshian
42 Sahaptin
43 Zuni

Mayan Peoples

44 Huastecs
45 Maya
46 Quiché
47 Mam

Otomí-Mixtec-Zapotecs

48 Otomí
49 Mixtec
50 Zapotecs

51 Mosquito (Miskitos)
52 × Caribs (incl. Black Caribs)
53 Chibcha

Others:

54 Totonac
55 Mixe-Zoque
56 Tarascans
57 Chorotega

Very sparsely populated area of the indigenous peoples

Uninhabited area

62/63
Pobeda
3147
Srednekolymsk
Bear Is.
Zyryanka
Kolyma
A R C T I C O C
Ambarchik
Yukagir
1185
Plateau
Cherskiy
Ayon I.
C. Shelagskiy
Omolon
Arctic Circle
Anyuy Ra.
Bilibino
Pevek
Wrangel I.
1096
1797
1853
Chukot Range
Evensk
R U S S I A
1503
1843
Markovo
Anadyr
Chukchi Sea
Barrow
Point Barrow
Penzhina Gulf
Kamenskoye
Vankarem
Prud. Bay
Point Hope
Anadyr
Koryak Range
Ilpyrskiy
Korf
Gora Ledyanaya
2562
Chukot Pen.
Kotzebue Sound
Brooks Range
Mt. Is
Karaginskiy I.
Pakhachi
Gulf of Anadyr
Uelen
C. Dezhnëv
Kotzebue
Bering Str.
Selawik
C. Olyutorskiy
Beringovskiy
Provideniya
C. Prince of Wales
Seward Pen.
Fort Yuko
Cape Navarin
C. Chukotskiy
Gambell
1437
Saint Lawrence Island
Nome
Alaska
Circ
Norton Sound
Unalakleet
Ruby
Fairbanks
UNITED STATE
Yukon
Kuskokwim Mts.
1374
Kantishna
Mt. McKinley
6194
Saint Matthew I.
C. Romanzof
Hooper Bay
Alaska Ra
Bering Sea
Bethel
Kuskokwim
Willow Lake
Palmer
Nunivak I.
Anchorage
Attu I.
Near Is.
Attu
Kuskokwim Bay
Kenai Pen.
Newhalen
Dillingham
3053
Cook Inlet
Seward
Homer
Pribilof Is.
Bristol Bay
Afognak I.
Rat Is.
Aleutian Range
Shelikof Str.
Kodiak
Aleutian Islands
Alaska Pen.
2507
Mt. Veniaminof
1353
Andreanof Is.
1806
Fox Islands
Cold Bay
Chignik
Kodiak I.
Atka
Umnak I.
Unalaska
Unimak I.
Shumagin Islands
Trinity Islands
Unalaska I.
P A C I F I C O C

140 J 130 K 120 L 110 M 100 N 90 O 112/113 80 Q
Devon I.
Borden I.
Mackenzie King I.
Parry Is.
Cornwallis I.
Lancaster Sound
Arctic Bay
Baffin Island
Prince Charles I.
Igloolik
Resolute Bay
Bathurst I.
Somerset I.
Brodeur Pen.
Gulf of Boothia
Melville Pen.
Foxe Basin
Foxe Pen.
Prince Patrick I.
Melville I.
Viscount Melville Sound
Prince of Wales Island
Boothia Pen.
Foxe Channel
Mould Bay
Eglinton I.
McClure Strait
McClintock Channel
Repulse Bay
Southampton I.
Coral Harbour
C. Prince Alfred
Banks Island
655
Victoria Island
King William I.
Roes Welcome Sound
543
Coats Island
Sachs Harbour
Ikaluktutiak/ Cambridge Bay
Queen Maud Gulf
Nunavut
Beaufort Sea
Cape Bathurst
Amundsen Gulf
Holman
Coronation Gulf
Baker Lake
Rankin Inlet
Hudson Bay
Mackenzie Bay
Bathurst Inlet
Back
Tuktoyaktuk
Coppermine
Arviat
Inuvik
Aklavik
Old Crow
Dubawnt Lake
Cape Churchill
Echo Bay
Churchill
Porcupine
Northwest Territories
Great Bear Lake
Reliance
Fort Norman
Yellowknife
Manitoba
Yukon
Mackenzie Mts.
Mackenzie
CANADA
Dawson
Keele Peak 2972
Mayo
Great Slave Lake
Fort Resolution
Uranium City
Wollaston Lake
Thompson
Reindeer L.
Lynn Lake
Fort Providence
Fort Smith
Slave
Wollaston Lake
Fort Simpson
Hay River
Territory
Faro
Lake Athabasca
Snow Lake
Carmacks
Flin Flon
Fort Vermilion
Athabasca
La Loche
The Pas
Whitehorse
Watson Lake
Liard
5950 Mount Logan
Fort Nelson
Fort McMurray
La Ronge
Skagway
Cassiar
Rocky Mountains
Mount Sylvia 2942
Saskatchewan
Yakutat
Ware
Prince Albert
Juneau
Coast Mountains
British Columbia
Peace
Peace River
Lac la Biche
Saskatchewan
Mt. Ratz 3136
St. Paul
Chichagof I.
Fort St. John
Alberta
Saskatoon
Sitka
Baranof I.
Alexander Arch.
Dawson Creek
Grande Prairie
Edmonton
Kupreanof I.
Edson
Wainwright
Regina
Wrangell
Stewart
Wetaskiwin
Prince of Wales Island
Mount Robson 3954
Red Deer
Swift Current
Ketchikan
Jasper
Drumheller
Prince George
Brooks
Dixon Entrance
Quesnel
Banff
Calgary
Prince Rupert
Kitimat
3618
Lethbridge
Queen
1250
Hecate Str.
Mt. Assiniboine
Havre
Charlotte Is.
Ocean Falls
Mount Waddington 4016
Kamloops
Revelstoke
Kimberley
Great Falls
Fraser
Vernon
Kelowna
Montana
Cape St. James
Queen Charlotte Sound
Billings
Port Hardy
Vancouver
Spokane
Helena
Vancouver Island
Port Alberni
Victoria
Everett
Washington
Seattle
Tacoma
Mt. Rainier
Idaho
Wyoming
Olympia
4392
Yakima
UNITED STATES
Portland
Boise
Pocatello
Salem
Oregon
Utah
65
60
55
50
45
4
5
6
7
8
9
112/113
140 J 130 K 120 114/115 L

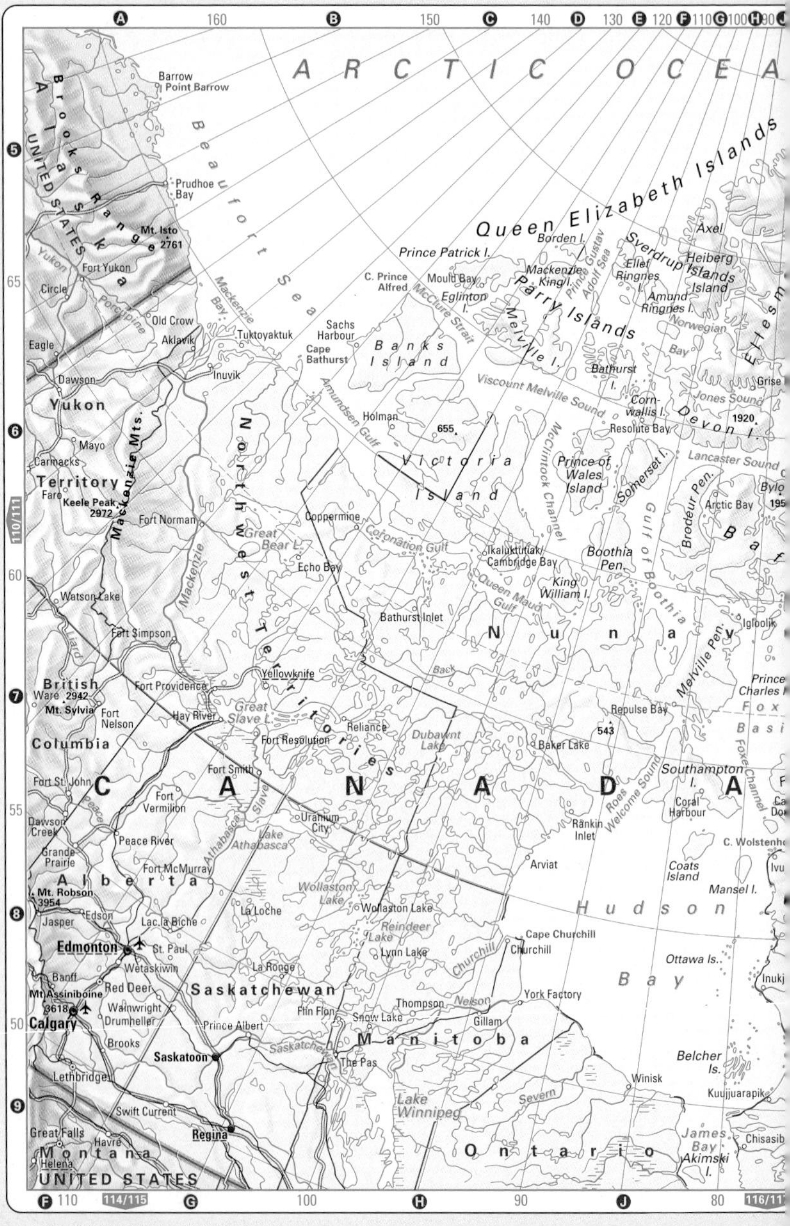
A
B
C
D
E
F
G
H
160
150
140
130
120
110
100
ARCTIC OCEAN
Barrow
Point Barrow
Brooks Range
Alaska
UNITED STATES
Beaufort Sea
Prudhoe Bay
Mt. Isto 2761
Yukon
Fort Yukon
Circle
Porcupine
Old Crow
Aklavik
Eagle
Mackenzie Bay
Tuktoyaktuk
Dawson
Inuvik
Yukon Territory
Mayo
Carmacks
Faro
Keele Peak 2972
Mackenzie Mts.
Fort Norman
Queen Elizabeth Islands
Borden I.
Prince Patrick I.
C. Prince Alfred
Mould Bay
Eglinton I.
Mackenzie King I.
Prince Gustav Adolf Sea
Sverdrup Islands
Ellef Ringnes I.
Amund Ringnes I.
Axel Heiberg Island
Parry Islands
Melville I.
McClure Strait
Sachs Harbour
Cape Bathurst
Banks Island
Norwegian Bay
Ellesmere
Bathurst I.
Viscount Melville Sound
Cornwallis I.
Jones Sound
Grise
Devon I.
1920
Resolute Bay
Amundsen Gulf
Holman
655
Victoria Island
Prince of Wales Island
McClintock Channel
Somerset I.
Lancaster Sound
Bylo
Brodeur Pen.
Arctic Bay
Gulf of Boothia
Northwest Territories
Coppermine
Coronation Gulf
Great Bear L.
Echo Bay
Ikaluktutiak/Cambridge Bay
Boothia Pen.
King William I.
Queen Maud Gulf
Baffin
Bathurst Inlet
Nunavut
Igloolik
Melville Pen.
Mackenzie
Watson Lake
Fort Simpson
Liard
Back
Yellowknife
British Columbia
Ware
2942
Mt. Sylvia
Fort Providence
Fort Nelson
Hay River
Great Slave L.
Reliance
Fort Resolution
Dubawnt Lake
Repulse Bay
543
Baker Lake
Prince Charles I.
Foxe Basin
Fort St. John
CANADA
Fort Smith
Fort Vermilion
Peace
Slave
Uranium City
Southampton I.
Foxe Channel
Coral Harbour
Roes Welcome Sound
Rankin Inlet
Dawson Creek
Peace River
Athabasca
Lake Athabasca
Grande Prairie
Fort McMurray
Alberta
Mt. Robson 3954
Wollaston Lake
Arviat
Coats Island
C. Wolstenholme
Mansel I.
Edson
Jasper
La Loche
Lac la Biche
Reindeer Lake
Hudson Bay
Edmonton
St. Paul
Lynn Lake
Cape Churchill
Churchill
Wetaskiwin
La Ronge
Ottawa Is.
Banff
Mt Assiniboine 3618
Red Deer
Saskatchewan
Wainwright
York Factory
Calgary
Drumheller
Flin Flon
Thompson
Nelson
Snow Lake
Gillam
Prince Albert
Manitoba
Brooks
Saskatoon
The Pas
Belcher Is.
Lethbridge
Winisk
Kuujjuarapik
Swift Current
Lake Winnipeg
Severn
Great Falls
Regina
Havre
Montana
Helena
UNITED STATES
Ontario
James Bay
Akimski I.
Chisasibi
Inukjuak
Churchill
Saskatchewan
65
60
55
50
5
6
7
8
9
110/111
114/115
116/117
F
G
H
J
90
80

L
M
N
O
P
Q
R
S
T
60
50
40
30
20
10
0
10
Nordost-
rundingen
C. Morris Jesup
Peary Land
Lincoln
Sea
Greenland
Sea
King Frederick
VIII Land
Danmarkshavn
Knud Rasmussen Land
Greenland
(Denm.)
2544
Jan Mayen
(Norw.)
Daneborg
Arctic Circle
King Christian X Land
Qaanaaq/Thule
Ittoqqortoormiit
Melville
Bay
Seyðisfjörður
Akureyri
ICELAND
Gunnbjørn Fjeld
3700
Vatna-
jökull
2119
Denmark Strait
Upernavik
3230
Baffin
Bay
Svartenhuk Pen.
Unmmannaq
Nuugssuaq
Reykjavík
Ilulissat
Qeqertarsuaq
Clyde
Qeqertarsuaq
Qasigiannguit
King Christian
IX Land
Ammassalik
Home
Bay
Davis Strait
Kangerlussuaq
Sisimiut
Penny Highland
2591
Cumberland
Pen.
Cape
Dyer
Maniitsoq
King Frederik VI Coast
Pangnirtung
Cumberland Sd.
Nuuk
(Godthåb)
Hall Pen.
1143
Iqaluit
Meta
Incognita Pen.
Frobisher Bay
Paamiut
2300
Qaqortoq
Ivittuut
Nanortalik
Cape Farewell
Resolution I.
Akpatok I.
Kangirsuk
Labrador Sea
Ungava
Bay
1595
ATLANTIC
OCEAN
Kuujjuaq
Nain
Newfoundland
Labrador
Québec
Hopedale
Rigolet
Smallwood
Res.
1150
Schefferville
Melville
L.
Port Hope Simpson
Labrador City
St. Anthony
65
60
55
50
5
6
7
8
9
46/47
70
60
50
40

110/111
Queen Charlotte Is.
Cape St. James
Queen Charlotte Sound
Ocean Falls
Port Hardy
Vancouver I.
Prince George
Quesnel
British Columbia
Coast Mts.
Mt. Waddington 4016
Golden Hinde 2200
Vancouver
Port Alberni
Nanaimo
Victoria
Kamloops
Fraser
Mt. Robson 3954
Jasper
Edson
Edmonton
St. Paul
Lloydminster
Wetaskiwin
Wainwright
Alberta
Red Deer
Drumheller
Banff
Mt. Assiniboine 3618
Calgary
Brooks
Revelstoke
Columbia
Vernon
Kelowna
Penticton
Hope
Kimberley
Trail
Lethbridge
Cut Bank
Seattle
Everett
Grand Coulee
Spokane
Tacoma
Washington
Ellensburg
Aberdeen
Olympia
4392
Mt. Rainier
Yakima
Longview
Astoria
Portland
Salem
Newport
Corvallis
Eugene
Kennewick
Pendleton
The Dalles
Lewiston
Grangeville
Coeur d'Alene
Kalispell
Thompson Falls
Missoula
Bovill
Bitterroot Range
Anaconda
Butte
Helena
Townsend
Bozeman
Great Falls
Lewistown
Baker
Oregon
Bend
Burns
Roseburg
Medford
Bly
Klamath Falls
Crescent City
Nampa
Boise
Idaho
Borah Peak 3859
Idaho Falls
Pocatello
Twin Falls
Grand Teton 4197
Snake
Mt. Shasta 4317
2744
Eureka
Cape Mendocino
Redding
Sacramento
Chico
Yuba C.
Great
Winnemucca
Lovelock
Elko
Great Salt Lake
Logan
Ogden
Salt Lake City
Provo
Uinta Mts.
Reno
Carson City
Nevada
Ely
Wheeler Peak 3982
Utah
Price
Richfield
Santa Rosa
Stockton
San Francisco
Oakland
San Jose
Monterey
Basin
Tonopah
Bishop
Cedar City
Mt. Whitney 4418
Fresno
Tulare
San Joaquin
Las Vegas
Henderson
Littlefield
L. Mead
Colorado
Page
Grand Canyon
Plateau
3862
Flagstaff
San Luis Obispo
Santa Maria
Point Conception
Bakersfield
Barstow
Santa Barbara
Kingman
Holbrook
Prescott
LOS ANGELES
San Bernardino
Arizona
Parker Dam
PHOENIX
Palm Springs
Miami
Channel Islands
Oceanside
SAN DIEGO
Brawley
Gila
Yuma
Tijuana
Ensenada
Mexicali
Tucson
Sonoyta
Nogales
Cerro de la Encantada 3096
San Quintín
Gulf of California
Isla Angel de la Guarda
Lower California
Guadalupe I.
Cedros I.
Hermosillo
Tiburón I.
Guaymas
Pta. Sta. Eugenia
Santa Rosalía
Ciudad Obregón
Huatabampo
PACIFIC OCEAN
Rocky Mts.
Cascade Range
Sierra Nevada
Coast Ranges
UNITED

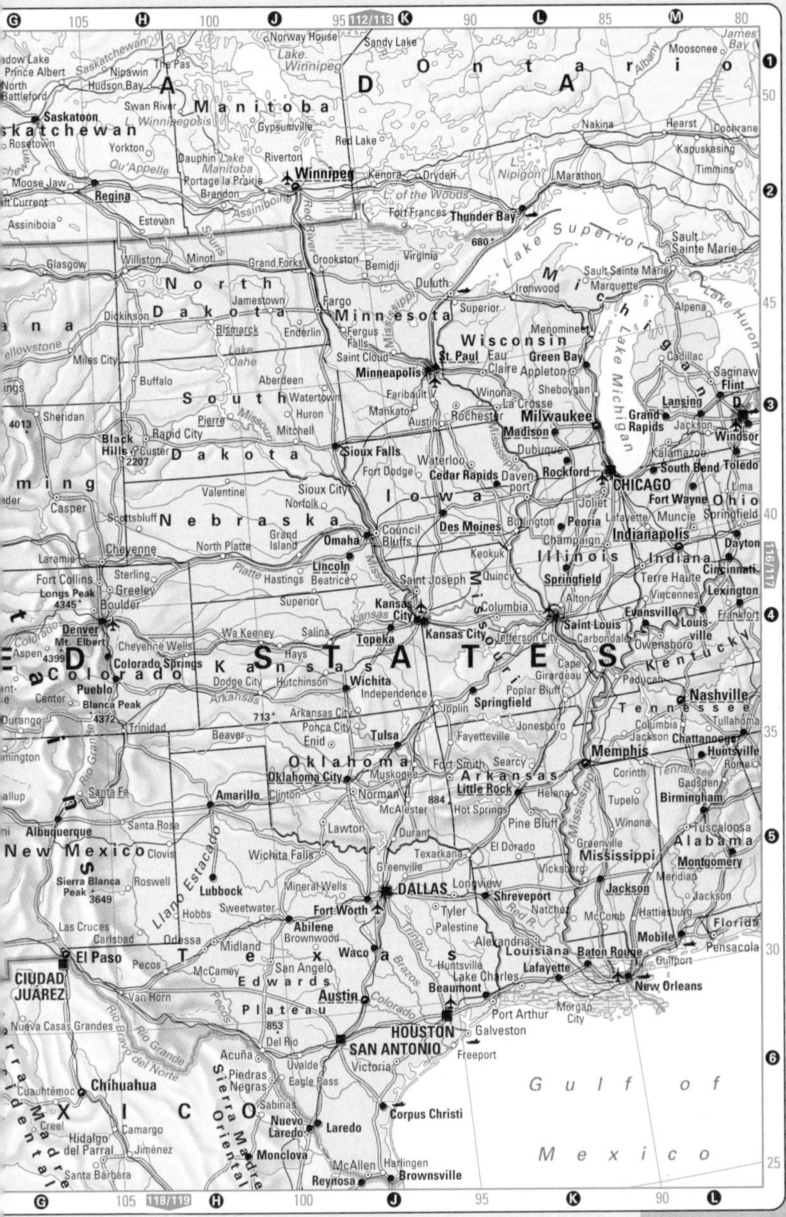
G
105
H
100
J
95
112/113
K
90
L
85
M
80
1
2
3
4
5
6
50
45
40
35
30
25
Norway House
Sandy Lake
James Bay
Moosonee
Saskatchewan
Prince Albert
Nipawin
The Pas
Lake Winnipeg
O n t a r i o
Albany
North Battleford
Hudson Bay
A
D
A
Saskatoon
Swan River
M a n i t o b a
L. Winnipegosis
Gypsumville
Nakina
Hearst
Cochrane
Rosetown
Yorkton
Red Lake
Kapuskasing
Riverton
Dauphin
Lake Manitoba
L. Nipigon
Timmins
Qu'Appelle
Winnipeg
Kenora
Dryden
Marathon
Moose Jaw
Portage la Prairie
Brandon
Regina
Assiniboine
L. of the Woods
Fort Frances
Thunder Bay
Assiniboia
Estevan
Souris
Red River
Lake Superior
680
Sault Sainte Marie
Glasgow
Williston
Minot
Grand Forks
Crookston
Bemidji
Virginia
Sault Sainte Marie
N o r t h
Jamestown
Duluth
Ironwood
Marquette
Fargo
Mississippi
Superior
Alpena
Lake Huron
Dickinson
D a k o t a
Minnesota
Bismarck
Enderlin
Fergus Falls
Wisconsin
Menominee
Yellowstone
Lake Oahe
Saint Cloud
St. Paul
Eau Claire
Green Bay
Cadillac
Miles City
Minneapolis
Appleton
Lake Michigan
Saginaw
Buffalo
Aberdeen
Winona
Sheboygan
Flint
S o u t h
Watertown
Faribault
La Crosse
Lansing
Sheridan
Huron
Mankato
Rochester
Milwaukee
Grand Rapids
Missouri
Pierre
Austin
Jackson
4013
Black Hills
Rapid City
Mitchell
Madison
Windsor
Custer
2207
D a k o t a
Sioux Falls
Dubuque
Kalamazoo
Waterloo
South Bend
Toledo
Fort Dodge
Cedar Rapids
Davenport
Rockford
m i n g
Valentine
Sioux City
CHICAGO
Lima
Casper
Norfolk
I o w a
Joliet
Fort Wayne
O h i o
Scottsbluff
N e b r a s k a
Council Bluffs
Des Moines
Burlington
Peoria
Lafayette
Muncie
Springfield
Grand Island
Omaha
Champaign
Indianapolis
Dayton
Cheyenne
North Platte
Keokuk
Laramie
Lincoln
Missouri
Illinois
Indiana
Cincinnati
116/117
Fort Collins
Sterling
Platte
Hastings
Beatrice
Saint Joseph
Quincy
Springfield
Terre Haute
Longs Peak
Greeley
Vincennes
Lexington
4345
Boulder
Superior
Kansas City
Columbia
Alton
Evansville
Frankfort
Kansas
Denver
Wa Keeney
Salina
Kansas City
Saint Louis
Louisville
Colorado
Mt. Elbert
Cheyenne Wells
Topeka
Jefferson City
Carbondale
Owensboro
Aspen
4399
D
S T A T E S
Hays
Kentucky
Colorado Springs
K a n s a s
Cape Girardeau
C o l o r a d o
Dodge City
Hutchinson
Wichita
Paducah
Pueblo
Independence
Poplar Bluff
Nashville
Center
Arkansas
Blanca Peak
Springfield
Tennessee
4372
713
Arkansas City
Joplin
Durango
Trinidad
Ponca City
Jonesboro
Columbia
Tullahoma
Beaver
Enid
Tulsa
Fayetteville
Jackson
Chattanooga
Memphis
Huntsville
Rio Grande
O k l a h o m a
Fort Smith
Searcy
Rome
Oklahoma City
Muskogee
A r k a n s a s
Corinth
Tennessee
Gadsden
Santa Fe
Amarillo
Clinton
Norman
884
Little Rock
Helena
Tupelo
Birmingham
McAlester
Hot Springs
Albuquerque
Santa Rosa
Lawton
Durant
Pine Bluff
Winona
Tuscaloosa
Alabama
Llano Estacado
Greenville
New Mexico
Clovis
Wichita Falls
Texarkana
El Dorado
Mississippi
Montgomery
Greenville
Vicksburg
Meridian
Sierra Blanca Peak
3649
Roswell
Lubbock
Mineral Wells
DALLAS
Longview
Jackson
Shreveport
Jackson
Hobbs
Sweetwater
Fort Worth
Tyler
Natchez
McComb
Hattiesburg
Red R.
Las Cruces
Abilene
Trinity
Palestine
Florida
Carlsbad
Odessa
Brownwood
Alexandria
Mobile
Midland
Louisiana
Baton Rouge
Pensacola
El Paso
Pecos
T e x a s
Waco
Brazos
Huntsville
Lake Charles
Gulfport
McCamey
San Angelo
Lafayette
CIUDAD JUAREZ
E d w a r d s
Beaumont
New Orleans
Van Horn
Austin
Colorado
Pecos
P l a t e a u
Port Arthur
Morgan City
853
HOUSTON
Nueva Casas Grandes
Rio Grande
Del Rio
Galveston
SAN ANTONIO
Rio Bravo del Norte
Acuña
Freeport
Uvalde
Victoria
Piedras Negras
Eagle Pass
G u l f o f
Cuauhtémoc
Chihuahua
Sabinas
M E X I C O
Corpus Christi
Sierra Madre Occidental
Sierra Madre Oriental
Nuevo Laredo
Laredo
Creel
Camargo
M e x i c o
Hidalgo del Parral
Jiménez
Monclova
McAllen
Harlingen
Santa Bárbara
Brownsville
Reynosa
G
105
118/119
H
100
J
95
K
90
L

100
95
90
85
80
75
112/113
114/115
120
50
45
40
35
30
25
Manitoba
Portage la Prairie
Brandon
Winnipeg
Assiniboine
L. of the Woods
Souris
Minot
Red Lake
Kenora
Dryden
CANADA
Ontario
James Bay
Fort Albany
Albany
Moosonee
Fort Rupert
Québec
Chibougamau
Nakina
Lake Nipigon
Fort Frances
Hearst
North Dakota
Grand Forks
Crookston
Thunder Bay
Marathon
Kapuskasing
Cochrane
Jamestown
Bismarck
Bemidji
680
Enderlin
Fargo
Virginia
Lake Superior
Timmins
Rouyn
Val-d'Or
Fergus Falls
Duluth
Lake Oahe
Minnesota
Mississippi
Superior
Ironwood
Marquette
Sault Sainte Marie
Sudbury
North Bay
Aberdeen
South Dakota
Saint Cloud
Pierre
Watertown
Huron
Wisconsin
Sault Sainte-Marie
Michigan
Ottawa
Mont-Laurier
Hull
St-Jérôme
Minneapolis
St. Paul
Menominee
Georgian Bay
Parry Sound
Pembroke
Mitchell
Faribault
Eau Claire
Lake Michigan
Lake Huron
Mankato
Green Bay
Alpena
Ottawa
Sioux Falls
Rochester
Winona
Appleton
Austin
Peterborough
Kingston
Missouri
Sioux City
La Crosse
Sheboygan
Cadillac
Owen Sound
Norfolk
Waterloo
Madison
Milwaukee
Saginaw
Toronto
Oshawa
Lake Ontario
Watertown
Nebraska
Fort Dodge
Iowa
Dubuque
Grand Rapids
Lansing
Flint
Sarnia
Hamilton
Rochester
New York
Grand Island
Cedar Rapids
Omaha
Council Bluffs
Davenport
Rockford
London
DETROIT
Utica
Syracuse
Buffalo
Des Moines
CHICAGO
Jackson
Kalamazoo
Windsor
Lake Erie
Olean
Binghamton
Hastings
Lincoln
Burlington
Joliet
South Bend
Toledo
Erie
Superior
Beatrice
Peoria
Fort Wayne
Cleveland
Bradford
Williamsport
Scranton
Saint Joseph
Keokuk
Indiana
Youngstown
Salina
Kansas City
Missouri
Champaign
Lima
Akron
Canton
Pennsylvania
Quincy
Illinois
Lafayette
Muncie
Mansfield
Pittsburgh
NEW YORK
Kansas
Topeka
Kansas City
Columbia
Springfield
Terre Haute
Springfield
Ohio
Harrisburg
Hutchinson
Jefferson City
Indianapolis
Dayton
Columbus
Wheeling
Johnstown
Allentown
Wichita
Cincinnati
Parkersburg
York
Baltimore
Arkansas City
Saint Louis
Vincennes
Louisville
Spruce Knob 1482
Dover
Independence
UNITED STATES
Evansville
West Virginia
Washington
Annapolis
Ponca City
Cape Girardeau
Carbondale
Frankfort
Lexington
Charleston
Delaware
Enid
Joplin
Springfield
Owensboro
Tulsa
Oklahoma City
Poplar Bluff
Kentucky
Virginia
Chesapeake
Fayetteville
Paducah
Roanoke
Richmond
Norman
Muskogee
Fort Smith
Jonesboro
Bluefield
Lynchburg
Newport News
Oklahoma
Nashville
Johnson City
Danville
Norfolk
Virginia Beach
McAlester
Searcy
Jackson
Oak Ridge
Winston-Salem
Greensboro
884
Arkansas
Hot Springs
Memphis
Tennessee
Columbia
Knoxville
Mt. Mitchell 2037
Durham
Elizabeth City
Durant
Little Rock
Helena
Tullahoma
Chattanooga
High Point
Raleigh
Pine Bluff
Corinth
Asheville
North Carolina
Greenville
Texarkana
Huntsville
Greenville
Charlotte
Fayetteville
New Bern
C. Hatteras
El Dorado
Tupelo
Spartanburg
Hamlet
DALLAS
Longview
Greenville
Winona
Gadsden
Rome
Anderson
Athens
Columbia
Wilmington
Tyler
Shreveport
Birmingham
Appalachian Mts.
Atlanta
South Carolina
Vicksburg
Mississippi
Tuscaloosa
Augusta
Georgetown
Palestine
Red R.
Jackson
Alabama
Macon
Charleston
Trinity
Texas
Louisiana
Natchez
Meridian
Montgomery
Georgia
Columbus
Alexandria
McComb
Jackson
Savannah
Brazos
Huntsville
Lake Charles
Hattiesburg
Beaumont
Baton Rouge
Mobile
Dothan
Albany
HOUSTON
Port Arthur
Lafayette
Pensacola
Valdosta
Brunswick
Gulfport
Galveston
Freeport
Morgan City
New Orleans
Warrington
Panama City
Tallahassee
Jacksonville
Cape San Blas
Saint Augustine
Ocala
Florida
Daytona Beach
Orlando
Gulf of Mexico
Cape Canaveral
Tampa
Saint Petersburg
Grand Bahama I.
BAHAMAS
West Palm Beach
Fort Myers
Fort Lauderdale
Marsh Harbour
Great Abaco
Miami
Cape Sable
Florida Keys
Straits of Florida
Key West
Tropic of Cancer
Eleuthera I.
Andros I.
Nassau

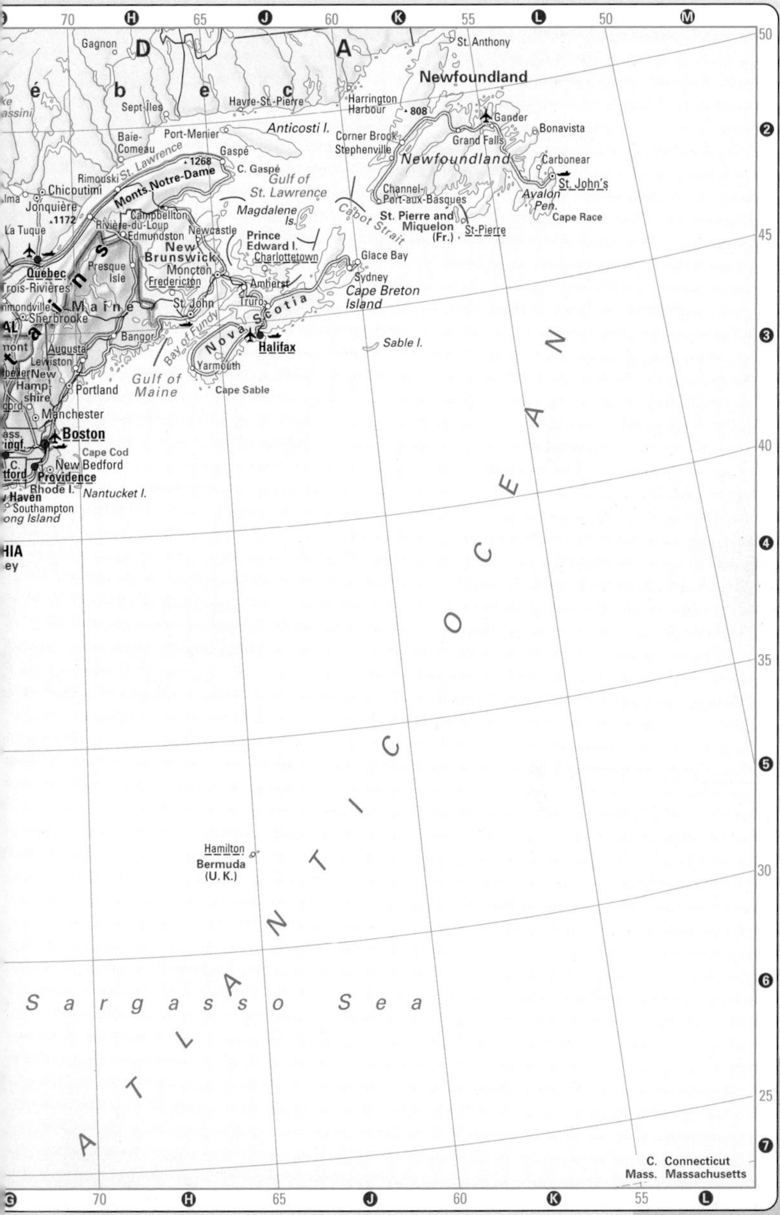
Gagnon
St. Anthony
Newfoundland
Havre-St.-Pierre
Harrington Harbour
808
Sept-Îles
Anticosti I.
Gander
Bonavista
Baie-Comeau
Port-Menier
Corner Brook
Stephenville
Grand Falls
Newfoundland
Carbonear
St. Lawrence
1268
Gaspé
C. Gaspé
Rimouski
Gulf of St. Lawrence
St. John's
Chicoutimi
Monts Notre-Dame
Jonquière
Channel-Port-aux-Basques
Avalon Pen.
1172
Campbellton
Magdalene Is.
Cabot Strait
St. Pierre and Miquelon (Fr.)
Cape Race
La Tuque
Rivière-du-Loup
Edmundston
Newcastle
Prince Edward I.
St-Pierre
New Brunswick
Charlottetown
Glace Bay
Québec
Presque Isle
Moncton
Sydney
Trois-Rivières
Fredericton
Amherst
Cape Breton Island
Maine
St. John
Truro
Nova Scotia
Sherbrooke
Bay of Fundy
Halifax
Bangor
Augusta
Sable I.
Lewiston
New Hampshire
Yarmouth
Gulf of Maine
Portland
Cape Sable
Manchester
Boston
Cape Cod
New Bedford
Providence
Rhode I.
Nantucket I.
Southampton
Hamilton
Bermuda (U. K.)
ATLANTIC OCEAN
Sargasso Sea
C. Connecticut
Mass. Massachusetts

114/115
SAN DIEGO
Oceanside
Calif.
Brawley
PHOENIX
Miami
Arizona
Gila
Yuma
Tijuana
Mexicali
Ensenada
Sonoyta
Tucson
Nogales
Douglas
Cananea
Cerro de la Encantada 3095
San Quintín
Guadalupe I.
Lower California
Gulf of California
Isla Ángel de la Guarda
Tiburón I.
Hermosillo
Ures
Cedros I.
Pta. Sta. Eugenia
Guaymas
Yaqui
Ciudad Obregón
Santa Rosalía
Navojoa
Huatabampo
Santo Domingo
Los Mochis
Co. Mohinora 3992
San Bernardo
Tropic of Cancer
La Paz
2406
Cape San Lucas
San José del Cabo
Culiacán
El Salto
Mazatlán
Islas Tres Marías
Tepic
GUADALAJARA
Cape Corrientes
Revillagigedo Islands (Mex.)
Zamora de Hidalgo
Nevado de Colima 4340
Manzanillo
Colima
Uruapan
Apatzingán
Morelia
Lázaro Cárdenas
Acapulco
3703
Chilpanc
Sierra Madr
Toluca
Cuernavaca
Popocat
(MEXICO C
MEXIC
Pac
Querétar
Irapuato
Guanajuato
LEÓN
2987
Aguascalientes
San Luis Potosí
Zacatecas
Fresnillo
Durango
Juan Aldama
Concepción del Oro
Matehuala
Cerro Peña Ne 3664
Río Grande de Santiago
Torreón
Saltillo
Gómez Palacio
Abasolo
Monclova
Sierra Madre Occidental
Sierra Madre Oriental
Hidalgo del Parral
Santa Bárbara
Jiménez
Camargo
Creel
Cuauhtémoc
Chihuahua
Nueva Casas Grandes
3200
CIUDAD JUÁREZ
El Paso
Río Bravo del Norte
Rio Grande
Van Horn
Pecos
New Mexico
Sierra Blanca Peak 3649
Roswell
Las Cruces
Carlsbad
Clovis
Llano Estacado
Hobbs
Lubbock
Odessa
Midland
McCamey
Sweetwater
Abil
Brown
San An
Wichita F
UNITED
Edwards Plateau
853
Del Rio
Acuña
Piedras Negras
Uvalde
Eagle P
Sabinas
Nuevo Laredo
La
Rey
MON
Mor
Li
Ci
Vic
MEXICO
PACIFIC OCEAN
Clipperton I. (French Polynesia)
120
115
110
105
100
30
25
20
15
10
A
B
C
D
E
1
2
3
4
5
6

F
95
G
90
H
116/117
85
J
80
K
75
1
2
3
4
5
6
30
25
20
15
10
120/121
Oklahoma
Durant
Arkansas
Pine Bluff
Texarkana
El Dorado
Greenville
Tupelo
Greenville
Winona
Birmingham
Tusc.
Gadsden
Atlanta
Augusta
South Carolina
Georgetown
Charleston
Macon
STATES
DALLAS
Longview
Shreveport
Mississippi
Vicksburg
Jackson
Meridian
Alabama
Montgomery
Columbus
Savannah
Georgia
Brunswick
Palestine
Tyler
Trinity
Red R.
Natchez
McComb
Hattiesburg
Dothan
Albany
Valdosta
Alexandria
Louisiana
Mobile
Pensacola
Tallahassee
Jacksonville
Brazos
Huntsville
Beaumont
Lake Charles
Baton Rouge
Gulfport
Warrington
Panama City
Saint Augustine
Colorado
Lafayette
New Orleans
Cape San Blas
Ocala
Daytona Beach
HOUSTON
Port Arthur
Morgan City
Orlando
Cape Canaveral
Galveston
Freeport
Tampa
Florida
Saint Petersburg
Grand Bahama I.
Great Abaco
West Palm Beach
Marsh Harbour
Corpus Christi
Fort Myers
Fort Lauderdale
Miami
Nassau
Gulf of Mexico
BAHAMAS
Harlingen
Brownsville
Matamoros
Cape Sable
Key West
Florida Keys
Straits of Florida
Andros I.
LA HABANA
(HAVANA)
Matanzas
Cárdenas
Artemisa
Colón
Santa Clara
Ciego de Avila
Pinar del Río
CUBA
Cienfuegos
Trinidad
Nuevitas
Camagüey
Tampico
Cape San Antonio
C. Catoche
Yucatán Channel
Isla de la Juventud
Progreso
Tizimín
Cancún
Mérida
Valladolid
Greater Antilles
Tuxpán
Bay of Campeche
Chichén-Itzá
Cozumel I.
Cayman Islands
(U. K.)
Grand Cayman
Georgetown
Montego Bay
JAMAICA
Campeche
Yucatán Pen.
Xalapa Enríquez
Veracruz
Pico de Orizaba
5675
Carmen
Chetumal
Francisco Escárcega
Caribbean Sea
Coatzacoalcos
Orange Walk
Belize City
Villahermosa
Río Usumacinta
Tikal
BELIZE
Flores
Belmopan
G. of Honduras
Bay Islands
Oaxaca
Tuxtla
San Cristóbal de las Casas
Juchitán
Tehuantepec
Salina Cruz
Puerto Barrios
La Ceiba
Gulf of Tehuantepec
Tonalá
Cobán
Puerto Cortés
Sierra Madre
GUATEMALA
3139
San Pedro Sula
Río Coco
C. Gracias a Dios
Tajumulco
4220
HONDURAS
Tapachula
Quezaltenango
2865
Tegucigalpa
1990
Puerto Cabezas
Providencia I.
(Col.)
CD. DE GUATEMALA
(GUATEMALA CITY)
Santa Ana
San José
San Miguel
NICARAGUA
San Salvador
EL SALVADOR
La Unión
Choluteca
San Andrés I.
Chinandega
Matagalpa
León
Bluefields
Managua
Granada
L. Nicaragua
Panama Canal
COSTA RICA
Limón
Puntarenas
Bocas del Toro
Colón
Pen. de Nicoya
San José
Panamá
Cabo Blanco
(Panama City)
S.M.
3820
Cortés
PANAMA
Santiago
David
Pen. de Azuero
Coiba
OCEAN

116/117
118/119
UNITED STATES
Texas
Louisiana
Mississippi
Alabama
Georgia
South Carolina
Florida
Houston
Beaumont
Lake Charles
Lafayette
Baton Rouge
New Orleans
Mobile
Montgomery
Columbus
Savannah
Charleston
Jacksonville
Tallahassee
Pensacola
Gulfport
Port Arthur
Galveston
Freeport
Morgan City
Huntsville
Alexandria
Natchez
McComb
Hattiesburg
Jackson
Meridian
Dothan
Albany
Valdosta
Brunswick
Warrington
Panama City
Cape San Blas
Saint Augustine
Daytona Beach
Ocala
Orlando
Cape Canaveral
Tampa
Saint Petersburg
Fort Myers
West Palm Beach
Fort Lauderdale
Miami
Cape Sable
Key West
Florida Keys
Straits of Florida
Gulf of Mexico
BAHAMAS
Grand Bahama I.
Marsh Harbour
Great Abaco
Eleuthera I.
Nassau
Andros I.
Cat I.
Clarence Town
Acklins I.
LA HABANA (HAVANA)
Artemisa
Matanzas
Cárdenas
Pinar del Río
Colón
Santa Clara
Cienfuegos
Trinidad
Ciego de Ávila
Nuevitas
Isla de la Juventud
CUBA
Camagüey
Holguín
Bayamo
Manzanillo
Baracoa
Sa. Maestra
1974
Santiago de Cuba
Cayman Islands (U. K.)
Georgetown
Grand Cayman
Montego Bay
Kingston
2256
JAMAICA
Navassa (U. S.)
Bay of Campeche
Progreso
C. Catoche
Tizimín
Mérida
Cancún
Valladolid
Chichén Itzá
Yucatán Pen.
Cozumel I.
Yucatan Channel
C. San Antonio
Campeche
Carmen
Villahermosa
Francisco Escárcega
Chetumal
MEXICO
Tuxtla
San Cristóbal de Las Casas
Sierra Madre
Tikal
Flores
Orange Walk
Belize City
BELIZE
Belmopan
GUATEMALA
Cobán
Tapachula
Tajumulco
4220
3139
Quezaltenango
CD. DE GUATEMALA (GUATEMALA C.)
San José
G. of Honduras
Bay Islands
Puerto Barrios
Puerto Cortés
La Ceiba
San Pedro Sula
HONDURAS
2865
Santa Ana
Tegucigalpa
San Salvador
EL SALVADOR
San Miguel
La Unión
Choluteca
Río Coco
C. Gracias á Dios
Puerto Cabezas
1990
Chinandega
NICARAGUA
Matagalpa
León
Managua
Granada
Bluefields
L. Nicaragua
Providencia I.
(Col.)
San Andrés I.
Caribbean Sea
COSTA RICA
Puntarenas
Pen. de Nicoya
Cabo Blanco
San José
Limón
3820
Cortés
Bocas del Toro
Panama Canal
Punta Manzanilla
Colón
PANAMA
Panama (Panama City)
San Miguelito
David
Santiago
Coiba
Azuero Pen.
Gulf of Panama
Punta Mala
La Palma
Santa Marta
BARRANQUILLA
Cartagena
El Carmen de Bolívar
Gulf of Darién
Sincelejo
Montería
Turbo
Cauca
Barrancabermeja
Bello
MEDELLÍN
Quibdó
La Dorada
PACIFIC OCEAN

F
G
H
J
K
70
65
60
55
30
25
20
15
10
5
1
2
3
4
5
6
7
Hamilton
Bermuda
(U. K.)
A T L A N T I C
O C E A N
S a r g a s s o S e a
Tropic of Cancer
Turks and Caicos Is.
(U. K.)
Grand Turk
DOMINICAN
REP.
San Francisco
de Macorís
Santiago
3175
La Romana
SANTO
DOMINGO
Barahona
Hispaniola
Mona Passage
San Juan
1338
Mayagüez
Ponce
Puerto Rico
(U. S.)
Virgin Is. of the U.S.
Charlotte Amalie
British Virgin Is. (U.K.)
Anegada Passage
Anguilla (U.K.)
St-Martin (Guad. / Neth. Ant.)
St-Barthélémy (Guad.)
Barbuda
St. Croix
(Neth. Antilles)
Basseterre
St. John's
ANTIGUA AND BARBUDA
SAINT KITTS AND NEVIS
Montserrat (U.K.)
Plymouth
Pointe-à-Pitre
1467
Guadeloupe (Fr.)
Basse-Terre
Marie-Galante
DOMINICA
Roseau
L e s s e r
A n t i l l e s
Fort-de-France
Martinique (Fr.)
SAINT LUCIA
Castries
BARBADOS
Bridgetown
SAINT VINCENT AND THE
GRENADINES
Kingstown
GRENADA
St. George's
S e a
Aruba
(Neth.)
Oranjestad
Netherlands Antilles
Curaçao
Bonaire
Willemstad
Blanquilla
Guajira
Pen.
G. of
Venezuela
Punto Fijo
Coro
Margarita
La Asunción
Carúpano
Port
of Spain
TRINIDAD
AND TOBAGO
Tobago
Trinidad
San Fernando
MARACAIBO
Cabimas
Lake
Maracaibo
Barquisimeto
San
Felipe
Puerto
Cabello
Maiquetía
CARACAS
Maracay
Valencia
San Juan de
los Morros
1931
Cumaná
Barcelona
Co. Turimiquire
2596
Maturín
Tucupita
Trujillo
Acarigua
San Carlos
El Tigre
Valera
Guanare
Pico Bolívar
Mérida
5007
Barinas
Apure
San Fernando
Ciudad Bolívar
Orinoco
Ciudad Guayana
Ciudad Piar
Guri
Res.
San Cristóbal
V E N E Z U E L A
Arauca
El Dorado
Bucaramanga
Cocuy
5493
Meta
Puerto Carreño
Puerto Ayacucho
Auyán Tebuy
2560
Caroní
Mt. Roraima
2810
Santa Elena
de Uairén
Morajuana
Matthews
Ridge
Charity
Georgetown
New
Amsterdam
Bartica
Linden
G U Y A N A
Paramaribo
Groningen
Nieuw
Nickerie
SURINAME
130/131

① Near Bucay, Ecuador
(Rother, Schwäbisch Gmünd)

② Lima
(Kroß, Bochum)

③ Altiplano, Bolivia
(Fuchs, Paderborn)

④ Patagonia
(Rother, Schwäbisch Gmünd)

⑤ Perito Moreno Glacier, Cordillera Patagonica
(Rother, Schwäbisch Gmünd)

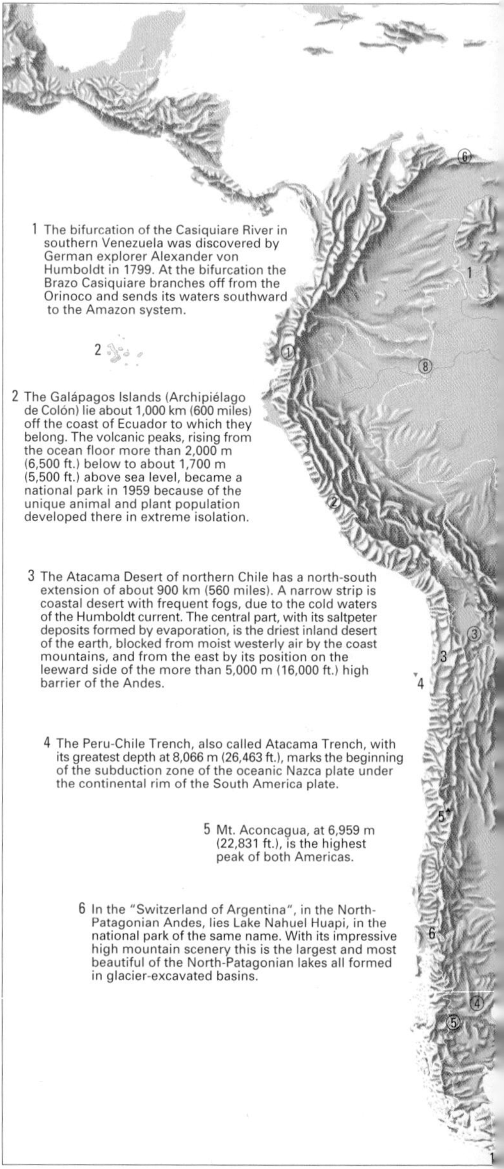

1 The bifurcation of the Casiquiare River in southern Venezuela was discovered by German explorer Alexander von Humboldt in 1799. At the bifurcation the Brazo Casiquiare branches off from the Orinoco and sends its waters southward to the Amazon system.

2 The Galápagos Islands (Archipiélago de Colón) lie about 1,000 km (600 miles) off the coast of Ecuador to which they belong. The volcanic peaks, rising from the ocean floor more than 2,000 m (6,500 ft.) below to about 1,700 m (5,500 ft.) above sea level, became a national park in 1959 because of the unique animal and plant population developed there in extreme isolation.

3 The Atacama Desert of northern Chile has a north-south extension of about 900 km (560 miles). A narrow strip is coastal desert with frequent fogs, due to the cold waters of the Humboldt current. The central part, with its saltpeter deposits formed by evaporation, is the driest inland desert of the earth, blocked from moist westerly air by the coast mountains, and from the east by its position on the leeward side of the more than 5,000 m (16,000 ft.) high barrier of the Andes.

4 The Peru-Chile Trench, also called Atacama Trench, with its greatest depth at 8,066 m (26,463 ft.), marks the beginning of the subduction zone of the oceanic Nazca plate under the continental rim of the South America plate.

5 Mt. Aconcagua, at 6,959 m (22,831 ft.), is the highest peak of both Americas.

6 In the "Switzerland of Argentina", in the North-Patagonian Andes, lies Lake Nahuel Huapi, in the national park of the same name. With its impressive high mountain scenery this is the largest and most beautiful of the North-Patagonian lakes all formed in glacier-excavated basins.

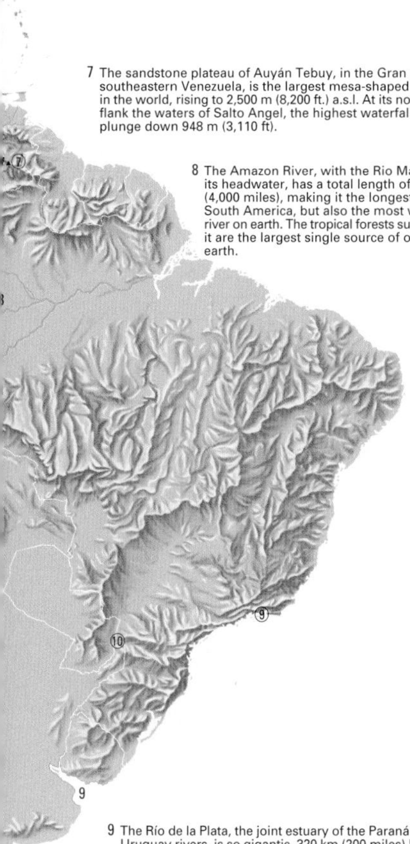

7 The sandstone plateau of Auyán Tebuy, in the Gran Sabana of southeastern Venezuela, is the largest mesa-shaped mountain in the world, rising to 2,500 m (8,200 ft.) a.s.l. At its northeastern flank the waters of Salto Angel, the highest waterfall on earth, plunge down 948 m (3,110 ft).

8 The Amazon River, with the Rio Madeira as its headwater, has a total length of 6,437 km (4,000 miles), making it the longest river of South America, but also the most water-rich river on earth. The tropical forests surrounding it are the largest single source of oxygen on earth.

9 The Río de la Plata, the joint estuary of the Paraná and Uruguay rivers, is so gigantic, 320 km (200 miles) long and up to 225 km (140 miles) wide, and the amount of freshwater discharging into it so enormous, that its discoverers, in 1515, first called it Mar Dulce, or Freshwater Sea.

10 Cape Horn on the Chilean Isla Hornos, at 55°59′ S, is the southernmost point of South America.

⑥ Caracas
(Rother, Schwäbisch Gmünd)

⑦ Guiana Highlands
(Rother, Schwäbisch Gmünd)

⑧ Amazon near Letícia
(Rother, Schwäbisch Gmünd)

⑨ Rio de Janeiro
(Rother, Schwäbisch Gmünd)

⑩ Iguaçu Falls
(Rother, Schwäbisch Gmünd)

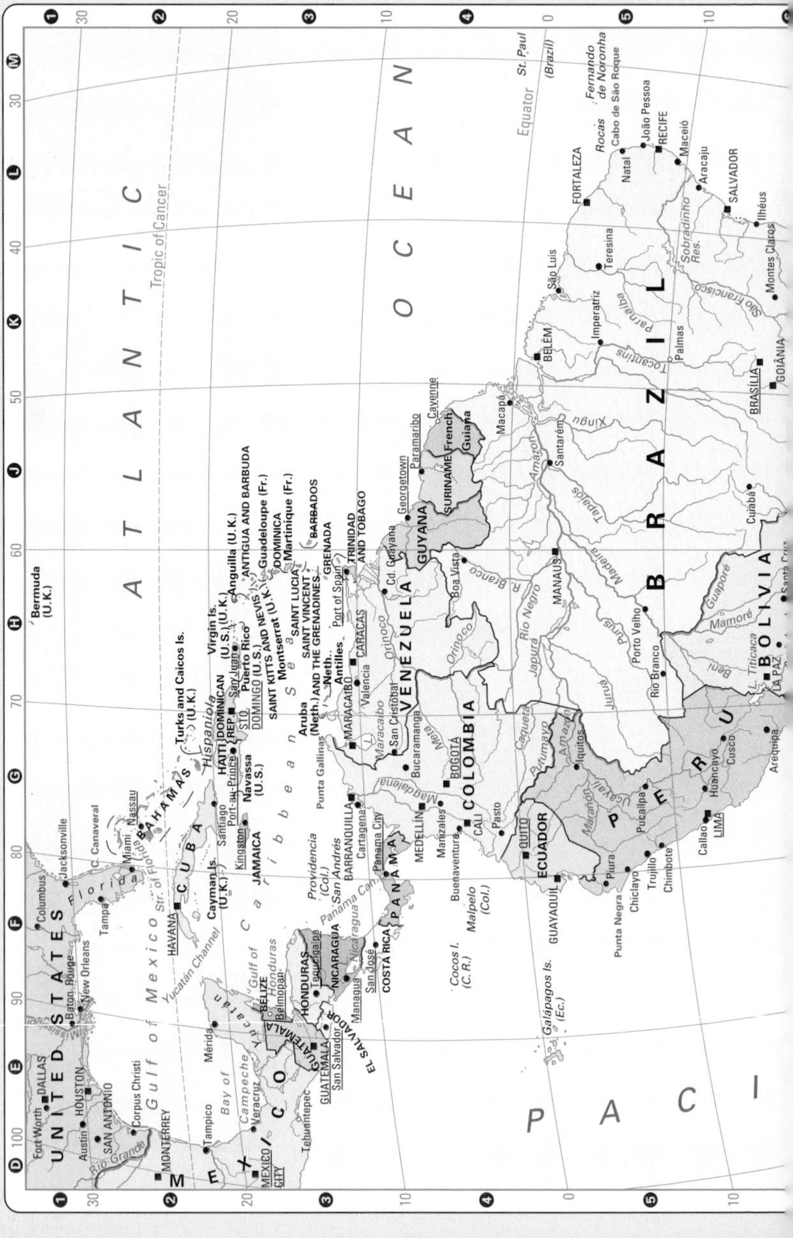
ATLANTIC OCEAN
Caribbean Sea
Gulf of Mexico
PACI
Tropic of Cancer
Equator
UNITED STATES
MEXICO
CUBA
BAHAMAS
JAMAICA
HAITI
DOMINICAN REP.
BELIZE
GUATEMALA
HONDURAS
EL SALVADOR
NICARAGUA
COSTA RICA
PANAMA
COLOMBIA
VENEZUELA
GUYANA
SURINAME
French Guiana
ECUADOR
PERU
BRAZIL
BOLIVIA
TRINIDAD AND TOBAGO
BARBADOS
GRENADA
SAINT VINCENT AND THE GRENADINES
SAINT LUCIA
DOMINICA
ANTIGUA AND BARBUDA
SAINT KITTS AND NEVIS
Bermuda (U.K.)
Turks and Caicos Is. (U.K.)
Cayman Is. (U.K.)
Virgin Is. (U.S.) (U.K.)
Anguilla (U.K.)
Montserrat (U.K.)
Guadeloupe (Fr.)
Martinique (Fr.)
Puerto Rico
Navassa (U.S.)
Aruba (Neth.)
Neth. Antilles
Hispaniola
Providencia (Col.)
San Andrés
Malpelo (Col.)
Cocos I. (C.R.)
Galápagos Is. (Ec.)
St. Paul
(Brazil)
Fernando de Noronha
Rocas
Cabo de São Roque
Bay of Campeche
Yucatán Channel
Yucatan
Gulf of Honduras
Str. of Florida
Florida
Panama Can.
Nicaragua
Punta Gallinas
Punta Negra
Rio Grande
Mississippi
Fort Worth
DALLAS
Austin
HOUSTON
SAN ANTONIO
Corpus Christi
Baton Rouge
New Orleans
Columbus
Jacksonville
Tampa
Miami
C. Canaveral
MONTERREY
Tampico
Veracruz
MEXICO CITY
Tehuantepec
Mérida
HAVANA
Santiago
Nassau
Kingston
Port-au-Prince
STO. DOMINGO
San Juan
GUATEMALA
San Salvador
Tegucigalpa
Belmopan
Managua
San José
Panama City
BARRANQUILLA
Cartagena
MARACAIBO
Maracaibo
Valencia
CARACAS
Port of Spain
Cd. Guayana
Georgetown
Paramaribo
Cayenne
San Cristobal
Bucaramanga
MEDELLÍN
BOGOTÁ
Manizales
Buenaventura
CALI
Pasto
QUITO
GUAYAQUIL
Piura
Chiclayo
Trujillo
Chimbote
Callao
LIMA
Huancayo
Cusco
Arequipa
Iquitos
Pucallpa
LA PAZ
Boa Vista
MANAUS
Porto Velho
Rio Branco
Santarém
Macapá
BELÉM
São Luís
Imperatriz
Teresina
FORTALEZA
Natal
João Pessoa
RECIFE
Maceió
Aracaju
SALVADOR
Ilhéus
Palmas
BRASÍLIA
GOIÂNIA
Cuiabá
Montes Claros
Orinoco
Meta
Magdalena
Caquetá
Putumayo
Amazon
Marañon
Ucayali
Japurá
Rio Negro
R. Branco
Juruá
Purus
Madeira
Tapajós
Xingu
Tocantins
Parnaíba
São Francisco
Sobradinho Res.
Guaporé
Mamoré
Beni
L. Titicaca
30
20
10
0
40
50
60
70
80
90
100

1 : 50 000 000

0 500 1000 1500 2000 km
0 500 1000 miles

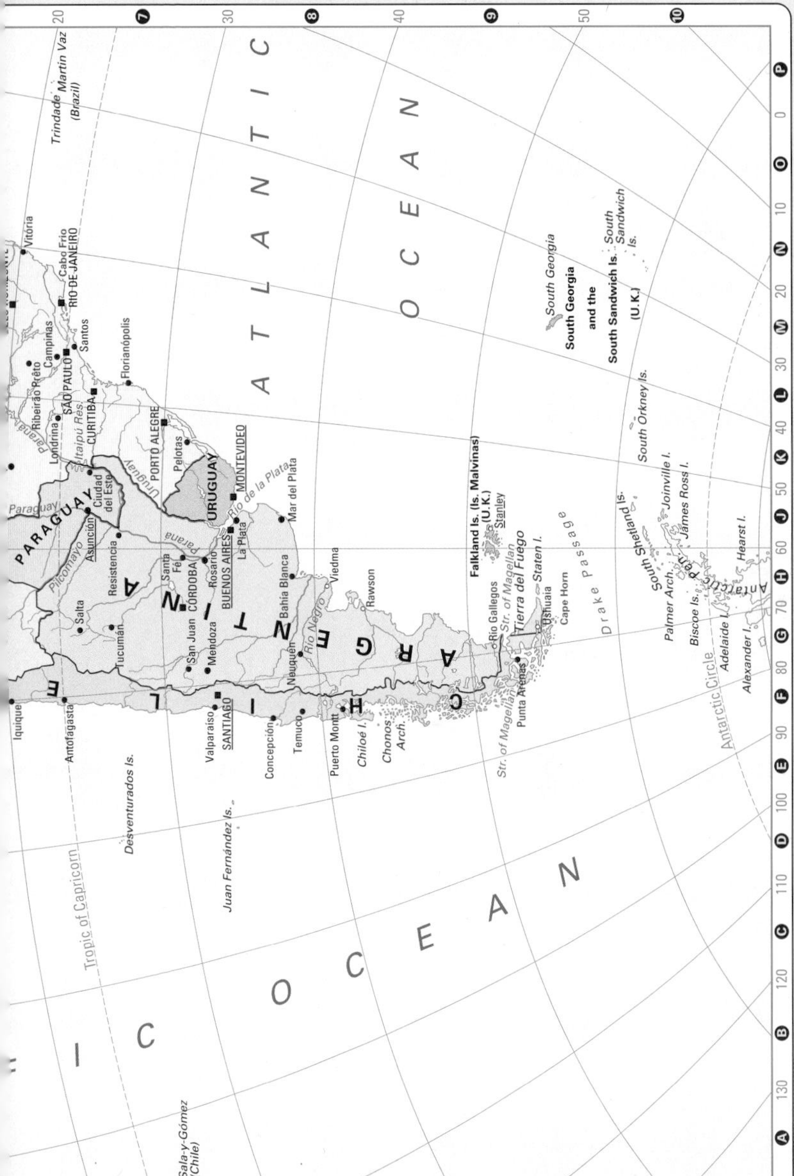

ATLANTIC OCEAN
OCEAN
Trindade
Martin Vaz
(Brazil)
Vitória
Cabo Frio
RIO DE JANEIRO
Santos
Campinas
SÃO PAULO
Ribeirão Prêto
Florianópolis
Londrina
Itaipú Res.
CURITIBA
Paraná
PORTO ALEGRE
Pelotas
Uruguay
URUGUAY
MONTEVIDEO
Río de la Plata
Mar del Plata
PARAGUAY
Paraguay
Ciudad del Este
Asunción
Pilcomayo
Resistencia
Santa Fé
CÓRDOBA
Rosario
BUENOS AIRES
La Plata
Salta
Tucumán
San Juan
Mendoza
ARGENTINA
CHILE
Bahía Blanca
Viedma
Rawson
Río Negro
Neuquén
Iquique
Antofagasta
Valparaíso
SANTIAGO
Concepción
Temuco
Puerto Montt
Chiloé I.
Chonos Arch.
Desventurados Is.
Juan Fernández Is.
Tropic of Capricorn
Sala-y-Gómez
(Chile)
Falkland Is. (Is. Malvinas)
(U.K.)
Stanley
Río Gallegos
Str. of Magellan
Tierra del Fuego
Staten I.
Ushuaia
Punta Arenas
Cape Horn
Drake Passage
South Georgia
South Georgia
and the
South Sandwich Is.
(U.K.)
South Sandwich Is.
South Orkney Is.
South Shetland Is.
Joinville I.
James Ross I.
Palmer Arch.
Antarctic Pen.
Biscoe Is.
Adelaide I.
Hearst I.
Alexander I.
Antarctic Circle

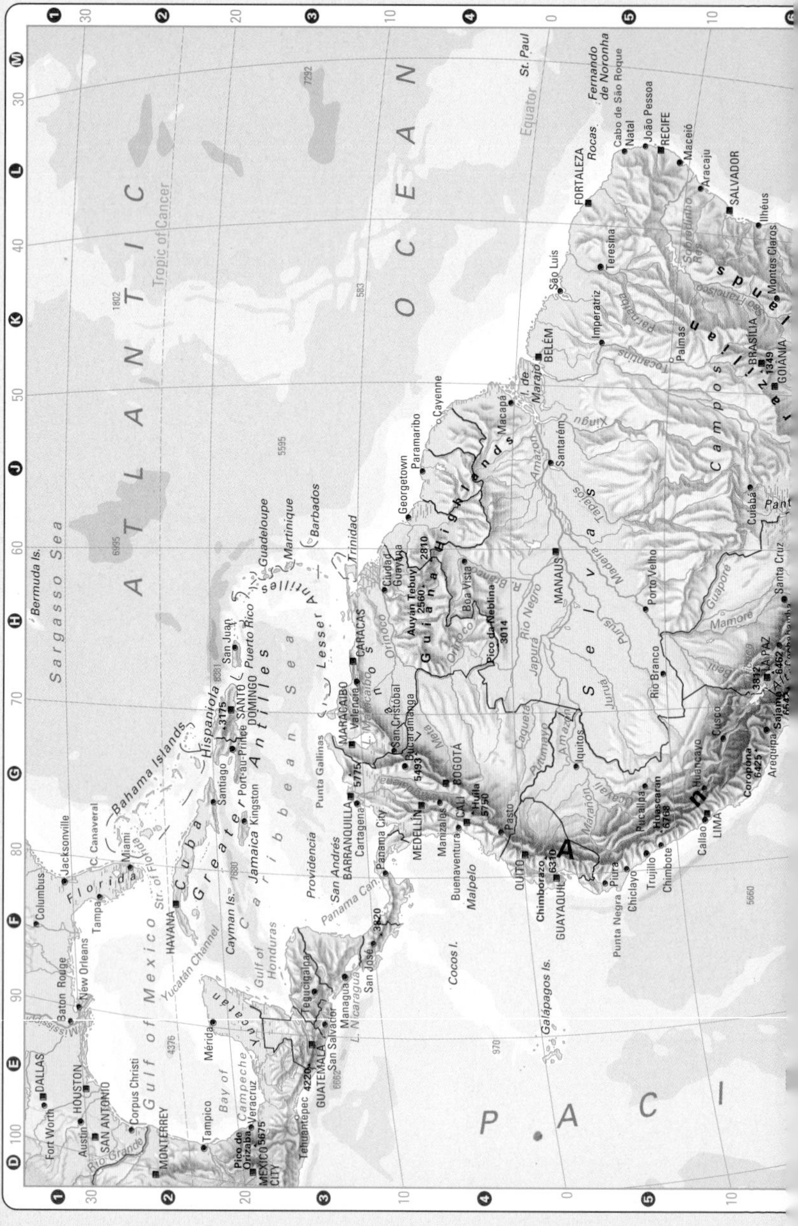
ATLANTIC OCEAN
PACIFIC
Sargasso Sea
Bermuda Is.
Tropic of Cancer
Equator
Gulf of Mexico
Bay of Campeche
Yucatán Channel
Str. of Florida
Bahama Islands
Cuba
Hispaniola
Greater Antilles
Lesser Antilles
Caribbean Sea
Puerto Rico
Jamaica
Cayman Is.
Guadeloupe
Martinique
Barbados
Trinidad
Gulf of Honduras
Providencia
San Andrés
Panama Can.
L. Nicaragua
Cocos I.
Malpelo
Galápagos Is.
Guiana Highlands
Selvas
Campos
Andes
Amazon
Orinoco
Rio Negro
Madeira
Tapajós
Xingu
Tocantins
Purus
Juruá
Japurá
Putumayo
Caquetá
Marañón
Ucayali
Guaporé
Mamoré
R. Branco
I. de Marajó
Rocas
Fernando de Noronha
Cabo de São Roque
St. Paul
DALLAS
Fort Worth
HOUSTON
Austin
SAN ANTONIO
Corpus Christi
Rio Grande
MONTERREY
Tampico
Veracruz
Pico de Orizaba 5675
MÉXICO CITY
Tehuantepec
GUATEMALA
4220
San Salvador
Tegucigalpa
Managua
San José
3820
Panama City
Mérida
Yucatán
Baton Rouge
New Orleans
Mississippi
Columbus
Jacksonville
C. Canaveral
Tampa
Miami
Florida
HAVANA
Santiago
Port-au-Prince
SANTO DOMINGO
3175
San Juan
Kingston
Punta Gallinas
MARACAIBO
L. Maracaibo
Valencia
CARACAS
BARRANQUILLA
Cartagena
5775
San Cristóbal
Bucaramanga
5493
BOGOTÁ
MEDELLÍN
Manizales
CALI
Huila 5750
Buenaventura
Pasto
QUITO
Chimborazo 6310
GUAYAQUIL
Ciudad Guayana
Auyán Tebuy 2560
2810
Boa Vista
Pico da Neblina 3014
MANAUS
Georgetown
Paramaribo
Cayenne
Macapá
Santarém
BELÉM
São Luís
Imperatriz
Teresina
FORTALEZA
Natal
João Pessoa
RECIFE
Maceió
Aracaju
SALVADOR
Ilhéus
Montes Claros
Palmas
BRASÍLIA
GOIÂNIA
1349
Cuiabá
Porto Velho
Rio Branco
Iquitos
Piura
Punta Negra
Chiclayo
Trujillo
Chimbote
Huascarán 6768
Pucallpa
Huancayo
Callao
LIMA
Cusco
Coropuna 6425
Arequipa
LA PAZ
3812
6462
Sajama
Santa Cruz
Sobradinho Res.
São Francisco
Parnaíba
Meta
Pant
6995
7292
1802
583
5595
7680
4376
6662
970
5660

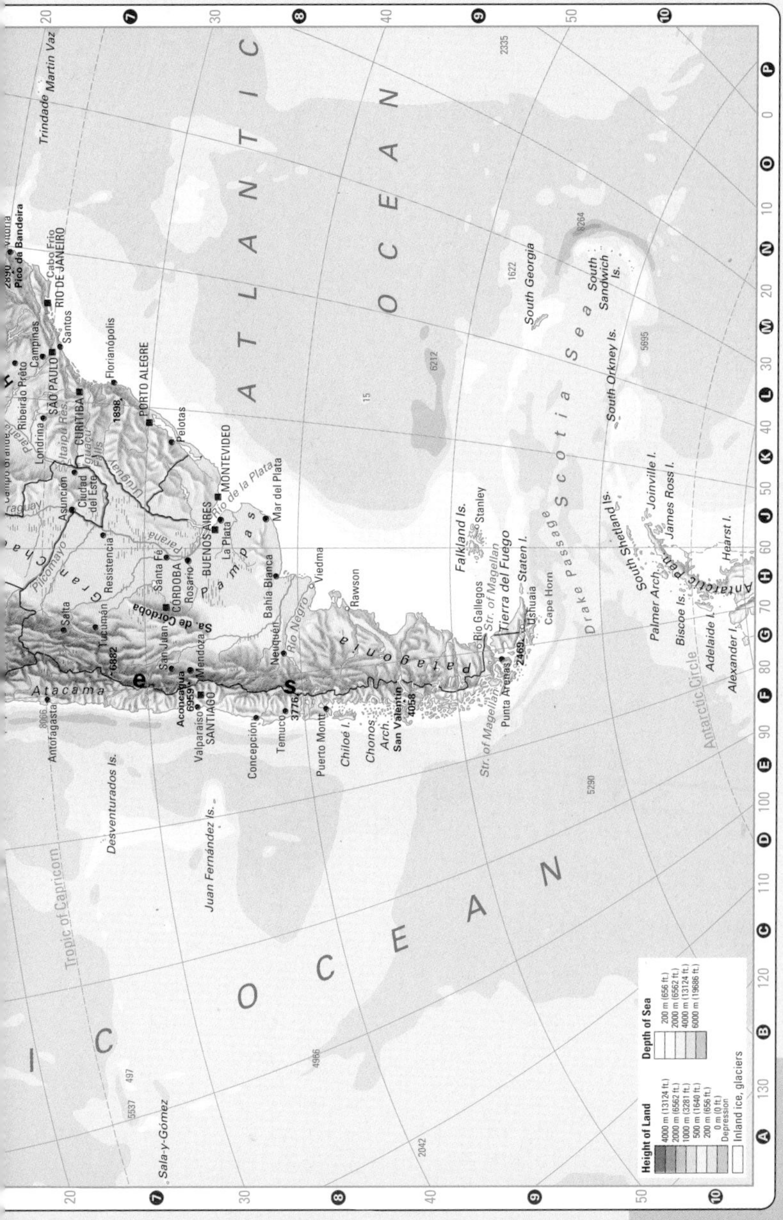
ATLANTIC OCEAN
OCEAN
Trindade
Martin Vaz
Pico da Bandeira
RIO DE JANEIRO
Cabo Frio
Santos
Campinas
SÃO PAULO
Ribeirão Prêto
Londrina
CURITIBA
Florianópolis
PORTO ALEGRE
Pelotas
Asunción
Ciudad del Este
Uruguay
MONTEVIDEO
Río de la Plata
BUENOS AIRES
La Plata
Mar del Plata
Resistencia
Santa Fé
Rosario
CÓRDOBA
Pampas
Gran Chaco
Pilcomayo
Paraná
Salta
Tucumán
Sa. de Córdoba
San Juan
Mendoza
Aconcagua
6959
6882
Atacama
Antofagasta
Valparaíso
SANTIAGO
Concepción
Temuco
3776
Neuquén
Bahía Blanca
Viedma
Rawson
Río Negro
Patagonia
Puerto Montt
Chiloé I.
Chonos Arch.
San Valentin
4058
Río Gallegos
Str. of Magellan
Punta Arenas
Tierra del Fuego
Ushuaia
2469
Staten I.
Cape Horn
Falkland Is.
Stanley
Drake Passage
Scotia Sea
South Georgia
South Sandwich Is.
South Orkney Is.
South Shetland Is.
Joinville I.
James Ross I.
Antarctic Pen.
Palmer Arch.
Biscoe Is.
Adelaide I.
Alexander I.
Hearst I.
Antarctic Circle
Tropic of Capricorn
Desventurados Is.
Juan Fernández Is.
Sala-y-Gómez
Height of Land
4000 m (13124 ft.)
2000 m (6562 ft.)
1000 m (3281 ft.)
500 m (1640 ft.)
200 m (656 ft.)
0 m (0 ft.)
Depression
Inland ice, glaciers
Depth of Sea
200 m (656 ft.)
2000 m (6562 ft.)
4000 m (13124 ft.)
6000 m (19686 ft.)

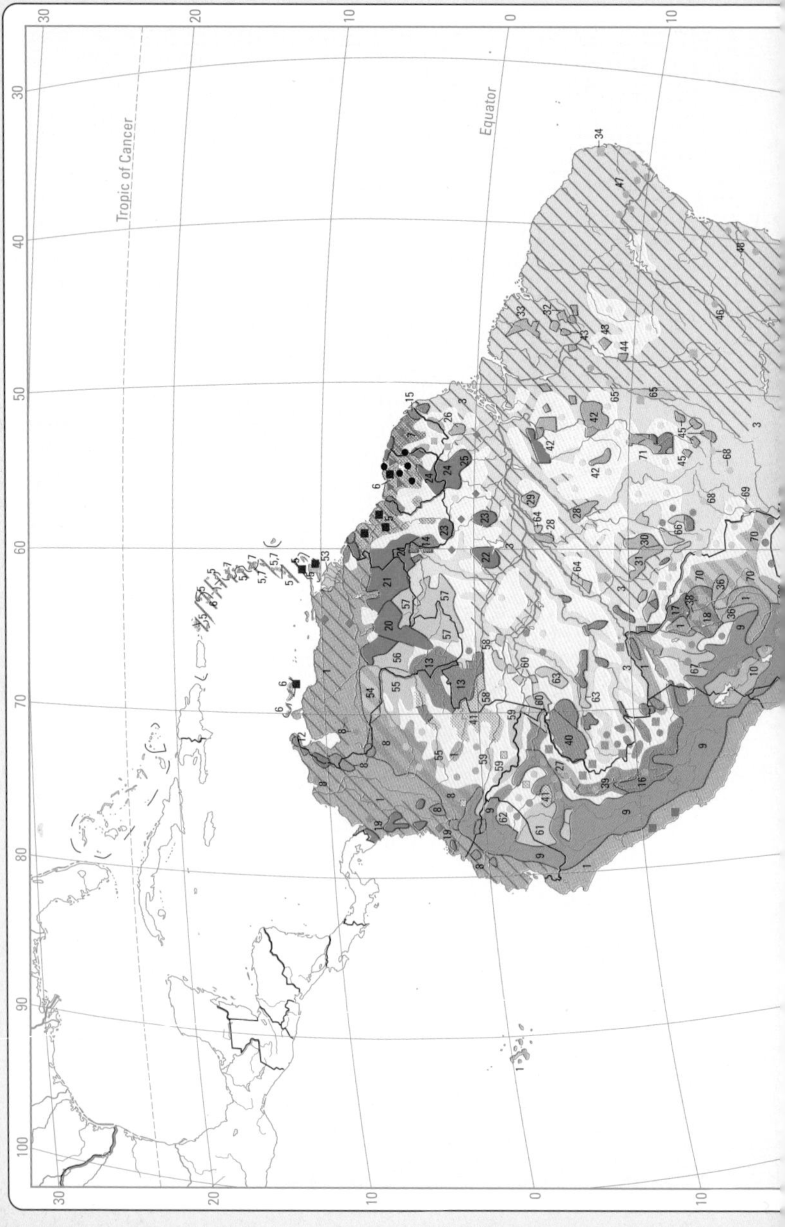
Tropic of Cancer
Equator

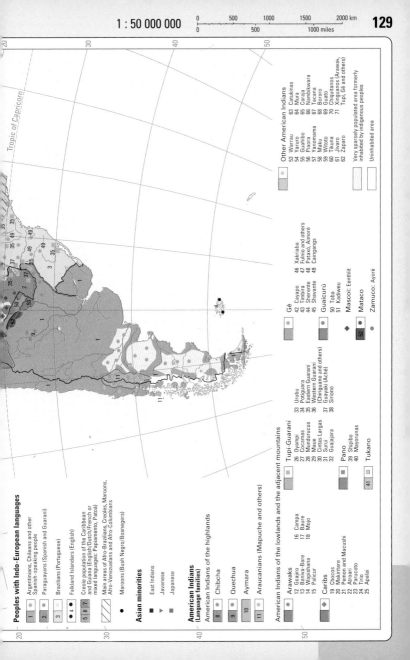

Peoples with Indo-European languages

- 1 Argentinians, Chileans and other Spanish-speaking people
- 2 Paraguayans (Spanish and Guaraní)
- 3 Brazilians (Portuguese)
- 4 Falkland Islanders (English)
- 5 6 7 Creole population of the Caribbean and Guiana (English/Dutch/French or mixed languages: Papiamento, Patoá)
- Main areas of Afro-Brazilians, Creoles, Maroons, Afro-Venezuelans and Afro-Columbians
- Maroons (Bush Negro/Bosnegers)

Asian minorities

- East Indians
- Javanese
- Japanese

American Indians
(Language families)

American Indians of the highlands

- 8 Chibcha
- 9 Quechua
- 10 Aymara
- 11 Araucanians (Mapuche and others)

American Indians of the lowlands and the adjacent mountains

Arawaks
12 Goajiro
13 Baniva-Bare
14 Wapishana
15 Palicur
16 Campa
17 Baure
18 Mojo

Caribs
19 Chocos
20 Makiritare
21 Pemon and Macushi
22 Atroari
23 Parucoto
24 Tirio
25 Apalai

Tupí-Guaraní
26 Oyampi
27 Cocamas
28 Mundurucus
29 Maue
30 Cintas Largas
31 Surui
32 Guajajara
33 Urubu
34 Potiguara
35 Eastern Guaraní
36 Western Guaraní (Chiriguano and others)
37 Guayaki (Aché)
38 Siriono

Pano
39 Shipibo
40 Mayorunas

41 **Tukano**

Gê
42 Cayapo
43 Timbira
44 Sherente
45 Shavante
46 Xakriaba
47 Fulnio and others
48 Pataxó, Aimoré
49 Caingangs

Guaicurú
50 Toba
51 Kadiweu

Mascoi: Eenthlit

52 **Mataco**

Zamuco: Ayoré

Other American Indians
53 Warrau
54 Yaruro
55 Guahibo
56 Piaora
57 Yanomama
58 Maku
59 Witoto
60 Tikuna
61 Jivaro
62 Zaparo
63 Catukinas
64 Mura
65 Caraja
66 Nambikwara
67 Tacana
68 Bororo
69 Guato
70 Chiquitanos
71 Xinguanos (Arawak, Tupi, Gê and others)

- Very sparsely populated area formerly inhabited by indigenous peoples
- Uninhabited area

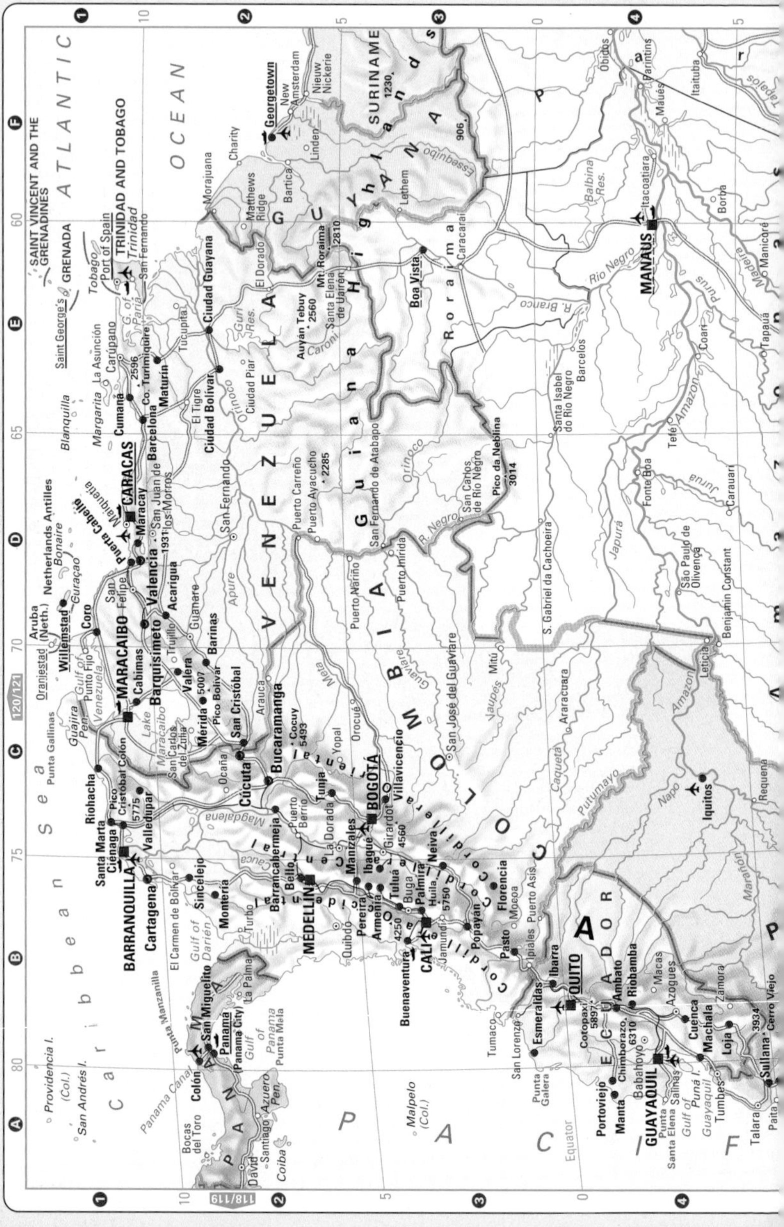
ATLANTIC
OCEAN
Caribbean Sea
PACIFIC
VENEZUELA
COLOMBIA
ECUADOR
PANAMA
GUYANA
SURINAME
Guiana Highlands
SAINT VINCENT AND THE GRENADINES
GRENADA
TRINIDAD AND TOBAGO
Port of Spain
Georgetown
CARACAS
BOGOTÁ
QUITO
MANAUS
MARACAIBO
BARRANQUILLA
MEDELLÍN
CALI
GUAYAQUIL
Cartagena
Valencia
Barquisimeto
Maracay
Ciudad Bolívar
Ciudad Guayana
Boa Vista
Iquitos
Leticia
Panamá (Panama City)
Colón
Netherlands Antilles
Aruba (Neth.)
Oranjestad
Willemstad
Bonaire
Curaçao
Lake Maracaibo
Gulf of Venezuela
Gulf of Darién
Gulf of Panama
Gulf of Guayaquil
Orinoco
Amazon
Rio Negro
Magdalena
Cauca
Meta
Putumayo
Caquetá
Napo
Japurá
Juruá
Purus
Madeira
Pico Cristóbal Colón 5775
Pico Bolívar 5007
Pico da Neblina 3014
Mt. Roraima 2810
Cotopaxi 5897
Chimborazo 6310
Equator
120/121
118/119

132/133
134/135
Cuiabá
Mato Grosso
Pantanal
Mato Grosso do Sul
Corumbá
Sinop
Diamantino
Poconé
Cáceres
Paraguay
Juruena
Roosevelt
Guaporé
Vilhena
Rondônia
Humaitá
Porto Velho
Jiparaná
Guajará-Mirim
Lábrea
Pimenta Bueno
Rio Branco
Boca do Acre
Sena Madureira
Cruzeiro do Sul
Tarauacá
Purus
Acre
Cobija
Riberalta
Beni
Mamoré
Puerto Siles
Piso Firme
Trinidad
Ascensión
San Ignacio
San José
Santa Cruz
Montero
Cabezas
BOLIVIA
Cochabamba
Todos Santos
Reyes
Apolo
La Paz
Illimani 6462
Ancohuma 6427
Lake Titicaca
Puerto Acosta
Guaqui
Viacha
Oruro
Challapata
Sucre
Potosí
Aiquile
Choreti
Villamontes
Tarija
Yacuiba
Pilcomayo
Uyuni
Salar de Uyuni
Tupiza
La Quiaca
L. Poopó
Altiplano
Sajama 6542
Aucanquilcha 6176
Chuquicamata 6020
Calama
Atacama Desert
Salar de Atacama
San Pedro de Atacama
San Antonio de los Cobres
Salar de Arizaro
Llullaillaco 6723
Iquique
Tocopilla
Antofagasta
Punta Angamos
Catalina
Taltal
Arica
Tacna
Ilo
Moquegua
Arequipa
Chachani 6084
Coropuna 6425
Mollendo
Juliaca
Puno
Sicuani
Sandia
Puerto Maldonado
Cusco
Quillabamba
Machupicchu
Salcantay 6271
Abancay
Ayacucho
Huancavelica
Huancayo
La Oroya
Puquio
Nazca
Chala
Ica
Pisco
Chincha Alta
Punta Carreta
LIMA
Callao
Huacho
Barranca
Huaraz
Huascarán
Huallanca 6768
Chimbote
Trujillo
Pacasmayo
Chiclayo
Cajamarca
Juanjuí
Pucallpa
Uchiza
Tingo María
Huánuco
Cerro de Pasco
Ucayali
Huallaga
Cordillera Central
Cordillera Occidental
Cordillera Oriental
PARAGUAY
Asunción
Villa Hayes
Caacupé
Villarrica
Concepción
Pedro Juan Caballero
Ponta Porã
Porto Murtinho
Fuerte Olimpo
Puerto Suárez
Capitán Pablo Lagerenza
General Eugenio A. Garay
Doctor Pedro P. Peña
Pozo Colorado
Aquidauana
Formosa
Las Lomitas
Bermejo
ARGENTINA
Salta
San Salvador de Jujuy
Tartagal
Embarcación
Metán
Monte Quemado
CHILE
OCEAN
Tropic of Capricorn
790
883
700

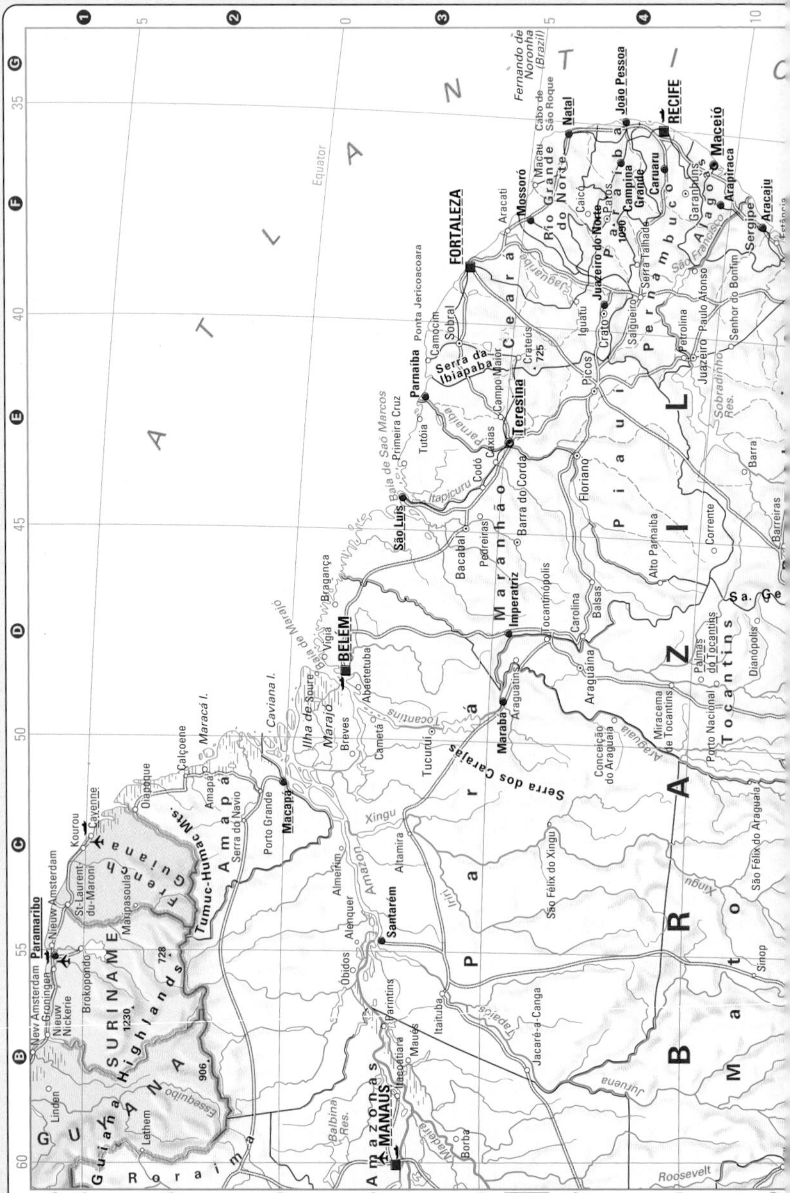
ATLANTIC
Equator
Fernando de Noronha (Brazil)
Cabo de São Roque
Natal
João Pessoa
RECIFE
Maceió
Aracaju
Arapiraca
Sergipe
Alagoas
Caruaru
Campina Grande
Paraíba
Rio Grande do Norte
Mossoró
Aracati
Macau
Caicó
Patos
FORTALEZA
Ceará
Jaguaribe
Juazeiro do Norte
Crato
Iguatu
Pernambuco
Serra Talhada
Salgueiro
Garanhuns
São Francisco
Paulo Afonso
Petrolina
Juazeiro
Senhor do Bonfim
Sobradinho Res.
Ponta Jericoacoara
Camocim
Sobral
Parnaíba
Serra da Ibiapaba
Campo Maior
Crateús
Teresina
Picos
Piauí
Floriano
Tutóia
Primeira Cruz
Baía de São Marcos
São Luís
Itapicuru
Codó
Caxias
Barra do Corda
Bacabal
Pedreiras
Maranhão
Imperatriz
Tocantinópolis
Carolina
Balsas
Alto Parnaíba
Corrente
Barra
Barreiras
Bragança
Baía de Marajó
Vigia
BELÉM
Abaetetuba
Ilha de Marajó
Soure
Breves
Cametá
Tocantins
Tucuruí
Marabá
Araguatins
Araguaína
Conceição do Araguaia
Araguaia
Miracema do Tocantins
Palmas do Tocantins
Porto Nacional
Dianópolis
Serra dos Carajás
Pará
Caviana I.
Maracá I.
Calçoene
Amapá
Oiapoque
Macapá
Porto Grande
Serra do Navio
Tumuc-Humac Mts.
Cayenne
Kourou
French Guiana
St-Laurent-du-Maroni
Maripasoula
Paramaribo
Nieuw Amsterdam
New Amsterdam
Groningen
Nieuw Nickerie
Brokopondo
SURINAME
Guiana Highlands
GUYANA
Linden
Lethem
Essequibo
Roraima
Xingu
Altamira
Almeirim
Amazon
Alenquer
Santarém
Óbidos
Parintins
Itaituba
Tapajós
Jacaré-a-Canga
São Félix do Xingu
Iriri
Amazonas
MANAUS
Itacoatiara
Maués
Balbina Res.
Madeira
Borba
Juruena
Roosevelt
Sinop
São Félix do Araguaia
Mato Grosso
BRAZIL
130/131

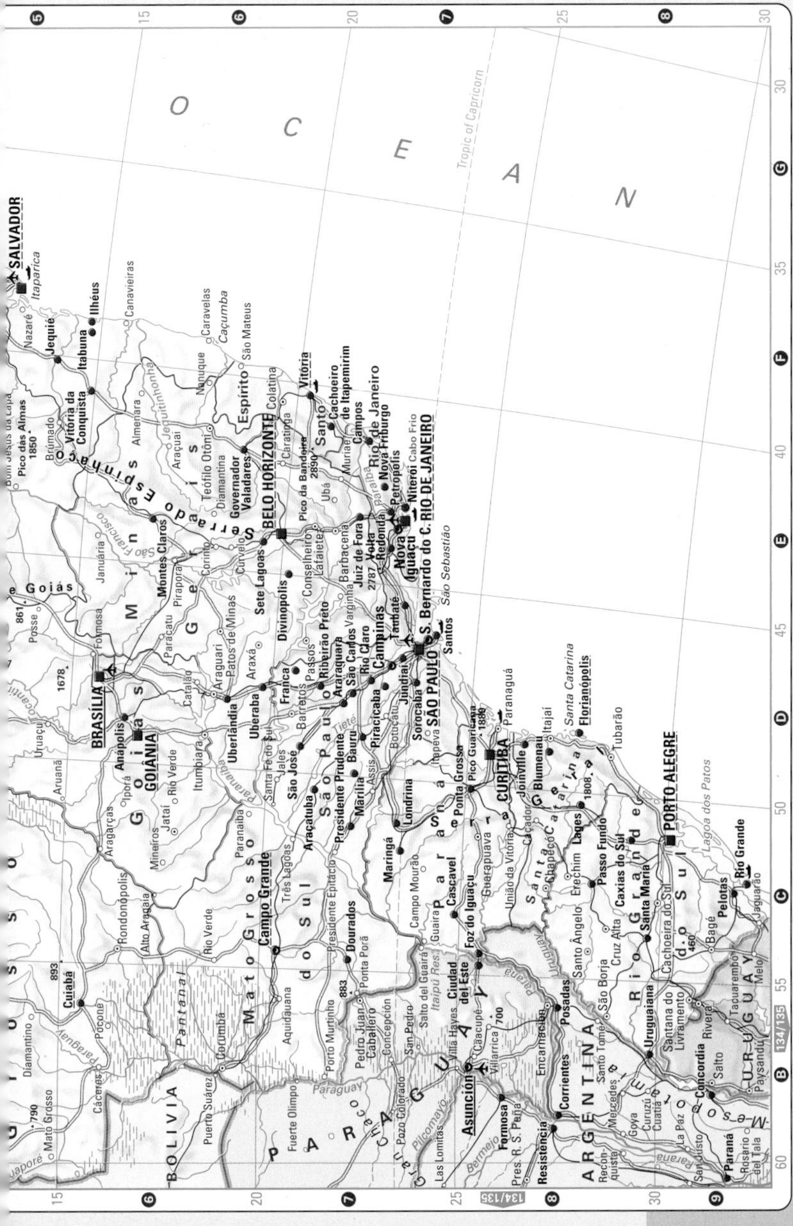
OCEAN
Tropic of Capricorn
SALVADOR
Itaparica
Ilhéus
Canavieiras
Itabuna
Jequié
Nazaré
Vitória da Conquista
Brumado
Pico das Almas 1850
Caravelas
Caçumba
São Mateus
Nanuque
Espírito Santo
Colatina
Vitória
Cachoeiro de Itapemirim
Campos
Rio de Janeiro
Nova Friburgo
Petrópolis
Niterói
Cabo Frio
RIO DE JANEIRO
Nova Iguaçu
Volta Redonda
Juiz de Fora
Barbacena
Conselheiro Lafaiete
Pico da Bandeira 2890
Governador Valadares
Teófilo Otôni
Diamantina
Almenara
Araçuaí
BELO HORIZONTE
Serra do Espinhaço
Minas Gerais
Montes Claros
São Francisco
Januária
Pirapora
Curvelo
Corinto
Sete Lagoas
Divinópolis
Paracatu
Patos de Minas
Araxá
Araguari
Uberlândia
Uberaba
Catalão
Franca
Ribeirão Preto
Passos
Varginha
São Carlos
Araraquara
Rio Claro
Campinas
Piracicaba
Jundiaí
Sorocaba
Taubaté
SÃO PAULO
S. Bernardo do C.
Santos
São Sebastião
São Paulo
Tietê
Bauru
Botucatu
Marília
Assis
Presidente Prudente
Araçatuba
São José
Jales
Barretos
Santa Fé do Sul
Itapeva
Londrina
Maringá
Ponta Grossa
CURITIBA
Paranaguá
Pico Guaricana 1889
Joinville
Blumenau
Itajaí
Florianópolis
Santa Catarina
Lages
Tubarão
Caçador
Chapecó
Erechim
Passo Fundo
Caxias do Sul
Santa Maria
PORTO ALEGRE
Lagoa dos Patos
Rio Grande
Pelotas
Jaguarão
Bagé
Cachoeira do Sul
Santo Ângelo
Cruz Alta
Rio Grande do Sul
Uruguaiana
Santana do Livramento
Rivera
Tacuarembó
Melo
URUGUAY
Salto
Paysandú
Concordia
Paraná
Rosario del Tala
Santa Fe
Paraná
BRASÍLIA
Goiás
Anápolis
GOIÂNIA
Rio Verde
Itumbiara
Paranaíba
Jataí
Iporá
Mineiros
Aragarças
Aruanã
Uruaçu
Formosa
Posse
Mato Grosso do Sul
Campo Grande
Três Lagoas
Dourados
Ponta Porã
Aquidauana
Corumbá
Pantanal
Cuiabá
Poconé
Cáceres
Rondonópolis
Alto Araguaia
Rio Verde
Diamantino
Mato Grosso
Guaporé
BOLIVIA
Puerto Suárez
PARAGUAY
Paraguay
Asunción
Villarrica
Caacupé
Villa Hayes
Ciudad del Este
Foz do Iguaçu
Itaipú Res.
Salto del Guairá
Guaíra
Cascavel
Campo Mourão
Guarapuava
União da Vitória
Paraná
Concepción
Pedro Juan Caballero
San Pedro
Pozo Colorado
Fuerte Olimpo
Porto Murtinho
Pilcomayo
Las Lomitas
Bermejo
Formosa
Resistencia
Corrientes
Posadas
Encarnación
Santo Tomé
São Borja
Mercedes
Goya
Curuzú Cuatiá
Reconquista
La Paz
San Justo
ARGENTINA
Pres. R. S. Peña
Uruguay
Chaco

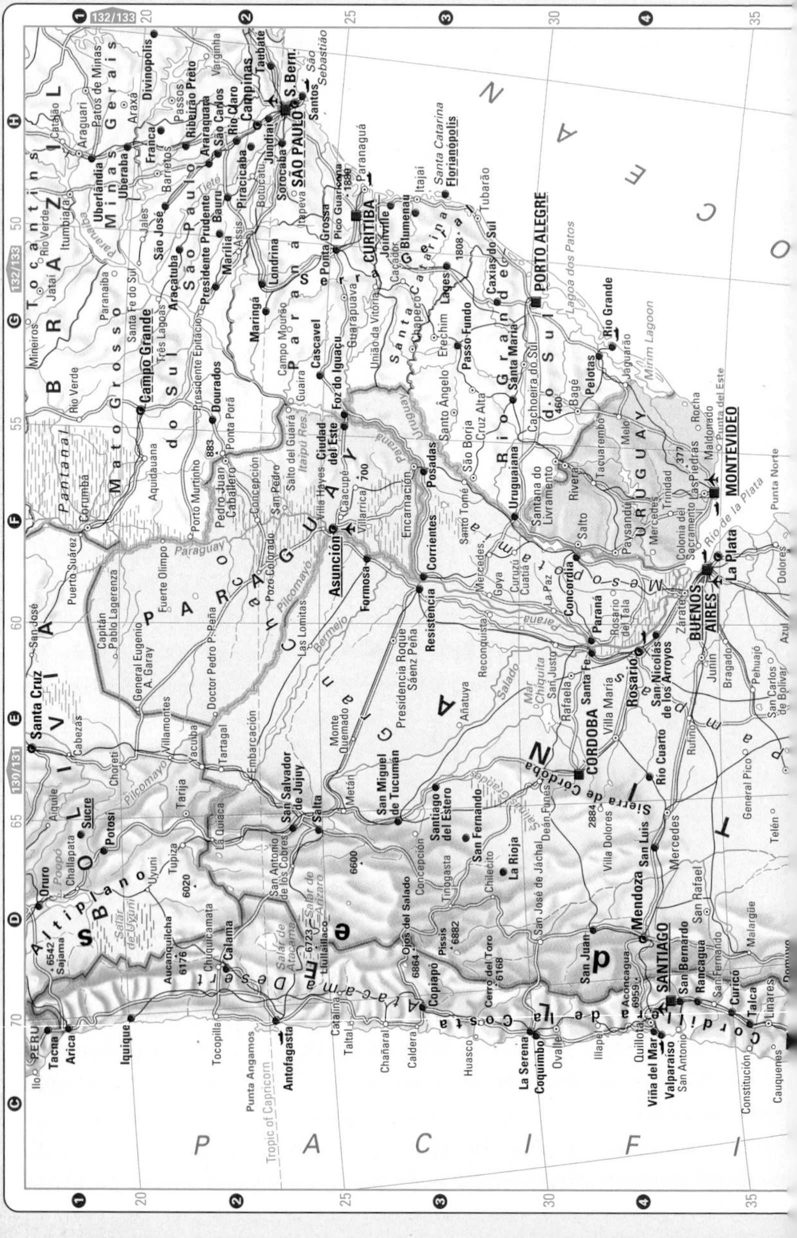

BRAZIL
PARAGUAY
URUGUAY
BOLIVIA
ARGENTINA
PERU
PACIFIC
ATLANTIC OCEAN
SÃO PAULO
CURITIBA
PORTO ALEGRE
MONTEVIDEO
BUENOS AIRES
La Plata
Asunción
Rosario
CÓRDOBA
Santa Fe
Paraná
Corrientes
Resistencia
Posadas
Formosa
San Miguel de Tucumán
Salta
San Salvador de Jujuy
Santiago del Estero
Mendoza
San Juan
San Luis
SANTIAGO
Valparaíso
Viña del Mar
Antofagasta
Iquique
Arica
Tacna
Calama
Copiapó
La Serena
Coquimbo
Sucre
Potosí
Oruro
Santa Cruz
Campo Grande
Florianópolis
Londrina
Maringá
Cascavel
Foz do Iguaçu
Ciudad del Este
Pelotas
Rio Grande
Santa Maria
Passo Fundo
Caxias do Sul
Campinas
Santos
Sorocaba
Ribeirão Preto
Uberlândia
Uberaba
Franca
Divinópolis
Blumenau
Joinville
Ponta Grossa
Lages
Concordia
Salto
Rivera
Uruguaiana
Tropic of Capricorn
Aconcagua 6959
Altiplano
Pantanal
Gran Chaco
Pampa
Sierra de Córdoba
Lagoa dos Patos
Mirim Lagoon
Río de la Plata

Mar del Plata
Necochea
Tandil
Tres Arroyos
Suárez
1243
Bahía Blanca
Punta Rasa
General Acha
Bahía Blanca
Colorado
Río Negro
Carmen de Patagones
Viedma
Gulf of San Matías
Valdés Pen.
Rawson
Trelew
Puerto Madryn
Neuquén
General Roca
Chos Malal
Zapala
Sierra Colorada
San Carlos de Bariloche
Lanín 3776
Tres Picos 2492
Esquel
Chubut
Las Plumas
390
C. Dos Bahías
Comodoro Rivadavia
Gulf of San Jorge
Caleta Olivia
C. Tres Puntas
Puerto Deseado
Chico
Las Heras
Sarmiento
L. Buenos Aires
Chile Chico
Gobernador Gregores
Puerto San Julián
Puerto Santa Cruz
Bahía Grande
L. San Martín
L. Viedma
L. Argentino
El Calafate
Río Gallegos
C. Vírgenes
Strait of Magellan
Puerto Natales
Punta Arenas
Porvenir
Río Grande
Tierra del Fuego
Ushuaia
Yogan 2469
Navarino I.
Wollaston Is.
Cape Horn
Hoste I.
Dawson I.
Brunswick Pen.
Riesko I.
Santa Inés I.
Cabo Deseado
Queen Adelaide Arch.
Madre de Dios I.
Wellington I.
Murallón 2831
Campana I.
Gulf of Peñas
Taitao Pen.
San Valentín 4058
Coihaique
Puerto Aisén
Chonos Arch.
Magdalena
Golfo Corcovado
Pta. Pabellón
Chiloé I.
Castro
Ancud
Puerto Montt
Osorno
Valdivia
Temuco
Angol
Los Angeles
Lebu
C. San Diego
Staten I.
Falkland Islands (Is. Malvinas) (U. K.)
West Falkland
705
Stanley
East Falkland
South Georgia (U. K.)
Grytviken
A T L A N T I C
O C E A N
P a t a g o n i a
C o r d i l l e r a
P a t a g o n i c a

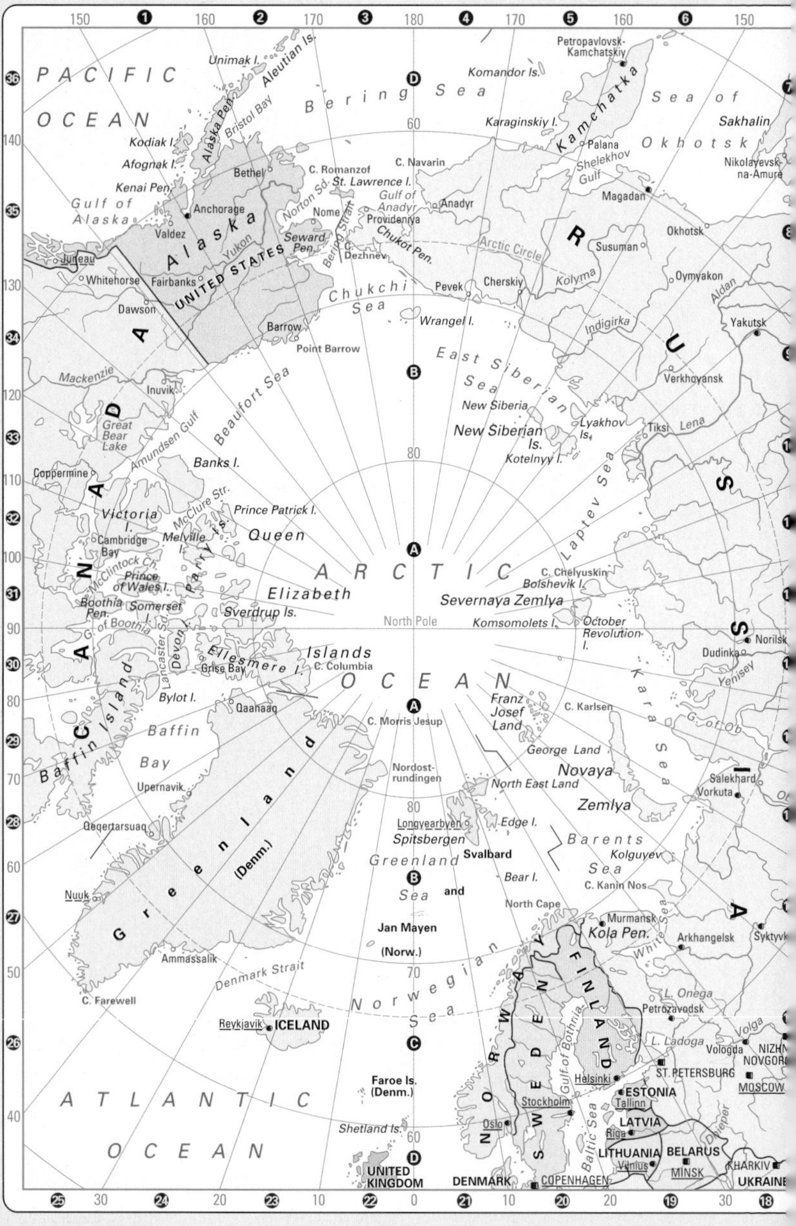
PACIFIC OCEAN
Bering Sea
Unimak I.
Aleutian Is.
Alaska Pen.
Bristol Bay
Kodiak I.
Afognak I.
Kenai Pen.
Gulf of Alaska
Anchorage
Valdez
Bethel
Alaska
Yukon
UNITED STATES
Juneau
Whitehorse
Fairbanks
Dawson
Norton Sd.
Nome
Seward Pen.
Bering Strait
C. Romanzof
St. Lawrence I.
C. Dezhnev
Komandor Is.
Karaginskiy I.
C. Navarin
Gulf of Anadyr
Anadyr
Provideniya
Chukot Pen.
Arctic Circle
Petropavlovsk-Kamchatskiy
Kamchatka
Palana
Shelekhov Gulf
Magadan
Sea of Okhotsk
Sakhalin
Nikolayevsk-na-Amure
Okhotsk
Susuman
Kolyma
Oymyakon
Aldan
Yakutsk
Verkhoyansk
Indigirka
Cherskiy
Pevek
Chukchi Sea
Wrangel I.
Barrow
Point Barrow
Beaufort Sea
Mackenzie
Inuvik
Great Bear Lake
Amundsen Gulf
Banks I.
Coppermine
Victoria I.
McClure Str.
Prince Patrick I.
Melville I.
Parry Is.
Cambridge Bay
McClintock Ch.
Prince of Wales I.
Boothia Pen.
Somerset I.
G. of Boothia
Lancaster Sd.
Devon I.
Ellesmere I.
Grise Bay
Sverdrup Is.
Queen Elizabeth Islands
C. Columbia
Bylot I.
Qaanaaq
Baffin Bay
Baffin Island
Upernavik
Qeqertarsuaq
Nuuk
Ammassalik
C. Farewell
Denmark Strait
Greenland (Denm.)
C. Morris Jesup
Nordostrundingen
CANADA
East Siberian Sea
New Siberia
New Siberian Is.
Kotelnyy I.
Lyakhov Is.
Tiksi
Lena
Laptev Sea
C. Chelyuskin
Bolshevik I.
Severnaya Zemlya
Komsomolets I.
October Revolution I.
North Pole
ARCTIC OCEAN
Norilsk
Dudinka
Yenisey
Kara Sea
Franz Josef Land
C. Karlsen
G. of Ob
George Land
Novaya Zemlya
North East Land
Salekhard
Vorkuta
Longyearbyen
Spitsbergen
Edge I.
Svalbard and Jan Mayen (Norw.)
Barents Sea
Kolguyev
Greenland Sea
Bear I.
C. Kanin Nos
North Cape
Murmansk
Kola Pen.
White Sea
Arkhangelsk
Syktyvk
RUSSIA
Norwegian Sea
L. Onega
Petrozavodsk
L. Ladoga
Volga
Vologda
NIZHN NOVGOR
ST. PETERSBURG
MOSCOW
FINLAND
NORWAY
SWEDEN
Gulf of Bothnia
Helsinki
ESTONIA
Tallinn
Stockholm
Oslo
Baltic Sea
LATVIA
Riga
LITHUANIA
Vilnius
BELARUS
MINSK
Dnieper
KHARKIV
UKRAINE
DENMARK
COPENHAGEN
UNITED KINGDOM
Shetland Is.
Faroe Is. (Denm.)
ICELAND
Reykjavík
ATLANTIC OCEAN

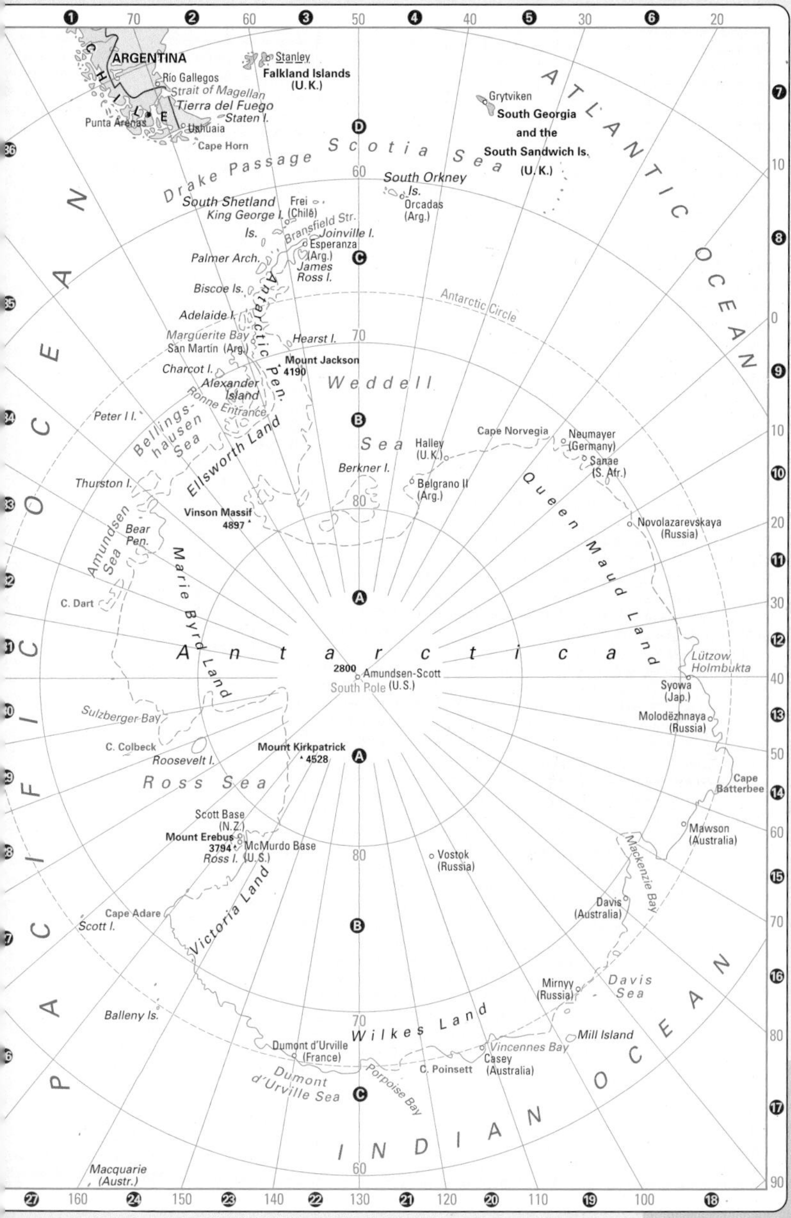
ARGENTINA
CHILE
Río Gallegos
Strait of Magellan
Tierra del Fuego
Staten I.
Punta Arenas
Ushuaia
Cape Horn
Stanley
Falkland Islands (U.K.)
Grytviken
South Georgia and the South Sandwich Is. (U.K.)
ATLANTIC OCEAN
Drake Passage
Scotia Sea
South Orkney Is.
Orcadas (Arg.)
South Shetland Is.
Frei (Chile)
King George I.
Bransfield Str.
Joinville I.
Esperanza (Arg.)
James Ross I.
Palmer Arch.
Biscoe Is.
Antarctic Pen.
Antarctic Circle
Adelaide I.
Marguerite Bay
San Martín (Arg.)
Hearst I.
Mount Jackson 4190
Charcot I.
Alexander Island
Ronne Entrance
Weddell Sea
Peter I I.
Bellingshausen Sea
Ellsworth Land
Cape Norvegia
Neumayer (Germany)
Halley (U.K.)
Sanae (S. Afr.)
Berkner I.
Belgrano II (Arg.)
Queen Maud Land
Thurston I.
Vinson Massif 4897
Novolazarevskaya (Russia)
Amundsen Sea
Bear Pen.
Marie Byrd Land
C. Dart
Antarctica
Lützow Holmbukta
2800
Amundsen-Scott South Pole (U.S.)
Syowa (Jap.)
Molodëzhnaya (Russia)
Sulzberger Bay
C. Colbeck
Roosevelt I.
Mount Kirkpatrick 4528
Ross Sea
Cape Batterbee
Scott Base (N.Z.)
Mount Erebus 3794
McMurdo Base (U.S.)
Ross I.
Mawson (Australia)
Vostok (Russia)
Mackenzie Bay
Victoria Land
Cape Adare
Scott I.
Davis (Australia)
PACIFIC OCEAN
Mirnyy (Russia)
Davis Sea
Balleny Is.
Wilkes Land
Mill Island
Dumont d'Urville (France)
Vincennes Bay
Casey (Australia)
C. Poinsett
Dumont d'Urville Sea
Porpoise Bay
INDIAN OCEAN
Macquarie (Austr.)

To complement the information provided in the preceding map section, the Pocket Atlas comprises 63 pages of additional data on the political and territorial entities of the world, i.e. above all on the 195 countries currently listed in the U.N. statistics.

The countries are arranged by the short form of their name in English; dependent territories and exclaves follow the respective nation.

As a rule, the names of the territorial units are listed by their
- short form in English
- full name in English
- short form in the official language
- full name in the official language,
if there are differences among them.

The area and population figures given for the territorial units are based on the "Statistisches Jahrbuch der Bundesrepublik Deutschland", the statistical yearbook of the Federal Republic of Germany. Figures for federal administrative units have mainly been taken from the "Britannica Book of the Year". Due to differences in the inclusion of inland waters, some area figures may deviate from those of other statistical surveys.

The representation of cities in the maps of the first section of this atlas has been done with a view to presenting the population density of a specific region as accurately as possible. To that end, scale permitting, the signature of a given city has been supplemented by the area covered by the agglomeration (cf. Los Angeles). Correspondingly, in the following statistics, in relevant cases the population figure of its agglomeration is added to the number of inhabitants of the city proper.

Population figures have primarily been taken from the "Britannica Book of the Year" and from the "Fischer Weltalmanach". Both publications have also served as the principal sources for information on language, religion and currency. Special care has been taken in each case to include the most recent population figure available.

Concerning the languages, emphasis has been put on the official languages separated by a slash. In some cases, though, additional important languages spoken in the respective nation have been added, separated by a comma.

Afghanistan

Islamic State of Afghanistan
Afghānestān
Dı Afgānistān Islāmī Dawlat/
Dowlat-e Eslāmī-ye Afghānestān

Area: 652,090 km^2
Population: 21,800,000 (1997)
Capital: Kābul (Pop. 400,000; A: 2,000,000)
Administration: 31 provinces
Languages: Pashto/Dari
Religions: Muslim 99%
Currency: 1 afghani = 100 puls
Major cities:
Kandahār (226,000), Herāt (177,000), Mazār-e Sharīf (128,000), Jalālābād (59,000), Kunduz (57,000), Baghlān (41,000), Meymaneh (40,000)

Albania

Republic of Albania
Shqipëria
Republika e Shqipërisë

Area: 28,748 km^2
Population: 3,430,000 (1997)
Capital: Tirana (Pop. 427,000)
Administration: 26 provinces
Languages: Albanian
Religions: Muslim 70%, Orthodox 20%, Roman Catholic 10%
Currency: 1 lek = 100 qindars
Major cities:
Durrës (85,400), Elbasan (83,300), Shkodër (81,900), Vlorë (73,800), Korçë (65,400), Fier (45,200), Berat (43,800)

Algeria

People's Democratic Republic of Algeria
Al-Jazair
Jumhuriya al-Jazairiya
ad-Dimuqratiya ash-Shabiya

Area: 2,381,741 km^2
Population: 29,500,000 (1997)
Capital: Algiers (Pop. 1,687,579; A: 3,700,000)
Administration: 48 provinces (wilayat)
Languages: Arabic, Berber
Religions: Muslim 99.9%
Currency: 1 Alger. dinar = 100 centimes
Major cities:
Oran (599,000), Constantine (450,000), Annaba (228,000), Sétif (186,000), Batna (185,000), Sidi bel Abbès (155,000), Blida (132,000)

Andorra

Principality of Andorra
Andorra
Principat d'Andorra

Area: 453 km^2
Population: 74,000 (1997)
Capital: Andorra la Vella (Pop. 22,000)
Administration: 7 parishes
Languages: Catalan, Spanish, French
Religions: Roman Catholic 92%
Currency: French franc and Spanish peseta
Major cities:
Escaldes-Engordany (15,300), Encamp (9,400), St. Juliá de Lòrio (7,400), La Massana (5,500)

Angola

Republic of Angola
Angola
República de Angola

Area: 1,246,700 km^2
Population: 11,600,000 (1997)
Capital: Luanda (Pop. 2,250,000)
Administration: 18 provinces
Languages: Portuguese, Bantu languages
Religions: Christian 89%
Currency: 1 readjusted kwanza = 100 lwei
Major cities:
Huambo (400,000), Benguela (155,000), Lobito (150,000), Lubango (105,000), Namibe (100,000)

Antigua and Barbuda

Antigua and Barbuda

Area: 442 km^2
Population: 66,000 (1997)
Capital: Saint John's (Pop. 22,000)
Administration: 6 parishes, 2 dependencies
Languages: English, Creole
Religions: predominantly Anglican
Currency: 1 Eastern Caribbean dollar = 100 cents
Major towns:
Codrington (1,200)

1 km^2 = 0.3861 square mile

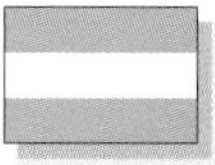

Argentina

Argentine Republic
Argentina
República Argentina

Area: 2,780,400 km^2
Population: 35,700,000 (1997)
Capital: Buenos Aires (Pop. 2,961,000; A: 10,990,000)
Administration: 23 provinces and 1 federal district
Languages: Spanish, Indian languages
Religions: Roman Catholic 91%
Currency: 1 peso = 100 centavos
Major cities:
Córdoba (1,148,000), Rosario (895,000), La Plata (521,000), Mar del Plata (520,000), San Miguel de Tucumán (471,000), Salta (367,000), Santa Fe (343,000), Corrientes (258,000), Bahía Blanca (255,000), Resistencia (228,000), Paraná (207,000), Posadas (202,000)

External Territory:

Argentine Antarctic Sector

Antártida Argentina
Claimed by Argentina

Area: 1,231,000 km^2
Research stations

Armenia

Republic of Armenia
Hayastan
Hayastani Hanrapetut'yun

Area: 29,800 km^2
Population: 3,640,000 (1997)
Capital: Yerevan (Pop. 1,283,000; A: 1,450,000)
Administration: 37 districts
Languages: Armenian, Russian
Religions: Armenian Apostolic Church
Currency: 1 dram = 100 lumas
Major cities:
Vanadzor (159,000), Gyumri (120,000), Hrazdan (61,000), Ejmiatsin (61,000), Abovyan (59,000)

Australia

Commonwealth of Australia

Area: 7,682,300 km^2
Population: 18,200,000 (1997)
Capital: Canberra (Pop. A: 345,000)
Administration: 6 states, 2 territories
Languages: English, Austr. languages
Religions: Christian 73%
Currency: 1 Australian dollar = 100 cents
Major cities:
Sydney (A: 3,879,000), Melbourne (A: 3,283,000), Brisbane (A: 1,521,000), Perth (A: 1,295,000), Adelaide (A: 1,079,000), Newcastle (A: 464,000), Gold Coast (A: 354,000), Wollongong (A: 256,000), Hobart (A: 196,000), Sunshine Coast (A: 156,000)

	Area km^2	Population 1996	Capital
States			
New South Wales	801,600	6,040,000	Sydney
Queensland	1,727,200	3,370,000	Brisbane
South Australia	984,000	1,430,000	Adelaide
Tasmania	67,800	460,000	Hobart
Victoria	227,600	4,370,000	Melbourne
Western Australia	2,525,500	1,730,000	Perth
Territories			
Australian Capital Territory	2,400	300,000	Canberra
Northern Territory	1,346,200	200,000	Darwin

External Territories:

Ashmore and Cartier Islands

Territory of Ashmore and Cartier Islands

Area: 2 km^2, uninhabited

Australian Antarctic Territory

Claimed by Australia

Area: c. 6,120,000 km^2
Research stations

Christmas Island

Territory of Christmas Island

Area: 135 km^2
Population: 2,500 (1994)

Cocos (Keeling) Islands

Territory of Cocos Islands

Area: 14 km^2

Coral Sea Islands
Territory of Coral Sea Islands

Reefs and islands scattered over a sea area of about 1 million km^2 (uninhabited)

Heard and the McDonald Islands
Territory of Heard and the McDonald Islands

Area: 412 km^2, uninhabited

Norfolk Island
Territory of Norfolk Island

Area: 35 km^2
Population: 2,000 (1997)
Seat of government:
Kingston

Bahamas, The
Commonwealth of The Bahamas

Area: 13,878 km^2
Population: 288,000 (1997)
Capital: Nassau (Pop. 172,000)
Administration: 18 districts
Languages: English, Creole
Religions: Protestant 76%, Roman Catholic 19%
Currency: 1 Bahamian dollar = 100 cents
Major cities/towns:
Freeport (26,600), High Rock (8,100), West End (7,800), Cooper Town (5,500)

Austria
Republic of Austria
Österreich
Republik Österreich

Area: 83,859 km^2
Population: 8,140,000 (1997)
Capital: Vienna (Pop. 1,610,000)
Administration: 9 federal states
Languages: German
Religions: Roman Catholic 78%, Protestant 5%
Currency: 1 schilling = 100 groschen
Major cities:
Graz (240,000), Linz (190,000), Salzburg (145,000), Innsbruck (110,000), Klagenfurt (91,000), Villach (57,000), Wels (55,000)

Bahrain
State of Bahrain
Al-Bahrayn
Dawlat al-Bahrayn

Area: 694 km^2
Population: 581,000 (1997)
Capital: Manama (Pop. 137,000)
Administration: 11 regions
Languages: Arabic, English
Religions: Muslim 90%
Currency: 1 Bahrain dinar = 1,000 fils
Major cities:
Al-Muharraq (74,000), Jidd Hafs (45,000)

Azerbaijan
Azerbaijani Republic
Azərbaycan
Azərbaycan Respublikasi

Area: 86,600 km^2
Population: 7,650,000 (1997)
Capital: Baku (Pop. 1,080,000; A: 1,660,000)
Administration: 54 districts, Nakhichevan Aut. Republic, Nagorno-Karabakh Aut. Region
Languages: Azerbaijani, Russian
Religions: Muslim 90%
Currency: 1 manat = 100 gopik
Major cities:
Gəncə (282,000), Sumqayıt (236,000)

Bangladesh
People's Republic of Bangladesh
Bangladesh
Gana Prajatantri Bangladesh

Area: 143,998 km^2
Population: 122,200,000 (1997)
Capital: Dhaka (Pop. 3,638,000; A: 7,832,000)
Administration: 5 divisions
Languages: Bengali, English
Religions: Muslim 87%, Hindu 12%
Currency: 1 taka = 100 paisa
Major cities:
Chittagong (1,566,000), Khulna (601,000), Rajshahi (325,000), Rangpur (221,000), Bhairab Bāzār (180,000), Jessore (176,000)

Barbados

Area: 430 km²
Population: 262,000 (1997)
Capital: Bridgetown (Pop. 6,700)
Administration: 11 parishes
Languages: English, Bajan
Religions: Anglican 33%, other Protestants 30%, non-denominational 20%
Currency: 1 Barbados dollar = 100 cents
Major cities/towns:
Speightstown (3,500), Bathsheba

Belarus

Republic of Belarus
Belarus
Respublika Belarus

Area: 207,600 km²
Population: 10,300,000 (1997)
Capital: Minsk (Pop. 1,680,000)
Administration: 6 provinces
Languages: Belarusian/Russian
Religions: Russian Orthodox 60%, Roman Catholic 8%
Currency: 1 rouble = 100 kopeks
Major cities:
Homyel (502,000), Mahilyow (368,000), Vitsyebsk (356,000), Hrodna (304,000), Brest (295,000)

Belgium

Kingdom of Belgium
Belgique/België/Belgien
Royaume de Belgique/Koninkrijk België/Königreich Belgien

Area: 30,519 km²
Population: 10,200,000 (1997)
Capital: Brussels (Pop. A: 948,000)
Administration: 3 regions: Flanders, Wallonia, Brussels-Capital
Languages: French/Dutch/German
Religions: Roman Catholic 81%
Currency: 1 Belg. franc = 100 centimes
Major cities:
Antwerp (456,000), Ghent (226,000), Charleroi (206,000)

Belize

Area: 22,696 km²
Population: 224,000 (1997)
Capital: Belmopan (Pop. 6,800)
Administration: 6 districts
Languages: English, English Creole, Spanish
Religions: Roman Catholic 58%, Protestant 28%
Currency: 1 Belize dollar = 100 cents
Major cities:
Belize City (54,000), Orange Walk (15,000)

Benin

Republic of Benin
Bénin
République du Bénin

Area: 112,622 km²
Population: 5,720,000 (1997)
Capital: Porto-Novo (Pop. 179,000)
Administration: 12 regions
Languages: French, Fon, Adja, Yoruba
Religions: Traditional beliefs 60%, Roman Catholic 21%
Currency: 1 CFA franc = 100 centimes
Major cities:
Cotonou (537,000), Djougou (134,000), Parakou (104,000)

Bhutan

Kingdom of Bhutan
Druk-Yul

Area: 47,000 km²
Population: 1,870,000 (1997)
Capital: Thimphu (Pop. 30,300)
Administration: 20 districts
Languages: Dzongkha, Nepali, Assamese
Religions: Buddhist 72%, Hindu 24%
Currency: 1 ngultrum = 100 chetrum
Major cities:
Punakha (district 16,700)

Bolivia

Republic of Bolivia
Bolivia
República de Bolivia

Area:	1,098,581 km^2
Population:	7,770,000 (1997)
Capital:	Sucre (judicial, Pop. 145,000), La Paz (administrative, Pop. A: 1,200,000)
Administration:	9 departments
Languages:	Spanish/Quechua/Aymara
Religions:	Roman Catholic 93%
Currency:	1 boliviano = 100 centavos

Major cities:
Santa Cruz (767,000), Cochabamba (449,000), El Alto (446,000), Oruro (202,000),

Bosnia and Herzegovina

Rep. of Bosnia and Herzegovina
Bosna i Hercegovina
Republika Bosna i Hercegovina

Area:	51,129 km^2
Population:	3,860,000 (1997)
Capital:	Sarajevo (Pop. 416,000)
Administration:	Croat-Moslem Federation and Serb Republic
Languages:	Bosnian/Croatian/Serbian
Religions:	Muslim 44%, Orth. Catholic 31%, Roman Catholic 15%
Currency:	1 dinar = 100 para

Major cities:
Banja Luka (143,000), Zenica (96,000), Tuzla (84,000), Mostar (76,000)

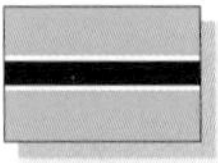

Botswana

Republic of Botswana

Area:	581,730 km^2
Population:	1,520,000 (1997)
Capital:	Gaborone (Pop. 133,000)
Administration:	11 districts
Languages:	English, Setswana
Religions:	Christian 50%, traditional beliefs 49%
Currency:	1 pula = 100 thebe

Major cities:
Francistown (65,000), Selebi-Pikwe (40,000), Molepolole (36,000), Kanye (31,000)

Brazil

Federative Republic of Brazil
O Brasil
República Federativa do Brasil

Area:	8,547,404 km^2
Population:	163,000,000 (1997)
Capital:	Brasília (Pop. 1,822,000)
Administration:	26 states, 1 federal district
Languages:	Portuguese
Religions:	Roman Catholic 75%, Protestant and other Christians 10%
Currency:	1 real = 100 centavos

Major cities:
São Paulo (9,839,000; A:16,420,000), Rio de Janeiro (5,552,000), Salvador (2,212,000), Belo Horizonte (2,091,000), Fortaleza (1,966,000), Curitiba (1,467,000), Recife (1,346,000), Pôrto Alegre (1,289,000), Manaus (1,157,000), Belém (1,144,000), Goiânia (1,004,000), Guarulhos (972,000), Campinas (909,000)

	Area km^2	Population 1996	Capital
States			
Acre	153,150	484,000	Rio Branco
Alagoas	27,933	2,633,000	Maceió
Amapá	143,454	380,000	Macapá
Amazonas	1,577,820	2,389,000	Manaus
Bahia	567,295	12,542,000	Salvador
Ceará	146,348	6,809,000	Fortaleza
Espírito Santo	46,194	2,803,000	Vitória
Goiás	341,289	4,515,000	Goiânia
Maranhão	333,366	5,222,000	São Luís
Mato Grosso	906,807	2,236,000	Cuiabá
Mato Grosso do Sul	358,159	1,928,000	Campo Grande
Minas Gerais	588,384	16,673,000	Belo Horizonte
Pará	1,253,165	5,511,000	Belém
Paraíba	56,585	3,306,000	João Pessoa
Paraná	199,709	9,004,000	Curitiba
Pernambuco	98,938	7,399,000	Recife
Piauí	252,378	2,673,000	Teresina
Rio de Janeiro	43,910	13,406,000	Rio de Janeiro
Rio Grande do Norte	53,307	2,559,000	Natal
Rio Grande do Sul	282,062	9,635,000	Pôrto Alegre
Rondônia	238,513	1,229,000	Pôrto Velho
Roraima	225,116	247,000	Boa Vista
Santa Catarina	95,443	4,875,000	Florianópolis
São Paulo	248,809	34,119,000	São Paulo
Sergipe	22,050	1,624,000	Aracaju
Tocantins	278,421	1,049,000	Palmas
Federal district			
Distrito Federal	5,822	1,822,000	Brasília
Disputed areas	2,977	–	

1 km^2 = 0.3861 square mile

Brunei

State of Brunei Darussalam
Brunei Darussalam
Negara Brunei Darussalam

Area: 5,765 km^2
Population: 306,000 (1997)
Capital: Bandar Seri Begawan (Pop. 45,867)
Administration: 4 districts
Languages: Malay, English
Religions: Muslim 67%, Buddhist 13%, Christian 10%
Currency: 1 Brunei dollar = 100 cents
Major cities:
Kuala Belait (21,000), Seria (21,000)

Burundi

Republic of Burundi
Burundi
Republika y'Uburundi/
République du Burundi

Area: 27,834 km^2
Population: 6,410,000 (1997)
Capital: Bujumbura (Pop. 300,000)
Administration: 15 provinces
Languages: Kirundi/French
Religions: Christian 68%, traditional beliefs
Currency: 1 Burundi franc =100 centimes
Major cities:
Gitega (102,000), Muyinga (79,000), Ngozi (74,000), Kayanza (63,000), Kirundo (63,000)

Bulgaria

Republic of Bulgaria
Bŭlgaria
Republika Bŭlgaria

Area: 110,912 km^2
Population: 8,430,000 (1997)
Capital: Sofia (Pop. 1,116,000)
Administration: 8 regions, 1 city commune
Languages: Bulgarian, Turkish
Religions: Bulgarian Orthodox 86%, Muslim 13%
Currency: 1 lev = 100 stotinki
Major cities:
Plovdiv (346,000), Varna (304,000), Burgas (200,000), Ruse (169,000), Stara Zagora (151,000), Pleven (128,000), Sliven (107,000)

Cambodia

Kingdom of Cambodia
Kampuchea
Preah Reach Ana Pak Kampuchea

Area: 181,035 km^2
Population: 10,500,000 (1997)
Capital: Phnom Penh (Pop. 920,000)
Administration: 21 provinces
Languages: Khmer, French, Chinese
Religions: Buddhist 88%, Muslim 2%
Currency: 1 riel = 100 sen
Major cities:
Bătdâmbâng (94,000), Siĕmréab (76,000), Kâmpóng Saôm (75,000)

Burkina Faso

Area: 274,000 km^2
Population: 11,100,000 (1997)
Capital: Ouagadougou (Pop. 634,000)
Administration: 45 provinces
Languages: French, Mossi, Fulani
Religions: Traditional beliefs 65%, Muslim 25%
Currency: 1 CFA franc = 100 centimes
Major cities:
Bobo-Dioulasso (269,000), Koudougou (105,000), Ouahigouya (39,000)

Cameroon

Republic of Cameroon
Cameroun/Cameroon
République du Cameroun/
Republic of Cameroon

Area: 475,442 km^2
Population: 13,900,000 (1997)
Capital: Yaoundé (Pop. 800,000)
Administration: 10 provinces
Languages: French/English
Religions: Christian 53%, traditional beliefs
Currency: 1 CFA franc = 100 centimes
Major cities:
Douala (1,200,000), Garoua (160,000), Maroua (140,000), Bafoussam (120,000)

Canada

Area: 9,970,610 km^2 (of wich 755,180 km^2 are freshwater)
Population: 29,900,000 (1997)
Capital: Ottawa (Pop. 314,000; A: 1,010,000)
Administration: 10 provinces, 2 territories
Languages: English/French
Religions: Roman Catholic 46%, Protestant 30%
Currency: 1 Canadian dollar = 100 cents
Major cities:
Toronto (635,000; A: 4,260,000), Montréal (1,018,000; A: 3,330,000), Vancouver (472,000; A: 1,830,000), Edmonton (A: 860,000), Calgary (A: 820,000), Québec (168,000; A: 670,000), Winnipeg (A: 670,000), Hamilton (318,000; A: 620,000), London (A: 400,000), Kitchener (A: 380,000), St. Catharines-Niagara (A: 370,000), Halifax (A: 330,000), Victoria (A: 300,000)

	Area km^2	Population 1996	Capital
Provinces			
Alberta	661,190	2,847,000	Edmonton
British Columbia	947,800	3,933,000	Victoria
Manitoba	649,950	1,145,000	Winnipeg
New Brunswick	73,440	762,000	Fredericton
Newfoundland	405,720	564,000	St. John's
Nova Scotia	55,490	948,000	Halifax
Ontario	1,068,580	11,408,000	Toronto
Prince Edward Island	5,660	137,000	Charlottetown
Québec	1,540,680	7,420,000	Québec
Saskatchewan	652,330	1,024,000	Regina
Territories			
Northwest Territories	1,224,920	46,000	Yellowknife
Nunavut	2,201,400	22,000	Iqaluit
Yukon Territory	483,450	32,000	Whitehorse

Cape Verde

Republic of Cape Verde
Cabo Verde
República de Cabo Verde

Area: 4,033 km^2
Population: 406,000 (1997)
Capital: Praia (Pop. 62,000)
Administration: 16 counties
Languages: Portuguese
Religions: Roman Catholic 96%
Currency: 1 Cape Verde escudo = 100 centavos
Major cities:
Mindelo (47,000)

Central African Republic

Ködrö tî Bê-Afrîka/
République centrafricaine

Area: 622,984 km^2
Population: 3,420,000 (1997)
Capital: Bangui (Pop. A: 706,000)
Administration: 16 prefectures and the capital
Languages: Sango/French
Religions: Traditional beliefs 57%, Christian 35%, Muslim 8%
Currency: 1 CFA franc = 100 centimes
Major cities:
Berbérati (47,000), Bouar (43,000), Bambari (41,000), Bossangoa (32,000)

Chad

Republic of Chad
Tchad/Tshad
République du Tchad/
Jumhuriya Tshad

Area: 1,284,000 km^2
Population: 6,690,000 (1997)
Capital: N'Djamena (Pop. 530,000)
Administration: 14 prefectures
Languages: French/Arabic
Religions: Muslim 50%, Christian 30%
Currency: 1 CFA franc = 100 centimes
Major cities:
Moundou (281,000), Sarh (198,000), Bongor (195,000), Abéché (188,000), Doba (185,000)

Chile

Republic of Chile
Chile
República de Chile

Area:	756,626 km^2
Population:	14,600,000 (1997)
Capital:	Santiago de Chile (Pop. 5,077,000)
Administration:	13 regions
Languages:	Spanish, Indian languages
Religions:	Roman Catholic 77%, Protestant 13%
Currency:	1 Chilean peso = 100 centavos

Major cities:
Concepción (350,000), Viña del Mar (322,000), Valparaíso (282,000), Talcahuano (261,000), Antofagasta (237,000), San Bernardo (206,000)

External Territories:

Islands in the Pacific Ocean:

Easter Island (Isla de Pascua/Rapa Nui)
Juan Fernández Islands
Sala-y-Gómez
Desventurados Islands
Diego Ramírez Islands

Chilean Antarctic Territory

Antártida Chilena
Claimed by Chile

Area:	1,250,000 km^2

Research stations

China

People's Republic of China
Zhongguo
Zhonghua Renmin Gonghe Guo

Area:	9,562,036 km^2
Population:	1,220,800,000 (1997)
Capital:	Peking (Pop. 6,600,000)
Administration:	22 provinces, 5 auton. regions, 4 municipalities
Languages:	Mandarin Chinese
Religions:	Non-religious 52%, Confucianist 20%, Buddhist 8%
Currency:	1 Renminbi (yuan) = 10 jiao

Major cities:
Shanghai (8,800,000), Hong Kong (6,500,000) Tianjin (5,000,000), Shenyang (3,900,000)

Colombia

Republic of Colombia
Colombia
República de Colombia

Area:	1,138,914 km^2
Population:	37,000,000 (1997)
Capital:	Bogotá (Pop. 6,005,000)
Administration:	32 departments, capital
Languages:	Spanish, Indian languages
Religions:	Roman Catholic 95%
Currency:	1 Col. peso = 100 centavos

Major cities:
Cali (1,986,000), Medellín (1,971,000), Barranquilla (1,158,000), Cartagena (813,000), Cúcuta (589,000), Bucaramanga (508,000), Pereira (434,000), Ibagué (420,000)

Comoros

Fed. Islamic Rep. of the Comoros
Comores/Al-Qumur
Rép. fédérale islamique des Comores/Jumhuriyat al-Qumur al-Ittihadiyah al-Islamiyah

Area:	1,862 km^2
Population:	651,000 (1997)
Capital:	Moroni (Pop. 23,400)
Administration:	3 districts
Languages:	Comorian/French/Arabic
Religions:	Muslim 99%, Roman Catholic 1%
Currency:	1 Comorian franc = 100 centimes

Major towns:
Moutsamudu (14,000), Foumbouni (7,000)

Congo,
Democratic Republic of the

République démocratique du Congo

Area:	2,344,858 km^2
Population:	47,900,000 (1997)
Capital:	Kinshasa (Pop. 4,655,000)
Administration:	11 regions
Languages:	French
Religions:	Roman Catholic 42%, Protestant 25%
Currency:	1 new zaïre = 100 makuta

Major cities:
Lubumbashi (851,000), Mbuji-Mayi (806,000), Kolwezi (418,000), Kisangani (418,000), Kananga (393,000), Likasi (299,000)

Congo, Republic of the

Congo
République du Congo

Area: 342,000 km^2
Population: 2,740,000 (1997)
Capital: Brazzaville (Pop. 938,000)
Administration: 9 regions, 6 communes
Languages: French, Kongo, Lingala
Religions: Roman Catholic 54%, traditional beliefs
Currency: 1 CFA franc = 100 centimes
Major cities:
Pointe-Noire (576,000), Loubomo (84,000), Nkayi (43,000)

Croatia

Republic of Croatia
Hrvatska
Republika Hrvatska

Area: 56,538 km^2
Population: 4,500,000 (1997)
Capital: Zagreb (Pop. 707,000)
Administration: 21 counties, 2 districts (at present under local Serbian control)
Languages: Croatian, Serbian, Hungarian
Religions: Roman Catholic 77%
Currency: 1 kuna = 100 lipa
Major cities:
Split (189,000), Rijeka (168,000), Osijek (105,000), Zadar (76,000), Pula (62,000)

Costa Rica

Republic of Costa Rica
Costa Rica
República de Costa Rica

Area: 51,100 km^2
Population: 3,570,000 (1997)
Capital: San José (Pop. 324,000; A: 959,000)
Administration: 7 provinces
Languages: Spanish, English Creole
Religions: Roman Catholic 89%, Protestant 8%
Currency: 1 Costa Rican colon = 100 céntimos
Major cities:
Limón (57,000), Alajuela (50,000)

Cuba

Republic of Cuba
Cuba
República de Cuba

Area: 110,861 km^2
Population: 11,100,000 (1997)
Capital: Havana (Pop. 2,241,000)
Administration: 14 provinces, 1 special municipality
Languages: Spanish
Religions: Non-denominational 56%, Roman Catholic 39%
Currency: 1 Cuban peso = 100 centavos
Major cities:
Santiago de C. (440,000), Camagüey (294,000), Holguín (242,000), Guantánamo (208,000)

Côte d'Ivoire

Republic of Côte d'Ivoire
(Ivory Coast)
Côte d'Ivoire
République de Côte d'Ivoire

Area: 322,463 km^2
Population: 14,300,000 (1997)
Capital: Yamoussoukro (Pop. 130,000)
Administration: 16 regions
Languages: French, Akran, Kru
Religions: Traditional beliefs 60%, Muslim 27%, Christian 12%
Currency: 1 CFA franc = 100 centimes
Major cities:
Abidjan (1,929,000, A: 2,800,000), Bouaké (330,000), Daloa (122,000), Korhogo (109,000)

Cyprus

Republic of Cyprus
Kýpros/Kıbrıs
Kypriaki Dimokratía/
Kıbrıs Cumhuriyeti

Area: 9,251 km^2
Population: 764,000 (1997)
Capital: Nicosia (Pop. 191,000)
Administration: 6 districts
Languages: Greek/Turkish
Religions: Greek Orthodox 80%, Muslim 19%
Currency: 1 Cyprus pound = 100 cents
Major cities:
Limassol (149,000), Lárnaka (66,000), Páfos (36,000)

1 km^2 = 0.3861 square mile

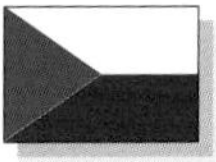

Czech Republic
Česká Republika

Area: 78,864 km^2
Population: 10,200,000 (1997)
Capital: Prague (Pop. 1,205,000)
Administration: 7 regions and the capital
Languages: Czech, Slovak, Romany
Religions: Roman Catholic 39%, non-denominational 40%
Currency: 1 koruna = 100 halura
Major cities:
Brno (388,000), Ostrava (324,000), Plzeň (170,000), Olomouc (104,000), Liberec (100,000), Hradec Králové (100,000), Č. Budějovice (100,000)

Denmark
Kingdom of Denmark
Danmark
Kongeriget Danmark

Area: 43,094 km^2
Population: 5,240,000 (1997)
Capital: Copenhagen (Pop. A: 1,360,000)
Administration: 14 counties, 2 municipalities
Languages: Danish, Faroese, Inuit
Religions: Protestant (Lutheran) 90%
Currency: 1 Danish krone = 100 øre
Major cities:
Århus (280,000), Odense (184,000), Ålborg (160,000), Esbjerg (83,000), Randers (62,000)

Faroe Islands
Føroyar/Færøerne

Area: 1,399 km^2
Population: 47,000 (1997)
Capital: Tórshavn (Pop. 15,000)
Languages: Faroese/Danish
Religions: Protestant (Lutheran) 95%
Currency: 1 Faroese krona = 100 oyru

Greenland
Kalaallit Nunaat/Grønland

Area: 2,175,600 km^2
Population: 58,000 (1997)
Capital: Nuuk (Pop. 13,300)
Languages: Inuit/Danish
Religions: Protestant (Lutheran) 98%
Currency: 1 Danish krone = 100 øre

Djibouti
Republic of Djibouti
Djibouti
Jumhuriya Jibuti/
République de Djibouti

Area: 23,200 km^2
Population: 634,000 (1997)
Capital: Djibouti (Pop. 383,000)
Administration: 4 districts
Languages: Arabic/French
Religions: Muslim 97%
Currency: 1 Djibouti franc = 100 centimes
Major towns:
Ali-Sabieh (4,000), Tadjoura (3,500), Dikhil (3,000)

Dominica
Commonwealth of Dominica

Area: 751 km^2
Population: 71,000 (1997)
Capital: Roseau (Pop. 16,500)
Administration: 10 parishes
Languages: English, French Creole
Religions: Roman Catholic 80%, Protestant 13%
Currency: 1 East Caribbean dollar = 100 cents
Major towns:
Portsmouth (3,600), Marigot (2,900), Atkinson (2,500)

Dominican Republic
República Dominicana

Area: 48,734 km^2
Population: 8,090,000 (1997)
Capital: Santo Domingo (Pop. 2,138,000)
Administration: 26 provinces and National District
Languages: Spanish, French Creole
Religions: Roman Catholic 90%
Currency: 1 Dom. peso = 100 centavos
Major cities:
Santiago (364,000), La Romana (133,000), San Francisco de Macorís (130,000)

Ecuador

Republic of Ecuador
El Ecuador
República del Ecuador

Area: 283,561 km^2
Population: 11,900,000 (1997)
Capital: Quito (Pop. 1,401,000)
Administration: 21 provinces
Languages: Spanish, Indian languages
Religions: Roman Catholic 93%
Currency: 1 sucre = 100 centavos
Major cities:
Guayaquil (1,877,000), Cuenca (240,000), Machala (185,000), Santo Domingo (165,000), Portoviejo (160,000), Ambato (151,000), Manta (149,000), Milagro (114,000)

Equatorial Guinea

Republic of Equatorial Guinea
Guinea Ecuatorial
República de Guinea Ecuatorial

Area: 28,051 km^2
Population: 420,000 (1997)
Capital: Malabo (Pop. 40,000)
Administration: 7 provinces
Languages: Spanish, Fang, Bubi, Portuguese patois
Religions: Roman Catholic 99%
Currency: 1 CFA franc = 100 centimes
Major cities:
Bata (40,000), Luba (15,000)

Egypt

Arab Republic of Egypt
Misr
Jumhuriyat Misr al-Arabiya

Area: 1,001,449 km^2
Population: 64,440,000 (1997)
Capital: Cairo (Pop. 6,800,000; A: 15,000,000)
Administration: 26 governorates
Languages: Arabic, French, English
Religions: Muslim 90%
Currency: 1 Egypt. pound = 100 piastres
Major cities:
Alexandria (3,380,000), El-Gîza (2,144,000), Shubrâ el-Khayma (834,000), Port Said (460,000), El-Mahalla el-Kubra (408,000)

Eritrea

Area: 117,600 km^2
Population: 3,410,000 (1997)
Capital: Asmara (Pop. 400,000)
Administration: 10 provinces
Languages: Tigrinya/Arabic
Religions: Coptic Christian 50%
Currency: 1 nakfa = 100 cents
Major cities:
Aseb (50,000), Keren (40,000), Massawa (40,000)

El Salvador

Republic of El Salvador
El Salvador
República de El Salvador

Area: 21,041 km^2
Population: 5,920,000 (1997)
Capital: San Salvador (Pop. A: 611,000)
Administration: 14 departments
Languages: Spanish, Indian languages
Religions: Roman Catholic 92%
Currency: 1 colón = 100 centavos
Major cities:
Santa Ana (202,000), Nueva San Salvador (192,000), San Miguel (183,000), Delgado (145,000), Mejicanos (139,000)

Estonia

Republic of Estonia
Eesti
Eesti Vabariik

Area: 45,100 km^2
Population: 1,460,000 (1997)
Capital: Tallinn (Pop. 421,000)
Administration: 15 counties
Languages: Estonian, Russian
Religions: Estonian Orthodox 20%, Protestant (Lutheran) 14%
Currency: 1 kroon = 100 sents
Major cities:
Tartu (102,000), Narva (75,000), Kohtla-Järve (54,000), Pärnu (52,000)

Ethiopia

Federal Democratic Republic of Ethiopia
Ityopia

Area: 1,104,300 km²
Population: 60,100,000 (1997)
Capital: Addis Ababa (Pop. 2,209,000)
Administration: 9 regions and the capital
Languages: Amharic, English
Religions: Muslim 45%, Ethiopian Orthodox 40%
Currency: 1 birr = 100 cents
Major cities:
Dirē Dawa (165,000), Hārer (131,000), Nazrēt (128,000), Gonder (112,000), Desē (97,000)

Fiji

Republic of Fiji/
Na Matanitu ko Viti

Area: 18,274 km²
Population: 809,000 (1997)
Capital: Suva (Pop. A: 200,000)
Administration: 14 provinces
Languages: English/Fijian
Religions: Christian 53%, Hindu 38%, Muslim 8%
Currency: 1 Fiji dollar = 100 cents
Major cities/towns:
Lautoka (28,000), Nandi (8,000)

Finland

Republic of Finland
Suomi/Finland
Suomen Tasavalta/
Republiken Finland

Area: 338,145 km²
Population: 5,140,000 (1997)
Capital: Helsinki (Pop. 532,000)
Administration: 11 provinces, 1 autonomous province
Languages: Finnish/Swedish
Religions: Protestant (Lutheran) 86%
Currency: 1 markka = 100 penniä
Major cities:
Espoo (196,000), Tampere (186,000), Vantaa (169,000), Turku/Åbo (167,000), Oulu (112,000)

France

French Republic
France
République française

Area: 543,965 km²
Population: 58,500,000 (1997)
Capital: Paris (Pop. 2,152,000; A: 9,320,000)
Administration: 22 regions
Languages: French, regional languages
Religions: Roman Catholic 81%
Currency: 1 franc = 100 centimes
Major cities:
Marseille (808,000, A: 1,090,000), Lyon (422,000), Toulouse (366,000), Nice (346,000), Strasbourg (256,000), Nantes (252,000), Bordeaux (213,000), Monpellier (211,000), Rennes (204,000), Saint-Étienne (202,000), Le Havre (197,000)

Overseas Departments:

French Guiana

Department of Guiana
Guyane française
Département de la Guyane

Area: 90,000 km²
Population: 153,000 (1997)
Capital: Cayenne (Pop. 42,000)

Guadeloupe

Department of Guadeloupe
Guadeloupe
Département de la Guadeloupe

Area: 1,705 km²
Population: 431,000 (1997)
Capital: Basse-Terre (Pop. 14,000)

Martinique

Department of Martinique
Martinique
Département de la Martinique

Area: 1,102 km²
Population: 384,000 (1997)
Capital: Fort-de-France (Pop. 100,000)

Réunion

Department of Réunion
Réunion
Département de la Réunion

Area: 2,510 km²
Population: 664,000 (1997)
Capital: Saint-Denis (Pop. 122,000)

Territorial Collectivities:

Mayotte
Territorial Collectivity of Mayotte
Mayotte
Collectivité territoriale de Mayotte

Area:	374 km^2
Population:	106,000 (1997)
Capital:	Mamoudzou (Pop. 20,000)

Saint Pierre and Miquelon
Territorial Collectivity of Saint Pierre and Miquelon
Saint-Pierre-et-Miquelon
Collectivité territoriale de Saint-Pierre-et-Miquelon

Area:	242 km^2
Population:	7,000 (1997)
Capital:	Saint-Pierre (Pop. 5,700)

Overseas Territories:

French Polynesia
Territory of French Polynesia
Polynésie française
Territoire de la Polynésie française

Area:	4,000 km^2
Population:	223,000 (1997)
Capital:	Papeete (Pop. 24,000)

French Southern and Antarctic Territories
Territoire des Terres australes et antarctiques françaises

The territories comprise:
Keguelen Islands (7,215 km^2)
Crozet Islands (515 km^2)
Amsterdam Island (54 km^2)
Saint-Paul Island (7 km^2)
Terre Adélie, claimed by France (432,000 km^2)

New Caledonia
Territory of New Caledonia
Nouvelle-Calédonie
Territoire de la Nouvelle-Calédonie et Dépendances

Area:	18,575 km^2
Population:	189,000 (1997)
Capital:	Nouméa (Pop. 65,000)

Wallis and Futuna
Territory of Wallis and Futuna
Wallis-et-Futuna
Territoire de Wallis-et-Futuna

Area:	274 km^2
Population:	15,000 (1997)
Capital:	Mata'utu (Pop. 815)

Gabon
Gabonese Republic
Gabon
République gabonaise

Area:	267,668 km^2
Population:	1,140,000 (1997)
Capital:	Libreville (Pop. 420,000)
Administration:	9 provinces
Languages:	French, Fang, Bantu languages
Religions:	Roman Catholic 52%, traditional beliefs 40%
Currency:	1 CFA franc = 100 centimes

Major cities:
Port Gentil (164,000), Masuku (75,000), Lambaréné (24,000), Moanda (23,000)

Gambia, The
Republic of The Gambia

Area:	11,295 km^2
Population:	1,160,000 (1997)
Capital:	Banjul (Pop. A: 271,000)
Administration:	5 rural divisions and the capital
Languages:	English, Mandinka, Fulani, Wolof
Religions:	Muslim 85%, Christian 10%
Currency:	1 dalasi = 100 bututs

Major cities:
Serekunda (103,000), Brikama (24,000), Bakau (19,000)

Georgia
Republic of Georgia
Sakartvelo
Sakartvelos Respublika

Area:	69,700 km^2
Population:	5,440,000 (1997)
Capital:	Tbilisi (Pop. 1,279,000)
Administration:	2 autonomous republics, 1 autonomous region, 79 regions/councils
Languages:	Georgian, Russian
Religions:	Predom. Georgian Orthodox
Currency:	1 lari = 100 tetri

Major cities:
Kutaisi (238,000), Rustavi (162,000), Batumi (138,000), Sukhumi (120,000), Gori (70,000)

1 km^2 = 0.3861 square mile

Germany

Federal Republic of Germany
Deutschland
Bundesrepublik Deutschland

Area: 357,021 km²
Population: 82,000,000 (1997)
Capital: Berlin (Pop. 3,459,000)
Administration: 16 federal states
Languages: German
Religions: Protest. 34%, Rom. Cath. 33%
Currency: 1 Dt. Mark = 100 pfennigs
Major cities:
Hamburg (1,708,000), Munich (1,226,000), Cologne (964,000), Frankfurt a. M. (647,000), Essen (613,000), Dortmund (597,000), Stuttgart (586,000), Düsseldorf (571,000), Bremen (549,000)

Ghana

Republic of Ghana

Area: 238,533 km²
Population: 18,300,000 (1997)
Capital: Accra (Pop. 949,000; A: 1,900,000)
Administration: 10 regions
Languages: English, about 75 languages
Religions: Christian 60%, traditional beliefs 35%
Currency: 1 cedi = 100 pesewas
Major cities:
Kumasi (385,000), Tamale (151,000), Tema (110,000), Sekondi-Takoradi (104,000)

Greece

Hellenic Republic
Ellás
Ellinikí Dimokratía

Area: 131,957 km²
Population: 10,500,000 (1997)
Capital: Athens (Pop. A: 3,070,000)
Administration: 13 regions and the Monastic Republic of Mount Athos
Languages: Greek
Religions: Greek Orthodox 97%
Currency: 1 drachma = 100 lepta
Major cities:
Thessaloníki (384,000), Piraeus (183,000), Patras (153,000), Irákleio (116,000), Lárisa (113,000), Vólos (77,000)

Grenada

State of Grenada

Area: 344 km²
Population: 99,000 (1997)
Capital: Saint George's (Pop. 4,400)
Administration: Information not available
Languages: English, English Creole, French Creole
Religions: Rom. Cath. 53%, Protest. 38%
Currency: 1 East Caribbean dollar = 100 cents
Major towns:
Gouyave (3,000), Grenville (2,000)

Guatemala

Republic of Guatemala
Guatemala
República de Guatemala

Area: 108,889 km²
Population: 11,200,000 (1997)
Capital: Guatemala City (Pop. 1,167,000)
Administration: 22 departments
Languages: Spanish, Mayan languages
Religions: Roman Catholic 80%, Protestant 19%
Currency: 1 quetzal = 100 centavos
Major cities:
Quezaltenango (104,000), Escuintla (70,000), Mazatenango (43,000), Retalhuleu (40,000)

Guinea

Republic of Guinea
Guinée
République de Guinée

Area: 245,857 km²
Population: 7,550,000 (1997)
Capital: Conakry (Pop. 950,000; A: 1,508,000)
Administration: 33 regions and the capital
Languages: French, Fulani, Malinke
Religions: Muslim 95%, Christian 1.5%
Currency: Guinea franc
Major cities:
Kankan (150,000), Labé (110,000), Kindia (80,000)

Guinea-Bissau

Republic of Guinea-Bissau
Guiné-Bissau
República da Guiné-Bissau

Area: 36,125 km²
Population: 1,110,000 (1997)
Capital: Bissau (Pop. 233,000)
Administration: 8 regions and the capital
Languages: Portuguese, Crioulo
Religions: Traditional beliefs 54%, Muslim 8%, Christian 8%
Currency: 1 CFA franc = 100 centimes
Major towns:
Bafatá (13,000), Gabú (7,800), Mansôa (5,400)

Guyana

Co-operative Republic of Guyana

Area: 214,969 km²
Population: 847,000 (1997)
Capital: Georgetown (Pop. 234,000)
Administration: 10 regions
Languages: English, Hindi, Urdu, Indian languages
Religions: Protestant 34%, Hindu 33%, Roman Catholic 20%
Currency: 1 Guyana dollar = 100 cents
Major cities:
New Amsterdam (25,000)

Haiti

Republic of Haiti
Haïti/Dayti
République d'Haïti/Repiblik Dayti

Area: 27,750 km²
Population: 7,390,000 (1997)
Capital: Port-au-Prince (Pop. 753,000; A: 1,300,000)
Administration: 9 departments
Languages: French/Creole
Religions: Roman Catholic 80%, Protestant 10%
Currency: 1 gourde = 100 centimes
Major cities:
Cap-Haïtien (101,000), Gonaïves (63,000)

Honduras

Republic of Honduras
Honduras
República de Honduras

Area: 112,088 km²
Population: 5,970,000 (1997)
Capital: Tegucigalpa (Pop. 814,000)
Administration: 18 departments and the Central District
Languages: Spanish, Indian languages, English
Religions: Roman Catholic 90%
Currency: 1 lempira = 100 centavos
Major cities:
San Pedro Sula (384,000), La Ceiba (89,000), El Progreso (85,000), Choluteca (76,000)

Hungary

Republic of Hungary
Magyarország
Magyar Köztársaság

Area: 93,032 km²
Population: 9,990,000 (1997)
Capital: Budapest (Pop. 1,907,000)
Administration: 19 counties and the capital
Languages: Hungarian, German, Slovak
Religions: Roman Catholic 68%, Protestant 25%
Currency: 1 forint = 100 filler
Major cities:
Debrecen (210,000), Miskolc (180,000), Szeged (167,000), Pécs (162,000), Győr (127,000), Nyíregyháza (113,000), Székesfehérvár (107,000)

Iceland

Republic of Iceland
Ísland
Lýðveldið Ísland

Area: 103,000 km²
Population: 274,000 (1997)
Capital: Reykjavík (Pop. 105,000)
Administration: 8 regions
Languages: Icelandic
Religions: Protestant (Lutheran) 93%
Currency: 1 króna = 100 aurar
Major cities:
Kópavogur (18,000), Hafnarfjörður (18,000), Akureyri (15,000)

1 km² = 0.3861 square mile

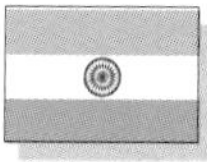

India

Republic of India
Bharat/India
Bharat Ganarajya/
Republic of India

Area: 3,165,596 km²
Population: 959,400,000 (1997)
Capital: New Delhi (Pop. 301,000)
Administration: 25 states, 7 union territories
Languages: Hindi/English, Telugu, Bengali, Marathi, Tamil, Urdu
Religions: Hindu 80%, Muslim 11%
Currency: 1 rupee = 100 paise
Major cities:
Mumbai/Bombay (9,926,000; A: 15,093,000), Delhi (7,207,000; A: 8,420,000), Calcutta (4,400,000; A: 11,020,000), Chennai/Madras (3,841,000; A: 5,420,000), Bangalore (3,302,000), Hyderābād (3,146,000), Ahmadābād (2,955,000), Kanpur (1,879,000), Nāgpur (1,625,000), Lucknow (1,619,000), Pune (1,567,000), Sūrat (1,506,000), Jaipur (1,458,000), Indore (1,092,000), Bhopāl (1,063,000), Vadodara (1,062,000), Ludhiāna (1,043,000), Kalyān (1,015,000), Hāora (950,000)

	Area km²	Population 1994	Capital
States			
Andhra Pradesh	275,045	71,800,000	Hyderābād
Arunāchal Pradesh	83,743	965,000	Itānagar
Assam	78,438	24,200,000	Dispur
Bihār	173,877	93,080,000	Patna
Goa	3,702	1,235,000	Panaji
Gujarāt	196,024	44,235,000	Gāndhīnagar
Haryāna	44,212	17,925,000	Chandīgarh
Himachal Pradesh	55,673	5,530,000	Shimla
Jammu and Kashmir	100,569[1]	8,435,000[1]	Srīnagar
Karnātaka	191,791	48,150,000	Bangalore
Kerala	38,863	30,555,000	Thiruvananthapuram
Madhya Pradesh	443,446	71,950,000	Bhopāl
Mahārāshtra	307,713	85,565,000	Mumbai
Manipur	22,327	2,010,000	Imphāl
Meghālaya	22,429	1,960,000	Shillong
Mizoram	21,081	775,000	Āīzawl
Nāgāland	16,579	1,410,000	Kohīma
Orissa	155,707	33,795,000	Bhubaneshwar
Punjab	50,362	21,695,000	Chandīgarh
Rājasthān	342,239	48,040,000	Jaipur
Sikkim	7,096	444,000	Gangtok
Tamil Nadu	130,058	58,840,000	Chennai
Tripura	10,486	3,065,000	Agartala
Uttar Pradesh	294,411	150,695,000	Lucknow
West Bengal	88,752	73,600,000	Calcutta
Union Territories			
Andaman and Nicobar Islands	8,249	322,000	Port Blair
Chandīgarh	114	725,000	Chandīgarh
Dādra and Nagar Haveli	491	153,000	Silvassa
Daman and Diu	112	111,000	Daman
Delhi	1,483	10,865,000	New Delhi
Lakshadweep	32	56,000	Kavaratti
Pondicherry	492	894,000	Pondicherry

[1] Exclusive of the area occupied by Pakistan and China.

Indonesia

Republic of Indonesia
Indonesia
Republik Indonesia

Area: 1,904,569 km²
Population: 203,400,000 (1997)
Capital: Jakarta (Pop. 9,341,000)
Administration: 27 prov., 3 auton. districts
Languages: Bahasa Indonesia, 250 (est.) languages or dialects
Religions: Muslim 87%
Currency: 1 rupiah = 100 sen
Major cities:
Surabaya (2,743,000), Bandung (2,429,000), Medan (1,942,000), Palembang (1,394,000) Semarang (1,367,000), Ujungpandang (1,121,000)

Iran

Islamic Republic of Iran
Iran
Jomhuri-ye Eslami-ye Iran

Area: 1,633,188 km²
Population: 71,500,000 (1997)
Capital: Tehrān (Pop. 6,759,000)
Administration: 28 provinces
Languages: Farsi (Persian), Turkic languages, Kurdish
Religions: Muslim 99%
Currency: 1 rial = 100 dinars
Major cities:
Mashhad (1,887,000), Isfahan (1,266,000), Tabrīz (1,191,000), Shīrāz (1,053,000), Karaj (941,000), Ahvāz (805,000), Qom (778,000)

Iraq

Republic of Iraq
Iraq
Jumhouriya al 'Iraqia

Area:	438,317 km^2
Population:	21,300,000 (1997)
Capital:	Baghdād (Pop. 4,044,000)
Administration:	18 governorates, three of the governorates form a (Kurdish) Autonom. Region
Languages:	Arabic, Kurdish, Turkish
Religions:	Muslim 95%
Currency:	1 Iraqi dinar = 1000 fils

Major cities:
Basra (617,000), Mosul (571,000), Arbīl (334,000), As-Sulaymānīyah (279,000)

Ireland

Republic of Ireland
Éire / Ireland
Poblacht na h'Éireann / Republic of Ireland

Area:	70,284 km^2
Population:	3,560,000 (1997)
Capital:	Dublin (Pop. A: 1,008,000)
Administration:	4 provinces (29 county councils, 5 county boroughs)
Languages:	Irish/English
Religions:	Roman Catholic 88%
Currency:	1 Irish pound = 100 pence

Major cities:
Cork (180,000), Limerick (79,000), Galway (57,000), Waterford (44,000)

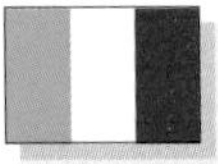

Italy

Italian Republic
Italia
Repubblica Italiana

Area:	301,268 km^2
Population:	57,200,000 (1997)
Capital:	Rome (Pop. 2,650,000)
Administration:	20 regions
Languages:	Italian, German, French
Religions:	Roman Catholic over 90%
Currency:	1 lira = 100 centesimi

Major cities:
Milan (1,306,000), Naples (1,047,000), Turin (921,000), Palermo (689,000), Genoa (656,000), Bologna (386,000), Florence (382,000), Catania (342,000), Bari (336,000), Venice (298,000)

Israel

State of Israel
Yisra'el/Isrā'īl
Medinat Yisra'el/Dawlat Isrā'īl

Area:	21,946 km^2, including the Golan Heights (1,176 km^2) and East Jerusalem (70 km^2)
Population:	5,740,000 (1997)
Capital:	Jerusalem (Pop. 579,000)
Administration:	6 districts
Languages:	Hebrew/Arabic, Yiddish
Religions:	Jewish 81%, Muslim 14%
Currency:	1 new sheqel = 100 agorot

Major cities:
Tel Aviv-Yafo (355,000), Haifa (247,000), Holon (164,000), Rishon LeZiyyon (160,000)

Palestinian-administered Territories:

West Bank

Area:	5,879 km^2
Population:	1,650,000 Palestinian Arabs (1997), 112,000 Israeli settlers (1993)

Major cities:
Nāblus (130,000), Hebron (120,000), Bet Lehem (40,000), Jericho (15,000)

Gaza Strip

Area:	378 km^2
Population:	1,020,000 Palest. Arabs (1997) 4,800 Israeli settlers (1993)

Major cities:
Gaza (273,000)

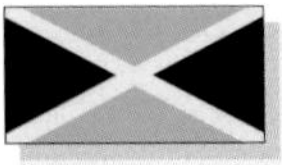

Jamaica

Area:	10,990 km^2
Population:	2,520,000 (1997)
Capital:	Kingston (Pop. A: 538,000)
Administration:	14 parishes
Languages:	English, Jamaican Creole
Religions:	Protestant 56%, Roman Catholic 5%
Currency:	1 Jamaican dollar = 100 cents

Major cities:
Spanish Town (110,000), Portmore (94,000), Montego Bay (82,000), May Pen (46,000)

Japan
Nihon, Nippon
Nihon Koku

Area: 377,801 km^2
Population: 125,600,000 (1997)
Capital: Tōkyō (Pop. A: 11,774,000)
Administration: 47 prefectures
Languages: Japanese, Korean, Chinese
Religions: Shinto 87%, Buddhist 74%
Currency: 1 yen = 100 sen
Major cities:
Yokohama (3,307,000), Ōsaka (2,602,000), Nagoya (2,152,000), Sapporo (1,757,000), Kyōto (1,464,000), Kōbe (1,424,000), Fukuoka (1,285,000), Kawasaki (1,203,000), Hiroshima (1,109,000)

Jordan
Hashemite Kingdom of Jordan
Al-Urdun
Al-Mamlaka al-Urduniya al-Hashemiya

Area: 89,342 km^2
Population: 4,320,000 (1997)
Capital: Ammān (Pop. 963,000)
Administration: 5 provinces
Languages: Arabic
Religions: Muslim 80%, Christian minority
Currency: 1 Jordan dinar = 1000 fils
Major cities:
Az-Zarqā (345,000), Irbid (208,000), As-Salt (187,000), Ar-Rusayfah (131,000)

Kazakhstan
Republic of Kazakhstan
Kazakstan
Kazak Respublikasy

Area: 2,717,300 km^2
Population: 16,900,000 (1997)
Capital: Astana (Pop. 287,000)
Administration: 15 regions
Languages: Kazakh, Russian, German
Religions: Muslim 47%
Currency: 1 tenge = 100 tiyn
Major cities:
Almaty (1,176,000), Karagandy (596,000), Shymkent (404,000), Pavlodar (349,000), Semey (342,000), Öskemen (334,000), Taraz (317,000), Aktöbe (264,000)

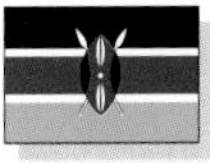

Kenya
Republic of Kenya
Kenya
Jamhuri ya Kenya

Area: 580,367 km^2
Population: 28,400,000 (1997)
Capital: Nairobi (Pop. 1,505,000)
Administration: 7 provinces and the capital
Languages: Swahili, English, Kikuyu
Religions: Traditional beliefs 60%, Roman Catholic 26%
Currency: 1 Kenya shilling = 100 cents
Major cities:
Mombasa (465,000), Kisumu (185,000), Nakuru (163,000), Machakos (116,000), Eldoret (105,000), Nyeri (89,000), Meru (78,000), Thika (57,000)

Kiribati
Republic of Kiribati
Kiribati
Ribaberikin Kiribati/ Republic of Kiribati

Area: 726 km^2
Population: 80,000 (1997)
Capital: Bairiki (Pop. 2,200)
Administration: 6 districts
Languages: Kiribati/English
Religions: Roman Catholic 53%, Protestant 39%
Currency: 1 Austral. dollar = 100 cents
Island Groups:
Gilbert Islands, Phoenix Islands, Line Islands

Korea, North
Democratic People's Republic of Korea
Chosun Minchu-chui Inmin Konghwa-guk

Area: 120,538 km^2
Population: 22,800,000 (1997)
Capital: P'yongyang (Pop. 2,355,000)
Administration: 9 provinces, 3 special cities
Languages: Korean, Russian, Chinese
Religions: Traditional beliefs 16%, Ch'ondogyo 14%, atheist 68%
Currency: 1 won = 100 chon
Major cities:
Hamhung (701,000), Ch'ongjin (520,000), Namp'o (370,000), Sinuiju (289,000), Wonsan (274,000), Kanggye (211,000), Haeju (195,000)

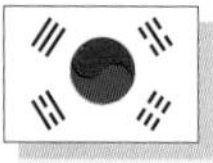

Korea, South

Republic of Korea
Daehan Min-kuk

Area: 99,274 km^2
Population: 45,700,000 (1997)
Capital: Seoul (Pop. 10,229,000)
Administration: 9 provinces, 6 special cities
Languages: Korean, English, Japanese
Religions: Protestant 33%, Confucianist 23%, Buddhist 21%
Currency: 1 won = 100 chon
Major cities:
Pusan (3,814,000), Taegu (2,449,000), Inch′on (2,308,000), Taejon (1,272,000), Kwangju (1,258,000), Ulsan (967,000), Songnam (869,000)

Kuwait

State of Kuwait
Al-Kuwait
Dowlat al-Kuwait

Area: 17,818 km^2
Population: 1,800,000 (1997)
Capital: Kuwait (Pop. 29,000)
Administration: 5 governorates
Languages: Arabic, English
Religions: Muslim 95%
Currency: 1 Kuwait dinar = 1000 fils
Major cities:
As-Sālimīyah (130,000), Qalīb ash-Shuyūkh (102,000), Hawallī (82,000), Abraq Khītān (64,000)

Kyrgyzstan

Kyrgyz Republic
Kyrgyzstan
Kyrgyz Respublikasy

Area: 198,500 km^2
Population: 4,490,000 (1997)
Capital: Bishkek (Pop. 584,000)
Administration: 6 provinces and the capital
Languages: Kyrgyz/Russian
Religions: Muslim 70%
Currency: 1 som = 100 tiyin
Major cities:
Osh (219,000), Dzhalal-Abad (80,000), Tokmak (71,000), Karaköl (64,300), Kara-Balta (55,000)

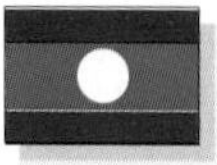

Laos

Lao People's Democratic Republic
Lao
Sathalanalat Paxathipatai Paxaxôn Lao

Area: 236,800 km^2
Population: 5,190,000 (1997)
Capital: Vientiane (Pop. 528,000)
Administration: 17 provinces and the capital
Languages: Lao, French, English
Religions: Buddhist 58%, tribal religionist 34%
Currency: 1 kip = 100 at
Major cities:
Louangphrabang (68,000), Khantabouli (51,000), Pakxé (47,000)

Latvia

Republic of Latvia
Latvija
Latvijas Republika

Area: 64,600 km^2
Population: 2,480,000 (1997)
Capital: Rīga (Pop. 816,000)
Administration: 26 districts, 7 special cities
Languages: Latvian, Russian
Religions: Lutheran 55%, Roman Catholic 24%
Currency: 1 lats = 100 santimi
Major cities:
Daugavpils (118,000), Liepāja (97,000), Jelgava (71,000), Jūrmala (59,000)

Lebanon

Republic of Lebanon
Lubnan
Jumhouriya al-Lubnaniya

Area: 10,400 km^2
Population: 3,120,000 (1997)
Capital: Beirut (Pop. 1,500,000)
Administration: 5 governorates and the capital
Languages: Arabic, French, English
Religions: Muslim 60%, Christian 40%
Currency: 1 Lebanese pound = 100 piastres
Major cities:
Tripoli (200,000), Zahlah (200,000), Sidon (100,000)

1 km^2 = 0.3861 square mile

Lesotho

Kingdom of Lesotho
Lesotho
Mmuso wa Lesotho/
Kingdom of Lesotho

Area: 30,355 km^2
Population: 2,130,000 (1997)
Capital: Maseru (Pop. 370,000)
Administration: 10 districts
Languages: Sesotho/English
Religions: Roman Catholic 44%, Protestant 30%
Currency: 1 loti = 100 lisente
Major towns:
Teyateyaneng (14,000), Mafeteng (13,000), Hlotse (10,000)

Liechtenstein

Principality of Liechtenstein
Liechtenstein
Fürstentum Liechtenstein

Area: 160 km^2
Population: 31,000 (1997)
Capital: Vaduz (Pop. 5,000)
Administration: 11 communes
Languages: German
Religions: Roman Catholic 83%, Protestant 7%
Currency: 1 Swiss franc = 100 centimes
Major towns:
Schaan (5,100), Balzers (4,000), Triesen (4,000)

Liberia

Republic of Liberia

Area: 111,369 km^2
Population: 2,520,000 (1997)
Capital: Monrovia (Pop. 1,000,000)
Administration: 13 counties
Languages: English, Gola, Kpelle
Religions: Traditional beliefs 70%, Muslim 20%, Christian 10%
Currency: 1 Liberian dollar = 100 cents
Major cities:
Harbel (60,000), Gbarnga (30,000), Buchanan (25,000)

Lithuania

Republic of Lithuania
Lietuva
Lietuvos Respublika

Area: 65,200 km^2
Population: 3,720,000 (1997)
Capital: Vilnius (Pop. 573,000)
Administration: 10 provinces
Languages: Lithuanian, Russian
Religions: Roman Catholic 80%
Currency: 1 litas = 100 centas
Major cities:
Kaunas (411,000), Klaipėda (202,000), Šiauliai (147,000), Panevėžys (132,000)

Libya

Socialist People's Libyan Arab Jamahiriya
Al-Jamahiriya
Al-Jamahiriya al-Arabiya al-Libiya ash-Shabiya al-Ishtirakiya

Area: 1,759,540 km^2
Population: 5,780,000 (1997)
Capital: Tripoli (Pop. 591,000)
Administration: 13 regions (baladiyat)
Languages: Arabic, Tuareg
Religions: Muslim 97%
Currency: 1 Libyan dinar = 1000 dirhams
Major cities:
Benghazi (446,000), Misrātah (122,000), Az-Zāwiyah (89,000)

Luxembourg

Grand Duchy of Luxembourg
Lëtzebuerg/Luxemburg/Luxembourg
Groussherzogtom Lëtzbuerg/
Großherzogtum Luxemburg/
Grand-Duché de Luxembourg

Area: 2,586 km^2
Population: 416,000 (1997)
Capital: Luxembourg (Pop. 78,000)
Administration: 12 cantons
Languages: Letzeburgish/German/French
Religions: Roman Catholic 95%
Currency: 1 Luxembourg franc = 100 centimes
Major cities:
Esch-sur-Alzette (25,000), Differdange (17,000)

Macedonia

Former Yugoslav Republic of Macedonia
Makedonija
Republika Makedonija

Area: 25,713 km^2
Population: 2,190,000 (1997)
Capital: Skopje (Pop. 444,000)
Administration: 123 communes
Languages: Macedonian, Albanian, Turkish
Religions: Macedonian Orthodox 67%, Muslim 30%
Currency: 1 denar = 100 deni
Major cities:
Bitola (78,000), Kumanovo (72,000), Prilep (68,000), Tetovo (50,000)

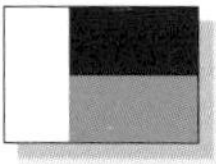

Madagascar

Republic of Madagascar
Madagasikara/Madagascar
Repoblikan'i Madagasikara/
République de Madagascar

Area: 587,041 km^2
Population: 15,800,000 (1997)
Capital: Antananarivo (Pop. 1,053,000)
Administration: 6 provinces
Languages: Malagasy/French
Religions: Trad. beliefs 52%, Roman Catholic 25%, Protestant 20%
Currency: 1 Malagasy franc = 100 centimes
Major cities:
Toamasina (127,000), Antsirabe (120,000)

Malawi

Republic of Malawi
Malaŵi/Malawi
Dziko la Malaŵi/
Republic of Malawi

Area: 118,484 km^2
Population: 10,200,000 (1997)
Capital: Lilongwe (Pop. 396,000)
Administration: 3 regions
Languages: Chichewa/English
Religions: Christian 75%, traditional beliefs 10%
Currency: 1 kwacha = 100 tambala
Major cities:
Blantyre (447,000), Mzuzu (63,000), Zomba (63,000)

Malaysia

Persekutuan Tanah Malaysia

Area: 329,758 km^2
Population: 21,000,000 (1997)
Capital: Kuala Lumpur (Pop. 1,145,000)
Administration: 13 states, 2 federal territories
Languages: Malay, Chinese, Tamil
Religions: Muslim 53%, Buddhist 17%
Currency: 1 ringgit = 100 sen
Major cities:
Ipoh (383,000), Johor Baharu (329,000), Melaka (296,000), Petaling Jaya (255,000), Tawai (245,000), Kelang (244,000), Kuala Terengganu (229,000)

Maldives

Republic of Maldives
Divehi Raajjeyge
Divehi Raajjeyge Jumhooriyyaa

Area: 298 km^2
Population: 270,000 (1997)
Capital: Malé (Pop. 63,000)
Administration: 20 districts (administrative atolls) and the capital district
Languages: Divehi (Maldivian)
Religions: Sunni Muslim 99%
Currency: 1 rufiyaa = 100 laari

Mali

Republic of Mali
Mali
République du Mali

Area: 1,240,192 km^2
Population: 11,500,000 (1997)
Capital: Bamako (Pop. 746,000)
Administration: 8 regions and the capital
Languages: French, Bambara
Religions: Muslim 80% , traditional beliefs 18%
Currency: 1 CFA franc = 100 centimes
Major cities:
Ségou (99,000), Mopti (78,000), Sikasso (73,000), Gao (55,000)

1 km^2 = 0.3861 square mile

Malta

Republic of Malta
Malta
Repubblika ta' Malta/
Republic of Malta

Area: 316 km^2
Population: 370,000 (1997)
Capital: Valletta (Pop. 9,100)
Administration: 6 regions
Languages: Maltese/English
Religions: Roman Catholic 93%
Currency: 1 Maltese lira = 100 cents
Major cities:
Birkirkara (22,000), Qormi (20,000), Hamrun (13,600), Rabat (13,500)

Marshall Islands

Republic of the Marshall Islands

Area: 181 km^2
Population: 57,000 (1997)
Capital: Uliga (Pop. 18,000)
Administration: 24 districts
Languages: English, Marshallese
Religions: Protestant 80%, Roman Catholic 15%
Currency: 1 U.S. dollar = 100 cents
Major towns:
Ebeye (8,300), Jaluit (1,600)

Mauritania

Islamic Republic of Mauritania
Muritaniyah
Al-Jumhuriyah al-Islamiyah
al-Muritaniyah

Area: 1,025,520 km^2
Population: 2,390,000 (1997)
Capital: Nouakchott (Pop. 480,000)
Administration: 13 regions
Languages: Arabic, French, Wolof
Religions: Muslim 99.6%
Currency: 1 ouguiya = 5 khoums
Major cities:
Nouâdhibou (59,000), Kaédi (31,000), Kiffa (29,000), Rosso (28,000)

Mauritius

Republic of Mauritius

Area: 2,040 km^2
Population: 1,140,000 (1997)
Capital: Port Louis (Pop. 146,000)
Administration: 9 districts, 3 dependencies
Languages: English, French Creole
Religions: Hindu 53%, Christian 30%
Currency: 1 Mauritius rupee = 100 cents
Major cities:
Beau Bassin-Rose Hill (98,000), Vacoas-Phoenix (96,000), Curepipe (78,000), Quatre Bornes (75,000)

Mexico

United Mexican States
México
Estados Unidos Mexicanos

Area: 1,958,201 km^2
Population: 94,200,000 (1997)
Capital: Mexico City (Pop. 11,708,000)
Administration: 31 states, Federal District
Languages: Spanish, Mayan dialects
Religions: Roman Catholic 90%
Currency: 1 Mex. peso = 100 centavos
Major cities:
Guadalajara (1,633,000), Puebla (1,123,000), Monterrey (1,088,000), León (1,042,000), Ciudad Juárez (1,012,000), Tijuana (992,000), Culiacán (696,000), Mexicali (696,000)

Micronesia

Federated States of Micronesia

Area: 702 km^2
Population: 109,000 (1997)
Capital: Palikir
Administration: 4 states
Languages: English, 8 indigenous languages
Religions: Roman Catholic 59%, Protestant 39%
Currency: 1 U.S. dollar = 100 cents
Major towns:
Weno (15,000), Kolonia (6,200), Colonia (3,500)

Moldova

Republic of Moldova
Moldova
Republica Moldova

Area: 33,700 km^2
Population: 4,450,000 (1997)
Capital: Chişinău (Pop. 667,000)
Administration: 40 rural districts, 10 cities
Languages: Moldovian, Russian
Religions: Predominantly Eastern Orthodox
Currency: 1 leu = 100 bani
Major cities:
Tiraspol (186,000), Bălţi (159,000), Tighina (Bendery) (133,000)

Monaco

Principality of Monaco
Monaco
Principauté de Monaco

Area: 1.95 km^2
Population: 32,000 (1997)
Capital: Monaco (Pop. 1,200)
Administration: 4 districts
Languages: French, Monegasque
Religions: Roman Catholic 90%, Protestant 6%
Currency: 1 French franc = 100 centimes

Mongolia

Mongol Uls

Area: 1,566,500 km^2
Population: 2,570,000 (1997)
Capital: Ulan Bator (Pop. 632,000)
Administration: 21 provinces and the capital
Languages: Khalkha Mongol, Russian, Kazakh
Religions: Buddhist 90%
Currency: 1 tugrik = 100 möngö
Major cities:
Darhan (87,000), Erdenet (59,000), Choybalsan (41,000)

Morocco

Kingdom of Morocco
Maghreb
Mamlaka al-Maghrebia

Area: 458,730 km^2 (without Western Sahara)
Population: 27,500,000 (1997)
Capital: Rabat (Pop. 623,000)
Administration: 16 regions
Languages: Arabic, Berber, French
Religions: Muslim 89%
Currency: 1 dirham = 100 centimes
Major cities:
Casablanca (3,079,000), Fez (735,000), Marrakech (665,000), Oujda (661,000), Meknès (495,000), Beni-Mellal (453,000), Kénitra (441,000)

Mozambique

Republic of Mozambique
Moçambique
República de Moçambique

Area: 801,590 km^2
Population: 18,100,000 (1997)
Capital: Maputo (Pop. 932,000)
Administration: 10 provinces and the capital
Languages: Portuguese, vernaculars
Religions: Traditional beliefs 60%, Christian 30%
Currency: 1 metical = 100 centavos
Major cities:
Beira (299,000), Nampula (251,000), Quelimane (146,000), Nacala (125,000), Tete (112,000)

Myanmar (Burma)

Union of Myanmar
Myanma Pyi
Pyidaungzu Myanma Naingngandaw

Area: 676,578 km^2
Population: 46,800,000 (1997)
Capital: Rangoon (Pop. 3,302,000)
Administration: 7 states, 7 divisions
Languages: Burmese, English
Religions: Buddhist 87%, Christian 6%
Currency: 1 kyat = 100 pyas
Major cities:
Mandalay (533,000), Moulmein (220,000), Pegu (151,000), Bassein (144,000), Taunggyi (108,000), Sittwe (108,000)

1 km^2 = 0.3861 square mile

Namibia
Republic of Namibia

Area: 824,292 km^2
Population: 1,610,000 (1997)
Capital: Windhoek (Pop. 161,000)
Administration: 13 regions
Languages: English, Afrikaans, German
Religions: Protestant 62%, Roman Catholic 20%
Currency: 1 Namibia dollar = 100 cents
Major cities:
Swakopmund (16,000), Rehoboth (15,000), Rundu (15,000), Keetmanshoop (14,000)

Nauru
Republic of Nauru
Naoero/Nauru

Area: 21 km^2
Population: 11,000 (1997)
Capital: Yaren (Pop. 4,000)
Administration: 14 districts
Languages: Nauruan/English
Religions: Protestant 60%, Roman Catholic 30%
Currency: 1 Australian dollar = 100 cents

Nepal
Kingdom of Nepal
Nepal
Nepal Adhirajya

Area: 147,181 km^2
Population: 22,600,000 (1997)
Capital: Kathmandu (Pop. 535,000)
Administration: 14 zones
Languages: Nepali, Maithili, Bhojpuri
Religions: Hindu 90%, Buddhist 5%
Currency: 1 Nepalese rupee = 100 paisa
Major cities:
Biratnagar (129,000), Lalitpur (116,000), Pokhara (48,000), Birganj (44,000)

Netherlands, The
Kingdom of The Netherlands
Nederland
Koninkrijk der Nederlanden

Area: 40,844 km^2
Population: 15,600,000 (1997)
Capital: Amsterdam (Pop. 724,000)
Administration: 12 provinces
Languages: Dutch/Frisian (regionally)
Religions: Roman Catholic 36%, Protestant 26%
Currency: 1 guilder = 100 cents
Major cities:
Rotterdam (599,000), The Hague (445,000), Utrecht (234,000), Eindhoven (196,000), Groningen (171,000), Tilburg (163,000), Haarlem (150,000), Apeldoorn (149,000), Enschede (148,000)

Overseas Territories:

Aruba
Area: 193 km^2
Population: 86,000 (1997)
Capital: Oranjestad (Pop. 20,000)

Netherlands Antilles
Nederlandse Antillen

Area: 800 km^2
Population: 195,000 (1997)
Capital: Willemstad (Pop. 119,000)

Nicaragua
Republic of Nicaragua
Nicaragua
República de Nicaragua

Area: 130,000 km^2
Population: 4,340,000 (1997)
Capital: Managua (Pop. 1,000,000)
Administration: 16 departments
Languages: Spanish, Indian languages
Religions: Roman Catholic 89%, Protestant 5%
Currency: 1 córdoba = 100 centavos
Major cities:
León (172,000), Chinandega (102,000), Masaya (102,000), Granada (89,000)

New Zealand

Area: 270,534 km^2
Population: 3,640,000 (1997)
Capital: Wellington (Pop. 158,000)
Administration: 90 counties, 3 urban districts
Languages: English, Maori
Religions: Christian 62%
Currency: 1 New Zeal. dollar = 100 cents
Major cities:
Auckland (A: 998,000), Christchurch (314,000), Dunedin (121,000), Hamilton (107,000)

Self-governing Overseas Territories:

Cook Islands

Area: 236 km^2
Population: 19,000 (1997)
Capital: Avarua

Niue

Area: 260 km^2
Population: 2,100 (1997)
Capital: Alofi (Pop. 900)

Overseas Territories:

Tokelau

Area: 12 km^2
Population: 1,800 (1992)

Ross Dependency

Claimed by New Zealand
Area: 750,310 km^2, research stat.

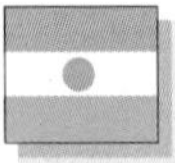

Niger

Republic of Niger
Niger
République du Niger

Area: 1,267,000 km^2
Population: 9,780,000 (1997)
Capital: Niamey (Pop. 398,000; A: 550,000)
Administration: 8 departments
Languages: French, Hausa, Djerma
Religions: Muslim 80%, traditional beliefs 10–15%
Currency: 1 CFA franc = 100 centimes
Major cities:
Zinder (121,000), Maradi (113,000), Tahoua (52,000), Agadèz (50,000)

Nigeria

Federal Republic of Nigeria

Area: 923,768 km^2
Population: 118,300,000 (1997)
Capital: Abuja (Pop. 298,000)
Administration: 36 states and the capital
Languages: English, French, Hausa
Religions: Muslim 45%, Protestant 26%
Currency: 1 naira = 100 kobo
Major cities:
Lagos (1,444,000; A: 5,700,000), Ibadan (1,362,000), Ogbomosho (694,000), Kano (641,000), Oshogbo (454,000), Ilorin (453,000), Abeokuta (407,000), Port Harcourt (390,000)

Norway

Kingdom of Norway
Norge
Kongeriket Norge

Area: 323,877 km^2
Population: 4,360,000 (1997)
Capital: Oslo (Pop. 495,000)
Administration: 19 counties
Languages: Norwegian, Lappish
Religions: Protestant (Lutheran) 89%
Currency: 1 Norw. krone = 100 øre
Major cities:
Bergen (224,000), Trondheim (145,000), Stavanger (105,000), Kristiansand (70,000)

Svalbard and Jan Mayen

Svalbard og Jan Mayen
Svalbard: 61,500 km^2; 3,200 inhabitants
Jan Mayen: 381 km^2, uninhabited

External Territories:

Bouvet Island

Bouvetøya
Area: 59 km^2, uninhabited

Peter I Island

Peter I Øy
Claimed by Norway
Area: 249 km^2, uninhabited

Queen Maud Land

Dronning Maud Land
Claimed by Norway
Area: 2,500,000 km^2, uninhabited

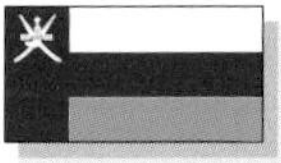

Oman

Sultanate of Oman
Uman
Saltanat 'Uman

Area: 212,457 km^2
Population: 2,400,000 (1997)
Capital: Muscat (Pop. 52,000)
Administration: 59 provinces
Languages: Arabic, Baluchi, English
Religions: Muslim 85%, Hindu 15%
Currency: 1 Omani rial = 1000 baiza
Major cities:
Suhār (92,000), Rustaq (66,000), Nizwa (63,000), Sūr (60,000)

Panama

Republic of Panama
Panamá
República de Panamá

Area: 75,517 km^2
Population: 2,720,000 (1997)
Capital: Panama City (Pop. 625,000)
Administration: 9 provinces, 1 Special Territory
Languages: Spanish, Indian languages, English Creole
Religions: Roman Catholic 96%
Currency: 1 balboa = 100 centesimos
Major cities:
San Miguelito (294,000), Colón (138,000), David (100,000), Santiago (68,000)

Pakistan

Islamic Republic of Pakistan
Pakistan
Islami Jamhuriya e Pakistan

Area: 796,095 km^2 (excluding the disputed area of Kashmir)
Population: 143,800,000 (1997)
Capital: Islāmābād (Pop. 350,000)
Administration: 4 provinces, federally administered tribal areas, capital
Languages: Urdu, Panjabi, Sindhi
Religions: Muslim 97%
Currency: 1 Pakistan rupee =100 paisa
Major cities:
Karāchi (5,181,000), Lahore (2,953,000), Faisalābād (1,104,000), Rawalpindi (795,000)

Papua New Guinea

Independent State of Papua New Guinea

Area: 462,840 km^2
Population: 4,500,000 (1997)
Capital: Port Moresby (Pop. 250,000)
Administration: 19 provinces, National Capital District
Languages: English/Pidgin/Motu
Religions: Protestant 58%, Roman Catholic 33%
Currency: 1 kina = 100 toea
Major cities:
Lae (81,000), Madang (27,000), Wewak (23,000), Goroka (18,000)

Palau

Republic of Palau
Belau/Palau
Belu'u era Belau/
Republic of Palau

Area: 459 km^2
Population: 17,000 (1997)
Capital: Koror (Pop. 11,000)
Administration: 16 states
Languages: Palauan/English
Religions: Roman Catholic 41%, Protestant 25%, traditional beliefs 25%
Currency: 1 U.S. dollar = 100 cents
Major towns:
Melekeok, Ngetbong, Airai

Paraguay

Republic of Paraguay
Paraguay
República del Paraguay/
Tetâ Paraguay

Area: 406,752 km^2
Population: 5,090,000 (1997)
Capital: Asunción (Pop. 502,000)
Administration: 17 departments and the capital
Languages: Spanish/Guaraní
Religions: Roman Catholic 94%
Currency: 1 guaraní = 100 céntimos
Major cities:
Ciudad del Este (134,000), Encarnación (55,000), Pedro Juan Caballero (54,000)

Peru
Republic of Peru
El Perú
República del Perú

Area:	1,285,216 km^2
Population:	24,400,000 (1997)
Capital:	Lima (Pop. A: 6,480,000)
Administration:	24 departments, constitutional province of Callao
Languages:	Spanish/Quechua/Aymara
Religions:	Roman Catholic 89%
Currency:	1 nuevo sol = 100 centimos

Major cities:
Arequipa (619,000), Callao (615,000), Trujillo (509,000), Chiclayo (412,000), Piura (286,000), Iquitos (266,000), Cusco (258,000), Huancayo (257,000)

Philippines
Republic of the Philippines
Pilipinas
Republika ng Pilipinas

Area:	300,000 km^2
Population:	70,600,000 (1997)
Capital:	Manila (Pop. 1,655,000, A: 7,830,000)
Administration:	16 regions
Languages:	Pilipino, Tagalog, English
Religions:	Roman Catholic 89%
Currency:	1 peso = 100 centavos

Major cities:
Davao (1,007,000), Cebu (662,000), Zamboanga (511,000), Cagayan de Oro (428,000), Bacolod (402,000), Iloilo (335,000), Iligan (273,000)

Poland
Republic of Poland
Polska
Rzeczpospolita Polska

Area:	323,250 km^2
Population:	38,630,000 (1997)
Capital:	Warsaw (Pop. 1,629,000)
Administration:	49 provinces (voivodships)
Languages:	Polish, German, Ukrainian
Religions:	Roman Catholic 91%
Currency:	1 złoty = 100 groszy

Major cities:
Łódź (818,000), Kraków (741,000), Wrocław (646,000), Poznań (581,000), Gdańsk (462,000), Szczecin (419,000), Bydgoszcz (387,000), Lublin (355,000), Katowice (351,000), Białystok (281,000)

Portugal
Portuguese Republic
Portugal
República Portuguesa

Area:	91,982 km^2
Population:	9,800,000 (1997)
Capital:	Lisbon (Pop. 681,000; A: 2,050,000)
Administration:	8 regions, 2 auton. regions
Languages:	Portuguese
Religions:	Roman Catholic 90%
Currency:	1 escudo = 100 centavos

Major cities:
Porto (309,000), Vila Nova de Gaia (247,000), Coimbra (148,000), Braga (144,000)

Autonomous Regions:

Azores
Autonomous Region of the Azores
Açores

Area:	2,330 km^2
Population:	241,000 (1995)
Capital:	Ponta Delgada

Madeira
Autonomous Region of Madeira

Area:	779 km^2
Population:	257,000 (1995)
Capital:	Funchal (Pop. 127,000)

Portuguese-administered Territory:

Macao *(12/20/1999 handed back to China)*

Area:	18 km^2
Population:	415,000 (1997)

Qatar
State of Qatar
Al-Qatar
Dawlat Qatar

Area:	11,000 km^2
Population:	568,000 (1997)
Capital:	Doha (Pop. 392,000)
Administration:	9 municipalities
Languages:	Arabic, Urdu, Farsi (Persian), English
Religions:	Muslim 92%
Currency:	1 Qatari riyal = 100 dirhams

Major cities:
Ar-Rayyān (165,000), Al-Wakrah (34,000)

1 km^2 = 0.3861 square mile

Romania
Romậnia

Area:	238,391 km^2
Population:	22,600,000 (1997)
Capital:	Bucharest (Pop. 2,037,000)
Administration:	41 counties
Languages:	Romanian
Religions:	Romanian Orthodox 87%
Currency:	1 leu = 100 bani

Major cities:
Constanța (347,000), Iași (347,000), Timișoara (332,000), Cluj-Napoca (332,000), Galați (328,000), Brașov (320,000), Craiova (311,000)

Russia
Russian Federation
Rossiya
Rossiyskaya Federatsiya

Area:	17,075,400 km^2
Population:	147,600,000 (1997)
Capital:	Moscow (Pop. 8,718,000; A: 12,410,000)

Administration:
21 republics,
6 territories (kray),
49 provinces (oblast),
10 autonomous areas (avtonomnyy okrug),
2 cities of federal status: Moscow, St. Petersburg,
Jewish Autonomous Region.

Languages:	Russian, languages of the minorities
Religions:	Russian Orthodox 24%, Muslim 10 – 15%
Currency:	1 rouble = 100 kopeks

Major cities:
St. Petersburg (4,837,000), Nizhniy Novgorod (1,383,000), Novosibirsk (1,369,000), Yekaterinburg (1,280,000), Samara (1,184,000), Omsk (1,163,000), Ufa (1,094,000), Chelyabinsk (1,086,000), Kazan (1,085,000), Perm (1,032,000), Rostov-n.-D. (1,026,000), Volgograd (1,003,000), Voronezh (908,000), Saratov (895,000), Krasnoyarsk (869,000), Tolyatti (702,000), Simbirsk (678,000), Izhevsk (654,000), Krasnodar (646,000), Vladivostok (632,000), Yaroslavl (629,000), Khabarovsk (618,000), Barnaul (596,000), Irkutsk (585,000), Novokuznetsk (572,000), Ryazan (536,000), Penza (534,000), Orenburg (532,000)

Rwanda
Rwandese Republic
Rwanda
Republika y'u Rwanda/
République rwandaise/
Rwandese Republic

Area:	26,338 km^2
Population:	6,070,000 (1997)
Capital:	Kigali (Pop. 234,000)
Administration:	11 prefectures
Languages:	Kinyarwanda/French/English
Religions:	Christian c. 50%, traditional beliefs c. 50%
Currency:	1 Rwanda franc = 100 centimes

Major cities:
Butare (43,000), Ruhengeri (29,000)

Saint Kitts and Nevis
Federation of Saint Kitts and Nevis

Area:	261 km^2
Population:	41,000 (1997)
Capital:	Basseterre (Pop. 12,000)
Administration:	14 parishes
Languages:	English, English Creole
Religions:	Anglican 36%, Methodist 32%, Roman Catholic 11%
Currency:	1 Eastern Caribbean dollar = 100 cents

Major towns:
Charlestown (1,700)

Saint Lucia

Area:	622 km^2
Population:	144,000 (1997)
Capital:	Castries (Pop. A: 55,000)
Administration:	10 districts
Languages:	English, English Creole
Religions:	Roman Catholic 77%, Protestant 19%
Currency:	1 Eastern Caribbean dollar = 100 cents

Major cities:
Vieux Fort (23,000), Micoud (15,000)

Saint Vincent and the Grenadines

Area: 388 km²
Population: 113,000 (1997)
Capital: Kingstown (Pop. 16,000)
Languages: English, English Creole
Religions: Protestant 75%, Roman Catholic 9%
Currency: 1 Eastern Caribbean dollar = 100 cents
Major towns:
Georgetown

Sao Tome and Principe

Dem. Rep. of Sao Tome and Principe
São Tomé e Príncipe
República Democrática de São Tomé e Príncipe

Area: 964 km²
Population: 135,000 (1997)
Capital: São Tomé (Pop. 43,000)
Administration: 6 districts on São Tomé, self-government of Príncipe
Languages: Portuguese, Portuguese Creole
Religions: Roman Catholic 93%
Currency: 1 dobra = 100 centimos
Major towns:
Santo António (1,000)

Samoa

Independent State of Samoa
Samoa
Malo Sa'oloto Tuto'atasi o Samoa/Independent State of Samoa

Area: 2,831 km²
Population: 169,000 (1997)
Capital: Apia (Pop. 34,000)
Administration: 11 districts
Languages: Samoan/English
Religions: Protestant 71%, Roman Catholic 22%
Currency: 1 tala = 100 sene
Major towns:
Sataua, Salelologa

Saudi Arabia

Kingdom of Saudi Arabia
Arabiya as-Sa'udiya
Al-Mamlaka al-'Arabiya as Sa'udiya

Area: 2,149,690 km²
Population: 19,500,000 (1997)
Capital: Riyadh (Pop. 1,800,000)
Administration: 13 regions
Languages: Arabic, English
Religions: Muslim 98%
Currency: 1 riyal = 100 halalas
Major cities:
Jiddah (1,500,000), Mecca (630,000), At-Tāif (410,000), Medina (400,000), Ad-Dammām (350,000)

San Marino

Republic of San Marino
San Marino
Repubblica di San Marino

Area: 61 km²
Population: 25,000 (1997)
Capital: San Marino (Pop. 4,400)
Administration: 9 districts (castelli)
Languages: Italian
Religions: Roman Catholic 93%
Currency: 1 Italian lira = 100 centesimi
Major towns:
Serravalle (7,300)

Senegal

Republic of Senegal
Sénégal
République du Sénégal

Area: 196,722 km²
Population: 8,770,000 (1997)
Capital: Dakar (Pop. 1,641,000)
Administration: 10 regions
Languages: French, Wolof
Religions: Muslim 95%
Currency: 1 CFA franc = 100 centimes
Major cities:
Thiès (216,000), Kaolack (193,000), Ziguinchor (162,000), Saint-Louis (132,000)

1 km² = 0.3861 square mile

Seychelles

Republic of Seychelles
Seychelles/Sesel
Repiblik Sesel/Republic of Seychelles/République des Seychelles

Area: 455 km^2
Population: 76,000 (1997)
Capital: Victoria (Pop. 25,000)
Administration: 23 districts
Languages: Creole/English/French
Religions: Roman Catholic 90%, Anglican 8%
Currency: 1 Seychelles rupee = 100 cents

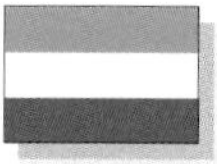

Sierra Leone

Republic of Sierra Leone

Area: 71,740 km^2
Population: 4,450,000 (1997)
Capital: Freetown (Pop. 669,000)
Administration: 4 provinces
Languages: English, Mende languages, Krio
Religions: Traditional beliefs 52%, Muslim 39%
Currency: 1 leone = 100 cents
Major cities:
Koidu (82,000), Bo (60,000), Kenema (52,000), Makeni (49,000)

Singapore

Republic of Singapore
Singapura/Hsin-chia-p'o/Singapore
Republik Singapura/Hsin-chia-p'o Kung-ho-kuo/Singapore Kudiyarasu

Area: 618 km^2
Population: 3,430,000 (1997)
Capital: Singapore (Pop. 3,040,000)
Administration: 5 divisions
Languages: Malay/Chinese (Mandarin)/Tamil/English
Religions: Buddhist 32%, Taoist 22%, Muslim 15%, Christian 3%
Currency: 1 Singapore dollar = 100 cents

Slovakia

Slovak Republic
Slovensko
Slovenská Republika

Area: 49,012 km^2
Population: 5,350,000 (1997)
Capital: Bratislava (Pop. 452,000)
Administration: 8 regions
Languages: Slovak, Hungarian
Religions: Roman Catholic 60%
Currency: 1 Slovak koruna = 100 haliers
Major cities:
Košice (242,000), Prešov (93,000), Nitra (88,000), Žilina (87,000), Banská Bystrica (85,000), Trnava (70,000), Martin (61,000)

Slovenia

Republic of Slovenia
Slovenija
Republika Slovenija

Area: 20,256 km^2
Population: 1,920,000 (1997)
Capital: Ljubljana (Pop. 276,000)
Administration: 62 districts
Languages: Slovene, Croatian, Hungarian
Religions: Christian 74%
Currency: 1 tolar = 100 stotins
Major cities:
Maribor (103,000), Celje (40,000), Kranj (37,000), Koper (25,000), Novo Mesto (23,000)

Solomon Islands

Area: 28,896 km^2
Population: 403,000 (1997)
Capital: Honiara (Pop. 35,000)
Administration: 8 provinces, Capital Territory
Languages: English, Melanesian languages
Religions: Christian c. 95%
Currency: 1 Solomon Islands dollar = 100 cents
Major towns:
Gizo (4,000), Auki (3,000), Kirakira (3,000), Buala (2,000)

Somalia

Somali Democratic Republic
Soomaaliya
Jamhuriyadda Dimugradiga ee Soomaaliya

Area: 637,657 km^2
Population: 10,300,000 (1997)
Capital: Mogadishu (Pop. 900,000)
Administration: 18 regions
Languages: Somali, Arabic, English, Italian
Religions: Muslim almost 100%
Currency: 1 Somali shilling = 100 cents
Major cities:
Hargeysa (c. 400,000), Kismaayo (c. 200,000), Marka (100,000), Berbera (65,000)

South Africa

Republic of South Africa
South Africa/Suid-Afrika
Republic of South Africa/
Republiek van Suid-Afrika

Area: 1,221,037 km^2
Population: 43,300,000 (1997)
Capital: Pretoria (Pop. 526,000; A: 1,100,000)
Administration: 9 provinces
Languages: Afrikaans/English/Ndebele/Pedi (North Sotho)/Sotho (South Sotho)/Swazi/Tsonga/Tswana (West Sotho)/Venda/Xhosa/Zulu
Religions: Christian 78%
Currency: 1 rand = 100 cents
Major cities:
Cape Town (855,000; A: 2,400,000), Durban (716,000; A: 1,100,000), Johannesburg (713,000; A: 1,900,000), Soweto (597,000), Port Elizabeth (303,000), Umlazi (299,000), Diepmeadow (241,000), Lekoa (218,000), Tembisa (209,000), Katlehong (202,000)

External Territory:

Prince Edward and Marion Islands

Prince Edward Island: 41 km^2, uninhabited
Marion Island: 388 km^2, uninhabited

Spain

Kingdom of Spain
España
Reino de España

Area: 505,992 km^2
Population: 39,700,000 (1997)
Capital: Madrid (Pop. 2,900,000; A: 5,000,000)
Administration: 17 autonomous communities
Languages: Castilian Spanish/Catalan/Galician/Basque
Religions: Roman Catholic 96%
Currency: 1 peseta = 100 céntimos
Major cities:
Barcelona (1,509,000; A: 4,600,000), Valencia (747,000), Seville (697,000), Zaragoza (602,000), Málaga (549,000), Bilbao (359,000), Las Palmas (356,000), Murcia (346,000), Valladolid (320,000), Córdoba (306,000), Palma de Mallorca (304,000), Vigo (287,000), Gijón (284,000), Alicante (275,000)

Places under Spanish Sovereignty in North Africa:

Ceuta

Place of Ceuta

Area: 19 km^2
Population: 69,000 (1996)

Melilla

Place of Melilla

Area: 13 km^2
Population: 60,000 (1996)

Sri Lanka

Democr. Socialist Rep. of Sri Lanka
Sri Lanka/Ilangai
Sri Lanka Prajatantrika Samajavadi Janarajaya/Ilangai Jananayaka Socialisa Kudiarasu

Area: 65,610 km^2
Population: 18,300,000 (1997)
Capital: Colombo (Pop. 1,994,000)
Administration: 9 provinces
Languages: Sinhala/Tamil, English
Religions: Buddhist 69%, Hindu 16%, Muslim 8%
Currency: 1 Sri Lankan rupee = 100 cents
Major cities:
Moratuwa (170,000), Jaffna (129,000), Anuradhapura (109,000) Kandy (104,000), Galle (84,000), Negombo (64,000)

Sudan, The

Republic of the Sudan
Sudan
Jumhuriyat as-Sudan

Area: 2,505,813 km^2
Population: 27,900,000 (1997)
Capital: Khartoum (Pop. 925,000)
Administration: 26 federal states
Languages: Arabic, English
Religions: Muslim 70%, traditional beliefs 20%
Currency: 1 Sudan. dinar = 100 piastres
Major cities:
Omdurman (1,267,000), Khartoum North (879,000), Port Sudan (305,000), Kassalā (234,000), Nyala (229,000), El-Obeid (228,000)

Sweden

Kingdom of Sweden
Sverige
Konungariket Sverige

Area: 449,964 km^2
Population: 8,830,000 (1997)
Capital: Stockholm (Pop. 727,000)
Administration: 24 counties (län)
Languages: Swedish, Finnish, Lappish
Religions: Protestant (Lutheran) 89%
Currency: 1 krona = 100 öre
Major cities:
Göteborg (457,000), Malmö (251,000), Uppsala (186,000), Linköping (132,000), Västerås (124,000), Norrköping (123,000), Örebro (122,000), Jönköping (116,000)

Suriname

Republic of Suriname
Suriname
Republiek Suriname

Area: 163,265 km^2
Population: 437,000 (1997)
Capital: Paramaribo (Pop. 201,000)
Administration: 9 districts, capital district
Languages: Dutch, English, Hindi
Religions: Hindu 27%, Roman Catholic 23%, Muslim 20%, Protestant 19%
Currency: 1 Suriname guilder = 100 cents
Major towns:
Nieuw Nickerie (6,100)

Switzerland

Swiss Confederation
Schweiz/Suisse/Svizzera/Svizera
Schweizerische Eidgenossenschaft/
Confédération suisse/Confederazione
Svizzera/Confederaziun Svizera

Area: 41,284 km^2
Population: 7,260,000 (1997)
Capital: Berne (Pop. 124,000)
Administration: 26 cantons and demi-cantons
Languages: German/French/Italian/Romansch
Religions: Roman Catholic 46%, Protestant 40%
Currency: 1 Swiss franc = 100 centimes
Major cities:
Zürich (339,000), Geneva (173,000), Basel (171,000), Lausanne (114,000)

Swaziland

Kingdom of Swaziland
kaNgwane/Swaziland
Umbuso weSwatini/
Kingdom of Swaziland

Area: 17,364 km^2
Population: 910,000 (1997)
Capital: Mbabane (Pop. 52,000)
Administration: 4 districts
Languages: Swazi/English
Religions: Christian 78%, traditional beliefs 21%
Currency: 1 lilangeni = 100 cents
Major cities:
Manzini (18,000)

Syria

Syrian Arab Republic
Suriya
Jumhuriya al-Arabiya as-Suriya

Area: 185,180 km^2, including the Golan Heights (1,176 km^2)
Population: 14,900,000 (1997)
Capital: Damascus (Pop. 1,394,000)
Administration: 14 districts (mohafaza)
Languages: Arabic, Kurdish, Armenian
Religions: Muslim 90%, Christian 9%
Currency: 1 Syrian pound = 100 piastres
Major cities:
Aleppo (1,583,000), Homs (540,000), Latakia (312,000), Hamāh (264,000), Ar-Raqqah (165,000), Al-Qāmishlī (144,000)

Taiwan

Republic of China
Chung-hua
Chung-hua Min-kuo

Area: 36,000 km^2
Population: 21,600,000 (1997)
Capital: T'aipei (Pop. 2,605,000)
Administration: 16 counties, 7 municipalities
Languages: Mandarin Chinese
Religions: Buddhist 43%, Taoist 34%
Currency: 1 New Taiwan dollar = 100 cents
Major cities:
Kaohsiung (1,434,000), T'aichung (876,000), T'ainan (711,000), Chungho (384,000)

Tajikistan

Republic of Tajikistan
Tojikiston
Jumkhurii Tojikiston

Area: 143,100 km^2
Population: 6,050,000 (1997)
Capital: Dushanbe (Pop. 529,000)
Administration: 3 provinces, Badakhshan Autonomous Republic and the capital
Languages: Tajik, Russian, Uzbek
Religions: Mainly Sunni Muslim
Currency: 1 Tajik rouble = 100 tanga
Major cities:
Khujand (162,000), Kulob (79,000)

Tanzania

United Republic of Tanzania
Tanzania
Jamhuri ya Muungano wa Tanzania/
United Republic of Tanzania

Area: 883,749 km^2
Population: 31,400,000 (1997)
Capital: Dodoma (Pop. 204,000; A: 1,800,000)
Administration: 25 regions
Languages: Swahili/English
Religions: Muslim 35%, Roman Catholic 33%, Protestant 13%
Currency: 1 Tanz. shilling = 100 cents
Major cities:
Dar es Salaam (1,463,000), Mwanza (223,000), Tanga (188,000), Zanzibar (158,000)

Thailand

Kingdom of Thailand
Prathet Thai/Muang Thai
Ratcha Anachak Thai

Area: 513,115 km^2
Population: 59,100,000 (1997)
Capital: Bangkok (Pop. 5,573,000)
Administration: 76 provinces (changwads)
Languages: Thai, Chinese, Malay, English
Religions: Buddhist 94%
Currency: 1 baht = 100 stangs
Major cities:
Nakhon Ratchasima (188,000), Chiang Mai (170,000), Hat Yai (149,000), Sara Buri (107,000), Ubon Ratchathani (106,000), Nakhon Sawan (97,000)

Togo

Togolese Republic
Togo
République togolaise

Area: 56,785 km^2
Population: 4,310,000 (1997)
Capital: Lomé (Pop. A: 513,000)
Administration: 5 regions
Languages: French/Ewe/Kabye
Religions: Traditional beliefs 50%, Christian 35%, Muslim 15%
Currency: 1 CFA franc = 100 centimes
Major cities:
Sokodé (55,000), Lama-Kara (41,000), Atakpamé (30,000), Tsévié (26,000)

Tonga

Kingdom of Tonga
Tonga
Pule'anga Fakatu'i'o Tonga

Area: 747 km^2
Population: 99,000 (1997)
Capital: Nuku'alofa (Pop. 34,000)
Administration: 5 divisions
Languages: Tongan, English
Religions: Protestant 70%, Roman Catholic 20%
Currency: 1 pa'anga = 100 seniti
Islands (Pop.):
Tongtapu (67,000), Vava'u (16,000), Ha'apai (8,000), Eua (5,000)

1 km^2 = 0.3861 square mile

Trinidad and Tobago

Republic of Trinidad and Tobago

Area: 5,130 km^2
Population: 1,310,000 (1997)
Capital: Port of Spain (Pop. 51,000)
Administration: 8 counties, 3 boroughs and Tobago
Languages: English, French, Spanish
Religions: Christian 40%, Hindu 24%, Muslim 6%
Currency: 1 Trinidad and Tobago dollar = 100 cents
Major cities:
San Fernando (30,000), Arima (30,000)

Turkmenistan

Turkmenostan
Turkmenostan Respublikasy

Area: 488,100 km^2
Population: 4,230,000 (1997)
Capital: Ashgabat (Pop. 517,000)
Administration: 5 regions
Languages: Turkmen, Russian, Uzbek
Religions: Mainly Sunni Muslim
Currency: 1 manat = 100 tenesi
Major cities:
Chärjew (166,000), Dashhovuz (117,000), Mary (95,000), Nebitdag (89,000), Turkmenbashi (60,000)

Tunisia

Republic of Tunisia
Tunisiya
Jumhuriya at-Tunisiya

Area: 163,610 km^2
Population: 9,320,000 (1997)
Capital: Tunis (Pop. 674,000; A: 1,600,000)
Administration: 23 governorates
Languages: Arabic, French
Religions: Muslim 99%
Currency: 1 Tun. dinar = 1,000 millimes
Major cities:
Sfax (231,000), Sousse (125,000), Kairouan (103,000), Binzert (99,000), Gabès (99,000), Gafsa (71,000)

Tuvalu

Area: 26 km^2
Population: 10,000 (1997)
Capital: Funafuti (Pop. 4,000 on island)
Administration: 9 atolls
Languages: Tuvaluan/English
Religions: Protestant 98%
Currency: 1 Australian dollar = 100 cents

Turkey

Republic of Turkey
Türkiye
Türkiye Cumhuriyeti

Area: 774,815 km^2
Population: 62,800,000 (1997)
Capital: Ankara (Pop. 2,838,000)
Administration: 67 provinces
Languages: Turkish, Kurdish, Arabic
Religions: Muslim 99%
Currency: 1 Turkish lira = 100 kurush
Major cities:
İstanbul (7,774,000), İzmir (2,018,000), Adana (1,067,000), Bursa (1,017,000), Gaziantep (730,000), Konya (585,000), Mersin (533,000)

Uganda

Republic of Uganda
Uganda
Jamhuriya ya Uganda/
Republic of Uganda

Area: 241,038 km^2
Population: 20,800,000 (1997)
Capital: Kampala (Pop. 773,000)
Administration: 38 districts
Languages: Kiswahili/English, Bantu languages
Religions: Roman Catholic 40%, Protestant 26%, Muslim 5%
Currency: 1 Uganda shilling = 100 cents
Major cities:
Jinja (61,000), Mbale (54,000), Masaka (49,000)

Ukraine

Ukraina

Area:	603,700 km^2
Population:	51,400,000 (1997)
Capital:	Kiev (Pop. 2,620,000)
Administration:	24 provinces, Aut. Republic of Crimea, capital
Languages:	Ukrainian, Russian
Religions:	Mainly Orthodox
Currency:	1 hryvna = 100 kopiykas

Major cities:
Kharkiv (1,536,000), Dnipropetrovsk (1,134,000), Donetsk (1,075,000), Odesa (1,037,000), Zaporizhzhya (871,000), Lviv (797,000)

United Arab Emirates

Imarat al-Arabiya al-Muttahida

Area:	83,600 km^2
Population:	2,300,000 (1997)
Capital:	Abu Dhabi (Pop. 363,000)
Administration:	7 emirates
Languages:	Arabic, Hindi, Urdu, Farsi, English
Religions:	Muslim 96%
Currency:	1 dirham = 100 fils

Major cities:
Dubai (585,000), Sharjah (125,000)

United Kingdom

United Kingdom of Great Britain and Northern Ireland

Area:	244,101 km^2
Population:	58,800,000 (1997)
Capital:	London (Pop. A: 7,074,000)
Administration:	*England:* 39 counties, 7 metropolitan counties *Wales:* 8 counties *Scotland:* 9 regions, 3 island authority areas *Northern Ireland:* 26 districts
Languages:	English, Welsh, Scottish, Gaelic
Religions:	Protestant 53%, Roman Catholic 10%
Currency:	1 pound sterling = 100 pence

Major cities:
Birmingham (1,021,000), Leeds (727,000), Glasgow (616,000), Sheffield (530,000), Bradford (483,000), Liverpool (468,000), Edinburgh (449,000), Manchester (431,000), Bristol (400,000), Kirklees (389,000), Wirral (329,000), Wakefield (317,000)

	Area km^2	Population 1997	Capital
England	130,423	49,085,000	London
Wales	20,766	2,925,000	Cardiff
Scotland	78,789	5,128,000	Edinburgh
Northern Ireland	14,144	1,663,000	Belfast

Crown Dependencies:

Channel Islands

Area:	194 km^2 (Jersey 116 km^2; Guernsey and dependencies 78 km^2)
Population:	149,000 (1997)
Major cities:	St. Helier (28,000), St. Peter Port (16,000)

Isle of Man

Area:	572 km^2
Population:	72,000 (1997)
Major cities:	Douglas (22,000)

Dependent Territories:

Anguilla

Crown Colony of Anguilla

Area:	96 km^2
Population:	10,000 (1997)
Capital:	The Valley (Pop. 600)

Bermuda

Area:	53 km^2
Population:	60,000 (1997)
Capital:	Hamilton (Pop. 1,100)

British Antarctic Territory

Claimed by the United Kingdom, Argentina and partly by Chile

Area:	c. 1,710,000 km^2 (South Orkney Is., South Shetland Is., Antarctic Pen., Filchner and Ronne Ice Shelves, Coast Land)

Research stations

1 km^2 = 0.3861 square mile

British Indian Ocean Territory
Claimed by Mauritius

Area: 60 km^2 (land area)
Population: No permanent population

British Virgin Islands

Area: 151 km^2
Population: 19,000 (1997)
Capital: Road Town (Pop. 2,500)

Cayman Islands

Area: 264 km^2
Population: 32,000 (1997)
Capital: Georgetown (Pop. 20,000)

Falkland Islands (Islas Malvinas)
Claimed by Argentina

Area: 12,173 km^2
Population: 2,000 (1997)
Capital: Stanley (Pop. 1,600)

Gibraltar
Colony of Gibraltar

Area: 6 km^2
Population: 27,000 (1997)

Montserrat

Area: 102 km^2
Population: 11,000 (1997)
Capital: Plymouth (Pop. 1,500)

Pitcairn

Area: Pitcairn 5 km^2, Henderson 31 km^2, Oeno 5 km^2, Ducie 4 km^2
Population: Adamstown is the only settlement (Pop. 54)

Saint Helena
Crown Colony of Saint Helena and Dependencies

Area: 410 km^2 (St. Helena 122 km^2)
Population: 7,000
Capital: Jamestown (Pop. 1,400)
Dependencies: Ascension (88 km^2, Pop. 1,000), Tristan da Cunha (98 km^2, Pop. 300), Gough (90 km^2, uninh.), Inaccessible (10 km^2, uninhabited), Nightingale (2 km^2, uninh.)

South Georgia and the South Sandwich Islands
Claimed by Argentina

Area: 3,755 km^2/337 km^2
Population: South Georgia: No permanent population
South Sandwich Islands: Uninhabited

Turks and Caicos Islands

Area: 430 km^2
Population: 15,000 (1997)
Capital: Grand Turk (Pop. 3,800)

United States / U.S.A.
United States of America

Area: 9,809,431 km^2
Population: 267,600,000 (1997)
Capital: Washington (Pop. 543,000; A: 3,920,000)
Administration: 50 states and the District of Columbia
Languages: English/regionally Spanish
Religions: Protestant 56%, Roman Catholic 28%, Jewish 2%
Currency: 1 dollar = 100 cents
Major cities:
New York (7,381,000; A: 18,090,000), Los Angeles (3,554,000; A: 14,530,000), Chicago (2,722,000; A: 8,070,000), Houston (1,744,000; A: 3,710,000), Philadelphia (1,478,600; A: 5,900,000), San Diego (1,171,000; A: 2,500,000), Phoenix (1,159,000; A: 2,120,000), San Antonio (1,068,000; A: 1,300,000), Dallas (1,053,000; A: 3,890,000), Detroit (1,000,000; A: 4,670,000), San Jose (839,000), Indianapolis (747,000), San Francisco (735,000; A: 6,250,000), Jacksonville (680,000), Baltimore (675,000; A: 2,380,000), Columbus (657,000), El Paso (600,000), Memphis (597,000), Milwaukee (591,000), Boston (558,000, A: 4,170,000), Austin (541,000), Seattle (525,000; A: 2,560,000), Nashville-Davidson (511,000)

States	Area* km²	Population** 1997	Capital
Alabama	135,775	4,319,000	Montgomery
Alaska	1,700,139	609,000	Juneau
Arizona	295,276	4,555,000	Phoenix
Arkansas	137,742	2,523,000	Little Rock
California	424,002	32,268,000	Sacramento
Colorado	269,620	3,893,000	Denver
Connecticut	14,358	3,270,000	Hartford
Delaware	6,447	723,000	Dover
District of Columbia	177	529,000	Washington
Florida	170,313	14,654,000	Tallahassee
Georgia	153,953	7,486,000	Atlanta
Hawaii	28,313	1,187,000	Honolulu
Idaho	216,456	1,210,000	Boise
Illinois	150,007	11,896,000	Springfield
Indiana	94,328	5,864,000	Indianapolis
Iowa	145,754	2,852,000	Des Moines
Kansas	213,110	2,595,000	Topeka
Kentucky	104,665	3,908,000	Frankfort
Louisiana	134,275	4,352,000	Baton Rouge
Maine	91,653	1,242,000	Augusta
Maryland	32,135	5,094,000	Annapolis
Massachusetts	27,337	6,118,000	Boston
Michigan	250,738	9,774,000	Lansing
Minnesota	225,182	4,686,000	Saint Paul
Mississippi	125,443	2,731,000	Jackson
Missouri	180,546	5,402,000	Jefferson City
Montana	380,850	879,000	Helena
Nebraska	200,358	1,657,000	Lincoln
Nevada	286,368	1,677,000	Carson City
New Hampshire	24,219	1,173,000	Concord
New Jersey	22,590	8,053,000	Trenton
New Mexico	314,939	1,730,000	Santa Fe
New York	141,089	18,137,000	Albany
North Carolina	139,397	7,425,000	Raleigh
North Dakota	183,123	641,000	Bismarck
Ohio	116,103	11,186,000	Columbus
Oklahoma	181,049	3,317,000	Oklahoma City
Oregon	254,819	3,243,000	Salem
Pennsylvania	119,291	12,020,000	Harrisburg
Rhode Island	4,002	987,000	Providence
South Carolina	82,898	3,760,000	Columbia
South Dakota	199,745	738,000	Pierre
Tennessee	109,158	5,368,000	Nashville
Texas	695,676	19,439,000	Austin
Utah	219,902	2,059,000	Salt Lake City
Vermont	24,903	589,000	Montpelier
Virginia	110,771	6,734,000	Richmond
Washington	184,674	5,610,000	Olympia
West Virginia	62,759	1,816,000	Charleston
Wisconsin	169,653	5,170,000	Madison
Wyoming	253,349	480,000	Cheyenne

*including inland water
**includes military personnel residing overseas

Outlying Territories in the Caribbean:

Navassa

Navassa Island

Area: 5 km², uninhabited

Puerto Rico

Commonwealth of Puerto Rico

Area: 8,875 km²
Population: 3,740,000 (1997)
Capital: San Juan (Pop. 438,000)
Languages: Spanish/English
Religion: Roman Catholic 81%
Major cities:
Bayamón (232,000), Ponce (190,000), Carolina (188,000), Caguas (140,000), Mayagüez (101,000)

Virgin Islands of the United States

Area: 347 km²
Population: 106,000 (1997)
Capital: Charlotte Amalie (Pop. 12,000)
Languages: English, Spanish

Outlying Territories in the Pacific Ocean:

American Samoa

Territory of American Samoa

Area: 199 km²
Population: 56,000 (1997)
Capital: Pago Pago (Pop. 3,500)
Languages: Samoan/English

Baker Island

Area: 2 km², uninhabited

Guam

Territory of Guam

Area: 549 km²
Population: 153,000 (1997)
Capital: Agaña (Pop. 1,100)
Languages: English, Chamorro

Howland Island

Area: 2 km², uninhabited

Jarvis Island

Area: 8 km², uninhabited

Johnston Atoll

Area: 3 km²
Population: 1,200 (1997)

Kingman Reef

Area: 8 km², uninhabited

Midway Islands

Area: 5 km^2
Population: c. 450 (1997)

Northern Mariana Islands

Commonwealth of the Northern Mariana Islands

Area: 464 km^2
Population: 49,000 (1997)

Palmyra Atoll

Area: 6 km^2, uninhabited

Wake Island

Area: 8 km^2
Population: c. 200 (1997)

Vanuatu

Republic of Vanuatu
Vanuatu
Ripablik blong Vanuatu/
Republic of Vanuatu/
République de Vanuatu

Area: 12,189 km^2
Population: 178,000 (1997)
Capital: Port Vila (Pop. 34,000)
Administration: 6 provinces
Languages: Bislama/English/French
Religions: Christian 80%
Currency: 1 vatu = 100 centimes
Major towns:
Luganville (10,000)

Uruguay

Oriental Republic of Uruguay
Uruguay
República Oriental del Uruguay

Area: 177,414 km^2
Population: 3,220,000 (1997)
Capital: Montevideo (Pop. 1,379,000)
Administration: 19 departments
Languages: Spanish
Religions: Roman Catholic 78%
Currency: 1 Uruguayan peso = 100 centésimos
Major cities:
Salto (81,000), Paysandú (76,000), Las Piedras (58,000), Rivera (57,000), Melo (43,000), Tacuarembó (41,000), Mercedes (37,000)

Vatican City

Vatican City State
Vaticanus/Vaticano
Status Civitatis Vaticanae/
Stato della Città del Vaticano

Area: 0.44 km^2
Population: 1,000 (1997)
Languages: Latin/Italian
Religions: Roman Catholic 100%
Currency: 1 Italian lira = 100 centesimi

Uzbekistan

Republic of Uzbekistan
Uzbekiston
Uzbekiston Respublikasy

Area: 447,400 km^2
Population: 23,600,000 (1997)
Capital: Tashkent (Pop. 2,130,000)
Administration: 12 provinces, Karakalpak Autonomous Republic
Languages: Uzbek, Russian
Religions: Muslim 88%
Currency: 1 sum = 100 teen
Major cities:
Samarqand (372,000), Namangan (333,000), Andizhon (302,000), Bukhoro (235,000), Farghona (193,000), Nukus (182,000)

Venezuela

Republic of Venezuela
Venezuela
República de Venezuela

Area: 912,050 km^2
Population: 22,700,000 (1997)
Capital: Caracas (Pop. 1,825,000)
Administration: 20 states, Federal District
Languages: Spanish, Indian languages
Religions: Roman Catholic 93%
Currency: 1 bolívar = 100 céntimos
Major cities:
Maracaibo (1,208,000), Valencia (903,000), Barquisimeto (603,000), Ciudad Guayana (453,000), Maracay (354,000), Ciudad Bolívar (226,000), Barcelona (222,000), San Cristóbal (221,000)

Vietnam

Socialist Republic of Vietnam
Viêt Nam
Công Hòa Xã Hôi Chu Nghĩa Viêt Nam

Area: 331,689 km^2
Population: 76,400,000 (1997)
Capital: Ha Nôi (Pop. 2,155,000)
Administration: 7 regions
Languages: Vietnamese, Chinese
Religions: Buddhist 55%
Currency: 1 dong = 100 xu
Major cities:
Hô Chi Minh City (Saigon) (4,322,000), Hai Phong (783,000), Đă Nâng (383,000), Buôn Ma Thuôt (282,000), Nha Trang (221,000), Huê (219,000), Cân Tho` (216,000)

Western Sahara

(Occupied and administered by Morocco)

Area: 266,000 km^2
Population: 260,000 (1997)
Capital: El-Aaiún (Pop. 139,000)
Administration: 4 provinces
Languages: Arabic, Spanish
Religions: Almost 100% Muslim
Major cities:
Ad-Dakhla (18,000), Smara (18,000)

Yemen

Republic of Yemen
Al-Yaman
Al-Jamhuriya al-Yamaniya

Area: 527,968 km^2
Population: 16,200,000 (1997)
Capital: Sanā (Pop. 927,000)
Administration: 17 governorates
Languages: Arabic
Religions: Muslim 99%
Currency: 1 rial = 100 fils (North)
1 dinar = 1,000 fils (South)
Major cities:
Aden (401,000), Taizz (290,000), Al-Hudaydah (246,000)

Yugoslavia

Federal Republic of Yugoslavia
Jugoslavija
Savezna Republika Jugoslavija

Area: 102,173 km^2
Population: 10,400,000 (1997)
Capital: Belgrade (Pop. 1,168,000)
Administration: 2 republics
Languages: Serbian, Croatian, Albanian
Religions: Serbian Orthodox 44%, Roman Catholic 31%,
Currency: 1 dinar = 100 para
Major cities:
Novi Sad (180,000), Niš (175,000), Priština (155,000), Kragujevac (147,000), Podgorica (118,000), Subotica (100,000)

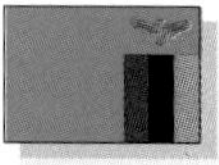

Zambia

Republic of Zambia

Area: 752,618 km^2
Population: 8,490,000 (1997)
Capital: Lusaka (Pop. 982,000)
Administration: 9 provinces
Languages: English, Bantu languages
Religions: Christian 72%, traditional beliefs 27%
Currency: 1 kwacha = 100 ngwee
Major cities:
Ndola (376,000), Kitwe (349,000), Chingola (187,000), Mufulira (175,000), Kabwe (167,000), Luanshya (148,000), Kalulushi (91,000)

Zimbabwe

Republic of Zimbabwe

Area: 390,757 km^2
Population: 11,700,000 (1997)
Capital: Harare (Pop. 1,189,000)
Administration: 8 provinces, 2 cities
Languages: English, Fanagalo, Bantu languages
Religions: Christian c. 55 %, traditional beliefs
Currency: 1 Zimbabwe dollar = 100 cents
Major cities:
Bulawayo (622,000), Chitungwiza (275,000), Mutare (131,000), Gweru (128,000)

1 km^2 = 0.3861 square mile

Countries and their Area

	Country	km²
1.	Russia	17,075,400
2.	Canada	9,970,610
3.	United States	9,809,431
4.	China	9,562,036
5.	Brazil	8,547,404
6.	Australia	7,682,300
7.	India	3,165,596
8.	Argentina	2,780,400
9.	Kazakhstan	2,717,300
10.	Sudan, The	2,505,813
11.	Algeria	2,381,741
12.	Congo, Democratic Republic of the	2,344,858
13.	Saudi Arabia	2,149,690
14.	Mexico	1,958,201
15.	Indonesia	1,904,569
16.	Libya	1,759,540
17.	Iran	1,633,188
18.	Mongolia	1,566,500
19.	Peru	1,285,216
20.	Chad	1,284,000
21.	Niger	1,267,000
22.	Angola	1,246,700
23.	Mali	1,240,192
24.	South Africa	1,221,037
25.	Colombia	1,138,914
26.	Ethiopia	1,104,300
27.	Bolivia	1,098,581
28.	Mauritania	1,025,520
29.	Egypt	1,001,449
30.	Nigeria	923,768
31.	Venezuela	912,050
32.	Tanzania	883,749
33.	Namibia	824,292
34.	Mozambique	801,590
35.	Pakistan	796,095
36.	Turkey	774,815
37.	Chile	756,626
38.	Zambia	752,618
39.	Myanmar (Burma)	676,578
40.	Afghanistan	652,090
41.	Somalia	637,657
42.	Central African Rep.	622,984
43.	Ukraine	603,700
44.	Madagascar	587,041
45.	Botswana	581,730
46.	Kenya	580,367
47.	France	543,965
48.	Yemen	527,968
49.	Thailand	513,115
50.	Spain	505,992
51.	Turkmenistan	488,100
52.	Cameroon	475,442
53.	Papua New Guinea	462,840
54.	Morocco	458,730
55.	Sweden	449,964
56.	Uzbekistan	447,400
57.	Iraq	438,317
58.	Paraguay	406,752
59.	Zimbabwe	390,757
60.	Japan	377,801
61.	Germany	357,021
62.	Congo, Rep. of the	342,000
63.	Finland	338,145
64.	Vietnam	331,689
65.	Malaysia	329,758
66.	Norway	323,877
67.	Poland	323,250
68.	Côte d'Ivoire	322,463
69.	Italy	301,268
70.	Philippines	300,000
71.	Ecuador	283,561
72.	Burkina Faso	274,000
73.	New Zealand	270,534
74.	Gabon	267,668
75.	Western Sahara	266,000
76.	Guinea	245,857
77.	United Kingdom	244,101
78.	Uganda	241,038
79.	Ghana	238,533
80.	Romania	238,391
81.	Laos	236,800
82.	Guyana	214,969
83.	Oman	212,457
84.	Belarus	207,600
85.	Kyrgyzstan	198,500
86.	Senegal	196,722
87.	Syria	185,180
88.	Cambodia	181,035
89.	Uruguay	177,414
90.	Tunisia	163,610
91.	Suriname	163,265
92.	Nepal	147,181
93.	Bangladesh	143,998
94.	Tajikistan	143,100
95.	Greece	131,957

1 km² = 0.3861 square mile

96. Nicaragua	130,000
97. Korea, North	120,538
98. Malawi	118,484
99. Eritrea	117,600
100. Benin	112,622
101. Honduras	112,088
102. Liberia	111,369
103. Bulgaria	110,912
104. Cuba	110,861
105. Guatemala	108,889
106. Iceland	103,000
107. Yugoslavia	102,173
108. Korea, South	99,274
109. Hungary	93,032
110. Portugal	91,982
111. Jordan	89,342
112. Azerbaijan	86,600
113. Austria	83,859
114. United Arab Emirates	83,600
115. Czech Republic	78,864
116. Panama	75,517
117. Sierra Leone	71,740
118. Ireland	70,284
119. Georgia	69,700
120. Sri Lanka	65,610
121. Lithuania	65,200
122. Latvia	64,600
123. Togo	56,785
124. Croatia	56,538
125. Bosnia and Herzegovina	51,129
126. Costa Rica	51,100
127. Slovakia	49,012
128. Dominican Rep.	48,734
129. Bhutan	47,000
130. Estonia	45,100
131. Denmark	43,094
132. Switzerland	41,284
133. Netherlands, The	40,844
134. Guinea-Bissau	36,125
135. Taiwan	36,000
136. Moldova	33,700
137. Belgium	30,519
138. Lesotho	30,355
139. Armenia	29,800
140. Solomon Islands	28,896
141. Albania	28,748
142. Equatorial Guinea	28,051
143. Burundi	27,834
144. Haiti	27,750
145. Rwanda	26,338
146. Macedonia	25,713
147. Djibouti	23,200
148. Belize	22,696
149. Israel	21,946
150. El Salvador	21,041
151. Slovenia	20,256
152. Fiji	18,274
153. Kuwait	17,818
154. Swaziland	17,364
155. Bahamas, The	13,878
156. Vanuatu	12,189
157. Gambia, The	11,295
158. Qatar	11,000
159. Jamaica	10,990
160. Lebanon	10,400
161. Cyprus	9,251
162. Brunei	5,765
163. Trinidad and Tobago	5,130
164. Cape Verde	4,033
165. Samoa	2,831
166. Luxembourg	2,586
167. Mauritius	2,040
168. Comoros	1,862
169. Sao Tome and Principe	964
170. Dominica	751
171. Tonga	747
172. Kiribati	726
173. Micronesia	702
174. Bahrain	694
175. Saint Lucia	622
176. Singapore	618
177. Palau	459
178. Seychelles	455
179. Andorra	453
180. Antigua and Barbuda	442
181. Barbados	430
182. St. Vincent and the Grenad.	388
183. Grenada	344
184. Malta	316
185. Maldives	298
186. Saint Kitts and Nevis	261
187. Marshall Islands	181
188. Liechtenstein	160
189. San Marino	61
190. Tuvalu	26
191. Nauru	21
192. Monaco	1.95
193. Vatican City	0.44

1 km^2 = 0.3861 square mile

Countries and their Population

	Inhabitants 1997
1. China	1,220,800,000
2. India	959,400,000
3. United States	267,600,000
4. Indonesia	203,400,000
5. Brazil	163,000,000
6. Russia	147,600,000
7. Pakistan	143,800,000
8. Japan	125,600,000
9. Bangladesh	122,200,000
10. Nigeria	118,300,000
11. Mexico	94,200,000
12. Germany	82,000,000
13. Vietnam	76,400,000
14. Iran	71,500,000
15. Philippines	70,600,000
16. Egypt	64,440,000
17. Turkey	62,800,000
18. Ethiopia	60,100,000
19. Thailand	59,100,000
20. United Kingdom	58,800,000
21. France	58,500,000
22. Italy	57,200,000
23. Ukraine	51,400,000
24. Congo, Democratic Republic of the	47,900,000
25. Myanmar (Burma)	46,800,000
26. Korea, South	45,700,000
27. South Africa	43,300,000
28. Spain	39,700,000
29. Poland	38,630,000
30. Colombia	37,000,000
31. Argentina	35,700,000
32. Tanzania	31,400,000
33. Canada	29,900,000
34. Algeria	29,500,000
35. Kenya	28,400,000
36. Sudan, The	27,900,000
37. Morocco	27,500,000
38. Peru	24,400,000
39. Uzbekistan	23,600,000
40. Korea, North	22,800,000
41. Venezuela	22,700,000
42. Nepal	22,600,000
Romania	22,600,000
44. Afghanistan	21,800,000
45. Taiwan	21,600,000
46. Iraq	21,300,000
47. Malaysia	21,000,000
48. Uganda	20,800,000
49. Saudi Arabia	19,500,000
50. Ghana	18,300,000
Sri Lanka	18,300,000
52. Australia	18,200,000
53. Mozambique	18,100,000
54. Kazakhstan	16,900,000
55. Yemen	16,200,000
56. Madagascar	15,800,000
57. Netherlands, The	15,600,000
58. Syria	14,900,000
59. Chile	14,600,000
60. Côte d'Ivoire	14,300,000
61. Cameroon	13,900,000
62. Ecuador	11,900,000
63. Zimbabwe	11,700,000
64. Angola	11,600,000
65. Mali	11,500,000
66. Guatemala	11,200,000
67. Burkina Faso	11,100,000
Cuba	11,100,000
69. Cambodia	10,500,000
Greece	10,500,000
71. Yugoslavia	10,400,000
72. Belarus	10,300,000
Somalia	10,300,000
74. Belgium	10,200,000
Czech Republic	10,200,000
Malawi	10,200,000
77. Hungary	9,990,000
78. Portugal	9,800,000
79. Niger	9,780,000
80. Tunisia	9,320,000
81. Sweden	8,830,000
82. Senegal	8,770,000
83. Zambia	8,490,000
84. Bulgaria	8,430,000
85. Austria	8,140,000
86. Dominican Rep.	8,090,000
87. Bolivia	7,770,000
88. Azerbaijan	7,650,000
89. Guinea	7,550,000
90. Haiti	7,390,000
91. Switzerland	7,260,000
92. Chad	6,690,000
93. Burundi	6,410,000
94. Rwanda	6,070,000
95. Tajikistan	6,050,000

96.	Honduras	5,970,000
97.	El Salvador	5,920,000
98.	Libya	5,780,000
99.	Israel	5,740,000
100.	Benin	5,720,000
101.	Georgia	5,440,000
102.	Slovakia	5,350,000
103.	Denmark	5,240,000
104.	Laos	5,190,000
105.	Finland	5,140,000
106.	Paraguay	5,090,000
107.	Croatia	4,500,000
	Papua New Guinea	4,500,000
109.	Kyrgyzstan	4,490,000
110.	Moldova	4,450,000
	Sierra Leone	4,450,000
112.	Norway	4,360,000
113.	Nicaragua	4,340,000
114.	Jordan	4,320,000
115.	Togo	4,310,000
116.	Turkmenistan	4,230,000
117.	Bosnia and Herzegovina	3,860,000
118.	Lithuania	3,720,000
119.	Armenia	3,640,000
	New Zealand	3,640,000
121.	Costa Rica	3,570,000
122.	Ireland	3,560,000
123.	Albania	3,430,000
	Singapore	3,430,000
125.	Central African Rep.	3,420,000
126.	Eritrea	3,410,000
127.	Uruguay	3,220,000
128.	Lebanon	3,120,000
129.	Congo, Rep. of the	2,740,000
130.	Panama	2,720,000
131.	Mongolia	2,570,000
132.	Jamaica	2,520,000
	Liberia	2,520,000
134.	Latvia	2,480,000
135.	Oman	2,400,000
136.	Mauritania	2,390,000
137.	United Arab Emirates	2,300,000
138.	Macedonia	2,190,000
139.	Lesotho	2,130,000
140.	Slovenia	1,920,000
141.	Bhutan	1,870,000
142.	Kuwait	1,800,000
143.	Namibia	1,610,000
144.	Botswana	1,520,000
145.	Estonia	1,460,000
146.	Trinidad and Tobago	1,310,000
147.	Gambia, The	1,160,000
148.	Gabon	1,140,000
	Mauritius	1,140,000
150.	Guinea-Bissau	1,110,000
151.	Swaziland	910,000
152.	Guyana	847,000
153.	Fiji	809,000
154.	Cyprus	764,000
155.	Comoros	651,000
156.	Djibouti	634,000
157.	Bahrain	581,000
158.	Qatar	568,000
159.	Suriname	437,000
160.	Equatorial Guinea	420,000
161.	Luxembourg	416,000
162.	Cape Verde	406,000
163.	Solomon Islands	403,000
164.	Malta	370,000
165.	Brunei	306,000
166.	Bahamas, The	288,000
167.	Iceland	274,000
168.	Maldives	270,000
169.	Barbados	262,000
170.	Western Sahara	260,000
171.	Belize	224,000
172.	Vanuatu	178,000
173.	Samoa	169,000
174.	Saint Lucia	144,000
175.	Sao Tome and Principe	135,000
176.	St. Vincent and the Gren.	113,000
177.	Micronesia	109,000
178.	Grenada	99,000
	Tonga	99,000
180.	Kiribati	80,000
181.	Seychelles	76,000
182.	Andorra	74,000
183.	Dominica	71,000
184.	Antigua and Barbuda	66,000
185.	Marshall Islands	57,000
186.	Saint Kitts and Nevis	41,000
187.	Monaco	32,000
188.	Liechtenstein	31,000
189.	San Marino	25,000
190.	Palau	17,000
191.	Nauru	11,000
192.	Tuvalu	10,000
193.	Vatican City	1,000

Earth Dimensions

Radius at the equator	6,378.160 km
Half axis	6,356.775 km
Amount of flattening of the geoid at the poles	1/298.254
Circumference at the equator	40,075.161 km
Circumference over the poles	40,008.006 km
Length of a degree at the equator	111.320 km
Average length of a meridian degree	111.133 km
Total surface	510.068 million km^2
Land surface (c. 29%)	c. 148.1 million km^2
Ocean surface (c. 71%)	c. 362.0 million km^2
Mass	5.976×10^{24} kg
Volume	1.083×10^{12} km^3
Mean density	5.517 g/cm^3
Sideric time per rotation	$23^h 56^m 4.09^s$
Mean distance Earth-Sun	149.598 million km
Distance Earth-Sun in aphelion (farthest from sun)	152.099 million km
Distance Earth-Sun in perihelion (nearest to sun)	147.096 million km
Length of the earth's orbit around the sun	939.886 million km
Tilt of the earth's axis in relation to its orbital plane (ecliptic), in 2000	23° 26′ 21″, 4
Average orbital speed around the sun	29.783 km/s
Sideric year	$365^d 6^h 9^m 9^s$
Tropical year	$365^d 5^h 48^m 46^s$
Average distance Earth-Moon	384,400 km
Distance Earth-Moon in apogee (farthest from earth)	406,740 km
Distance Earth-Moon in perigee (nearest to earth)	356,410 km
Sideric month	$27^d 7^h 43^m 12^s$
Synodic month	$29^d 12^h 44^m 3^s$

The Continents

	Area million km^2	Population 1998 million inh.
Europe	10.5	729.4
Asia	44.4	3,588.9
Australasia	8.5	29.5
Africa	30.3	778.5
North America	21.5	304.1
Central and South America	20.5	462.6
World	135.7	5,893.0

1 km = 0.6214 mile *1 km^2 = 0.3861 square mile*

Selected Mountains, Rivers, Islands and Lakes

Mountains

Europe

Mont Blanc (Western Alps)	4,807 m
Dufourspitze, Monte Rosa (Pennine Alps)	4,634 m
Matterhorn (Pennine Alps)	4,478 m
Finsteraarhorn (Bernese Alps)	4,274 m
Jungfrau (Bernese Alps)	4,158 m
Pelvoux (Western Alps)	4,102 m
Gran Paradiso (Graian Alps)	4,061 m
Bernina (Rhaetian Alps)	4,049 m
Ortles (Central Alps)	3,905 m
Mount Viso (Cottian Alps)	3,841 m
Großglockner (Hohe Tauern)	3,798 m
Mulhacén (Sierra Nevada)	3,481 m
Aneto (Pyrenees)	3,404 m
Marmolada (Dolomites)	3,342 m
Etna (Sicily)	3,323 m
Argentera (Maritime Alps)	3,297 m
Zugspitze (Bavarian Alps)	2,962 m
Musala (Rila)	2,925 m
Ólympus (Piería)	2,917 m
Vihren (Pirin)	2,914 m
Gran Sasso d'Italia (Abruzzi)	2,912 m
Triglav (Julian Alps)	2,864 m
Monte Cinto (Corsica)	2,706 m
Jezerca (North Albanian Alps)	2,694 m
Gerlachovský Štít (High Tatra)	2,655 m
Picos de Europa (Cantabrian Mountains)	2,648 m
Almanzor (Sierra de Gredos)	2,592 m
Grintavec (Karawanken)	2,559 m
Moldoveanu (Transylvanian Alps)	2,544 m
Durmitor (Dinaric Alps)	2,522 m
Galdhøpiggen (Scandinavia)	2,469 m
Ídi (Crete)	2,456 m
Ágios Ilías (Taïgetos)	2,407 m
Botev (Balkan Mountains)	2,376 m
Pietrosu (Carpathian Mountains)	2,303 m
Golyam Pereli (Rhodope Mountains)	2,191 m
Oræfajökull (Iceland)	2,119 m
Kebnekaise (Scandinavia)	2,111 m
Ďumbier (Low Tatra)	2,043 m
Estrêla (Portugal)	1,991 m
Narodnaya (Ural Mountains)	1,895 m
Monts Dore (Massif Central)	1,886 m
Monti del Gennargentu (Sardinia)	1,834 m
Newtontoppen (Spitsbergen)	1,712 m
Sněžka (Sudetes)	1,602 m
Roman-Kash (Crimean Mountains)	1,545 m
Feldberg (Black Forest)	1,493 m
Großer Arber (Bohemian Forest)	1,456 m
Grand Ballon (Vosges)	1,426 m
Ben Nevis (Grampian Mountains)	1,343 m
Halti (Northern Finland)	1,328 m
Vesuvius (Italy)	1,277 m
Klínovec (Ore Mountains)	1,244 m
Fichtelberg (Ore Mountains)	1,214 m
Brocken (Harz)	1,142 m
Snowdon (Cambrian Mountains)	1,085 m
Carrauntoohil (Ireland)	1,041 m
Kékes (Mátra)	1,015 m
Scafell Pikes (Cumbrian Mountains)	979 m

Asia

Mount Everest (Himalayas)	8,848 m
K 2 (Karakoram Range)	8,611 m
Dhaulagiri (Himalayas)	8,167 m
Nanga Parbat (Himalayas)	8,125 m
Muztag Feng (Kunlun Shan)	7,723 m
Kongur Shan (Kunlun Shan)	7,719 m
Tirich Mir (Hindu Kush)	7,690 m
Gongga Shan (Daxue Shan)	7,556 m
Communism Peak (Pamirs)	7,495 m
Pik Pobedy (Tien Shan)	7,439 m

1 m = 3.2808 feet

Lenin Pik (Trans Alai)	7,134 m
Nyainqêntanglha (Nyainqêntanglha Shan)	7,111 m
Demavend (Elburz Mountains)	5,671 m
Elbrus (Caucasus)	5,642 m
Pik Piramidalnyy (Turkestan Range)	5,621 m
Chimtarga (Zeravshan Range)	5,489 m
Ararat (Armenian Highlands)	5,165 m
Klyuchevskaya Sopka (Kamchatka)	4,750 m
Zard Kūh (Zagros Mountains)	4,548 m
Belukha (Altai)	4,506 m
Munkchairchan (Altai)	4,362 m
Uludoruk (Eastern Taurus Mountains)	4,135 m
Kinabalu (Borneo)	4,101 m
Ich Bogd (Govi Altayn Nuruu)	3,957 m
Kaçkar (Pontine Mountains)	3,932 m
Erciyeş (Anatolia)	3,917 m
Otgon Tenger (Khangai)	3,905 m
Kerinci (Sumatra)	3,805 m
Mount Fuji (Honshu)	3,776 m
Rinjani (Lombok)	3,726 m
Semeru (Java)	3,676 m
Nabī Shuayb (Yemen)	3,620 m
Munku-Sardyk (Eastern Sayan)	3,491 m
Rantekombola (Celebes)	3,455 m
Pobeda (Cherskiy Range)	3,147 m
Phan Si Pang (Hoanglien Son)	3,143 m
Kyzyl Taiga (Western Sayan)	3,121 m
Qurnat as Sawdā (Lebanon Mountains)	3,083 m
Jabal ash Shām (Oman Mountains)	2,980 m
Mount Apo (Mindanao)	2,954 m
Mount Pulog (Luzon)	2,929 m
Baitou Shan (China/Korea)	2,744 m
Anai Mudi (Western Ghats)	2,695 m
Mount Catherine (Sinai Peninsula)	2,637 m
Pidurutalagala (Ceylon)	2,524 m
Tahan (Malay Peninsula)	2,187 m
Tardoki-Jani (Sikhote Alin Range)	2,077 m
Huangganliang (Great Khingan Range)	2,029 m
Ólympos (Cyprus)	1,953 m
Topko (Dzhugdzhur Range)	1,906 m
Devodi Munda (Eastern Ghats)	1,680 m
Aksoran (Kazakh Uplands)	1,566 m

Australasia

Puncak Jaya (Maoke Range)	5,030 m
Mount Wilhelm (Bismarck Range)	4,509 m
Mauna Kea (Hawaii)	4,205 m
Mount Victoria (Owen Stanley Range)	4,073 m
Mount Cook (Southern Alps)	3,764 m
Mount Ruapehu (North Island, New Zealand)	2,797 m
Mount Balbi (Bougainville Island)	2,685 m
Mount Popomanaseu (Guadalcanal)	2,331 m
Mount Orohena (Tahiti)	2,241 m
Mount Kosciusko (Australian Alps)	2,228 m
Mount Tabwemasana (Espiritu Santo)	1,879 m
Mont Panié (New Caledonia)	1,628 m
Mount Ossa (Tasmania)	1,617 m
Mount Victoria (Viti Levu)	1,322 m

Africa

Kilimanjaro (Tanzania)	5,895 m
Mount Kenya (Kenya)	5,200 m
Margherita (Ruwenzori)	5,109 m
Ras Dashen (Ethiopian Highlands)	4,620 m
Toubkal (High Atlas)	4,165 m
Cameroon Mountain (Cameroon)	4,095 m
Pico de Teide (Tenerife)	3,718 m
Thabana Ntlenyana (Drakensberg)	3,482 m
Emi Koussi (Tibesti)	3,415 m

Kinyeti (Lolibai)	3,187 m
Jebel Marra (Darfur)	3,071 m
Piton des Neiges (Réunion)	3,069 m
Santa Isabel (Bioko)	3,008 m
Sapitwa (Mlanje)	3,002 m
Tahat (Ahaggar)	2,918 m
Maromokotro (Madagascar)	2,876 m
Môco (Bié Plateau)	2,619 m
Brandberg (Namibia)	2,574 m
Kompasberg (Sneeuberg)	2,504 m
Shimbiris (Somalia)	2,416 m
Kartala (Ngazidja)	2,361 m
Bintimani (Loma Mountains)	1,948 m
Pico Ruivo (Madeira)	1,847 m
Shere Hill (Jos Plateau)	1,780 m
Monts Nimba (Liberia/Guinea)	1,752 m
Tamgue (Fouta Djallon)	1,538 m
Table Mountain (South Africa)	1,087 m

North America

Mount McKinley (Alaska Range)	6,194 m
Mount Logan (Saint Elias Mountains)	5,950 m
Pico de Orizaba (Mexico)	5,675 m
Popocatépetl (Mexico)	5,452 m
Mount Whitney (Sierra Nevada)	4,418 m
Mount Elbert (Rocky Mountains)	4,399 m
Mount Rainier (Cascade Range)	4,392 m
Nevado de Colima (Sierra Madre Occidental)	4,340 m
Tajumulco (Sierra Madre)	4,220 m
Mount Waddington (Coast Mountains)	4,016 m
Cerro Mohinora (Sierra Madre Occidental)	3,992 m
Mount Robson (Rocky Mountains)	3,954 m
Chirripó Grande (Cordillera de Talamanca)	3,820 m
Gunnbjørn Fjeld (Greenland)	3,700 m
Cerro Peña Nevada (Sierra Madre Oriental)	3,992 m
Pico Duarte (Hispaniola)	3,175 m
Blue Mountain Peak (Jamaica)	2,256 m
Mount Mitchell (Appalachian Mountains)	2,037 m
Pico Turquino (Sierra Maestra)	1,974 m

South America

Aconcagua (Andes)	6,959 m
Pissis (Andes)	6,882 m
Ojos del Salado (Andes)	6,864 m
Huascarán (Andes)	6,768 m
Llullaillaco (Andes)	6,723 m
Sajama (Andes)	6,542 m
Illimani (Andes)	6,462 m
Chimborazo (Andes)	6,310 m
Cotopaxi (Andes)	5,897 m
Pico Cristóbal Colón (Sierra Nevada de Santa Marta)	5,775 m
Huila (Andes)	5,750 m
Pico Bolívar (Cordillera de Mérida)	5,007 m
San Valentín (Cordillera Patagónica)	4,058 m
Pico da Neblina (Guiana Highlands)	3,014 m
Pico da Bandeira (Brazilian Highlands)	2,890 m
Yogan (Tierra del Fuego)	2,469 m

Antarctica

Vinson Massif	4,897 m
Mount Kirkpatrick	4,528 m
Mount Jackson	4,190 m
Mount Erebus	3,794 m

Rivers

Europe

Volga	3,531 km
Danube	2,858 km
Ural	2,428 km
Dnieper	2,201 km
Kama	2,032 km
Don	1,870 km
Pechora	1,809 km
Oka	1,480 km
Belaya	1,430 km
Dniester	1,352 km
Rhine	1,320 km
Vyatka	1,314 km
Northern Dvina/Sukhona	1,302 km
Elbe	1,165 km
Desna	1,130 km
Vychegda	1,130 km
Donets	1,053 km
Vistula	1,047 km
Western Dvina	1,020 km
Loire	1,020 km
Tagus	1,007 km
Tisza	966 km
Prut	950 km
Meuse/Maas	933 km
Oder	912 km
Ebro	910 km
Rhône	812 km
Seine	776 km
Klarälven/Göta Älv	720 km
Po	652 km
Glomma	598 km
Maritsa	533 km
Kemijoki	483 km
Tevere	393 km
Shannon	361 km
Thames	346 km

Asia

Yangtze	5,526 km
Yellow River	5,464 km
Amur/Shilka/Onon	4,416 km
Ob/Katun	4,345 km
Lena	4,313 km
Irtysh	4,248 km
Mekong	4,184 km
Yenisey	4,102 km
Syr Darya/Naryn	3,012 km
Lower Tunguska	2,989 km
Indus	2,897 km
Brahmaputra	2,896 km
Tarim/Yarkand	2,750 km
Euphrates	2,736 km
Amu Darya/Panj/Vakhan	2,574 km
Kolyma	2,513 km
Ganges	2,511 km
Salween	2,414 km
Aldan	2,242 km
Xi Jiang	2,129 km
Irrawaddy	2,092 km
Sungari	1,927 km
Tigris	1,899 km

Australasia

Darling	2,740 km
Murray	2,570 km
Murrumbidgee	2,160 km
Lachlan	1,480 km
Sepik	1,127 km
Fly	1,120 km
Flinders	832 km
Waikato (New Zealand)	425 km

Africa

Nile/Kagera	6,671 km
Congo	4,374 km
Niger	4,184 km
Zambezi	2,736 km
Ubangi/Uele	2,300 km
Kasai	2,153 km
Orange River	2,092 km
Cubango/Okavango	1,800 km
Juba	1,650 km
Limpopo	1,600 km
Volta	1,600 km
Lomami	1,450 km

Senegal	1,430 km
Chari	1,400 km
Vaal	1,251 km
Gambia	1,127 km

North America

Mississippi/Missouri	6,420 km
Mackenzie/Peace River	4,241 km
Mississippi	3,778 km
Missouri	3,725 km
Yukon	3,185 km
Rio Grande (Rîo Bravo del Norte)	2,840 km
Nelson/Saskatchewan	2,575 km
Arkansas	2,348 km
Colorado	2,333 km
Ohio/Allegheny	2,101 km
Columbia	2,000 km
Snake	1,670 km
Churchill	1,609 km
Brazos	1,485 km
Tennessee/French Broad	1,421 km
Fraser	1,368 km
Saint Lawrence	1,287 km
Hudson	492 km

South America

Amazon	6,437 km
Paraná/Rîo de la Plata	4,264 km
Madeira	3,240 km
Purus	3,211 km
São Francisco	3,199 km
Japurá/Caquetá	2,816 km
Tocantins	2,699 km
Orinoco	2,575 km
Paraguay	2,549 km
Rîo Negro	2,253 km
Tapajós/Juruena	2,200 km
Xingu	2,100 km
Uruguay	1,609 km
Magdalena	1,538 km

Islands
(In some cases small adjacent islands are included.)

Europe

Great Britain	219,081 km^2
Iceland	103,000 km^2
Ireland	84,420 km^2
Novaya Zemlya (North Island)	48,904 km^2
Spitsbergen	39,044 km^2
Novaya Zemlya (South Island)	33,275 km^2
Sicily	25,426 km^2
Sardinia	23,813 km^2
North East Land	14,530 km^2
Corsica	8,682 km^2
Crete	8,263 km^2
Sjælland	7,016 km^2
Kolguyev	5,250 km^2
Euboea	3,655 km^2
Mallorca	3,505 km^2
Vaigach Island	3,383 km^2
Gotland	3,001 km^2
Fyn	2,977 km^2
Saaremaa	2,714 km^2
Hinnøy	2,198 km^2
Lésvos	1,630 km^2
Rhodes	1,398 km^2
Öland	1,344 km^2
Lolland	1,241 km^2
Hiiumaa	965 km^2
Rügen	926 km^2
Menorca	683 km^2
Corfu	592 km^2
Bornholm	588 km^2
Isle of Man	572 km^2
Krk	410 km^2
Malta	246 km^2
Fehmarn	185 km^2
Île d'Oléron	175 km^2

Asia

Borneo (Kalimantan)	736,000 km^2
Sumatra	425,000 km^2
Honshu	227,414 km^2

1 km = 0.6214 mile   1 km^2 = 0.3861 square mile

Celebes (Sulawesi)	180,000 km^2
Java	126,650 km^2
Luzon	104,700 km^2
Mindanao	94,600 km^2
Hokkaido	78,073 km^2
Sakhalin	76,400 km^2
Ceylon	65,610 km^2
Kyushu	36,554 km^2
Taiwan	36,000 km^2
Hainan	34,000 km^2
Timor	33,850 km^2
Shikoku	18,256 km^2
Halmahera	17,800 km^2
Seram	17,150 km^2
Flores	14,250 km^2
October Revolution Island	14,200 km^2
Sumbawa	13,280 km^2
Samar	13,080 km^2
Negros	12,700 km^2
Bangka	11,930 km^2
Palawan	11,785 km^2
Kotelnyy Island	11,665 km^2
Panay	11,515 km^2
Bolshevik Island	11,312 km^2
Sumba	11,150 km^2
Mindoro	9,735 km^2
Buru	9,500 km^2
Cyprus	9,251 km^2
Komsomolets Island	9,200 km^2
Wrangel Island	7,300 km^2
New Siberia	6,200 km^2

Australasia

New Guinea	771,600 km^2
South Island (New Zealand)	151,971 km^2
North Island (New Zealand)	114,489 km^2
Tasmania	64,410 km^2
New Britain	36,500 km^2
New Caledonia	16,177 km^2
Viti Levu	10,429 km^2
Hawaii (Big Island)	10,414 km^2
Bougainville Island	10,050 km^2
New Ireland	8,600 km^2
Guadalcanal	6,475 km^2
Melville Island	5,800 km^2
Vanua Levu	5,556 km^2
Kangaroo Island	4,350 km^2
Espíritu Santo	3,677 km^2
Savai'i	1,715 km^2
Tahiti	1,042 km^2

Africa

Madagascar	587,041 km^2
Socotra	3,580 km^2
Réunion	2,510 km^2
Tenerife	2,057 km^2
Bioko	2,017 km^2
Mauritius	1,865 km^2
Zanzibar	1,658 km^2
Ngazidja	1,148 km^2
Santiago	991 km^2
Pemba	984 km^2
Madeira	740 km^2

North America

Greenland	2,175,600 km^2
Baffin Island	688,808 km^2
Victoria Island	217,291 km^2
Ellesmere Island	196,237 km^2
Newfoundland	112,300 km^2
Cuba	105,007 km^2
Hispaniola	75,606 km^2
Banks Island	70,028 km^2
Devon Island	55,247 km^2
Axel Heiberg Island	43,178 km^2
Melville Island	42,150 km^2
Southampton Island	41,215 km^2
Prince of Wales Island	33,338 km^2
Vancouver Island	31,285 km^2
Somerset Island	24,786 km^2
Bathurst Island	16,042 km^2
Prince Patrick Island	15,848 km^2
King William Island	13,111 km^2
Ellef Ringnes Island	11,250 km^2
Bylot Island	11,067 km^2
Jamaica	10,962 km^2
Cape Breton Island	10,311 km^2
Puerto Rico	8,644 km^2

Andros Island	5,957 km²
Long Island	4,463 km²
Guadeloupe	1,433 km²

South America

Tierra del Fuego	47,000 km²
Chiloé Island	8,395 km²
East Falkland	6,605 km²
Isabela Island	5,825 km²
Trinidad	4,820 km²
West Falkland	4,532 km²

Antarctic Region

Kerguelen Islands	5,820 km²
South Georgia	3,755 km²
Ross Island	2,300 km²

Lakes (*excluding islands)

Europe

Lake Ladoga	18,135 km²
Lake Onega	9,720 km²
Vänern*	5,584 km²
Lake Peipus	3,550 km²
Vättern*	1,899 km²
Saimaa	1,460 km²
Lake Seg	1,200 km²
Mälaren*	1,140 km²
Beloye Ozero	1,125 km²
Inari Lake*	1,085 km²
Päijänne*	1,054 km²
Lake Ilmen	982 km²
Oulu Lake	893 km²
Balaton	592 km²
Lake Geneva	580 km²
Lake Constance	572 km²
Hjälmaren	484 km²
Lough Neagh	388 km²
Lake Garda	370 km²
Mjøsa	368 km²
Torne Lake	322 km²
Lake Neusiedl	320 km²
Lake Neuchâtel	218 km²
Lago Maggiore	212 km²
Müritz	110 km²
Chiemsee	80 km²
Loch Ness	65 km²

Asia

Caspian Sea	367,000 km²
Aral Sea*	c. 33,600 km²
Lake Baykal	31,499 km²
Lake Balkhash	18,428 km²
Ysyk-Köl	6,099 km²
Koko Nor	5,000 km²
Lake Urmia	4,686 km²
Lake Taimyr	4,560 km²
Lake Khanka	4,401 km²
Lake Van	3,713 km²
Lake Sevan	1,360 km²
Dead Sea	910 km²
Lake Biwa	672 km²

1 km² = 0.3861 square mile

Australasia	
Lake Eyre	c. 9,300 km²
Lake Torrens	c. 5,700 km²
Lake Gairdner	c. 4,700 km²
Lake Taupo	606 km²

Africa	
Lake Victoria	69,484 km²
Lake Tanganyika	32,893 km²
Lake Nyasa	28,878 km²
Lake Chad	16,316 km²
Lake Turkana	6,405 km²
Lake Albert	5,374 km²
Lake Mweru	4,920 km²
Lake Tana	3,630 km²
Lake Kivu	2,650 km²
Lake Edward	2,200 km²

North America	
Lake Superior	82,103 km²
Lake Huron	59,570 km²
Lake Michigan	57,757 km²
Great Bear Lake	31,328 km²
Great Slave Lake	28,568 km²
Lake Erie	25,667 km²
Lake Winnipeg	24,387 km²
Lake Ontario	19,011 km²
Lake Nicaragua	8,029 km²
Lake Athabasca	7,935 km²
Reindeer Lake	6,651 km²
Great Salt Lake	5,905 km²
Nettilling Lake	5,542 km²
Lake Winnipegosis	5,374 km²
Lake Manitoba	4,624 km²

South America	
Lake Maracaibo	13,512 km²
Lake Titicaca	8,288 km²
Lake Poopó	2,530 km²
Lago Argentino	1,415 km²
Lake Nahuel Huapi	550 km²

How to use the index

Contents and arrangement of names

- The index contains all the names occurring in the atlas maps.

- The names are arranged alphabetically.
  Letters with diacritical marks are treated like the same letters without them.
  The ligatures æ and œ are treated like separate letters; the special letter
  ð is regarded as dh, þ as th, and the German ß as ss.

- Names abbreviated in the maps are always spelled in full in the index:
  Liechtenstein [= Liecht.]

- Additions (in brackets) to names are referred to the primary name:
  Venezia (Venice)
  Venice → Venezia

Additional information

- Except for place names almost all entries in the index are marked with generic symbols.
  To distinguish between identical place names additional geographic information is added in brackets; the same is done for names having the same generic symbol:
  Aberdeen *[U.K.]*
  Aberdeen *[U.S., South Dakota]*
  Aberdeen *[U.S., Washington]*

  Long Island ☗ *[Bahamas]*
  Long Island ☗ *[Papua New Guinea]*
  Long Island ☗ *[U.S.]*

- Names beginning with a frequently used generic term are listed in the inverse form. There is a general reference for each generic term. Place names are excepted from this rule.
  Canaveral, Cape ❯≋
  Cape ... ❯≋ → ..., Cape
  Cape Town
  Carbonara, Cape ❯≋

Location

- The location of each name in the index is given by a number for the left-hand side of the respective map, plus a letter for column and another number for row.
  Alaska, Gulf of ≋❯ 110 H 6
  Baltimore 116 F 4

- For peoples and ethnic groups the index refers to the terms and numbers used in the legends of the ethnic maps.

Independent Nation
Dependency, Admin. Terr.
State, Province, Territory
People, Ethnic Group, Tribe
∴ Historic Ruins
Research Station
Region, Peninsula
Mountain Range, Mountains
▲ Peak
)(Pass
✱ Ice Shelf, Glacier

∽ River, Canal
⤳ Waterfall
◒ Lake, Lakes, Reservoir
⍨ Swamp
⍦ Saline Swamp
≋ Sea
≍ Strait
≈) Bay, Gulf
)≋ Cape
⌓ Island, Islands
⇄ Ocean Current
◷ Time Zone

Independent Nation
Dependency, Admin. Terr.
State, Province, Territory
People, Ethnic Group, Tribe
Historic Ruins
Research Station
Region, Peninsula
Mountain Range, Mountains
▲ Peak
)(Pass
* Ice Shelf, Glacier

River, Canal
Waterfall
Lake, Lakes, Reservoir
Swamp
Saline Swamp
Sea
Strait
Bay, Gulf
Cape
Island, Islands
Ocean Current
Time Zone

■ Independent Nation
Dependency, Admin. Terr.
State, Province, Territory
People, Ethnic Group, Tribe
∴ Historic Ruins
Research Station
Region, Peninsula
Mountain Range, Mountains
▲ Peak
)(Pass
* Ice Shelf, Glacier

River, Canal
Waterfall
Lake, Lakes, Reservoir
Swamp
Saline Swamp
Sea
Strait
Bay, Gulf
Cape
Island, Islands
Ocean Current
Time Zone

Independent Nation
Dependency, Admin. Terr.
State, Province, Territory
People, Ethnic Group, Tribe
Historic Ruins
Research Station
Region, Peninsula
Mountain Range, Mountains
▲ Peak
Pass
Ice Shelf, Glacier

River, Canal
Waterfall
Lake, Lakes, Reservoir
Swamp
Saline Swamp
Sea
Strait
Bay, Gulf
Cape
Island, Islands
Ocean Current
Time Zone

Independent Nation
Dependency, Admin. Terr.
State, Province, Territory
People, Ethnic Group, Tribe
Historic Ruins
Research Station
Region, Peninsula
Mountain Range, Mountains
▲ Peak
)(Pass
∗ Ice Shelf, Glacier

River, Canal · Waterfall · Lake, Lakes, Reservoir · Swamp · Saline Swamp · Sea · Strait · Bay, Gulf · Cape · Island, Islands · Ocean Current · Time Zone

Independent Nation
Dependency, Admin. Terr.
State, Province, Territory
People, Ethnic Group, Tribe
∴ Historic Ruins
Research Station
Region, Peninsula
Mountain Range, Mountains
▲ Peak
)(Pass
∗ Ice Shelf, Glacier

- River, Canal
- Waterfall
- Lake, Lakes, Reservoir
- Swamp
- Saline Swamp
- Sea
- Strait
- Bay, Gulf
- Cape
- Island, Islands
- Ocean Current
- Time Zone

Independent Nation
Dependency, Admin. Terr.
State, Province, Territory
People, Ethnic Group, Tribe
Historic Ruins
Research Station
Region, Peninsula
Mountain Range, Mountains
Peak
Pass
Ice Shelf, Glacier

∽ River, Canal
⥱ Waterfall
⌣ Lake, Lakes, Reservoir
⌔ Swamp
⌔ Saline Swamp
≋ Sea
≋ Strait
≋⟩ Bay, Gulf
⟩≋ Cape
⌓ Island, Islands
⇄ Ocean Current
◷ Time Zone

Independent Nation
Dependency, Admin. Terr.
State, Province, Territory
People, Ethnic Group, Tribe
∴ Historic Ruins
Research Station
Region, Peninsula
Mountain Range, Mountains
▲ Peak
)(Pass
∗ Ice Shelf, Glacier

River, Canal · Waterfall · Lake, Lakes, Reservoir · Swamp · Saline Swamp · Sea · Strait · Bay, Gulf · Cape · Island, Islands · Ocean Current · Time Zone

Independent Nation
Dependency, Admin. Terr.
State, Province, Territory
People, Ethnic Group, Tribe
Historic Ruins
Research Station
Region, Peninsula
Mountain Range, Mountains
▲ Peak
)(Pass
* Ice Shelf, Glacier

River, Canal — Waterfall — Lake, Lakes, Reservoir — Swamp — Saline Swamp — Sea — Strait — Bay, Gulf — Cape — Island, Islands — Ocean Current — Time Zone

■ Independent Nation
⛊ Dependency, Admin. Terr.
⛉ State, Province, Territory
⚇ People, Ethnic Group, Tribe
∴ Historic Ruins
⌂ Research Station
⌂ Region, Peninsula
⛰ Mountain Range, Mountains
▲ Peak
)(Pass
∗ Ice Shelf, Glacier

River, Canal
Waterfall
Lake, Lakes, Reservoir
Swamp
Saline Swamp
Sea
Strait
Bay, Gulf
Cape
Island, Islands
Ocean Current
Time Zone

G

Independent Nation
Dependency, Admin. Terr.
State, Province, Territory
People, Ethnic Group, Tribe
∴ Historic Ruins
Research Station
Region, Peninsula
Mountain Range, Mountains
▲ Peak
)(Pass
✱ Ice Shelf, Glacier

River, Canal
Waterfall
Lake, Lakes, Reservoir
Swamp
Saline Swamp
Sea
Strait
Bay, Gulf
Cape
Island, Islands
Ocean Current
Time Zone

Independent Nation
Dependency, Admin. Terr.
State, Province, Territory
People, Ethnic Group, Tribe
∴ Historic Ruins
Research Station
Region, Peninsula
Mountain Range, Mountains
▲ Peak
)(Pass
* Ice Shelf, Glacier

River, Canal
Waterfall
Lake, Lakes, Reservoir
Swamp
Saline Swamp
Sea
Strait
Bay, Gulf
Cape
Island, Islands
Ocean Current
Time Zone

■ Independent Nation
◘ Dependency, Admin. Terr.
◻ State, Province, Territory
People, Ethnic Group, Tribe
∴ Historic Ruins
Research Station
Region, Peninsula
▲▲ Mountain Range, Mountains
▲ Peak
)(Pass
∗ Ice Shelf, Glacier

∽ River, Canal
⥲ Waterfall
◡ Lake, Lakes, Reservoir
⩊ Swamp
⩋ Saline Swamp
≋ Sea
≊ Strait
≋) Bay, Gulf
)≋ Cape
⌓ Island, Islands
⇄ Ocean Current
◷ Time Zone

J

Independent Nation
Dependency, Admin. Terr.
State, Province, Territory
People, Ethnic Group, Tribe
∴ Historic Ruins
Research Station
Region, Peninsula
Mountain Range, Mountains
▲ Peak
)(Pass
∗ Ice Shelf, Glacier

∽ River, Canal
⥽ Waterfall
◡ Lake, Lakes, Reservoir
⩌ Swamp
⩊ Saline Swamp
≋ Sea
≍ Strait
≋⟩ Bay, Gulf
⟩≋ Cape
⌓ Island, Islands
⇄ Ocean Current
◷ Time Zone

Independent Nation
Dependency, Admin. Terr.
State, Province, Territory
People, Ethnic Group, Tribe
Historic Ruins
Research Station
Region, Peninsula
Mountain Range, Mountains
▲ Peak
)(Pass
∗ Ice Shelf, Glacier

River, Canal
Waterfall
Lake, Lakes, Reservoir
Swamp
Saline Swamp
Sea
Strait
Bay, Gulf
Cape
Island, Islands
Ocean Current
Time Zone

Independent Nation · Dependency, Admin. Terr. · State, Province, Territory · People, Ethnic Group, Tribe · ∴ Historic Ruins · Research Station · Region, Peninsula · Mountain Range, Mountains · ▲ Peak ·)(Pass · ✱ Ice Shelf, Glacier

River, Canal · Waterfall · Lake, Lakes, Reservoir · Swamp · Saline Swamp · Sea · Strait · Bay, Gulf · Cape · Island, Islands · Ocean Current · Time Zone

L

Independent Nation
Dependency, Admin. Terr.
State, Province, Territory
People, Ethnic Group, Tribe
∴ Historic Ruins
Research Station
Region, Peninsula
Mountain Range, Mountains
▲ Peak
)(Pass
∗ Ice Shelf, Glacier

River, Canal · Waterfall · Lake, Lakes, Reservoir · Swamp · Saline Swamp · Sea · Strait · Bay, Gulf · Cape · Island, Islands · Ocean Current · Time Zone

Independent Nation
Dependency, Admin. Terr.
State, Province, Territory
People, Ethnic Group, Tribe
Historic Ruins
Research Station
Region, Peninsula
Mountain Range, Mountains
▲ Peak
)(Pass
* Ice Shelf, Glacier

M

River, Canal · Waterfall · Lake, Lakes, Reservoir · Swamp · Saline Swamp · Sea · Strait · Bay, Gulf · Cape · Island, Islands · Ocean Current · Time Zone

Independent Nation
Dependency, Admin. Terr.
State, Province, Territory
People, Ethnic Group, Tribe
∴ Historic Ruins
Research Station
Region, Peninsula
Mountain Range, Mountains
▲ Peak
)(Pass
* Ice Shelf, Glacier

River, Canal · Waterfall · Lake, Lakes, Reservoir · Swamp · Saline Swamp · Sea · Strait · Bay, Gulf · Cape · Island, Islands · Ocean Current · Time Zone

Independent Nation
Dependency, Admin. Terr.
State, Province, Territory
People, Ethnic Group, Tribe
Historic Ruins
Research Station
Region, Peninsula
Mountain Range, Mountains
Peak
Pass
Ice Shelf, Glacier

River, Canal · Waterfall · Lake, Lakes, Reservoir · Swamp · Saline Swamp · ≋ Sea · Strait · Bay, Gulf · Cape · Island, Islands · Ocean Current · Time Zone

Independent Nation
Dependency, Admin. Terr.
State, Province, Territory
People, Ethnic Group, Tribe
Historic Ruins
Research Station
Region, Peninsula
Mountain Range, Mountains
▲ Peak
)(Pass
∗ Ice Shelf, Glacier

River, Canal
Waterfall
Lake, Lakes, Reservoir
Swamp
Saline Swamp
Sea
Strait
Bay, Gulf
Cape
Island, Islands
Ocean Current
Time Zone

Independent Nation · Dependency, Admin. Terr. · State, Province, Territory · People, Ethnic Group, Tribe · ∴ Historic Ruins · Research Station · Region, Peninsula · Mountain Range, Mountains · ▲ Peak ·)(Pass · ∗ Ice Shelf, Glacier

River, Canal
Waterfall
Lake, Lakes, Reservoir
Swamp
Saline Swamp
Sea
Strait
Bay, Gulf
Cape
Island, Islands
Ocean Current
Time Zone

Independent Nation
Dependency, Admin. Terr.
State, Province, Territory
People, Ethnic Group, Tribe
∴ Historic Ruins
Research Station
Region, Peninsula
Mountain Range, Mountains
▲ Peak
)(Pass
* Ice Shelf, Glacier

∽ River, Canal
⥲ Waterfall
≎ Lake, Lakes, Reservoir
⩦ Swamp
⩧ Saline Swamp
≋ Sea
≂ Strait
≋) Bay, Gulf
)≋ Cape
⩍ Island, Islands
⇄ Ocean Current
◷ Time Zone

P

Independent Nation
Dependency, Admin. Terr.
State, Province, Territory
People, Ethnic Group, Tribe
Historic Ruins
Research Station
Region, Peninsula
Mountain Range, Mountains
Peak
Pass
Ice Shelf, Glacier

∿ River, Canal
≒ Waterfall
⊖ Lake, Lakes, Reservoir
⌣ Swamp
⌣ Saline Swamp
≋ Sea
≊ Strait
≋) Bay, Gulf
)≋ Cape
⌓ Island, Islands
⇄ Ocean Current
◷ Time Zone

Independent Nation
Dependency, Admin. Terr.
State, Province, Territory
People, Ethnic Group, Tribe
∴ Historic Ruins
Research Station
Region, Peninsula
Mountain Range, Mountains
▲ Peak
)(Pass
* Ice Shelf, Glacier

River, Canal
Waterfall
Lake, Lakes, Reservoir
Swamp
Saline Swamp
Sea
Strait
Bay, Gulf
Cape
Island, Islands
Ocean Current
Time Zone

Q

R

Independent Nation
Dependency, Admin. Terr.
State, Province, Territory
People, Ethnic Group, Tribe
∴ Historic Ruins
Research Station
Region, Peninsula
Mountain Range, Mountains
▲ Peak
)(Pass
∗ Ice Shelf, Glacier

River, Canal
Waterfall
Lake, Lakes, Reservoir
Swamp
Saline Swamp
Sea
Strait
Bay, Gulf
Cape
Island, Islands
Ocean Current
Time Zone

S

■ Independent Nation
◧ Dependency, Admin. Terr.
▢ State, Province, Territory
People, Ethnic Group, Tribe
∴ Historic Ruins
Research Station
Region, Peninsula
Mountain Range, Mountains
▲ Peak
)(Pass
∗ Ice Shelf, Glacier

River, Canal
Waterfall
Lake, Lakes, Reservoir
Swamp
Saline Swamp
Sea
Strait
Bay, Gulf
Cape
Island, Islands
Ocean Current
Time Zone

Independent Nation
Dependency, Admin. Terr.
State, Province, Territory
People, Ethnic Group, Tribe
Historic Ruins
Research Station
Region, Peninsula
Mountain Range, Mountains
▲ Peak
Pass
Ice Shelf, Glacier

∽ River, Canal
⩳ Waterfall
⌣ Lake, Lakes, Reservoir
⏝ Swamp
⋓ Saline Swamp
≋ Sea
≍ Strait
≈) Bay, Gulf
)≈ Cape
⌓ Island, Islands
⇄ Ocean Current
◷ Time Zone

☗ Independent Nation
◧ Dependency, Admin. Terr.
▢ State, Province, Territory
⚇ People, Ethnic Group, Tribe
∴ Historic Ruins
⌂ Research Station
⌇ Region, Peninsula
⛰ Mountain Range, Mountains
▲ Peak
)(Pass
✱ Ice Shelf, Glacier

River, Canal
Waterfall
Lake, Lakes, Reservoir
Swamp
Saline Swamp
Sea
Strait
Bay, Gulf
Cape
Island, Islands
Ocean Current
Time Zone

■ Independent Nation
◘ Dependency, Admin. Terr.
□ State, Province, Territory
ꙮ People, Ethnic Group, Tribe
∴ Historic Ruins
⌂ Research Station
⌐ Region, Peninsula
▲▲ Mountain Range, Mountains
▲ Peak
)(Pass
* Ice Shelf, Glacier

River, Canal · Waterfall · Lake, Lakes, Reservoir · Swamp · Saline Swamp · Sea · Strait · Bay, Gulf · Cape · Island, Islands · Ocean Current · Time Zone

Independent Nation
Dependency, Admin. Terr.
State, Province, Territory
People, Ethnic Group, Tribe
Historic Ruins
Research Station
Region, Peninsula
Mountain Range, Mountains
▲ Peak
)(Pass
* Ice Shelf, Glacier

River, Canal
Waterfall
Lake, Lakes, Reservoir
Swamp
Saline Swamp
Sea
Strait
Bay, Gulf
Cape
Island, Islands
Ocean Current
Time Zone

● Independent Nation	ﻌ People, Ethnic Group, Tribe	≌ Region, Peninsula	▲ Peak
◐ Dependency, Admin. Terr.	∴ Historic Ruins	▲ Mountain Range, Mountains	)(Pass
○ State, Province, Territory	⌂ Research Station		✳ Ice Shelf, Glacier

River, Canal
Waterfall
Lake, Lakes, Reservoir
Swamp
Saline Swamp
Sea
Strait
Bay, Gulf
Cape
Island, Islands
Ocean Current
Time Zone

Independent Nation
Dependency, Admin. Terr.
State, Province, Territory
People, Ethnic Group, Tribe
∴ Historic Ruins
Research Station
Region, Peninsula
Mountain Range, Mountains
▲ Peak
)(Pass
* Ice Shelf, Glacier

River, Canal · Waterfall · Lake, Lakes, Reservoir · Swamp · Saline Swamp · Sea · Strait · Bay, Gulf · Cape · Island, Islands · Ocean Current · Time Zone

■ Independent Nation
◧ Dependency, Admin. Terr.
▽ State, Province, Territory
⚇ People, Ethnic Group, Tribe
∴ Historic Ruins
⌂ Research Station
⊵ Region, Peninsula
▲▲ Mountain Range, Mountains
▲ Peak
)(Pass
∗ Ice Shelf, Glacier

W

River, Canal
Waterfall
Lake, Lakes, Reservoir
Swamp
Saline Swamp
Sea
Strait
Bay, Gulf
Cape
Island, Islands
Ocean Current
Time Zone

Independent Nation
Dependency, Admin. Terr.
State, Province, Territory
People, Ethnic Group, Tribe
∴ Historic Ruins
Research Station
Region, Peninsula
Mountain Range, Mountains
▲ Peak
)(Pass
∗ Ice Shelf, Glacier

River, Canal
Waterfall
Lake, Lakes, Reservoir
Swamp
Saline Swamp
Sea
Strait
Bay, Gulf
Cape
Island, Islands
Ocean Current
Time Zone

■ Independent Nation
◐ Dependency, Admin. Terr.
◯ State, Province, Territory
👥 People, Ethnic Group, Tribe
∴ Historic Ruins
⌂ Research Station
Region, Peninsula
Mountain Range, Mountains
▲ Peak
)(Pass
∗ Ice Shelf, Glacier